MARRIED PRIESTS IN THE CATHOLIC CHURCH

Married Priests
in the
Catholic Church

Edited by
ADAM A. J. DeVILLE

University of Notre Dame Press
Notre Dame, Indiana

University of Notre Dame Press
Notre Dame, Indiana 46556
undpress.nd.edu
All Rights Reserved

Copyright © 2021 by the University of Notre Dame

Published in the United States of America

Library of Congress Control Number: 2021931599

ISBN: 978-0-268-20009-1 (Hardback)
ISBN: 978-0-268-20010-7 (Paperback)
ISBN: 978-0-268-20008-4 (WebPDF)
ISBN: 978-0-268-20011-4 (Epub)

CONTENTS

Acknowledgments   ix

Introduction—Adam A. J. DeVille   xi

PART I. *History Ancient and Modern*

ONE
Priestly Celibacy—An Apostolic Tradition? The Theological Stakes of a Historical Argument—David G. Hunter   3

TWO
From Antioch to America via Smyrna: Rethinking Married Priesthood and Parish Life with Ignatius, Alexis, and Polycarp —Dellas Oliver Herbel   21

THREE
Mandatory Celibacy among Eastern Catholics: A Church-Dividing Issue—James S. Dutko   32

PART II. *Canon Law East and West*

FOUR
Canonical Reflections on Clergy and Marriage —Patrick Viscuso   53

FIVE
Recent Papal Pronouncements on the Admission of Married Eastern Catholic Men to the Priesthood: An Ecumenical Issue —Alexander M. Laschuk   74

PART III.   *Ecumenical Considerations*

SIX
Married Clergy in the Anglican Tradition—John Hunwicke   91

SEVEN
The Gift to the Church of Married Clergy—Edwin Barnes   102

EIGHT
Official Catholic Pronouncements Regarding Presbyteral Celibacy: Their Fate and the Implications for Catholic-Orthodox Relations —Peter Galadza   108

PART IV.   *Pastoral-Familial Life*

NINE
Reflections on Two Vocations in Two Lungs of the One Church —David Meinzen   137

TEN
Growing Up in a Rectory: Using *Oikonomia* to Answer the Tough Questions Posed by the Children of Priestly Families —Julian Hayda   146

ELEVEN
The Vocation of the *Presbytera*: Icon of the Theotokos in the Midst of the Ministerial Priesthood—Irene Galadza   155

TWELVE
The Joys and Crosses of Clerical Families —Nicholas Denysenko   167

THIRTEEN
Marriage and Ministry: An Eastern Orthodox Perspective
—William C. Mills   175

FOURTEEN
"What Did You Expect?" A Reflection on Married Clergy
and Pastoral Ministry—Andrew Jarmus   186

PART V.   *Theology*

FIFTEEN
Celibacy and the Married Priesthood:
Rediscovering the Spousal Mystery—Thomas J. Loya   199

SIXTEEN
Married Priests: At the Heart of Tradition
—Lawrence Cross and Basilio Petrà   210

SEVENTEEN
Married Priesthood: Some Theological "Resonances"
—Basilio Petrà   228

EIGHTEEN
Conclusion: Toward a Theology of Married Priesthood
—Adam A. J. DeVille   246

APPENDIX 1. The Toronto Tempest—Victor Pospishil,
edited by Adam A. J. DeVille   258

APPENDIX 2. Recent Views on the Origins of Clerical Celibacy:
A Review of the Literature from 1980 to 1991
—J. Kevin Coyle, edited by Adam A. J. DeVille   299

Contributors   340

Index   344

ACKNOWLEDGMENTS

I thank all the contributors to this volume for their patience and willingness to see this project through. I thank in particular Fr. Peter Galadza, who organized one of the conferences (in Rome) that, together with my own presentation and that of others in Chicago at the American Academy of Religion conference in 2012, formed the initial impetus for this volume. It has since grown to be the much larger, more comprehensive project that has resulted in the volume you have before you today, and that is due in part to the "blind" reviewers of the University of Notre Dame Press, whom I also very much thank. Their comments and suggestions were extremely important and helpful in strengthening this book.

In an age when the ideology of efficiency ruthlessly tempts administrators to get rid of editors and seduces authors to publish as quickly as possible without peer review in any number of myriad places on the Internet, the University of Notre Dame Press proves to me once more (as they did with my 2011 book) how utterly invaluable the processes of peer review and professional editing both remain. This is especially so when the process is guided by such competent hands as those of Stephen Little, whose many insightful ideas, not least regarding the structure and organization of this book, were graciously and wisely conveyed. I thank him and others at the press (especially Marilyn Martin for her impeccable copyediting) very much indeed.

I dedicate this book to the late archpriest Robert Anderson, a priest of the Toronto Eparchy of the Ukrainian Greco-Catholic Church whom I first met in Ukraine in 2001. When we were both back in Canada the following year, he—who was celibate—would prove himself to be a prolific and bountiful spiritual father to many of us in Ottawa in those early years of this century, and also a dear friend to me and my family in many ways. Not a few of us have felt ourselves orphans since his very sudden death in December 2010. May his memory continue to be eternal!

Introduction

Adam A. J. DeVille

For more than fifteen years now, through three papacies, one has regularly heard expressed, especially in the popular media, the hope that perhaps this pope or the next will change certain things perceived as unpopular or old-fashioned, most of them having to do with sexual ethics. Invariably in that list is the question of abolishing a celibate priesthood in the Latin Church and replacing it with a married priesthood, a process indolent writers facilely assume will consist of a snap of papal fingers bringing instant change.

One of the several purposes of the present volume is to show that a married presbyterate is a much more complex reality than many assume and that its renewed advent among Catholics—especially in the Latin Church—will require careful consideration of many things. It is a multifaceted reality with its own history and theology deserving of careful consideration—and not as some kind of "concession" to the "lesser brethren," either. A married priesthood is as fully Catholic, as theologically grounded, and as venerable a tradition as priestly celibacy ever was.

No other book yet published offers so careful an analysis, so detailed a history, and so comprehensive a treatment of married Catholic priests as this one does. It looks at history in the first and second millenniums; at theology from the apostles to their papal successors John Paul II and Francis; at canon law ancient and modern; at Ukrainian Catholic, Russian Catholic, and Ruthenian Catholic experiences in Europe, North America, and Australia; at Anglican experiences in the Church of England and now in the Latin Church's ordinariates for Anglicans in England and

North America; and at Eastern Orthodox pastoral experience and family life in Canada and the United States. It includes the voices of some wives and children of married clergy (though I sought many more); of historians and scholars; and of priests (both Latin and Byzantine), some of whom are celibate, some widowed, and some happily married.

All this is by design to show the global reality of married clergy today and the great diversity in their origins and circumstances. When this volume was first conceived, it was thought sufficient to discuss married priests in the context of the Eastern Catholic Churches, and indeed their experiences still dominate here. But the changes in Catholic life since 2009 (the introduction of the Anglican ordinariates), and especially since the election of Pope Francis in 2013, mean that increasingly when we speak of "married Catholic priests" we do not find such men confined within some kind of "reservation" (to borrow a phrase of the late but still eminent historian Robert Taft) among ethnonationalist churches such as my own Ukrainian Greco-Catholic Church. Increasingly today, married priests are found precisely in the Latin Church, and their numbers have grown since the inauguration of the ordinariates, welcoming in a more organized fashion new numbers of Anglican clergy who had previously come into the Latin Church on an individual basis through such mechanisms as the Pastoral Provision in the United States.[1]

Will there be yet more married priests in the Latin Church? Certainly through late 2019 and the early part of 2020, as final edits were made to this volume, the debate over married Latin clergy has reached a fever pitch. It has long been a staple of Catholic debates going back, as noted above, several decades at least, but recent discussion has engendered even more controversy, not least because some of those stirring the pot this time are highly placed bishops.

In early 2018, three articles defending priestly celibacy appeared in rapid succession, as such things do with some regularity. The first of these articles shambled along, aware, its author claimed, of what it called "very bad" arguments in favor of celibacy,[2] most of which are apparently derived from an Augustinian hostility to sex, which the author proceeded to attempt, rather diffidently, to dismiss. But he then fell into extremely bad "arguments" of his own, the implications of which he seemed blithely to ignore. The central claim this high-profile author (Bishop Robert Barron) makes is that "the appropriateness of linking priesthood and celibacy comes, I think, from the priest's identity as a Eucharistic person."

This claim is never really developed, and the major problem with it comes—as we have seen in past attempts that take this approach—from its subtle denigration of the Eucharist offered by married priests, which is somehow made to seem suspect or at best second-rate—a notion several authors in this book explicitly critique for its clear implication that married priests are somehow lesser "Eucharistic persons." (In their more lurid forms, proponents of this view suggest that priestly hands which have touched their wives are rendered impure and unfit for touching the Eucharist, indeed even to consecrate the bread and wine.)

Such insinuations are offensive enough, but the article blithely carries on with this admission: "There are, I realize, a couple of major problems with offering arguments for celibacy. First, it can make everything seem so pat, rational, and resolved." Immediately we are treated to a brief autobiographical sketch about the author's own struggles with celibacy before he lurches into a quotation of *A Man for All Seasons* to say that, whether it is Thomas More facing martyrdom or a man facing the choice of celibacy, "finally it's a matter of love." And so the article comes to its final claim that "celibacy is finally . . . a form of life adopted by people in love with Jesus Christ." Once more the unspoken implication is that those priests who are not celibate somehow have a diminished love for Christ that is lacking in some way or other.

This is, of course, merely a restatement of the hoary old claim that married priests are "divided" in their loves between parish and home, a claim subjected to withering scrutiny by David Meinzen in this volume. The assumption that goes with Barron's claim is that to serve fellow human beings in one's own family is somehow to detract from serving Christ and His Church. But unless a priest is married to and the father of hostile, atheistic pagans wanting nothing to do with Christ, his serving his family *is* ipso facto serving the Church—the domestic church, no less valuable a "unit" of the body of Christ for either its size or its domesticity. It is high time we moved past this zero-sum idea that a priest serving his family is detracting from serving the Church.[3] There are some serious arguments in favor of celibacy, but this is not one of them.

The third apologia for celibacy was attempted by the cardinal-prefect of the Roman dicastery charged with liturgy and sacraments. In May 2018, during a Pentecost celebration in Chartes Cathedral, Robert Cardinal Sarah, in an incoherent and often apocalyptic "homily," lurched into a discussion of celibacy at one point, using this as an opportunity to voice his hostility to even the possibility of married priests:

Dear fellow priests, always keep this certainty: to be with Christ on the Cross is what priestly celibacy proclaims to the world! The plan, again advanced by some, to detach celibacy from the priesthood by conferring the sacrament of the Order on married men ("viri probati") for, they say, "pastoral reasons or necessities," would have serious consequences, in fact, to definitively break with the Apostolic Tradition. We would [have] to manufacture a priesthood according to our human dimension, but without perpetuating, without extending the priesthood of Christ, obedient, poor and chaste. Indeed, the priest is not only an "alter Christus," but he is truly "ipse Christus," he is Christ himself! And that is why, following Christ and the Church, the priest will always be a sign of contradiction!

The cardinal's claims were given even more publicity in early 2020 as the furor erupted over the book he put together with some kind of input from the retired bishop of Rome, Joseph Ratzinger. The "blurbs" from the publisher, along with other quotes, in both English and French, splashed by the cardinal and his publishers and votaries all over social media, have both repeated and also amplified the bogus notion that there is an "ontological link" between celibacy and priesthood. This was also attempted by the sometime cardinal secretary of the Congregation for the Clergy, Crescenzio Sepe, who several years ago similarly claimed that "the force binding celibacy to the priesthood lies in the ontology of the priest" and that "it is on the strength of this essential, ontological and existential assimilation to Christ that the extreme congruity and relevance of priestly celibacy can and should be judged."[4] This kind of nonsense (which shows up nowhere in Vatican II's *Presbyterorum ordinis* or in Pope Paul VI's 1967 *Sacerdotalis Caelibatus*) must be challenged sharply, as we shall later do. Perhaps such a transparently desperate claim, lacking as it does all basis in the tradition of East and West alike, and being conjured out of thin air sometime after 1992, is a sign of fear on the part of certain people who know unconsciously at least that celibacy's unqualified claims to historicity and apostolicity have fallen apart.

That such historical evidence has indeed fallen apart—if it was ever coherent and trustworthy to begin with—is demonstrated by our opening chapter in the first section of this book. The book unfolds in five sections. We begin with a series of historical reflections on diverse debates and disciplines surrounding marriage, celibacy, ordination, and continence.

David Hunter of the University of Kentucky begins this section for us with his chapter on priesthood and sexual continence and the origins of a Western tradition. Hunter treats debates, especially those around the fourth century, over whether clergy were expected to be celibate, married but sexually continent, or neither, and concludes that those in the West who attempt to insist on a so-called apostolic tradition of celibacy and continence have failed to make the case because the evidence for their claims is lacking. In some cases, such lacking is covered over or twisted in a tendentious fashion so as to provide cover for claims that celibacy was the original apostolic tradition that must still be observed everywhere today by all priests. As the English literary scholar and psychoanalyst Adam Phillips likes to say, "Memories always have a certain future in mind."

Next the Orthodox historian D. O. Herbel looks at the history of married priests in the North American context of the past 125 years, focusing in particular on the Alexis Toth fiasco, which is also treated in the chapter by James Dutko, which rounds out this section. Both men, Orthodox priests, write with an admirable irenicism about an issue that, at the time and for many decades afterward, caused bitterness and division (on the part of Eastern Catholics) and deep suspicion (on the part of Orthodox looking askance at Roman ecumenical moves). Roman intransigence on this issue drove tens of thousands of people out of the Catholic Church earlier in the twentieth century. In many ways it is no exaggeration to say that at least two entire Orthodox churches on this continent today (the Orthodox Church of America and the Carpatho-Russian Orthodox Diocese under Constantinople's jurisdiction) owe their very existence in considerable measure at Roman Catholic bishops, in the United States especially, who refused to have not merely married priests anywhere on the continent, but even previously married—that is, *widowed*—priests! So these men left, taking scores of faithful with them.

One such man, Archpriest James Dutko, is a son of a priest who experienced all of this firsthand. Dutko's chapter on mandatory celibacy among Eastern Catholics and the way it led to Church divisions is based on a talk he gave in Rome in November 2012 at a symposium on married Eastern Catholic priests and is published here for the first time. Dutko serenely recounts shocking events through the lens of his familial history, which functions as a microcosmic example of the large-scale struggles that destroyed families and parishes, especially in the inter-war years.

And yet, as the reader will see, Dutko and his father before him were able graciously to move on with their lives without bitterness or rancor at the unjust and terribly shabby way they and so many other people were treated by their so-called fellow Christians.

Our second section treats canonical issues. Its first chapter is from Patrick Viscuso, who is North America's leading scholar of Eastern, especially Byzantine, canon law. Viscuso, also a member of the long-standing official North American Orthodox-Catholic Theological Consultation, presented a paper to that consultation that we publish here for the first time. Here Viscuso reviews the requirements for ordination in the Greek Orthodox Church in the United States—the largest Orthodox church in this country—and then also reviews the ancient and controverted canonical literature, especially around Trullo, to debunk some of the more common Western assumptions and misrepresentations of those canons and that council.

The following chapter is from a young married Ukrainian Greco-Catholic priest who is a canonist in the Archdiocese of Toronto, one of the largest Latin tribunals in North America. Alexander Laschuk gives us fascinating insights into recent changes in canon law, some of them quite recondite, under Pope Francis. Laschuk analyzes a recent, seemingly minor rule change promulgated by the pope in a document made all the more remarkable for citing a critical source also included in this book.

As the plan for this book was initially taking shape in late 2012, it was decided that of the historical documents to be included, Victor Pospishil's text was high on the list. Pospishil was a very learned but little-known Ukrainian Catholic canonist, some of whose writings only ever circulated in private, almost "samizdat," editions due to the controversy surrounding discussions of married Catholic priests at the time. I had no idea that he would, two years later, be "rehabilitated," as it were, and by Rome herself! In November 2014, the original version of Pospishil's text, contained in the present volume, was cited in a footnote of a document published by the prefect of the Congregation for the Oriental churches. In *Pontificia Praecepta de clero Uxorato Orientali*, signed on 14 June 2014 by Leonardo Cardinal Sandri and published with papal approbation, footnote 7 avers that Pospishil was the source for the document's claim that "Being deprived of ministers of their own rite, an estimated number of around 200,000 Ruthenian faithful passed to Orthodoxy" (Privato dei ministri del loro proprio rito, un numero stimato a circa 200.000 fedeli ruteni passò all'ortodossia).[5] By itself, a footnote may seem a trifling matter indeed, but to those who know how carefully Vatican documents are vetted and how they invariably give overwhelming preference to citing "magisterial" sources (usually, in the modern period, other popes predominantly) and only very rarely works of theologians or canonists, this is significant. The significance, moreover, is amplified when, as readers will discover presently, Pospishil was an unsparing critic of Vatican policies on enforced celibacy, calling them "wholly unrealistic" and noting that "the Roman Curia must *nolens volens* own up to the dubious merit of having presided over the creation of several Eastern Orthodox churches in North America from Catholics who left the Church because of the refusal by Rome to permit the ordination of married priests." Needless to say, most Vatican documents do not habitually quote their critics by name, so the fact that this 2014 document did *not* ignore a critic such as Pospishil is indeed very revealing in many ways, as Laschuk makes clear in his chapter in this volume.

Our third section focuses on ecumenical implications. After 2009 (though, in practice, on an ad hoc basis, for many years before that), Anglican clergy began to be ordained to function as married Catholic priests in the newly created ordinariates in the United Kingdom, North America, and Australia.[6] Several such men, including some here in the United States, were asked to contribute to this book. In the end we were able to include a chapter from the inimitable John Hunwicke of England and the former Church of England bishop Edwin Barnes, who became Catholic. Both have written singular chapters based on their long pastoral and ecumenical experience as both Anglican and now Catholic priests. These chapters are helpful snapshots of married priests as they have lived in two quite distinct ecclesial contexts: first in Anglicanism and now as part of the Latin Church. Latin Catholics have too often been inclined to view the East—if they know of the existence of Eastern Catholics at all—through a colonial lens as inhabiting some kind of quaint ethnic "reservation" (to use the Jesuit historian Robert Taft's phrase) having nothing to do with the Latin Church. But the experience of the Anglican ordinariates is *within the Latin Church herself*, and thus harder to dismiss as some kind of extraneous exotica. Whether this arrangement and experience of married Anglican-cum-Catholic clergy does indeed penetrate further into the life of the Latin Church—and the implications of this for ordering her internal life—are questions the men whose chapters are in this section of the book take up in their chapters in different ways.

Of those, we begin with the droll John Hunwicke, who has had a long pastoral and scholarly ministry in the Church of England and now in the Catholic Church via the ordinariate. His chapter begins, appropriately enough, with the patron of the ordinariate and of all those who move from Canterbury to Rome, the recently canonized John Henry Cardinal Newman, and his thoughts on marriage and ordination in the Anglican and Roman churches. Though the arrangements of the ordinariate are, as Hunwicke acknowledges, still young and new, nothing in that experience so far has been anything other than positive. There are, in other words (*pace* John Ireland), no scandalized Latin lay faithful who collapse on their fainting couches at the sight of a married Catholic priest.

Married bishops, of course, are a different story. One such included here is the late Edwin Barnes, Anglican bishop of Richborough in the Church of England from 1995 to 2002. He was himself received into the Latin Catholic Church in 2011 and within weeks ordained a Catholic deacon and then priest.[7] He died in early 2019. His chapter is second in this section and, in addition to some of the ecumenical history it fascinatingly tells, is useful especially in challenging his fellow Latin Catholics to face some very practical—and especially financial—challenges of supporting a married presbyterate.

Our third section ends with a chapter that knits together James Dutko and Victor Pospishil (whose text is in Appendix 1): Peter Galadza's chapter on the ecumenical implications for Catholic-Orthodox relations today. Galadza, a well-known liturgical scholar and longtime married priest of the Ukrainian Greco-Catholic Church, reviews what has been said on married and celibate priests from the Second Vatican Council onward, paying special attention to the Council, Pope John Paul II, and prominent Catholic canonists such as George Nedungatt, as well as prominent theologians such as Hans Urs von Balthasar. Galadza then turns his attention to what the current pope said while still an archbishop in Argentina. Galadza concludes by expressing the very cautious hope that, whatever currents are afloat today in the Latin Church, they will not again rise up to try to drown Eastern Christians under a tide of reimposed celibacy, for then we would only divide Eastern and Western Christians anew and show that we have learned nothing from the damage and division of the past century.

Our fourth section is the most personal, and this by design. It features as many voices from priestly families as possible, including but not limited to married priests themselves, talking about the very real challenges of life in a pastoral context. This is also the largest section, and I should very much have liked it to be larger still. To that end I solicited many additional contributions, especially from the wives and family members of priests whom I know in North America, Europe, and the Middle East. They were all very diffident about the prospects of writing, and I could secure only two chapters. They seem to have a strong sense that their lives have already been so much under the microscope that any residual privacy has to be guarded carefully (a point Irene Galadza addresses). Additionally, priestly families are used to seeing and overhearing things that cannot then be talked about to preserve parochial confidences, so the reticence to write about them is understandable.

Nonetheless, we have several unique chapters here. We begin with a singular voice: that of David Meinzen, son of a Lutheran pastor and sometime Lutheran (Missouri Synod) seminarian, who became a priest in the Orthodox Church of America nearly twenty years ago and was pastor of one of her larger parishes. Then, in late 2010 he entered the Ukrainian Greco-Catholic Church (UGCC). Today he ministers at a UGCC mission parish in Fort Wayne, Indiana, where he is also the full-time chaplain at the VA hospital, serving bi-ritually by offering the Roman Mass and other sacraments during the week and the Byzantine liturgy and other sacraments on Sundays and feasts at St. Andrew's UGCC mission. With Lutheran ministers in his immediate family and experience living as a "preacher's kid," he reflects on being a married priest in three distinct ecclesial contexts—Eastern Orthodox, Eastern Catholic, and Roman Catholic. His chapter is noteworthy for debunking the oft-heard claim that a married priest will be "distracted" from pastoral responsibilities by having a family. Meinzen turns this on its head by showing that if a married priest does not take care of his family *first* he will be far from effective in looking after his parish "family"—a point also made later in this section of the book by Irene Galadza from the perspective of a wife who has seen how problems arise in the parish when the priest is not able to properly look after himself and his family. In this Meinzen is ahead of many others today in appropriating what psychotherapists and other clinicians increasingly stress as necessary for themselves, their colleagues, and their trainees: "self-care" (and in this case, family care, too) as a sine qua non of effective pastoral care.

At least two contributors here are intimately familiar with playing a series of roles in a parish as part of a priestly family. Julian Hayda, a graduate of DePaul University in Chicago, is the son of a well-known Ukrainian Chicago priest who, sadly, was killed in a cycling accident in 2007 in downtown Chicago. He offers a rare and singular glimpse into what he aptly calls the "fishbowl" of rectory life and the challenges it offers not just priests and parishioners but especially the young children of clerical families.

The second, from a Ukrainian Orthodox context, also in the Midwest, is Nicholas Denysenko, himself a deacon in the Orthodox Church of America and a prolific scholar. His grandfather, as he recounts, was a married priest from Ukraine who came to America and in effect tutored Nick in all the joys and challenges of pastoral life, some of which he shares with us in his chapter.

The challenges to a priestly family, and the culture of parishes, are given insightful and wise reflection in another chapter here: that of Irene Galadza. Her chapter is born out of Galadza's many decades in parish ministry alongside her husband, the mitered archpriest Roman Galadza, and their six children. Together they helped to build what is arguably the most unique and one of the most influential Ukrainian Catholic parishes in the world, St. Elias Church in Brampton, Ontario. Galadza reflects on not only her role as presbytera but also what it takes for husband and wife alike to survive together in parish ministry, with its myriad challenges and countless strains. With discernment and a very gentle and gracious spirit, she offers advice for young couples starting out in parish ministry.

The existence of married priests in the Orthodox churches is often the only thing that many Roman Catholics know about Orthodoxy. Two such married Orthodox priests, William Mills of North Carolina and Andrew Jarmus of Indiana (originally from Canada), round out this section with sometimes funny and sometimes sobering reflections on the experiences of their families' living in rectories now for many years. Both chapters admirably give intimate glimpses into priestly family life while also respecting the boundaries and privacy of their spouses and children. In doing so, Mills and Jarmus remind us that more widespread ordinations of married men in the Latin Church would require that priests learn about just such boundaries and respect. (I am reminded here of the possibly apocryphal story that Wilfred Knox, a prominent theologian in the Church of England in the early twentieth century, once proposed to write a two-volume treatment of moral theology: Volume I: *Respect for Clergy*; Volume II: *Lesser Virtues*!)

Our final section is more explicitly theological. We begin with Fr. Thomas Loya, who, while himself celibate, helpfully begins by first reflecting on the experience of his own family, in which there have been many married priests whose children and spouses have played integral parts supporting the lives of their parishes and helping their priests become better men and fathers, and vice versa. Indeed it is one of this author's most striking and important claims that, deprived of families, celibate Eastern Catholic priests have been *less* able to serve their parishes as well as their married counterparts once did. A wife and children often play an enormous and invaluable series of roles in the economy of a parish, roles that, in their absence, are often abandoned or else performed by paid staff without the same élan.

Next we have a chapter jointly written by an Eastern Catholic archpriest (now widowed) in Australia, Lawrence Cross, and a celibate Roman Catholic priest teaching in Italy, Basilio Petrà. The authors examine what Latin Church apologists for celibacy have been saying in the past few years, especially in the dangerous new tendency to suggest that celibacy is an "ontological" requirement for ordination itself, an utterly novel theory invented out of thin air in the mid-1990s and thus with no support in the tradition of East or West.

Petrà is himself perhaps the most important person writing on this topic today, having authored a number of recent studies in Italian on this very topic.[8] In 2009, one of those studies appeared as "Married Priesthood: Some Theological Resonances" and was published in the academic journal *Logos: A Journal of Eastern Christian Studies*, of which I am the editor.[9] To give that study wider circulation, as well as to introduce anglophone readers to Petrà's thinking, we have reproduced here a condensed version of his article. It builds on his previous piece with Cross in once again showing the absurdities in arguing for an "ontological" status to priestly celibacy.

The final chapter is my own, both forming the book's conclusion and also laying out what I think are the main elements of a theology of married priesthood. I begin that project by drawing on *Familiaris Consortio* (*FC*), the 1981 document Pope John Paul II published after a 1980 synod in Rome on marriage and family. That document offers a theology of marriage such that *nothing* it says could not be applied equally to married priestly families as to all others. *FC* also offers several short, if underdeveloped, reflections on the importance of sacrifice and askesis in sustaining marriage, and to flesh those out further I turn in my second part to Paul Evdokimov's book *The Sacrament of Love*, whose "apologia" for marriage bears a striking resemblance to the late pope's in some ways but then surpasses John Paul and uncannily anticipates the proponents of the "ontology" thesis by turning that very language against those who elevate ordination over marriage. After I reviewed both works, it became overwhelmingly evident that both East and West have today moved beyond any suspicion of marriage or any denigration of it vis-à-vis holy orders. Indeed, what we have today in both East and West is a very "thick" theological defense of marriage and family as an "icon of the Trinity." Nothing in that theology can be gainsaid to call into doubt the validity and equality of a married priesthood alongside a celibate one. Even if, in pastoral and canonical practice, the Catholic Church has not yet fully begun to treat married and celibate priests on the same level everywhere, at the level of theology any lingering suspicion of marriage is now gone and in its place is a vibrant and healthy theology from which the Church can only continue to benefit and grow in the years ahead.

The book ends with two appendixes consisting of historical texts we have chosen to reproduce here because of the importance of their arguments and the relative obscurity of their earlier publication. In the first instance—proceeding chronologically—we reprint (with only light and minor edits) a crucial document long out of print and very hard to find even when it was first printed almost forty-five years ago now: Victor Pospishil's "Compulsory Celibacy for Eastern Catholics in the Americas."[10] Though Pospishil wrote many well-received and conventionally published studies on canon law and pastoral matters, this text from 1976 was almost a species of samizdat literature privately printed and discreetly circulated not in the Gulag, but in Canada.[11] It contains a wealth of detail still not widely known today but deserving to be understood, not least because it provides support and context for the book's earlier chapters by Dutko and Herbel.

Pospishil begins using a case-study method, reviewing the stories of several then-young men whose lives had been yanked around by Rome after these men—believing the Second Vatican Council's call to the Eastern Catholic Churches to recover their own traditions, including that of married priests—went to seminary, studied for the priesthood, presented themselves (with the consent of their wives) to be ordained, and then, after their ordination, were forbidden from functioning as priests after brutal Latin intervention.[12] Pospishil demolishes the transparently manipulative ways in which canon law was abused in the twentieth century to justify a ban on married priests, pleading in the end for the games to be ended because of the damage done directly to Eastern Catholics and indirectly to the Latin Church and her relations with Orthodoxy.

The second text, reproduced in a slightly abbreviated form, is that of J. Kevin Coyle, a longtime professor of patristics and Church history at St. Paul University in Ottawa, Canada, before his sudden death in 2010. At the time of his death, Coyle had been married for twenty-one years, though vanishingly few of even his closest colleagues knew this because he had been ordained an Augustinian priest at one point in his life.

Coyle's text began life as a very long and highly detailed review essay, "Recent Views on the Origins of Clerical Celibacy: A Review of the Literature from 1980–1991," in the journal of which I have been the editor since 2008, *Logos: A Journal of Eastern Christian Studies*. His essay was published in our thirty-fourth volume in 1993, but that volume has long been out of print and enjoyed very limited circulation at the time (since the journal was only then being revived after a long hiatus).

Coyle's essay continues to deserve an audience today because major advocates of clerical celibacy (Alfons Stickler, Christian Cochini, and Roman Cholij especially) continue, in certain apologetic tracts and at websites, to be taken as authoritative and reliable. Coyle shows them very clearly to be neither. His knowledge of the sources, and careful review of the evidence in multiple languages, supports the arguments of David Hunter made at the beginning of this book. Both Coyle and Hunter conclude that it is not possible to appeal to early "apostolic" tradition as a justification for mandatory priestly celibacy because the evidence for such appeals is insufficient to nonexistent.

Notes

1. The history is told here: http://www.pastoralprovision.org. And D. P. Sullins, himself a married Anglican-cum-Catholic priest and professional sociologist, has analyzed the lives of some of these early married Catholic clerics in

Keeping the Vow: The Untold Story of Married Catholic Priests (Oxford University Press, 2016).

2. Bishop Robert Barron, "A Case for Priestly Celibacy," https://www.realclearreligion.org/articles/2018/03/16/a_case_for_priestly_celibacy_110187.html. This was a reprint from the following: https://www.wordonfire.org/resources/article/a-case-for-priestly-celibacy/5726. I give additional examples in my conclusion.

3. The second article, published in May 2018, was from a longtime apologist of celibacy, Peter Stravinskas, who was merely repeating what he has claimed for years now in other collections and articles, as in *Catholic World Report*, 24 May 2018: https://www.catholicworldreport.com/2018/05/24/christ-the-eternal-high-priest-and-the-meaning-of-priestly-celibacy/.

4. Cf., from earlier in the same text: "The problem of celibacy is closely connected with that of the ontological identity of the sacrament of Order," according to a speech of the secretary of the Congregation for the Clergy, Crescenzio Cardinal Sepe, "The Relevancy of Priestly Celibacy Today": http://www.vatican.va/roman_curia/congregations/cclergy/documents/rc_con_cclergy_doc_01011993_revel_en.html. In an earlier speech, whose honesty about the ultimate agenda deserves credit, Sepe claimed that "the reduction of Celibacy to a mere ecclesiastical law, common in some environments, is to be absolutely overcome in light of the papal Magisterium": http://www.clerus.org/clerus/dati/2011-01/25-13/Ars_Celibacy_2010_EN.html.

5. The official version is in *Acta Apostolicae Sedes*, 106, no. 6 (6 June 2014), available at http://www.vatican.va/archive/aas/documents/2014/acta-giugno2014.pdf, 496–499.

6. When, some time ago, I posted news of the forthcoming book on Facebook, the suggestion of Anglican names was made by Mark Woodruff of the United Kingdom. I wish to acknowledge with gratitude my debt to him for this suggestion and for facilitating contacts in England.

7. His own blog tells some of the story here: http://bishedwins.blogspot.com/2011/01/thanks.html.

8. One of those short studies, *Preti celibi e preti sposati: Due carismi della Chiesa cattolica* (Budapest: Cittadella, 2011), 106 pp., has been translated into English by David Hunter—I have a copy in my possession—and is awaiting publication once the vast and vexing complexities of Italian copyright law can be sorted out.

9. "Married Priesthood: Some Theological Resonances," *Logos: A Journal of Eastern Christian Studies* 50 (2009): 459–480.

10. See Andriy Chirovsky's necrology for Pospishil, "Archimandrite Victor Pospishil (1915–2006): An Appreciation of a Pastoral and Scholarly Life," *Logos: A Journal of Eastern Christian Studies* 46 (2006): 287–289.

11. A version of Pospishil's text was apparently published in the United States in the now-defunct journal *Diakonia*. In the version presented here, I have taken the liberty of adding annotations in the footnotes to explain some of Pospishil's otherwise recondite references to past events, texts, and personages.

12. I recently spoke in confidence to a Russian Orthodox Church Outside Russia (ROCOR) priest who was one such man driven out of the Catholic Church but ordained by the Russian Church.

PART I

History Ancient and Modern

CHAPTER ONE

Priestly Celibacy—An Apostolic Tradition?
The Theological Stakes of a Historical Argument

David G. Hunter

I would like to begin this chapter with a quotation from the "Decree on the Life and Ministry of Priests" (*Presbyterorum ordinis*), promulgated in 1965 at the final session of the Second Vatican Council. Describing the role of sexual continence in the life of the priest, the Council fathers stated: "[Perfect and perpetual continence] is not of course required by the very nature of the priesthood, as is clear from the practice of the early Church and the tradition of the Eastern churches: in these there are admirable married priests side by side with those who, together with all the bishops, have the grace of choosing to observe celibacy."[1] The conciliar document went on to reaffirm the commitment of the Latin Church to its traditional discipline of priestly celibacy or sexual continence. However, an important theological principle had been explicitly stated, namely, that this discipline did not belong to the priesthood "by its very nature" (*suapte natura*). It is noteworthy that the Council fathers based this key theological point on two historical realities: "the practice of the early Church" and "the tradition of the Eastern churches." My aim in the present chapter is to address the evidence for the first historical claim, that is, that a married priesthood was the practice of the early Church. I will discuss a recent challenge to this claim, namely, the argument that priestly sexual continence is founded on apostolic tradition and goes back to Jesus himself. I will examine the historical grounds of this argument and its theological ramifications. My central contention is that the hypothesis of an apostolic origin of priestly sexual continence is without any historical foundation and that its perpetuation within the Catholic community today is best understood as an effort to circumvent the teaching of *Presbyterorum ordinis* and the theological implications of the historical claims in that text from Vatican II.

The Historical Argument

At the time of the Second Vatican Council—and indeed, for most of the twentieth century—it was considered an undisputed historical fact that Christian clergy in the West were often married men and that a requirement of complete sexual abstinence for the higher clergy arose in the Western Church only at the end of the fourth century. At that time evidence for it first appears in the decrees of Bishops Damasus and Siricius and in the writings of Ambrose, Jerome, and Ambrosiaster.[2] At the end of the nineteenth century, two German scholars, Gustav Bickell and Franz Xaver von Funk, vigorously debated the issue.[3] Funk's arguments were widely regarded to have carried the day, and a strong consensus of Catholic scholarship in the first half of the twentieth century supported this view. For example, it was enshrined in authoritative surveys on the topic by Henri Leclercq in Hefele and Leclercq, *Histoire des conciles* and the *Dictionnaire d'archéologie chrétienne et de liturgie*, and by Elphège Vacandard in the *Dictionnaire de théologie catholique* and elsewhere.[4]

In the immediate aftermath of Vatican II there was an extraordinary output of historical scholarship on the question of priestly celibacy. Book-length studies appeared by Jean-Paul Audet, Martin Boelens, Edward Schillebeeckx, Roger Gryson, and Georg Denzler, among others, as well as important articles by Charles A. Frazee, Jean-Claude Guy, John E. Lynch, and Henri Crouzel and others.[5] All of these studies agreed that permanent sexual continence did not become a requirement for the higher clergy in the West until the fourth century. The possibility of an apostolic origin of the requirement was not seriously entertained in the immediate post-conciliar literature.

But beginning in the early 1980s and continuing into the later 1990s, a new view (or rather a revival of the earlier view of Bickell) appeared in Catholic circles: namely, that a requirement of complete sexual abstinence for the higher clergy goes back to the apostolic age, indeed to Jesus himself. The proponents of this theory include a Jesuit historian, Christian Cochini, a German cardinal and canon lawyer, the late Alfons Maria Stickler, and, most recently, a German priest and theologian, Stefan Heid.[6] Each of these writers is aware that his view goes beyond the explicit evidence, which dates only from the fourth century, so all of them try in various ways to argue that there must have been an unstated, but universal, tradition of clerical sexual continence that existed apart from and prior to any explicit legislation. All of these attempts are historically problematic.[7]

For example, in his book *The Case for Clerical Celibacy*, Cardinal Stickler attempted to trace priestly celibacy back to some of the radical sayings of Jesus. He cited Luke 18:28–30, where Jesus tells Peter, who was evidently married, that anyone who has left house, wife, brothers, parents, or children for the sake of the kingdom of God will be given repayment many times over in this present time and, in the world to come, eternal life. Although the text does not refer to priests or to any other church officials (which, of course, would have been an anachronism in the days of Jesus), the cardinal comments: "Here we clearly already have the first obligation of clerical celibacy, namely, the commitment to continence in the use of marriage after ordination."[8]

There are several problems with this argument. Stickler rightly noted that Jesus placed radical demands on some of his disciples, although he discreetly ignored Jesus's equally well-attested affirmation of the permanence of marriage (cf. Mark 10:5–9). But there is no good historical reason to identify the radical discipleship of an apostle with what later became the Catholic priesthood. Stickler has assumed that there is a simple identity between the ministry of Jesus's disciples and the office of later Church leaders known as bishops, presbyters, and deacons. The historical reality of early Christianity was more complex. From the earliest times, there were apostles who were generally itinerant missionaries. Besides these traveling preachers, there were local officials administering the individual churches, who were sometimes called "elders" or *presbyteroi* and sometimes "overseers" or *episcopoi*.[9] Initially both types of leaders existed simultaneously, and there is no evidence that celibacy was required of either one. Even in the case of the itinerant missionaries, we have explicit evidence that married couples served as apostles (e.g., 1 Cor. 9:5 and Rom. 16:3–7) and no indication that they were sexually continent.

One might add that Stickler's treatment of the biblical evidence is problematic from another angle. In a recent discussion of the New Testament texts on ministry and celibacy, biblical scholar Raymond F. Collins observed that Stickler has conflated accounts from different gospels in order to create the desired dialogue between Jesus and his disciple Peter:

> To assist him in making a case for clerical celibacy, Stickler has created a conversation between Peter and Jesus from two different gospel accounts. He begins with Matthew's version of Peter's question not only because it was the gospel narrative that had been most commonly used in the Church for centuries but also because it presents Peter as saying that he and the other apostles had left everything—whereas Luke says only that they left their homes. Then Stickler quotes Jesus' response according to Luke. Luke is the only evangelist who describes Jesus as speaking about those who had left their wives.

As Collins has convincingly demonstrated, by blending Peter's words in Matthew 19:27 ("Look, we have left everything and followed you") with Luke's account in Luke 18:29–30 ("Truly I tell you, there is no one who has left house or wife or brothers or parents or children, for the sake of the kingdom of God, who will not get back very much more in this age, and in the age to come eternal life"), Stickler has produced "his own literary creation, not one found in the canonical Scriptures."[10]

In the case of the resident officials (that is, the bishops, presbyters, and deacons), there are some texts in the New Testament that suggest exactly the opposite of a requirement of sexual continence. The Pastoral Epistles, which probably date from the end of the first century or the early second century, portray the dutiful husband and father as the ideal steward of the church.[11] In 1 Timothy 3:2–5, for example, we find the following description of the suitable overseer: "Now a bishop must be above reproach, a husband of one wife, temperate, sensible, respectable, hospitable, an apt teacher, not a drunkard, not violent but gentle, not quarrelsome, and not a lover of money. He must manage his own household well, keeping his children submissive and respectful in every way—for if someone does not know how to manage his own household, how can he take care of God's Church?" Parallel passages exist in 1 Timothy 3:12 for deacons and in Titus 1:6 for presbyters. The Pastoral Epistles present marriage and family life as virtual prerequisites for pastoral ministry as a bishop, presbyter, or deacon. Nothing is said about sexual continence as a requirement for these married officials; indeed, the very opposite is suggested.

Proponents of the apostolic origins hypothesis, of course, are aware of these texts. To take account of them, they are forced into some arguments that are historically dubious. For Stefan Heid, the interpretation of the Pastorals is the entire hinge of his argument. He focuses on the words "a husband of one wife" (*mias gunaikos andra*, which could also be translated as "a man of one woman"). He argues that it means that a candidate for the clergy must not have married more than once. This is a legitimate interpretation, although it is not the only possible one or even the most likely one. Some commentators, for example, take the phrase "man of one woman" to mean simply a man who has lived in faithful monogamy with his wife, and not necessarily the prohibition of a second marriage.[12] In his commentary on this verse in the Anchor Bible series, Luke Timothy Johnson lists four possible interpretations for the phrase "a man of one wife." The bishop should be (1) monogamous (i.e., not polygamous) or (2) faithful to one wife (i.e., abstaining from extramarital sexual activities) or (3) married only once (i.e., not remarried, if widowed); or (4) a married man (i.e., required to be married). He declines to decide among these options.[13] More recently Raymond Collins has argued that "a husband of one wife" refers only to a man who has been faithful in marriage, not a prohibition of remarriage.[14]

There were even a few patristic interpreters who took the phrase "a man of one wife" to signify simply a commitment to sexual fidelity within marriage rather than a prohibition of a second marriage. Theodore of Mopsuestia, for example, held that the author of the Pastorals taught that a bishop should be a man "who, marrying a wife, continued to live chastely (*sôphronôs*) with her, keeping to her and limiting the appetite of nature to her."[15] According to Theodore, the apostle did not intend to bar twice-married men from advancement to the episcopate. Theodoret of Cyrrhus later supported Theodore's view, citing Paul's willingness to approve of remarriage.[16] While most patristic commentators understood the phrase to mean a prohibition of remarriage, the interpretations of Theodore and Theodoret, along with the reservations of modern scholars, should make us cautious about claiming that the meaning of the phrase from the Pastorals is clear.

Nevertheless, there may be good reasons to take "a man of one wife" as stating a prohibition of remarriage, as Heid does. Several second-century texts show a strong disapproval of second marriages for all Christians and not just for the clergy. Athenagoras, for example, stated that a second marriage was merely "respectable-looking adultery."[17] Somewhat more moderate views were expressed by Hermas, the early second-century author of *The Shepherd*: while not totally rejecting remarriage, Hermas suggested that a Christian who abstains from a second marriage gains "greater honor and great glory with the Lord."[18] It is possible that the author of the Pastoral Epistles might have wished to make binding on the clergy that same standard of marital conduct that Hermas and Athenagoras hoped for from the laity. Moreover, by the third century it seems to have been a common expectation that clergymen would not remarry and that twice-married Christians would not be ordained.[19]

Heid's reading of the phrase "a man of one wife" as a prohibition of second marriage for the clergy, therefore, may be correct. But what he proceeds to derive from it is untenable. The reason for the prohibition of a second marriage, Heid argues, is that a second marriage shows a lack of self-control. And why is a lack of self-control an impediment to membership in the clergy? Heid's answer: Because complete sexual abstinence was required of the clergy from the moment of their ordination. The circularity of this argument is clear. Heid has assumed the existence of an absolute requirement of sexual abstinence, even though the passage in question says nothing about it. He argues that there would be no reason for the author of the Pastoral Epistles to forbid a second marriage for a prospective clergyman unless he was expected to be sexually abstinent from the moment of his ordination. But this argument ignores the fact that many Christians in the second century considered second marriages to be problematic, whether or not one was in the clergy, and this implies nothing about sexual abstinence in the first marriage.[20] The requirement of strict monogamy for Church leaders—if that is what we have in the Pastoral Epistles—would have been an expression of these more general reservations about remarriage. There is no reason to think it entailed a requirement of complete sexual abstinence even within the first marriage.[21]

Once 1 Timothy 3:2 and the parallel passages from the Pastorals are removed from consideration as bases on which to establish the apostolic origins of clerical sexual continence, the weakness of the apostolic origins case becomes fully apparent. The reason is that prior to the fourth century there is no evidence of such a requirement, and those who want to pursue the case have to produce explanations for the lack of evidence. Cochini and Stickler have similar ways of accounting for this lack of evidence. Cochini appeals to what he calls the "principle of progressive explicitation," that is, the notion that a teaching could be included in the oral tradition of the apostles and held universally in the Church before being explicitly defined dogmatically.[22] Stickler, likewise, arguing from the perspective of a canon lawyer, suggests that it is usual for an oral law (*ius*) to exist prior to its formulation as a written law (*lex*).[23]

There may be an element of truth in these claims; for example, it is likely that an informal custom of clerical sexual continence may have arisen in the third century and pre-existed the appearance of the fourth-century Western requirement. As I will note below, Tertullian mentioned that there were some clergymen (and women) who had adopted complete sexual continence, and Origen expressed his personal preference for clerical sexual continence. But Cochini and Stickler have offered no compelling reason to project this development all the way back into the first century. Indeed, their appeals to an alleged "oral tradition" appear to be futile attempts to conjure evidence where it does not exist. Moreover, both Cochini and Stickler seem to be led astray by the way in which the fourth-century popes and the Council of Carthage in 390 *claimed* that the tradition of clerical sexual continence was an apostolic one.[24] But these appeals to fourth-century popes and councils do not provide adequate historical grounds on which to construct the existence of a genuine tradition that extends all the way back to the time of the apostles.[25]

There are yet further reasons to question whether a requirement of clerical sexual continence existed prior to its appearance in the explicit fourth-century evidence. On the one hand, we have a number of texts that speak of the qualifications for bishops in the third century. Both the *Apostolic Tradition*, attributed to Hippolytus, and the Syriac *Didascalia Apostolorum* address the issue of qualifications of the clergy, but without any mention of a requirement of sexual continence. On the other hand, those writers who do allude to a practice of priestly continence prior to the fourth century seem to assume that the practice was optional. For example, in the late second century Clement of Alexandria could write as though it was well known that married clerics would continue to engage in sexual relations and procreation with their wives. In the third book of his *Stromateis*, he comments on the passage from 1 Timothy 3 that we have just examined: "[The apostle Paul] entirely approves of the man who is husband of one wife, whether he is a presbyter, deacon, or layman, if he makes use of marriage blamelessly (1 Tim. 2:15)."[26]

Later, in the third century, both Tertullian and Origen spoke approvingly of clergy who remained sexually abstinent, but their comments do not indicate that such a practice was universally required and, in fact, may suggest just the opposite. In his writings against second marriage, Tertullian frequently mentioned that bishops were to be married only once, but he never referred to a requirement of permanent sexual abstinence. In his treatise *De exhortatione castitatis* Tertullian stated that "many men and women in ecclesiastical orders" were distinguished for their continence.[27] But Tertullian did not say that this sexual continence was a requirement, and his statement could imply that such clergy were especially noteworthy and not the norm.

A similar observation may be made regarding a passage in Origen's *Homilies on Leviticus*, in which he alluded briefly to the practice of sexual continence among "priests." Origen noted that although priests in the Old Testament were allowed to produce offspring to continue the priestly line, he would not endorse such a practice for Christian priests: "For sometimes concessions were granted concerning the posterity of the race and the succession of offspring. But I would not introduce such an understanding for the priests of the Church, for I see something else suggested in the mystery."[28] Origen's preference for a celibate clergy is clear, although he, too, does not speak of a law of sexual continence.[29] Moreover, in the passage in question Origen went on to interpret the abstinence of the Christian priest in an entirely allegorical sense: It refers to the Christian teacher who abstains from "begetting," that is, from giving birth to children in the preaching of the gospel. Such "abstinence" is in order, Origen argues, when the teacher sees that the hearers do not have ears that are receptive to the gospel.[30]

One further argument can be given against the assumption that clerical sexual continence was an apostolic tradition. In addition to the absence of any evidence of such a requirement prior to the fourth century, we have considerable evidence from the late fourth century indicating that the requirement was still seen as a novelty by many of the clergy upon whom it was being imposed. Bishops Damasus and Siricius of Rome and Ambrose of Milan acknowledged that many bishops and presbyters were simply unaware that any such requirement existed. In *De officiis*, for example, Ambrose observed: "In quite a number of out-of-the-way places, men who have been exercising a ministry—even, in some cases, the priesthood itself—have fathered children. They defend this behavior by claiming that they are following an old custom, one which used to obtain when the sacrifice was offered only at lengthy intervals."[31] Similarly, in the decretal *Ad Gallos episcopos* (probably composed by Damasus, though sometimes attributed to Siricius), the author stated that "many bishops" (*multos episcopos*) had regularly ignored ecclesiastical tradition on the matter of clerical sexual continence.[32] Likewise, in a letter to the Spanish bishop Himerius, Siricius indicated that some clergy in Spain appeared to be completely unaware of the requirement, while others refused to accept it.[33] Proponents of the apostolic origins hypothesis can account for this ignorance only by maintaining that the apostolic injunction to sexual continence—which they believe was preserved in oral tradition for three centuries—was then forgotten in many places by the fourth century. While such an occurrence is possible, it seems more reasonable to conclude that the sexual continence requirement was not an apostolic tradition, but rather a development that crystallized in the fourth-century Western Church.

The Theological Stakes

My aim in the first part of this chapter has been to subject the hypothesis of an apostolic origin of priestly sexual continence to serious historical scrutiny. I have argued that the views of Cochini, Stickler, and Heid lack a firm historical foundation and appear to be based on a combination of wishful thinking and special pleading. Despite the weakness of their arguments, the views of these scholars continue to be propagated actively in the Catholic Church today. To cite one recent example, on March 4–5, 2010, the Pontifical University of the Holy Cross, an Opus Dei foundation, held a symposium on priestly celibacy that featured a lecture by Stefan Heid. One could also mention a similar colloquy at Ars, convoked on April 24–26, 2011, at which Fr. Christian Cochini spoke on "Les origines apostoliques du célibat sacerdotal."[34] The fact that these views persist, despite their conflict with several generations of solid Catholic scholarship and despite their clear contradiction of the teaching of the Second Vatican Council, raises the following question: Why are such strenuous efforts being made on behalf of an argument that is so historically problematic?

The answer, of course, is that there is something greater at stake on the issue of the apostolic origins of clerical sexual continence than simply a historical point. As indicated in the passage cited above from *Presbyterorum ordinis*, the Council fathers had appealed to both "the practice of the early Church" and "the tradition of the Eastern churches" in order to support the theological claim that complete sexual continence was not required of the priesthood by its very nature. In order to appreciate the significance of this theological claim in its historical context, we must digress for a moment into the wider discussion of priestly celibacy that surrounded the Second Vatican Council and then continued in the subsequent decades. Attention to this broader context will enable us to understand better the persistence of the apostolic origins hypothesis and its theological implications.

There is little doubt that the future of the discipline of clerical celibacy was in the minds of many Catholics, both clergy and laity, at the time of the Second Vatican Council. Like the issue of artificial contraception, this was a matter that Pope Paul VI decided to reserve for his own judgment rather than to entrust to the bishops at the Council. In October of 1965, Pope Paul VI decided that the bishops at Vatican II would not be allowed to discuss publicly the question of celibacy in the Latin Church. His aim was probably to forestall what would have been an explosive discussion.[35] Later that year the bishops issued the "Decree on the Ministry and Life of Priests" (*Presbyterorum ordinis*). As we have seen, this document acknowledged the value of the married priesthood in the Eastern churches and affirmed that a similar practice was observed in the early Church. Nevertheless, despite its clear acknowledgment of the ancient and contemporary tradition of a married priesthood, most of the Council's decree concerned itself with demonstrating the "very many ways in which celibacy is appropriate to the priesthood."[36]

The years immediately after the close of the Council witnessed an intense outpouring of historical and theological writing on clerical celibacy. Much of this work seems to have been motivated by a desire to change the Church's contemporary practice, an aim that had been frustrated at the Council itself. Jean-Paul Audet probably spoke for many when he wrote in his 1967 book: "Is there a possibility that we shall honestly reconsider our law of clerical celibacy in the near future? It seems to me that we can only hope so."[37] As a result, we see many Catholic scholars emphasizing the negative factors motivating the sexual continence legislation and thus raising questions about the legitimacy of the development.

Perhaps the most dominant historical explanation of the sexual continence discipline to emerge in the decades after Vatican II was that some kind of "ritual" or "cultic impurity" lay at its root. Because the cultic rationale was no longer persuasive for many critics, it raised further questions about the value of the Church's discipline. One sees this position taken by numerous authors. Jean-Paul Audet, for example, argued that the perception of sexual activity as a source of "impurity" was "one of the most evidently regressive elements in our entire inheritance as human beings."[38] Edward Schillebeeckx suggested that there was a strong "pagan" element in the cultic purity motive, although it had been transformed into a "Christian" one in the light of the Augustinian doctrine of original sin. In such a view, according to Schillebeeckx, "sex is not degrading simply as such (anthropological dualism), but on account of the historic sinfulness of mankind (original sin)."[39]

A somewhat different tack was taken by Bernard Verkamp in an article on the ritual purity motivation. Verkamp noted that, although Catholic leaders had championed the ritual purity argument for centuries (he cited the most recent examples of Popes Pius XI and Pius XII), it was no longer being invoked by popes or councils: "Pope John XXIII, Pope Paul VI, and the Second Vatican Council all reaffirmed the law of celibacy, but did so without any explicit appeal to the notion of cultic purity. In fact, one gets the impression from reading the pertinent documents of Vatican II and Paul VI's encyclical *Sacerdotalis caelibatus* that the cultic purity rationale is being consciously and purposely rejected."[40] Such a shift, Verkamp noted, was certain to call into question the law itself.

Similarly, in a lengthy survey of the role of cultic purity in Catholic justifications of clerical celibacy, Georg Denzler observed that one no longer finds such arguments in official Catholic pronouncements. Citing a statement from the Sacred Congregation for Catholic Education published on April 11, 1974, which explicitly rejected "ritual purity" as a rationale for priestly celibacy, Denzler noted: "For the first time, a chief motive since the beginning of the church in favour of priestly abstinence and celibacy was officially abandoned."[41]

The upshot of all this post-conciliar discussion was to raise serious questions about the historical origins of the celibacy requirement and serious doubts about its validity in the Church of the late twentieth century. The writings of Cochini, Stickler, and Heid, then, can be interpreted as an effort to counteract the influence of the "ritual purity" perspective and to reinforce the Church's contemporary discipline in opposition to the movement for change that followed Vatican II. By tracing the development of clerical celibacy and sexual continence back to the apostolic age, these Catholic authors were attempting to circumvent the historical claims of Vatican II, as well as the difficulties implied in the "ritual purity" hypothesis, and trying to establish firmer grounds for the Church's traditional practice.

Moreover, there were also ecumenical implications in these historical questions. If, as Cochini, Stickler, and Heid wished to argue, the discipline of permanent sexual continence for priests could be traced back to the apostolic age, the tradition of the Eastern churches would also be impugned. The Eastern Christian practice of allowing deacons and presbyters to exercise their marital rights could then be seen as a departure from apostolic tradition (a justifiable "accommodation" to human weakness, perhaps, but still something short of the ideal). In this way, both of the historical bases on which *Presbyterorum ordinis* based its teaching would be removed. The way then would be cleared to consider the discipline of clerical sexual continence not only an apostolic tradition but also an essential aspect of the priesthood *suapte natura*. These are the "theological stakes" involved in this "historical argument."

Conclusion

My primary aim here has been to raise questions about the validity of the historical arguments that have been advanced in favor of the apostolic origins of priestly celibacy. But I hope I have also shown that these historical arguments were themselves provoked by conflicts within Roman Catholicism in the wake of Vatican II. Both the opponents and the proponents of a requirement of sexual continence for the clergy made use of historical arguments about the origins and character of the requirement to advance agendas that were essentially theological in nature, namely, to stake a position on the question of the validity of the requirement in the Church today. There is still a need for a historical account of the origins of clerical sexual continence that treats the issue, as much as possible, *sine ira et studio*, that is, without excessive hostility or partiality. While it is impossible to write a history without some perspective or presuppositions, rules of evidence and interpretation must still be respected. When they are, such a history will have a legitimate stake in theological argument.

Notes

1. *Presbyterorum Ordinis* 16; text and translation in Norman P. Tanner, S.J., *Decrees of the Ecumenical Councils*, vol. 2: *Trent–Vatican II* (London: Sheed & Ward; Washington, DC: Georgetown University Press, 1990), 1062: "Non exigitur quidem a sacerdotio suapte natura, uti apparet et praxi ecclesiae primaevae et ex traditione ecclesiarum orientalium, ubi praeter illos qui cum omnibus episcopis ex dono gratiae coelibatum eligunt servandum, sunt etiam optime meriti presbyteri coniugati." When it references "the practice of the early Church," the document cites 1 Timothy 3:2–5 and Titus 1:6.

2. Canon 33 of the Synod of Elvira (c. 305) is sometimes cited as the earliest evidence of a canonical prohibition of sexual relations for the higher clergy: "Placuit in totum prohibere episcopis, presbyteris et diaconibus vel omnibus clericis positis in ministerio abstinere se a coniugibus suis et non generare filios. Quicumque vero fecerit, ab honore clericatus exterminetur." Text in José Vives, ed., *Concilios Visigóticos et Hispano-Romanos* (Barcelona and Madrid: Consejo Superior de Investigaciones Científicas Instituto Enrique Flórez, 1963), 7. But the reader should know that serious doubts have been raised about the authenticity of this and other canons from Elvira; see the recent discussion by Josep Vilella Masana in "Las sanciones de los cánones pseudoiliberritanos," *Sacris erudiri* 46 (2007): 5–87. In any case, the ruling at Elvira would have had only local application. For an excellent overview of the problems surrounding the supposed Council of Elvira and its canons, as well as a history of the historiography, see Miguel J. Lázaro Sánchez, "L'état actuel de la recherché sur le concile d'Elvire," *Revue des sciences religieuses* 82 (2008): 517–546.

3. G. Bickell, "Der Cölibat eine apostoliche Anordnung," *Zeitschrift für katholische Theologie* 2 (1878): 26–64 and "Der Cölibat dennoch eine apostolische Anordnung," *Zeitschrift für katholische Theologie* 3 (1879): 792–799; F. X. von Funk, "Der Cölibat keine apostolische Anordnung," *Theologische Quartalschrift* 61 (1879): 208–247; "Der Cölibat noch lange keine apostolische Anordnung,"

Theologische Quartalschrift 62 (1880): 202–221; and "Cölibat und Priesterehe im christlichen Altertum," in his *Kirchengeschichtliche Abhandlungen und Untersuchungen*, I (Paderborn: F. Schöningh, 1897), 121–155.

4. Leclercq: "La legislation conciliaire relative au célibat ecclésiastique," in C. J. Hefele and H. Leclercq, *Histoire des conciles d'après les documents originaux*, II, 2, and Appendice VI (Paris: Librairie Letouzey et Ané, 1908), 1321–1348, and "Célibat," *Dictionnaire d'archéologie chrétienne et de liturgie* (Paris: Librairie Letouzey et Ané), 2:2802–2832. Vacandard: "Les origines du célibat ecclésiastique," *Revue du clergé français* 42 (1905): 252–289, reprinted in Vacandard's *Études de critique et d'histoire religieuse*, vol. 1 (Paris: Librairie V. Lecoffre, 1905), 71–120, and "Célibat ecclésiastique," *Dictionnaire de théologie catholique*, 2:2068–2088.

5. Audet: *Mariage et célibat dans le service pastoral de l'église: Histoire et orientations* (Paris: Éditions de l'Orante, 1967, reprinted in Québec: Éditions des sources, 1999), English translation by Rosemary Sheed, *Structures of Christian Priesthood* (New York: Macmillan, 1968). Boelens: *Die Klerikerehe in der Gesetzgebung der Kirche unter besonderer Berücksichtigung der Strafe: Eine rechtsgeschichtliche Untersuchung von den Anfängen der Kirche bis zum Jahre 1139* (Paderborn: F. Schöningh, 1968). Schillebeeckx: The original Dutch edition appeared in 1966: *Het ambts-celibaat in de branding: Een kritische bezinning* (Bilthoven: H. Nelissen, 1966), English translation by C.A.L. Jarrott, *Clerical Celibacy under Fire* (London and Sydney: Sheed and Ward, 1968). A less inflammatory title was used in the American edition: *Celibacy* (New York: Sheed and Ward, 1968). Gryson: *Les origines du célibat ecclésiastique du premier au septième siècle* (Gembloux, Belgium: Éditions J. Duculot, 1970). Crouzel and others: Denzler: *Das Papsttum und der Amtszölibat*, 2 vols., Päpste und Papsttum, Band 5, 1–2 (Stuttgart: Anton Hiersemann, 1973). See also Denzler's later book, *Die Geschichte des Zölibats* (Freiburg: Herder, 1993). Frazee: "The Origins of Clerical Celibacy in the Western Church," *Church History* 41 (1972): 149–167, reprinted in *Church History* 57 (1988, supplement): 108–126. Guy: "Le célibat sacerdotal: Approches historiques," *Études* 335 (1971): 93–106. Lynch: "Marriage and Celibacy of the Clergy: The Discipline of the Western Church; An Historico-Canonical Synopsis," *Jurist* 32 (1972): 14–38, 189–212. Crouzel's essay "Le célibat et la continence dans l'Église primitive: Leurs motivations," in *Celibacy and Ecclesiastical Continence in the Early Church: The Motives Involved*, along with other important studies, appeared in Joseph Coppens, ed., *Sacerdoce et célibat: Études historiques et théologiques* (Gembloux, Belgium: Duculot and Louvain: Peeters, 1971), 333–371. See also the useful collection of essays edited by William Bassett and Peter Huizing, *Celibacy in the Church* (New York: Herder, 1972).

6. Cochini: *The Apostolic Origins of Priestly Celibacy*, trans. Nelly Marans (San Francisco: Ignatius Press, 1990). Cochini's book, originally presented as his doctoral thesis at the Institut Catholique, was first published as *Origines apostoliques du célibat sacerdotal* (Paris: Éditions Lethielleux, 1981). Cochini has re-

cently restated his views in "Les origines apostoliques du célibat sacerdotal," in Vincent Siret, ed., *Le célibat sacerdotal, fondements, joies, defis: Colloque à Ars, 24-25-26 janvier 2011* (Paris: Parole et Silence, 2011), 37–64. Stickler: *The Case for Clerical Celibacy: Its Historical Development and Theological Foundations*, trans. Brian Ferme (San Francisco: Ignatius Press, 1995). Stickler's book was originally published as *Der Klerikerzölibat: Seine Entwicklungsgeschichte und seine theologischen Grundlagen* (Abensberg: Kral, 1993). Heid: *Celibacy in the Early Church: The Beginnings of a Discipline of Obligatory Continence for Clerics in East and West*, trans. Michael J. Miller (San Francisco: Ignatius Press, 2000). Heid's book originally appeared as *Zölibat in der frühen Kirche: Die Anfänge einer Enthaltsamkeitspflicht für Kleriker in Ost und West* (Paderborn: Ferdinand Schöningh, 1997). For a recent statement of his views, see Heid, "Il celibato e la continenza clericale nella Chiesa dei primi secoli: Un'ermeneutica storica per una retta comprensione del celibato nella Chiesa," in Laurent Touze and Marcos Arroyo, eds., *Il celibato sacerdotale: Teologia e vita* (Rome: EDUSC, 2012), 43–62.

7. In addition to the three studies mentioned, another work has defended the "apostolic origins" thesis: Roman Cholij, *Clerical Celibacy in East and West* (Leominster: Fowler Wright, 1989). I will not discuss Cholij here because his book deals primarily with the Council of Trullo (691) and its decrees on the celibacy of bishops and because he relies on Cochini for his account of the origins of clerical continence. See the thorough critique of Cholij and Cochini by J. Kevin Coyle, "Recent Views on the Origins of Clerical Celibacy: A Review of the Literature from 1980–1991," *Logos* 34 (1993): 480–531 (reprinted in this volume).

8. Stickler, *The Case for Clerical Celibacy*, 12.

9. For a reliable survey of the early evidence, see Joseph T. Lienhard, *Ministry* (Message of the Fathers of the Church 8) (Wilmington, DE: Michael Glazier, 1984), esp. 11–21.

10. Raymond F. Collins, *Accompanied by a Believing Wife: Ministry and Celibacy in the Earliest Christian Communities* (Collegeville, MN: Liturgical Press, 2013), 162–163. As Collins shows on pp. 82–83, Luke had a tendency to use hyperbole to underscore the radical nature of discipleship.

11. Plausible dates for the Pastorals range from 80 to 120. The outer limit is suggested by Helmut Koester, *Introduction to the New Testament*, vol. 2: *History and Literature of Early Christianity*, 2nd ed. (New York and Berlin: W. de Gruyter, 2000), 307–308.

12. A detailed case for this view has been made by Sydney Page, "Marital Expectations of Church Leaders in the Pastoral Epistles," *Journal for the Study of the New Testament* 50 (1993): 105–120.

13. See *The First and Second Letters to Timothy: A New Translation with Introduction and Commentary* (The Anchor Bible) (New York: Doubleday, 2001), 213–214. A similar ambivalence regarding the phrase is found in the commentary

of M. Dibelius and H. Conzelmann, *The Pastoral Epistles* (Philadelphia: Fortress Press, 1972), 52.

14. Collins, *Accompanied by a Believing Wife*, 184–214.

15. *Comm. in epistulam I ad Timotheum* (*PG* 66, 939); I have adopted the translation of Rowan Greer, *Theodore of Mopsuestia: The Commentaries on the Minor Epistles of Paul* (Writings from the Greco-Roman World; Leiden: Brill, 2010), 571.

16. See Theodoret's commentary on 1 Timothy 3:2 (*PG* 82, 805).

17. Athenagoras, *Legatio* 33.6: *euprepês estin moicheia*.

18. *Mandata* 4.4.32; text and translation in Michael W. Holmes, *The Apostolic Fathers: Greek Texts and English Translations*, 3rd ed. (Grand Rapids, MI: Baker Academic, 2007), 514–515.

19. See, e.g., Tertullian, *De exhortatione castitatis* 7.2 (CCSL 2, 1024); Origen, *Hom. in Luc.* 17.10 (SC 87, 262); *Comm. in Mt.* 14.22 (GCS 40, 336–337).

20. Single marriage was a widespread cultural ideal, one amply attested in pagan and Jewish inscriptions. See Majorie Lightman and William Zeisel, "Univira: An Example of Continuity and Change in Roman Society," *Church History* 46 (1977): 19–32; Bernard Kötting, "'Univira' in Inschriften," in W. den Boer et al., eds., *Romanitas et Christianitas: Studia Iano Henrico Waszink A.D. VI Kal. Nov. A. MCMLXXIII XIII lustra complenti oblata* (Amsterdam and London: North-Holland Publishing, 1973), 195–206; and Jean-Baptiste Frey, "La signification des termes ΜΟΝΑΝΔΡΟΣ et univira: Coup d'oeil sur la famille romaine aux premiers siécles de notre ère," *Recherches de science religieuse* 20 (1930): 48–60.

21. As Raymond Collins has observed, in *Accompanied by a Believing Wife*, 198, regarding Heid's interpretation of "a man of one wife": "Excluding sexual intercourse from the marriages of ministers of the Church is based on eisegesis of the biblical texts. It is reading something into the texts that the texts themselves do not imply." For further critique of Heid's interpretation of 1 Timothy, see Joseph T. Lienhard, "The Origins and Practice of Priestly Celibacy in the Early Church," in John C. Cavadini, ed., *The Charism of Priestly Celibacy: Biblical, Theological, and Pastoral Reflections* (Notre Dame, IN: Ave Maria Press, 2012), 47–64, esp. 49–53, and also the review of Heid's book by Hubertus Drobner in *Römische Quartalschrift für christliche Altertumskunde und Kirchengeschichte* 94 (1999): 311–312.

22. Cochini, *Apostolic Origins of Priestly Celibacy*, 62–63. But Cochini also claims that the teaching may have been stated explicitly in texts that are now lost. See the cogent critique of Cochini on this point by Coyle, "Recent Views," 484–485.

23. Stickler, *The Case for Clerical Celibacy*, 17–19.

24. Cochini, on pp. 3–17, begins his account with a presentation of the documents from the Council of Carthage of 390 and the *decreta* of Siricius in order to

establish that these magisterial documents teach the apostolic origins of clerical sexual continence. Similarly, Stickler, in *The Case for Clerical Celibacy*, 27–28, cites the same evidence and asserts: "From these texts there is clear evidence of a tradition that is based not only on a general conviction, which no one doubted, but also on solid documentary evidence."

25. See also the critique of Cochini by Roger Balducelli, who faults him for appealing to the realm of faith rather than history: "The Apostolic Origins of Clerical Continence: A Critical Appraisal of a New Book," *Theological Studies* 43 (1982): 693–705.

26. *Strom.* 3.12.90 (GCS 52, 237). In general, Clement was reluctant to grant that a life of celibacy was superior to one spent in marriage. See *Strom.* 3.12.79 and 7.12.70 and also my discussion in *Marriage, Celibacy, and Heresy in Ancient Christianity: The Jovinianist Controversy* (Oxford: Oxford University Press, 2007), 111–113.

27. *De exhortatione castitatis* 13.4 (CChr 2: 1035): "Quanti igitur et quantae in ecclesiasticis ordinibus de continentia censentur, qui Deo nubere maluerunt, qui carnis suae honorem restituerunt,—quique se iam illius aeui filios dicauerunt, occidentes in se concupiscentiam libidinis et totum illud, quod intra paradisum non potuit admitti." Translated by William P. Le Saint, S.J., in *Tertullian: Treatises on Marriage and Remarriage*. ACW 13 (New York: Newman Press, 1951), 64: "How many men and women there are whose chastity has obtained for them the honor of ecclesiastical orders! How many who have chosen to be wedded to God! How many who have restored to their flesh the honor it had lost! They have already set themselves apart as children of the world to come by killing concupiscence and, with it, all else that has no place in Paradise."

28. *Hom. in Lev.* 6.6.2–3, translated by Gary Wayne Barkley in *Origen: Homilies on Leviticus 1–16* (Fathers of the Church 83) (Washington, DC: Catholic University of America Press, 1990), 127.

29. Henri Crouzel, in "Le célibat et la continence dans l'Église primitive," 349, says he doubts that Origen is referring to a requirement of clerical sexual continence in this passage. Origen spoke obliquely of the sexual continence of priests in several other places. See *Hom. on Numbers* 23.3.2 and *Contra Celsum* 7.48.

30. We must be careful, however, not to assume that by "priest" Origen necessarily means an ordained official of the Church. "Priest" and "apostle" were terms that Origen often used to describe the "charismatic intellectual" in contrast to the ecclesiastic official. See the discussion in Joseph W. Trigg, "The Charismatic Intellectual: Origen's Understanding of Religious Leadership," *Church History* 50 (1981): 5–19. According to Trigg, 12, Origen applied the notions of "priest" and "apostle" to the charismatic teacher as "a way to oppose the pretensions of official authority, which was rapidly appropriating these very symbols to legitimate episcopal authority."

31. *De officiis* 1.249; text and translation in Ivor J. Davidson, *Ambrose: De officiis* (Oxford: Oxford University Press, 2001), 260.

32. *Ad Gallos episcopos* 2; text in Y.-M. Duval, ed., *La décrétale Ad Gallos Episcopos: Son texte et son auteur* (supplements to *Vigiliae Christianae* 73) (Leiden and Boston: Brill, 2005), 26. See also Ursula Reutter, *Damasus, Bischof von Rom (366–384): Leben und Werk* (Tübingen: Mohr Siebeck, 2009), 192–233, who also attributes the letter to Damasus, though she seems to be unaware of Duval's study.

33. Siricius, ep. 1.7.11 (PL 13: 1140) allowed that a clergyman who lapsed out of ignorance could keep his office as long as he embraced continence thereafter.

34. See n. 15 above.

35. See Mauro Velati, "Completing the Conciliar Agenda," in Giuseppe Alberigo, ed., *History of Vatican II*, vol. 5: *The Council and the Transition: Fourth Period and the End of the Council, September 1965–December 1965* (Leuven: Peeters; Maryknoll: Orbis, 2006), 231–237.

36. *Presbyterorum ordinis* 16: "Coelibatus vero multimodam convenientiam cum sacerdotio habet."

37. *Structures of Christian Priesthood*, 108.

38. Ibid., 91.

39. Schillebeeckx, *Clerical Celibacy under Fire*, 52. The study of Gryson, cited in n. 5 above, offered the most sustained account of the "ritual purity" argument, though without the negative judgments offered by Audet and Schillebeeckx.

40. "Cultic Purity and the Law of Celibacy," *Review for Religious* 30 (1971): 199–217, quotation at 217.

41. *Die Geschichte des Zölibats*, 78–79. Denzler has in mind the following passage from *Orientamenti educative per la formazione al celibato sacerdotale* (Rome: Sacred Congregation for Christian Education, 1974), 13: "Essa non è mossa da ragioni di 'purezza rituale' o dal concetto che solo per mezzo del celibato si possa giungere alla santificazione." In his broad survey of the history of clerical celibacy, Denzler had acknowledged that additional factors were at work in the formation of the tradition, including ascetic purity, social prestige, economic interests, power struggles, and theological arguments.

CHAPTER TWO

From Antioch to America via Smyrna

Rethinking Married Priesthood and Parish Life with Ignatius, Alexis, and Polycarp

Dellas Oliver Herbel

In some Orthodox circles (especially American Orthodox circles), the confrontation between Alexis Toth, an Eastern Catholic priest, and Archbishop John Ireland of Minneapolis has become the stuff of legend. Many sources provide what we know, based on Toth's later recounting.[1] Archbishop Ireland objected to Toth's presence, due to his being married (even though a widower by that time). Soon after their falling out, Toth and his congregation joined the Russian Orthodox Church, becoming part of the Russian Mission to North America. I have argued elsewhere that Toth converted not simply because of his falling out with Ireland but also because his falling out with Ireland was a catalyst for Toth to follow through on theological and Russophile convictions he already held.[2] Put simply, Toth believed the Russian Orthodox Church was the true church of his Carpatho-Rusyns ancestors and that he and all other Carpatho-Rusyns should return to that same church.

My intention here is not to explore the Toth Movement anew, much less repeat my previous work, but to revisit how having married clergy was a factor that has helped Orthodox Christianity in its "mission parish" enterprise, starting with the Toth Movement. With that in place, I will suggest ways a married priesthood might continue to face the challenge of mission parish work in the twenty-first century. When doing that, I will use my previous work on Orthodox converts and restorationism but turn that restorationism on its head. I will revisit second-century ecclesiology and use the writings of Ignatius of Antioch and Polycarp of Smyrna not as a means to a destination (the current Orthodox Church) but as a creative launching pad for rethinking how a married clergy might help Orthodox parishes going forward into the next century. In so doing, in this chapter I will at times blur the line between being "academic" and being "personal." I hope the reader will be patient with me for using this approach, but I also hope that the reader will ultimately benefit from it.

Before continuing, however, it might be wise for me to define what I mean by "mission parish." A contemporary mission parish may have any demographic makeup regarding age, race, and gender, but typically has no more than a hundred parishioners (often fewer). Geographically, these parishes exist in a range of situations, from suburbs and parts of cities within commuting distances of other Orthodox parishes to smaller American cities with no Orthodox presence for miles, sometimes hundreds of miles. Therefore, there are both similarities and dissimilarities between them and churches planted earlier by immigrants. The early mission-planting enterprises of immigrants were also often separated over vast geographical regions. Fr. Theoklitos Triantafilides (†1916), for example, could find himself at his parish in Galveston, Texas, helping out in San Francisco, or providing sacraments in Colorado.[3] The earlier missions, however, were often much larger than today's mission parishes, as they were not planned around a group of people consciously deciding to start an Orthodox parish but rather were responses to large influxes of immigrants who already belonged to an Orthodox church (Russian, Greek, etc.). Both the similarities and dissimilarities will be kept in mind as I proceed, but the reader should know that my main aim will be to press for how the married priesthood helps in a mission setting in the twenty-first century.

American Catholicism, the Married Priesthood, and the Growth of American Orthodox

Archbishop Ireland's negative assessment of Toth and his fellow Eastern Christian clergy might come as a surprise to many of us today. In an era in which we desire racial integration in parishes and wrestle with how to respond to social issues such as homosexuality and transgender concerns, a bishop upset over a heterosexual married priest might seem passé at best, especially given that the priest was a widower by that time. It is important to remember, though, that there were two major forces at play in Ireland's reaction.

First, there was the Americanist controversy. Americanists were those who believed that all Roman Catholics in America should conform to a single Catholic ethos, or culture. Two of the more prominent Americanists were Archbishops John Ireland and James Gibbons of Baltimore. Prominent opponents included Archbishop Michael Corrigan of New York City and Bishop Bernard McQuaid of Rochester, New York. Americanism had become a point of contention in the 1890s, and Ireland was at the forefront. The last thing he wanted was a group of clergy who did not conform to his Americanist vision.[4]

The second factor was that western, Latin-rite Catholic clergy genuinely felt threatened by a married priesthood they believed could not perform duties at the level of a celibate priesthood. In 1885, Metropolitan Sylvestr Sembratovych assigned Fr. Ivan Volans'kyĭ (1857–1926) to the Eastern Catholic parish in Shenandoah, Pennsylvania.[5] Volans'kyĭ helped organize not only the Shenandoah parish but also parishes in other areas of Pennsylvania and the East Coast as well as Denver and Minneapolis (Toth's future parish).[6] Volans'kyĭ's interactions with Catholic hierarchs in America foreshadowed what Toth later experienced. In Minneapolis, Archbishop Ireland refused to let Volans'kyĭ serve liturgy in any of the Latin parishes.[7] In Philadelphia, Archbishop John Ryan refused to meet with him, forcing Volans'kyĭ to write both to Sembratovych and to the Roman Congregation for the Propagation of the Faith.[8] Volans'kyĭ later went to Brazil as a missionary and ended his career back in Galicia.

It should be pointed out that bishops were not the only ones who held such views. For example, Fr. Albert A. Lings, Archbishop Corrigan's dean in New York, expressed relief in 1892 that the wife of Fr. Eugene Szatala, a Carpatho-Rusyn Eastern Catholic priest, remained in Europe.[9] An 1898 trip to L'viv, however, would force Lings to admit later that married priests could be effective.[10] Although Lings should be commended for changing his mind on the effectiveness of married priests (at least in the European context), his is but a more tolerant example of the sort of prejudice the Eastern Catholics encountered from both bishops and priests of the Latin Church.[11]

One can see how these two factors could mutually reinforce one another. Catholic clergy at the time were concerned with how they engaged American society and culture and would be perceived by such. Although it might be hard to appreciate today, at the time, many Catholic clergy feared that only a dedicated celibate Latin clergy could engage American Catholicism fruitfully. This attitude, even prejudice, ultimately served as a factor for tens of thousands of Eastern Catholics turning to the Orthodox Church, even beyond the initial Toth Movement.[12]

A married priesthood, however, cannot simply be reduced to a catalyst pushing Eastern Catholic immigrants and their clergy into the Orthodox Churches in America. A married priesthood also assisted the growth and development of Orthodoxy in America. Although we do not have much by way of documentation that can tell us what early American Orthodox clergy thought marriage brought to their ministries, we do know that they highly valued their families, including their co-workers in the mission field, their wives. For example, in the case of Fr. Nicola Yancey, his wife, Martha, helped him homestead near Kearney, Nebraska. Although he was ordained after her death, he always mourned her and would not have been in a position to help his children were it not for having had her as a partner in their homesteading.[13] Additionally, priests' wives would assist their husbands in parish duties, such as leading educational programming.[14]

The Married Priesthood in American Orthodoxy Today

Today's American Orthodox parish reality differs quite a bit from what it had been in the early to mid-twentieth century. Indeed, it may be difficult to see just how the married priesthood specifically can help Orthodoxy in any significant way. Certainly, Roman Catholic clergy in America no longer have deep-seated prejudices against Eastern clergy merely for being married. Orthodox churches today experience no new growth due to priests' being married.

One area of continuity, however, would be the way the married priesthood helped early Orthodox mission and parish building. Here the role played by the wife of the priest was pivotal. She often was his co-laborer and partner both in the home and in the parish. We continue to see this today, and it merits further exploration here to show just how significant the married priesthood may be for American Orthodoxy in the next century.

It is not unusual for a mission parish to have a priest because the priest's wife earns a full-time salary.[15] This is often the case in more established parishes as well, but in mission parishes it can be an absolute necessity. In such cases, the parish is able to focus on expenses other than the priest's salary. The parish often benefits in two ways: first, by having someone who pitches in with parish activities (Sunday School, serving meals, etc.), as many priests' wives have done throughout American Orthodoxy's history, and second, by having someone subsidize the parish budget.

As in many cases, however, the benefits come at a cost. How the costs are paid out will vary from situation to situation, but one can quickly imagine just what they might be: burnout, perhaps even resentment, by the clergy couple, who tire of being the primary financial sacrificers for the mission parish; inattentiveness to the priest's salary by the mission parish (because the priest's wife has a "good job"); impediments to the priest's availability because he must help watch his children while his wife works; and so on.

Perhaps one solution to this problem might be for the priest to accept a full-time job and to serve the mission parish on the side. There are many examples of this in American Orthodoxy as well, but this approach, too, comes with costs, all very similar to those noted above with a priest's wife working a full-time job outside of the home. Indeed, this approach may exacerbate some of those same detriments, as the priest will have even more burdens placed upon his time.

Despite these family constraints, however, the married priesthood is in a position to address the twenty-first-century mission parish realities in a way that is flexible and even innovative. As significant as it is that clergy wives underwrite the parish budget at times and sustain parish ministries as well, one of the most important things a married priesthood brings to the parish is a flexibility to rethink ecclesiology on the parish level. The current ecclesiology centers upon one priest operating on behalf of the diocesan bishop, with a parish council. This singular priest not only serves as the lead pastor and administrator but is also expected to perform myriad liturgical services and pastoral functions.

This standard model of mission parish church structure has served the Orthodox churches in America quite well for a long time. The twenty-first century, however, will be the century of small Orthodox parishes in America. Recent research by Alexei Krindatch at the Hartford Research Institute provides data that shows this is Orthodoxy's current trajectory for the twenty-first century.[16] Orthodoxy increased the number of its parishes by 17 percent during 2000–2012.[17] As a general rule, however, Orthodoxy is no longer adding large parishes from influxes of thousands of immigrants.[18] Additionally, there is a direct negative correlation between parish size and parishioners' attendance.[19] Smaller parishes are the most active in terms of membership dedication. Moreover, unlike in the late nineteenth and early twentieth centuries, the Orthodox churches in America can no longer presume that the majority of the children of immigrants will remain in the Orthodox Church (that is, if they ever could so presume in the first place).[20] In many places in America, especially in Pennsylvania and other regions of the Northeast and/or mining centers, one encounters small and even dying parishes. Small parishes, including small mission parishes, are becoming the American Orthodox norm.

In the midst of this trend, American Orthodox Christianity has an opportunity to leverage the married priesthood into a form that hearkens back to a model witnessed by Ignatius of Antioch and Polycarp of Smyrna. Although it is often thought that Ignatius's view of a local church headed by a bishop, surrounded and supported by a group of presbyters and deacons, is simply a description of the ecclesiology of the second century, the reality is more complex. As Allen Brent has cogently argued, it is much more likely that Ignatius used his procession to Rome (where he was to be martyred) as an opportunity to argue for his particular ecclesiological view (even if it was one in play at Antioch itself).[21] In contrast, a church leader like Polycarp of Smyrna would have seen himself as a bishop among other bishops.

On its surface, leveraging ecclesiological inspiration for twenty-first-century America from the second century might seem outrageous, but American Orthodoxy's twenty-first-century trajectory has been, and will likely continue to be, influenced significantly by a restorationism that finds the early Church within the contemporary Orthodox Church.[22] Therefore, I propose that American Orthodoxy embrace this reality for what it is but do so in a way that seeks inspiration from the Church of the past rather than furthering a claim that it simply is the Church of the past. The way forward, then, is one of change, but change in communication with the past. The married priesthood in twenty-first-century American Orthodoxy is in a prime position to create and implement a Neo-Polycarpian model of parish ecclesiology.

What would this look like? Well, first it would maintain the diocesan structure we have, keeping a bishop in place, as the historical outgrowth of Ignatius's model. It is too strongly entrenched historically and canonically at this time to reconfigure. A monarchical bishop is Ignatius's legacy to the Church, but the context in which he advocated for that is one shaped very much by what Polycarp represented, and that is an emphasis on the local parish, where the local bishop-presbyter saw himself as one among many—the first among equals, to borrow a phrase from later Church history.

This opens us to the second feature of the Neo-Polycarpian model I propose: a community of local clergy serving the needs of a small local parish. Like Polycarp, one's priest would be the "priest-in-charge," or the "first among equals," but would be co-serving with several other priests and deacons. This approach yields several advantages. First, the position of rector could rotate, which might help alleviate the burden of traveling to conventions and convocations as well as the burden of being the one with whom the buck stops, as it were. That burden could rotate. Additionally, this community of priests and deacons could serve together on the parish council with lay members. Regardless of whether the position of rector rotated, having a community of priests and deacons could also spread out the load of sacraments, services, and educational programming. The community would do this by simultaneously addressing the financial needs of the clergy, for they and their wives would all be gainfully employed outside the parish. No longer would their well-being depend on a minuscule parish budget. Yet, with employment affecting a priest's schedule, having other priests in the parish would allow needs to be met.

Indeed, breaking the priests' financial dependence on the parish would have additional benefits. Priests would have significant lives (including contacts and friends) outside of the parish. They would therefore also avoid the error of reducing their lives to the priesthood itself. This is no small matter, for I personally know of priests who have done just that, burnt out, and are no longer priests—some no longer in the ministry at all. Other priests, who strike me as overly strident and overly focused on their priestly identity, may have simply gone the way of being embittered priests rather than former priests. Either way, if my anecdotal description is at all accurate, a robust life outside the parish would benefit priests and their parishes.

Furthermore, no longer needing the financial graces of a local parish, priests might find their ethical backbones when relating to bishops. Currently, priests are caught between bishops who can move them, suspend them, and depose them at a moment's notice and parishes that determine salaries and sometimes balance budgets to the detriment of clergy salaries. The result is that bishops can more easily get away with unethical behavior because priests are less likely to speak up and criticize them for fear of losing their livelihood. An ecclesiastical structure based on a group of priests employed outside of the parish but serving the parish would better enable clergy to hold their archpastors (the bishops) to ethical standards. True, there will always be some priests who believe their role is simply to defend or excuse the bishop and/or circle the wagons, but a parish ecclesiology along the lines of what is proposed here would lessen this dynamic in two ways: Priests would no longer feel financial pressure to maintain the status quo of an errant bishop, and fewer priests would have a top-down emphasis on obedience more generally if ministry itself was seen as a collegial, synodal activity.

Of course, there is no reason that what I have outlined here must be used only by married priests. There is no reason a community of celibate priests could not serve a local parish or the local college of presbyters could not include a mixture of married and celibate priests, but to be truly successful, this model requires that a married priesthood be involved. One need only look at the clerical shortage in the Roman Catholic Church in America to see just how difficult it is to staff parishes on the basis of celibate priests alone.[23] Furthermore, a married priesthood would include families that are plugged into the societal organizations around them (via children's activities, if nothing else). For the model I've articulated here, a married priesthood is a requisite component.

Conclusion

The married priesthood has had and continues to have a significant effect on the presence of the Orthodox churches in America. It can also help guide the Orthodox into a new and reinvigorated way of living parish life in the twenty-first century and beyond. Toth and fellow Eastern priests brought many Catholics into the Orthodox Church and did so during a time in which their married priesthood was an important reason that many Western Catholic clergy looked at them with skepticism and prejudice. During the twentieth century, many Orthodox priests' wives ministered right alongside their husbands, and to this day, nearly every single priest's wife ministers to the parish in at least one capacity (and often in several capacities). This is all well and good, but the twenty-first century is showing signs of straining the current parish model, placing much burden and stress on priests and their families and furthering a system that has long allowed for corruption to be ignored, swept under the rug, or left unaddressed. By building on the restorationist impulse that is so strong in American Orthodoxy, however, the Orthodox have recourse to an earlier parish model of leadership and ministry. If the Orthodox churches were willing to turn to the sort of ecclesiology found in Ignatius of Antioch and Polycarp of Smyrna, not in order to try to imitate them, but for the purpose of creative inspiration, a healthier way forward could be tried. A parish ministry model based on a college of presbyters employed outside the parish but ministering as a team to the parish would create a means of better addressing the trajectory Orthodoxy is on toward the continuing prevalence of small parishes. It would also better enable priests to create safer, more ethical churches at the diocesan level. This model does not exclude celibate priests, but it does derive its strength from married priests, who, together with their families, are engaged in the world around them.

Notes

1. This encounter has been recounted by numerous authors at numerous times. Although far from all-inclusive, the following list should suffice: Keith S. Russin, "Father Alexis G. Toth and the Wilkes-Barre Litigations," *St. Vladimir's Theological Quarterly* 16 (1972): 132–133; James Jorgenson, "Father Alexis Toth and the Transition of the Greek Catholic Community in Minneapolis to the Russian Orthodox Church," *St. Vladimir's Theological Quarterly* 32 (1988): 127–128; Mark Stokoe, in collaboration with Leonid Kishkovsky, *Orthodox Christians in North America, 1794–1994* (Syosset, NY: Orthodox Christian Publications Center, 1995), 26–27; Peter G. Kochanik, *Rus' i pravoslavie v sievernoi Amerikie:*

K XXV lietiiu Russkago pravoslavnago obshchestva vzaimopomoshchi, 1895–1920 (Wilkes-Barre, PA: Russian Orthodox Catholic Mutual Aid Society, 1920), 20–21, and "Primiernoe i muzhestvennoe vysuplenie otsa Aleksiya Tovta na zashchitu pravoclavnych" i russko narodnych" idealov," *Svit* 62 (May 1959): 18–19. Konstantin Simon notes that one will not find any reference to this encounter in Ireland's correspondence. See Konstantin Simon, "Alexis Toth and the Beginnings of the Orthodox Movement among the Ruthenians in America (1891)," *Orientalia Christiana Periodica* 54 (1988): 391.

2. See *Turning to Tradition: Converts and the Making of an American Orthodox Church* (New York: Oxford University Press, 2014), 25–60.

3. For more on Triantafilides and other Greek priests who served the Russian Mission in the late nineteenth and early twentieth centuries, see my article "An Old World Response to a New World Situation: Greek Clergy in the Service of the Russian Mission to America," *Logos: A Journal of Eastern Christian Studies* 53 (2012): 177–195.

4. For more on Americanism, see Robert D. Cross, *The Emergence of Liberal Catholicism in America* (Cambridge: Harvard University Press, 1958); James Hennesey, *American Catholics* (New York: Oxford University Press, 1981); and Thomas T. McAvoy, *The Americanist Heresy in Roman Catholicism* (Notre Dame: University of Notre Dame Press, 1963).

5. Konstantin Simon, "The First Years of Ruthenian Church Life in America," *Orientalia Christiana Periodica* 60 (1994): 188. Further background information may be found in Konstantin Simon, "Before the Birth of Ecumenism: The Background Relating to the Mass 'Conversion' of Oriental Rite Catholics to Russian Orthodoxy in the U.S.," *Diakonia* 20 (1986): 128–151.

6. Ibid. See also Greek Catholic Union, *Opportunity Realized: The Greek Catholic Union's First One Hundred Years, 1892–1992* (Beaver, PA: Greek Catholic Union of the U.S.A., 1994), 6–7.

7. See James Jorgenson, "Father Alexis Toth and the Transition of the Greek Catholic Community in Minneapolis to the Russian Orthodox Church," *St. Vladimir's Theological Quarterly* 32, no. 2 (1988): 122. See also Simon, "Alexis Toth and the Beginnings of the Orthodox Movement," 389–390.

8. Simon, "Alexis Toth and the Beginnings of the Orthodox Movement," 188–89.

9. Thomas J. Shelley, "Dean Lings's Church: The Success of Ethnic Catholicism in Yonkers in the 1890's," *Church History* 65 (1996): 32.

10. Ibid., 36 n 22.

11. Indeed, Eastern European immigrants could encounter difficulties even when the immigrants were clearly Western Rite Roman Catholics. See Victor R. Greene, "For God and Country: The Origins of Slavic Catholic Self-Consciousness in America," *Church History* 35 (1963): 446–460. Greene recounts the difficulties faced in a Polish community in Chicago and charts its division into separate parishes.

12. For more on later Carpatho-Rusyn conversions to Orthodoxy, see Lawrence Barringer, *Good Victory!* (Brookline, MA: Holy Cross Orthodox Press, 1985).

13. See Christopher Morris, "A Man of Sorrows and of Faith," http://orthodoxhistory.org/2015/03/04/a-man-of-sorrows-and-of-faith/.

14. One prominent example may be found in the work of Mary Gelsinger, who greatly aided her husband, Fr. Michael Gelsinger. See idem, *Handbook for Orthodox Sunday Schools with Bible Stories, Selections for Memorizing and the Small Cathecism* (Brooklyn, NY: Syrian Antiochian Orthodox Archdiocese of New York and All North America, 1938).

15. Within my deanery alone, I can think of several examples of priests who are able to serve because of their wives' employment. This was my own situation from 2007–2014, thanks to the hard work of my wife, Lorie.

16. See http://www.hartfordinstitute.org/research/orthodoxindex.html.

17. Alexei Krindatch, "Fast Facts about U.S. Orthodox Churches," http://www.hartfordinstitute.org/research/orthodoxindex.html.

18. This isn't to say it never happens, especially among the "Oriental Orthodox," but it is no longer the norm, as it was at the beginning of the twentieth century.

19. Alexei D. Krindatch, "Eight Facts about Church Attendance," http://www.hartfordinstitute.org/research/orthodoxindex.html.

20. See Alexei D. Krindatch, "Orthodox (Eastern Christian) Churches in the United States at the Beginning of a New Millennium: Questions of Nature, Identity, and Mission," *Journal for the Scientific Study of Religion* 41 (2002): 562.

21. See Allen Brent, *Ignatius of Antioch: A Martyr Bishop and the Origin of Episcopacy* (London and New York: T&T Clark, 2009).

22. On this front, see my *Turning to Tradition*.

23. Not everyone agrees with my assessment. See Mary Rezac, "Why Married Priests Won't Really Fix the Shortage," *Catholic News Agency*, http://www.catholicnewsagency.com/news/why-married-priests-wont-really-fix-the-shortage-80190/. On the other hand, there are good, serious reasons to reconsider this and believe a married priesthood could, in fact, stem the shortage of priests in the Roman Catholic Church. See Thomas Reese, "Now Is the Time for Married Priests," *National Catholic Reporter*, https://www.ncronline.org/blogs/faith-and-justice/now-time-married-priests.

CHAPTER THREE

Mandatory Celibacy among Eastern Catholics

A Church-Dividing Issue

James S. Dutko

It was the summer of 1977. Archbishop Iakovos had convened a gathering of Orthodox seminary faculty from around the world to a conference at the Holy Cross Greek Orthodox School of Theology in Brookline, Massachusetts. As I left the chapel following vespers, I saw a statue of the late patriarch Athenagoras in the courtyard.

As a college and then graduate student in the early 1960s, I considered the late patriarch as a special hero. For me, he embodied a vision of the restoration of communion between Catholic West and Orthodox East in the fractured Body of Christ. In the wake of Vatican II and the historic meetings of Patriarch Athenagoras and Pope Paul VI in Jerusalem (1964), Rome (1965), and Constantinople (1967), the journey toward reconciliation had actually begun.

The statue of this twentieth-century giant of ecumenism stood there holding a chalice in one hand and bestowing a blessing with the other. The base of the status contains his words, "Come and let us look into one another's eyes." It was then that I noticed a crack at the base, as if to symbolize the fracture in the Body of Christ. It was, in totality, an image both of reality and of what was possible with our minds, hearts, and hands and the grace of God.

I have been an Orthodox priest of the Carpatho-Russian Orthodox Diocese for over forty years and have had the unique blessing and privilege to serve as a member of the North American Orthodox-Catholic Theological Consultation since 1989. Over the years, the dialogue within that group has produced an incredible body of work on issues that both divide and unite the Church. Even major topics such as the *filioque* ("The Filioque: A Church-Dividing Issue?") and primacy ("Steps towards a Reunited Church: A Sketch of an Orthodox-Catholic Vision for the Future") have been addressed.[1]

I was a young man when Patriarch Athenagoras offered a vision of hope, and now I am an old man who still dreams his dream of unity and reconciliation. As the Book of Acts (2:17) notes, *"Your young men will see visions and your old men will dream dreams."* I may be a dreamer, but I believe that there is reason to believe that the vision of Athenagoras can be realized. The ecumenical encounters over the years at the highest and lowest levels give reason for hope. Likewise, the work done both by the North American Consultation and by the Joint International Commission for Theological Dialogue between the Catholic Church and the Orthodox Church provides me reason to believe that when the millennial anniversary of the schism of 1054 arrives in forty-two years, the schism could very well be a matter of historical record rather than an existing reality. The very prayer of Our Lord Himself, offered on the night before His death, could be answered: "Holy Father, keep through your name those whom You have given Me, that they may be one as We are."[2]

In the spring of 2012, I was looking forward to returning to Holy Cross for the meeting of the consultation at which we would be continuing our work on the role of the laity in both churches. I was startled, however, on May 15 to discover that the Catholic News Service had just published an article suggesting that an issue long ignored in most ecumenical circles had risen to prominence once again. It was a past but ongoing Church-dividing issue in Eastern Catholic communities in North America: clerical celibacy. The issue was raised by Cardinal Leonardo Sandri, prefect of the Congregation for Eastern Churches, during the *ad limina* visits to the Vatican of Eastern Catholic hierarchs from North America. According to the news report: "The cardinal urged care in helping young people discern their vocation, 'maintaining formation programs, integrating immigrant priests (and) embracing celibacy in respect of the ecclesial context' of the United States where mandatory celibacy is the general rule for priests."[3] In one's life there are at times triggers that touch emotions that run deep within one's own psyche. The recommendation of a cardinal in the twenty-first century that the injustice leveled against Eastern Catholics in the nineteenth and twentieth centuries forbidding married priests to serve (and thus be ordained) in North America touched a nerve in my life for I am, after all, the son of one of the first Orthodox priests ordained in the Carpatho-Russian Diocese created in 1938 by the Patriarchate of Constantinople. This diocese was established for former Greek Catholic clergy and laity who, in response to their understanding of the Union of Uzhorod and the celibacy controversy, sought to return to their Orthodox roots.

A Church-Dividing Issue of the Past

The restriction on the immigration of married Greek Catholic priests to North American parishes and the ban on ordaining married Greek Catholic seminarians here have a long and sorrowful history. It was nothing less than a Church-dividing issue late in the nineteenth century and throughout the twentieth century. This insistence on priestly celibacy was evident in the *Instruction* of October 1890 addressed by the Holy See to the Austro-Hungarian bishops demanding that they recall at once to their original jurisdiction all the married priests who had settled in the United States, leaving only celibate priests.[4] This ban on married priests was also clearly articulated in an issue of *Ea Semper* dated 14 June 1907: "The priests who minister at present to the Ruthenian faithful are almost exclusively emigrants from Austria-Hungary. In future, their places are to be filled from the ranks of candidates educated in America, either in theological seminaries of their own rite, or (so long as such seminaries have not been established) in the Latin seminaries of the American dioceses in which they were born or have acquired domicile. Only such candidates as take the vow of celibacy will be henceforth admitted to ordination in the United States."[5]

Twenty-two years later, the Sacred Congregation for the Oriental Church issued a decree on the administration of the Greek-Ruthenian jurisdictions in the United States of North America known as *Cum Data Fuerit*. This statement again affirmed that "priests of the Greek-Ruthenian Rite who wish to go to the United States of North America and stay there, must be celibates."[6]

The Greek Catholic clergy and laity in the United States believed that these policies were a direct violation not only of their ancient sacred Eastern tradition but also of the spirit and intent of both the Union of Brest in 1595–1596 and that of Uzhorod in 1646, which served as the basis for their entrance into communion with the Church of Rome.[7]

A House Divided

Bishop John Martin once reflected that too often as a Church "we multiply by division." His words profoundly reflected the consequences of the intolerance by Rome toward the presence of married Greek Catholic clergy in America, one of the first of whom was the widower Fr. Alexis Toth. Toth was treated with scorn and rejection when he arrived in Minneapolis and presented his credentials to Archbishop John Ireland on 19 December 1890.[8] As a result, Toth and 365 members of St. Mary's in Minneapolis presented themselves to Bishop Vladimir of the Russian Orthodox Church in San Francisco on 25 March 1891 and were received into the Orthodox faith. In total, before his death in 1909, Toth—who would be canonized as a saint in 1994—had been instrumental in the reception of fifteen parishes and some 20,000 souls into Orthodoxy. These faithful became the foundation of today's Orthodox Church in America.

A second fracture in the body of the Greek Catholic Church in North America directly linked to the issue of clerical celibacy took place in the 1930s. After decades of ferment, revolution broke out among Greek Catholic clergy and laity when Bishop Takach was unable to persuade Rome to remove the celibacy clause in *Cum Data Fuerit*, which dealt with the structure of the Greek Catholic Church in America. In 1932, clergy were mandated by the Holy See through the apostolic delegate in Washington to sign a loyalty petition. In it were these lines:

> I profess myself a faithful subject of the Holy See and always ready to abide by the general and individual orders, decrees and decisions of the Roman Pontiff and their substitutes . . . promising to observe

exactly their general and particular orders, as they were issued in the past, at the present and in the future, concerning the Universal Church or its part, especially those that have to do with the Rite and the Eparchy to which I belong, namely all those ordinances contained in the Decree of the Sacred Congregation for the Oriental Church "Cum Data Fuerit" issued March 1, 1929.[9]

In the next four years, positions polarized between those loyal to Bishop Takach and those who continued to appeal for the end to the celibacy clause in America. As a result, several priests, including Fr. Orestes Chornock, pastor of St. John the Baptist Greek Catholic Church in Bridgeport, Connecticut, were suspended and eventually excommunicated.

Clergy and faithful who believed that the Union of Uzhorod had been violated, not only on the issue of celibacy but also on the right of clergy to nominate a candidate for the episcopacy, gathered in Pittsburgh in February 1936. They established the Carpatho-Russian Greek Catholic Diocese of the Eastern Rite of the United States. Fr. Chornock was nominated as administrator and was installed as such on 3 March 1936. In its formative state, the new diocese had no intention of breaking away from Rome, but merely sought that the principles of the Union of Uzhorod be operative in America.[10]

That was not to be, and a split with Rome came about, thus proving all over again that celibacy was indeed a Church-dividing issue. Within a year, those within the new diocese of Fr. Chornock moved beyond reconciliation with Rome to embrace a return to their historic roots in the Orthodox faith within the Patriarchate of Constantinople.

On 22 November 1937, clergy gathered at a council in Pittsburgh, cast ballots, and unanimously elected Fr. Orestes to serve as their bishop. Having broken ties with Rome, the assembly decided to petition the Ecumenical Patriarchate through the offices of Greek Orthodox archbishop Athenagoras in New York to receive the diocese into the Orthodox Church and consecrate Fr. Orestes to the episcopacy.[11] On 16 September 1938, Fr. Orestes was elected and consecrated as bishop of the titular see of Agathonikeia by the synod of the Ecumenical Patriarchate to serve as the shepherd of the new established Orthodox Carpatho-Russian diocese.

The ban on ordaining married men to the priesthood of the Eastern Catholic Church in North America was thus, without a doubt, a Church-dividing issue. It served as the major catalyst for the very growth of Orthodox Christianity in North America by the return of thousands of former Greek Catholics to Orthodoxy. It might even be said with some truth that perhaps the real fathers of Orthodoxy in North America were not Fr. Alexis Toth and Fr. Orestes Chornock, but rather Archbishop Ireland and Bishop Takach.

The Celibacy Controversy at the Parish Level

It is absolutely necessary to also look at the impact of this division over celibacy in the Greek Catholic Church at the parish level. The matter was hardly limited to intellectual or historical discussions by hierarchs, clerics, and academics from a distance. Rather, this issue dominated the entire body of the faithful in every Greek Catholic parish in America for decades, but especially during the 1930s following the promulgation of the ban of married priests in *Cum Data Fuerit*.

Most Greek Catholic priests in America were married. Their status as such simply mirrored the ongoing historic Eastern tradition with roots that went far deeper than the Unions of Brest and Uzhorod. The news of the implementation of the celibacy edict by Bishop Takach was dominant in every parish and was simply seen as an attempt to Latinize an Eastern Church in communion with Rome—in violation of Brest and Uzhorod.

Although no media tools like Twitter, Facebook, and email were operative in those days, the issue at hand was widely circulated and discussed, not only through publications such as *Svoboda* and the *Amerikanskl Russky Viestnik*, but also and especially through the voices of scores of married priests who protested the imposition of celibacy for the future clergy of the Greek Catholic Church in America.

The immigrants who had fled the oppression of the Habsburgs came to America with a clear vision. Although they would work hard, America was a place not only where their children could become anything they wished to be but a country where religious freedom was not just an idea, but also a reality. Their only wish was that they could worship God in "their own way."

In such a context, the battle lines were clearly drawn. Protesting priests would be relieved of their duties during the height of the Great Depression. As a result, many submitted, but only with a heavy heart. In these cases, submission was a matter of coercion rather than conversion!

I have had the privilege of serving a parish that was in the center of the dispute. Organized in 1904, Saint Michael's was involved in a bitter struggle in the 1930s that ultimately was resolved in the New York Supreme Court. At issue were some parishioners who wanted to remain Greek Catholic, while others had become Orthodox. This latter group retained use of the property, while the Catholics, led by Fr. Michael Staurovsky and loyal to their bishop, Basil Takich, were forced to worship elsewhere. In June of 1939, the first Orthodox priest, Fr. Joseph Mihaly of Bishop Orestes' diocese, was assigned to the parish. The two factions here in Binghamton were at bitter odds with each other. Having been the pastor here for more than twenty years, I learned how divisive this issue was even decades after the great struggle known as the "Borba." Let me give a few examples.

1. Name calling was common: *"Pindilindies"* was used to ridicule those who were seen as "Independents," in other words, no longer under Rome, and *"Celibatnicks"* was used for those whose priests would now be celibates.
2. Times of mourning were often set in such a way that a death in one parish would result in a lack of presence of both families and friends from the other church.
3. People who might have been members of a wedding party or sponsors at a baptism were barred if they attended the other church.
4. Family members of one church could not be buried in the cemetery of the other church, and at times bodies were even moved from one cemetery to the other.
5. Unfortunately, there were cases of family members and friends who, having chosen different sides in the dispute, ceased speaking to each other, some for a few days or weeks, others a few years. There were even some who never spoke to each other again.
6. An elderly man decorated as a hero in battles in the South Pacific during WWII still talked about his attendance as a high school student at the church trial in the New York Supreme Court as a "highlight" of his life.

7. Perhaps worst of all, more than a few faithful were so resentful of the ongoing and seemingly endless strife that they ceased going to any church at all.

In countless cities and towns in the coalfields and steel and industrial towns of the northeastern United States, the churches multiplied by division. Where there had been one church, there were now two, one Orthodox and one united with Rome. There is no question that the celibacy in the Eastern Catholic Church was a Church-dividing issue.

Celibacy as a Church-Dividing Issue Today

With the coming of Vatican II there was hope that the divisive issue of mandatory celibacy for Eastern Catholics in North America could be overcome. The Council's decree on the Eastern churches, *Orientalium Ecclesiarum*, offered hope, clearly proclaiming:

> All members of the Eastern Rite should know and be convinced that they can and should always preserve their legitimate liturgical rite and their established way of life, and that these may not be altered except to obtain for themselves an organic improvement. All these, then, must be observed by the members of the Eastern rites themselves. Besides, they should attain to an ever-greater knowledge and a more exact use of them, and, if in their regard they have fallen short owing to contingencies of times and persons, they should take steps to return to their ancestral traditions.[12]

There is no question but that both a monastic celibate and married clergy were part of the sacred tradition of the Christian East, including both Orthodox and Eastern Catholics. In spite of the Council's hopeful words, penned now more than a half-century ago, restrictions on married clergy serving and/or being ordained in North America were in effect all the way until 2014—a full fifty years after the Council's decree!

In 1977, His Beatitude Patriarch Maximos V of the Melkite Church received a letter from Pope Paul VI indicating that the ban enacted in the past was still in effect:

> We wish to assure the Melkite Pastors that questions concerning the life and progress of their Church are felt by the common Father as his own. There is no doubt that among these questions there is that of the preservation of the spiritual, liturgical and canonical traditions of the Melkites in the communities, which are outside the patriarch territory itself.... Specifically in the matter of the married clergy, we know that it touches on an extremely delicate point, one of the current practices of the Latin Church. It appeared to us—to Ourself and to the Holy See in general—that the discipline of the celibate priesthood must remain unchanged in the Latin Church. This is because we are convinced of its deep meaning and its usefulness for the Church—without, on the other hand, prejudicing the different tradition of the Eastern Church.
>
> ---
>
> In those areas where the Latin Church has been established for centuries, it is understandable that the presence of married Eastern priests, constituting a rather unusual and new fact, poses some delicate problems for the Latin Rite communities. That is why the Holy See, as Your Beatitude has been informed from time to time, has decided on this particular point to suspend the application for the general principle of the preservation of the traditions proper to the Eastern communities outside their patriarchal territories. This has been decided not for the Melkite Church only, but also for other communities which would have liked to apply it in all its extended areas, even in territories not comprised within their patriarchate. Thus the Melkite hierarchy might as well make its own these concerns which for the good of all the Church, have been those of the Holy See.[13]

In 1998, Metropolitan Judson and the bishops of the Pittsburgh Metropolia of the Byzantine Catholic Church canonically sought to restore a married priesthood. They argued that the retention of the married priesthood was a condition of the Union of Uzhorod, that the prohibition of married clergy in America caused great harm to the Church, that the Latin Church already had more than 100 married Roman Catholic priests in service, and that the retention of celibacy had ecumenical implications vis-à-vis the Orthodox churches.[14] Even though the 1990 *Code of Canons for the Eastern Churches* allowed each Eastern Catholic Church to proceed with the crafting of its own particular laws, the *Ruthenian Particular Law*, which would allow Byzantine bishops in the United States to ordain married men without special permission, was blocked, the final version reaffirming the right of the pope to regulate whether married men could be ordained on a case-by-case basis:[15]

> In 2010, reports circulated that the Italian episcopal conference was blocking the introduction of married Romanian Greek Catholic priests to serve the estimated 500,000 Romanian Catholics in Italy to "prevent possible confusion among the faithful"—precisely the same line of argumentation we heard in North America a century ago.[16]

Likewise, in October 2010, Bishop Aziz Mina of the Coptic Catholic Church at the special assembly for the Middle East of the Roman "synod" of bishops addressed this issue:

> Since the 1930s there has been a ban on the ordination of and the practice of the ministry by married priests outside the territories of the Patriarchy and the "Historically Eastern regions." I think, in line with whatever the Holy Father decides, that the time has come to take this step in favor of the pastoral care of the Eastern faithful throughout the Diaspora.[17]

When the assembly concluded, the bishops addressed the issue of married clergy outside of their territorial area:

> Married Priests: Clerical celibacy has always and everywhere been respected and valued in the Catholic Churches, in the East as in the West. Nonetheless, with a view to the pastoral service of our faithful, wherever they are to be found, and to respect the traditions of the Eastern Churches, it would be desirable to study the possibility of having married priests outside the patriarchal territory.[18]

The issue of the value of married priests was addressed in Beirut during the visit of Pope Benedict XVI in October 2012. There Benedict noted:

> Priestly celibacy is a priceless gift of God to his Church, one which ought to be received with appreciation in East and West alike, for it represents an ever timely prophetic sign. Mention must also be made of the ministry of married priests, who are an ancient part of the Eastern tradition. I would like to encourage those priests who, along with their families, are called to holiness in the faithful exercise of their ministry and in sometimes difficult living conditions. To all I repeat that the excellence of your priestly life will doubtless raise up new vocations which you are called to cultivate.[19]

In looking at the clerical celibacy issue in the Eastern Catholic Church today, it is apparent that during the decades since the proclamation of *Cum Data Fuerit* the call to eliminate the ban on a married clergy in North America has grown. It is important to note that these efforts are carefully watched and often applauded by many in the Orthodox Church.

Until the matter is resolved, however, the issue of restricting marriage to Eastern Catholic seminarians in North America remains a Church-dividing issue. The reason for this is clear, and it is ecclesiological: It has to do with whether the union between Eastern Christians and Rome is a real "marriage" of equal partners. If so, in any such union worthy of the name, respect and equality ought to reign rather than the subordination of one to the other. Over the decades, Rome has professed a profound respect for the Eastern tradition in the abstract. But what about in fact, in relations with the Eastern churches already in communion with her? Here Rome's words need to be put more clearly and irrevocably into action for the sake of the restoration of unity in the fractured Body of Christ.

Today, the ecumenical encounters between Rome and the Orthodox are akin to a courtship, so both parties get along rather well. But I am convinced that there will never be a marriage of the Orthodox East and Rome if the core of such a relationship is akin to subordination rather than equality—as it has so often been with the Eastern Catholics. It is for this reason that enforced celibacy will remain a Church-dividing issue. This restriction must be relegated to the dustbin of history.

Arguments have been made that the right of a married clergy must be limited to the historical territorial bases of the Eastern churches. This claim is hardly valid in today's world, where mass immigration has brought Christians of every tradition into each other's "historical territory" and where, for instance, there are now more Eastern Christians living outside the Middle East than there are in it. Moreover, in the twenty-first century faithful no longer live in the parochial villages of the past. To the contrary, people live in a totally interconnected world. No one is a stranger to the other any longer. The issue is not that faithful would be scandalized by the presence of married clergy in the Eastern Catholic churches but rather that they are by its absence.

The Way to Healing

In the year 2054, the Church will mark the millennial anniversary of the Great Schism of 1054. By or before then, can we make possible what our Lord prayed for, "that they may be one as you and I are one"? Will it be possible for both Catholics and Orthodox to share the blessing of the communion of faith and brotherhood in the one chalice and cup of salvation? Such a reality of restored harmony and unity in the Body of Christ can come into being with the grace of the Holy Spirit, aided in part by theological work, prayer, scholarship, action, and love.

An outline of challenges and possibilities is evident in a joint document issued in 2010 by the North American Orthodox-Catholic Theological Consultation titled "Steps towards a Reunited Church: A Sketch of an Orthodox Catholic Vision for the Future." One of its points deals directly with the issue of a mutual recognition of and respect for the traditions of one another:

> c) *Accepted Diversity*: different parts of this single Body of Christ, drawing on their different histories and different cultural and spiritual traditions, would live in full ecclesial communion with each other without requiring any of the parts to forego its own traditions and practices (see *Unitatis Redintegratio* 16).[20]

While the theological work of healing continues at the international and national levels, it is imperative that this issue of the ban regarding married clergy in the Eastern Catholic Church in North America be resolved once and for all. It is, after all, not only a matter of discipline but, even more importantly, a matter of justice. From an Orthodox perspective, the ban on a married priesthood has always been an injustice, a violation of the very spirit of the reunions of Brest and Uzhorod. It manifested itself in the treatment of the iconic figures of Fr. Alexis Toth and Fr. Orestes Chornock and in the lives of countless clergy and laity who simply sought the recognition of their just cause.

More than eight decades have now passed since the issuance of *Cum Data Fuerit*. Generations of Eastern Catholic seminarians in America, in order to fulfill their vocation to priesthood, were mandated to accept celibacy—not as a charism, but as a mandate—in order to be able to serve the people of God as priests. What untold damage was done to them, to their families and parish families, and to the cause of Christian unity because of this mandate!

Lawrence Barriger, writing in the *Church Messenger* on the eightieth anniversary of *Cum Data Fuerit*, offered a path to healing the wounds in the Body of Christ caused by this edict:

> If Pope Benedict really wanted to demonstrate his understanding of and regret for the divisions in families and the heartaches that *Cum Data Fuerit* had caused in the Byzantine Church since 1929 he could do two things. In the external forum he could rescind the excommunication of Metropolitan Orestes Chornock with the admission that his return to Orthodoxy was done out of the love of his Church and people which Rome, wittingly or unwittingly, was in the process of destroying. Internally the Pope could rescind the celibacy provision of *Cum Data Fuerit* to demonstrate that Rome no longer regards our Eastern Rite brothers and sisters as unwanted and unloved, subject to the needs and prejudices of the American Roman Catholic Church.[21]

Personal Reflections on an Icon of Healing

The division of Christian East and West has been a work in process for more than 1,000 years. It can be healed, but such an event requires far more than encounters and proclamations of popes and patriarchs and research by church theologians. It demands prayer and good will, compassion and understanding, and finally, forgiveness and love from and to everyone.

I was privileged to witness many of these gifts from people in my own life who had suffered much from the controversies arising from *Cum Data Fuerit*. It was my mother, Pani Mary, as she was known in our parish family, who once said to me as a young graduate student: "Nothing is ever so bad that some good can't come out it." And it was my father, one of the first married seminarians ordained to the priesthood by Bishop Orestes, who offered a model of how to be a source of healing in the midst of division through the example of his priestly life.

One week following his marriage to Mary Dzuback, then-seminarian Stephen Dutko was ordained to the holy priesthood on 10 May 1942. He was blessed to serve as a priest of priests for sixty-six years. At the age of 92, he fell asleep in the Lord during Bright Week of 2009. Pani Mary died on the feast of the Transfiguration, 19 August (Julian) 1991.

Fr. Stephen was a model of a practical ecumenist in his actions of love. He was a man of prayer, and his life was a reflection of the "way of life" to which all believers are called. His story reflects how one can move a seemingly immovable mountain with faith in action. His role of an ecumenist is not one that many might have attributed to someone who came of age in the midst of this "civil war" that raged in the Greek Catholic parishes in America in the 1930s. Born in 1917 in Nesquehoning, Pennsylvania, he grew up in Elizabeth, New Jersey. It was there that his parents and his priest, Fr. Orestes Koman, nurtured him in his knowledge of faith, his love of the liturgy and the Carpathian *Prostopenia* (plain chant), and his growing desire to serve the Lord in his life as a priest.

Yet as his childhood days of the 1920s passed into those of his youth in the 1930s, his family, like countless others in Greek Catholic communities across America, was deeply affected by both the growing controversy over priestly celibacy and the Latinization of the Church. In their loving defense of the faith and traditions of the Christian East, his family supported Fr. Orestes Chornock and the clergy and faithful who responded to the violation of the Union of Uzhored and the injustice of the celibacy demands in *Cum Data Fuerit*. Although Fr. Stephen was ordained as an Orthodox priest in the formative years of the new diocese, he never lost his love for his roots and heritage in the Greek Catholic Church. Throughout his life, he longed to see a reconciliation not only between his kinsmen but between the Church of Rome and the Orthodox East.

It was as a teenager that I became aware of the fact that besides our parish of St. Michael's, where my father was priest, there was another church in my hometown of Freeland, Pennsylvania. I learned that at St. Mary's Greek Catholic Church, at the top of Fern Street, where we lived, they had a liturgy almost identical to our own. They sang the same plain chant, cherished the same carols at Christmas, and even ate the same Slavic delights at Pascha. Moreover, almost all their families were related to the people in our parish.

From an old scrapbook with newspaper articles dating to the mid-1930s, I discovered the details of the "civil war" in the Greek Catholic Church in Freeland and that things were so bad that occasionally state police were stationed inside the church during liturgy to prevent disorder. Some people I knew in our parish had even spent time in jail because of disputes within the church. In spite of these things, however, neither my father nor my mother ever spoke ill of anyone. Both of them were known, loved, and respected in the coal-mining town of Freeland by everyone.

During my college years, Fr. Stephen rejoiced in the "seemingly major" events in the journey toward unity: the meeting of Patriarch Athenagoras and Pope Paul VI in Jerusalem in 1964 and the lifting, in 1965, of the bans of excommunication of 1054. As the years went by, he closely followed the subsequent encounters of popes and patriarchs, kept informed by his constant subscriptions to not only Orthodox publications but also those of the Eastern Catholic Church as well. I have memories of coming home as a grad student and finding copies of the Eastern Catholic journal *Diakonia* that he read cover to cover.

But beyond these events so distant from his daily walk, it was the seemingly "little" things in the sight of the world that brought joy to his soul. I can still remember a Christmas holiday around 1966 when the rectory doorbell rang. Opening the door, we were greeted by a group of teenagers and the assistant priest from Holy Spirit Byzantine Catholic Church. They began to sing the carols of Christmas that he had treasured since his youth. It was a small act of love that generated waves rather than ripples of hope in his life! In his soul, after the years of strife and division, it was as if an angelic choir had sung the tidings of great joy on his porch on a cold winter's night: *Znami Boh*! God was indeed with us!

At an ecumenical Thanksgiving service at St. Michael's in 1988, Fr. Stephen had the joy of asking his guest, Fr. John Cigan, pastor of Holy Spirit, to go to the altar and proclaim the gospel at that service. It was the first time since the division in 1939 that a Greek Catholic priest stood in the sanctuary. To anyone outside the household of faith, it might have seemed irrelevant, but to those whose lives had been tainted by the divisions reaching back three decades, it was as if the miracle of healing old wounds had begun.

It was no small matter to my father that, at Metropolitan Nicholas's celebrations of his fifty years of priesthood and twenty-five in the episcopacy, Orthodox as well as Byzantine and Ukrainian Catholic hierarchs were guests of honor in the liturgies celebrated at Christ the Saviour Cathedral in Johnstown, Pennsylvania, and St. John's in Perth Amboy, New Jersey.

A few months prior to my father's death, a group of Greek Catholic seminarians from Uzhorod sang a concert of folk and liturgical music at Holy Spirit Byzantine Catholic Church. He attended the performance and then spent two hours talking with the students (in their own language) over coffee about their lives in Europe, sharing their visions of being priests and singing the Carpatho-Rusyn folk songs he had cherished since his youth.

Years ago, Archbishop Demetrios, then a professor at Holy Cross Greek Orthodox School of Theology, offered concluding remarks at a Florovsky lecture at St. Vladimir's on the dialogue of Justin Martyr and Trypho the Jew. His memorable words typified Fr. Stephen's relationship with his former priests and friends of the Greek Catholic Church: "Although we did not agree, we departed as friends."[22]

When Fr. Stephen died, hundreds of people shared in the memorial services at St. Michael's, where he had been pastor from 1961 to 1991 and pastor emeritus until his death in 2009. To the casual observer, there were many floral arrangements in his honor by the icon screen. One was from the parish family of Holy Spirit Byzantine Catholic Church, and another was addressed to the "Beloved Monsignor" by a Ukrainian Catholic priest who once had served in the Binghamton area.

It is my hope and belief that having "crossed the finish line" in faith he now shares in the joy that the Lord has prepared for those who love Him. There he is not alone. He is joined by people of faith from both East and West who have truly loved their brothers and who have served the Lord. Together we pray that they are "invited to the marriage supper of the Lamb."

Fr. Stephen Dutko, one of the first married priests in the Carpatho-Russian diocese, shared in his final Paschal celebration five days prior to his death. As the matins of the resurrection were drawing to a conclusion, he joined his voice with those of hundreds of faithful as we sang those magnificent hymns of the feast, including these words penned by St. John Damascene so long ago: "This is the Resurrection Day. Let us be enlightened by this Feast. Let us embrace one another. Let us call 'brothers,' even those who hate us, and in the Resurrection, forgive everything and let us sing: Christ is risen from the dead, trampling down death by death, and to those in the tombs, bestowing life."[23] In retrospect, it is apparent to me that this was a prayer that he transformed daily into the actions of his priestly life. Although he was a son of a controversy that he did not create, he was a magnificent agent for its healing. Like him, we also are called to be agents of healing. As we do that, let us ask ourselves five important questions:

1. Must the convergence of unity be discovered only in death, or is it possible to discern, experience, and realize it along this pilgrimage of life?
2. Are we really willing to believe that what unites us far outweighs what divides us?
3. What would the Lord want us to do to heal the wounds that have divided us?
4. What will it take for the wounded healers of East and West to taste together the fountain of immortality, the cup of salvation?
5. Can the Eucharistic gifts be the source of healing, or must these gifts be only the end of the quest for reconciliation?

I have concluded these reflections on celibacy as a Church-dividing issue with stories of my priestly father's life because I am convinced that the priesthood of Christ is analogous to a coin that has two sides: celibate and married. Both share fully and necessarily in the fullness of the essence of the priesthood of our Lord. Both are esteemed, both are venerable, both are historical, and both are part of the tradition of the Church we love.

Jim Forest, in a reflection on the life of Henri Nouwen, noted that, like Thomas Merton, Nouwen believed that the healing of East-West divisions among Christians is assisted more by a process of East-West integration in the spiritual life than by academic theological conferences.

He often referred to a passage by Merton in his *Conjectures of a Guilty Bystander*:

> If I can unite in myself the thought and devotion of Eastern and Western Christendom, the Greek and the Latin Fathers, the Russian and the Spanish mystics, I can prepare in myself the reunion of divided Christians. From that secret and unspoken unity in myself can eventually come a visible and manifest unity of all Christians. If we want to bring together what is divided, we cannot do so by imposing one division upon the other. If we do this, the union is not Christian. It is political and doomed to further conflict. We must contain all the divided worlds in ourselves and transcend them to Christ.[24]

As I close, I come back to my beginning. As a young man, I had seen the statue of Patriarch Athenagoras, a model of ecumenism, extending the chalice of the Lord in one hand and offering the blessing of the Lord with the other. The memory of this moment has encouraged me to grow in his vision. And now that I am much older, like others along this journey, I still dream that our Lord's prayer for unity will be fulfilled and that we will all work to bring healing to all the churches of Christ everywhere.

Notes

1. The texts are available online at http://www.usccb.org/beliefs-and-teachings/dialogue-with-others/ecumenical/orthodox/orthodox-dialogue-documents.cfm and at http://www.scoba.us/resources/orthodox-catholic.html.

2. John 17:11 (NKJV).

3. Cindy Wooden, "Eastern Catholics Have Much to Offer US Church, Cardinal Tells Bishops," Catholic News Service, 15 May 2012.

4. "The Appointment of a Greek Bishop in the United States," *Ecclesiastical Review* 7 (November 1907): 457.

5. Ibid., 462.

6. *Cum Data Fuerit*, article 12.

7. Fr. Lawrence Barriger, *Good Victory* (Brookline, MA: Holy Cross Orthodox Press), 9, 11.

8. Ibid., 25–27.

9. "Declaration," 15 October 1932, in John Slivka, *Historical Mirror: Sources of the Rusin and Hungarian Greek Rite Catholics in the United States, 1884–1963* (Brooklyn, NY: n.p., 1978), 179.

10. Barriger, *Good Victory*, 94–97.
11. Ibid., 111–112, 118–119.
12. *Orientalium Ecclesiarium*, no. 6.
13. As cited in Philip Khairallah, "The Ecumenical Vocation of the Melkite Church," *St. Vladimir's Theological Quarterly* 20 (1986): 208–209.
14. For details, see "Can East & West Coexist with Married Priests? A Critical Consideration of the Case for Clerical Celibacy," at http://orthocath.wordpress.com/2010/01/24/can-east-west-coexist-with-married-priests.
15. Ibid.
16. Ibid.
17. Remarks by Aziz Mina, Bishop of Guizeh of the Copts, "Synodus Episcoporum Bulletin," available at http://www.vatican.va/news_services/press/sinodo/documents/bollettino_24_speciale-medio-oriente-2010/02_inglese/b01_02.html.
18. Proposition 23, available in ibid.
19. Post-synodal apostolic exhortation *Ecclesia in Medio Oriente*, no. 8 (14 September 2012): http://www.vatican.va/holy_father/benedict_xvi/apost_exhortations/documents/hf_ben-xvi_exh_20120914_ecclesia-in-medio-oriente_en.html.
20. http://www.usccb.org/beliefs-and-teachings/ecumenical-and-interreligious/ecumenical/orthodox/steps-towards-reunited-church.cfm.
21. "The Eightieth Anniversary of Cum Data Fuerit," *Church Messenger* (22 February 2009): 4.
22. Archbishop Demetrious, Florovsky Lecture, St. Vladimir's Seminary, Yonkers, New York, 1992.
23. Resurrection Matins, *Diocesan Service Book* (Johnstown, PA, 1992), 70.
24. Jim Forest, "Henri Nouwen: A Western Explorer of the Christian East," in *Remembering Henri*, ed. Gerry Twomey and Claude Pomerleau (New York: Orbis, 2006).

PART II

Canon Law East and West

CHAPTER FOUR

Canonical Reflections on Clergy and Marriage

Patrick Viscuso

In recent theological discussions within Catholicism, certain authors have asserted that there exists an ontological identity of celibacy with the Christian priesthood.[1] When examining Byzantine canonical texts, these same writers defend the view that a purported requirement for the perpetual continence of priests and their wives after ordination was an apostolic and doctrinal teaching. In particular, writers represented by Roman Cholij assert that the impediment to remarriage for priests and their spouses cannot be understood other than in light of such a requirement for perpetual continence.[2]

These authors and others employing their approach, such as Robert Cardinal Sarah, the prefect of the Congregation for Divine Worship and the Discipline of the Sacraments, continue to enjoy currency in Catholic thought.[3] I believe that such an approach will prevent Catholicism from recognizing the married priesthood as an authentic expression of the Church's tradition and will contribute to misunderstandings and intolerance of the Christian East's canonical tradition.

From Cholij's perspective, the Council in Trullo (691/692)—which the Orthodox Church recognizes as ecumenical—innovated when permitting the nuptial relations of married clergy. Consequently, he also views the subsequent explanations of the Byzantine canonist Theodōros Balsamōn, patriarch of Antioch (d. after 1195), as theologically inconsistent with the teachings of the Universal Church. In contrast, the Orthodox Church recognizes Balsamōn as an important representative of its canonical tradition, whose works continue to be referenced in its ecclesial life.[4]

In order to show the doctrinal consistency of marriage and marital life with the priesthood, in this study I will briefly examine the Byzantine canonical prohibition on the remarriage of widowed priest wives. I will do this through an analysis of Balsamōn's commentaries on legislation regarding this impediment to remarriage and one of his canonical works dealing with the sanctity of matrimony in general. And I will reach conclusions regarding the distortion of the Church's teachings on marriage and priesthood in the thought of writers such as Cholij.

Discussion of the Impediment to Remarriage by Widowed Priest Wives

Certain Catholic scholars view the Byzantine canonical impediment to remarriage for widowed priests as comprehensible only if their spouses were bound to perpetual continence through priestly ordination and view it as inconsistent with the prescriptions of Canon 13 of the Council in Trullo, which permitted an active marital life for priests and their wives. Roman Cholij is representative of this approach when examining the writings of the medieval canonist Theodōros Balsamōn:

> Balsamon's explanation would be thoroughly consistent and indeed quite obvious but for one fact: priests and other clerics, by dint of Trullo Canon 13, were allowed to use their marriage rights and therefore did not live perfect celibacy. Only a celibate could be considered as being truly "consecrated." Balsamon tried to give a doctrinal concordance of the various disciplinary norms of the Byzantine Church including Trullo 13. The fact that there is doctrinal inconsistency in the theology used by Balsamon does not, in the judgment of this author, throw a disfavourable light on the latter but rather, as we will demonstrate later, highlights the inconsistency of the discipline of

the canon. It is because of the priest's consecration of his body at the moment of his ordination that he was bound to celibacy; his wife took her own part in this act by promising perpetual continence. Without celibacy, the impediment to remarriage is unintelligible.[5]

Notwithstanding Cholij's personification of Balsamōn as representing the totality of Orthodox canonical tradition, the following discussion of widowed priest wives will show that Balsamōn's explanation of the impediment to remarriage, in fact, *presupposed* the prior existence of such nuptial relations and reveals the *doctrinal consistency* of marriage and marital union with the priesthood.

Theodōros Balsamōn on the Impediment to Remarriage

It should be stated as a matter of introduction that legislation prohibiting such remarriage on the part of widowed priest wives is not contained in the legislation of the apostolic canons, the seven ecumenical councils, early local councils, or the writings of certain Fathers recognized as having canonical authority by Byzantine canonists. Nevertheless, an impediment to second marriage by wives of priests was discussed by Theodōros Balsamōn in his commentaries on Canons 48 of the Council in Trullo and 44 of St. Basil the Great.

In both these cases, the discussion may be characterized as "implied"—that is to say, although not directly the subject of the legislation in question, Balsamōn introduced the question as being related. A third source, the canonist's treatise titled *Decision Regarding the Question That Was Discussed in a Synod, Concerning Whether It Is Possible for One and the Same Man to Be Joined to Two Second Cousins*,[6] has important theological implications regarding the nature of the union shared between the priest wife and her husband.

Canon 48 of Trullo legislated that the wives of candidates for the episcopacy separate from their husbands by mutual consent and take up residence in a monastery far from the episcopal see.[7] Balsamōn explained: "For by seeing each other frequently, they would continually remind each other of their former way of life and marriage, and kindle passion for one another."[8]

The first issue raised in the commentary is whether the dissolution, to which the wife must agree, was in violation of the civil law, which forbade divorce by consent—"one will ask, since *Novel* 127 of Justinian ... prohibited that marriages be dissolved by the consent of the spouses, how does the present canon rule that the wife be separated by consent from a bishop-elect husband?"[9] Balsamōn replied that such an agreement by the wife did not actually constitute the cause of the dissolution. The just cause was monastic tonsure, a basis for divorce recognized under the legislation of the emperor Justinian I and subsequent Byzantine law.[10]

The wife consented to the ordination, and to the tonsuring, the latter of which alone is the grounds for the divorce. As Balsamōn stated, "Since she chose the divorce on account of the ordination, she will be compelled by means of tonsuring to complete the divorce, and 'not trifle with things that are no subject for trifling.'"[11] When such consent did not take place, the ordination did not proceed. However, once the consent was given, the wife's agreement was fulfilled by the tonsuring, which incontrovertibly had to follow, consistent with a decision rendered under the Byzantine emperor Isaakios II Angelos (r. 1185–1195, 1203–1204), to which Balsamōn makes explicit reference.[12]

Balsamōn also stated that the separated wife's eligibility for the rank of deaconess as expressed by the canon was not evidence that tonsuring was unrequired, since both laywomen and nuns were considered worthy of the order. The canonist then made the following point:

> Otherwise, if it happened that the wife of the one being ordained was in a monastery with a lay *schēma*, she would reasonably seek to live outside of it, and perhaps also be wedded to another man or even live with the one that became a bishop; which would be an outrageous thing and something not according to the will of the divine canons. Note all these things on account of those who deem the wives of priests worthy to marry a second time. For I think that from the present canon they are not permitted to marry a second time.[13]

The parallel was drawn between the impediments to remarriage resulting from ordination to the episcopate and the priesthood.

Nevertheless, in the case of the bishop's spouse, monastic tonsure provided the grounds for the prohibition of remarriage. Such tonsuring did not occur in the case of married parish clergy unless one of the spouses adopted the monastic life, grounds for divorce under Byzantine legislation that would normally leave the remaining spouse free to remarry. The monastic tonsure of a spouse was regarded in Byzantine inheritance law as having the same effects as death.[14] It may thus be inferred that even without the adoption of the monastic life by her spouse, the wife of a priest was unable to contract another marriage. This would point to an impediment to remarriage based on grounds other than monastic tonsure, namely, the ordination of her husband.

Canon 44 of St. Basil the Great dealt with a deaconess who committed fornication with a pagan by prohibiting her from receiving communion for seven years. She was ordered to live in purity. In the words of the canon, the pagan, "after converting who again commits sacrilege, returns to vomit. Therefore, we no longer permit the body of the deaconess as consecrated to be used sensually."[15] In his commentary, Balsamōn stated that although the deaconess was defrocked on account of fornication, the canon "does not allow the woman formerly consecrated to God, even if defrocked, to be joined with him at any time whatsoever, because of her body being consecrated, and required to be further preserved from any profane and sensual use, according to the general principle which states, 'The sacred does not become defiled' (κατὰ τὸν καθόλου κανόνα τὸν λέγοντα, τὸ ἱερὸν μιαρὸν οὐ γίνεται)."[16] The canonist then added the following statement:

> Bear these points in mind also for clergy and monks who change their *schēma*, indeed also nuns and female ascetics, who wish to be joined with legal wives or husbands. I believe from this canon the wives of priests are rightly prohibited from marrying a second time, just as those who are ordained (οἱ ἱερωμένοι) that repudiate the priesthood will not be allowed to spend their lives as laity and marry a second time.[17]

Balsamōn was thus drawing a parallel here between the impediment to remarriage by priest wives and that of those priests who renounce their ordination and seek a second marriage. His commentary then continued in the following manner:

> For the wives of priests, who are reckoned one body and one priestly flesh through union with priests (μὲν γὰρ γυναῖκες τῶν ἱερέων

ἓν σῶμα καὶ μία σὰρξ ἱερατικὴ διὰ τῆς μετὰ τῶν ἱερέων συναφείας χρηματίσασαι), who consequently also are ordained so to speak (κἀντεῦδεν οἷον ἱερωθεῖσθαι), will not be profaned (οὐ βεβηλωθήσονται) by the second marriage. The priests who once for all renounced second marriage on account of being ordained, and who vowed this very thing to God, will not be allowed to repudiate the priestly office (τὴν ἱερατικὴν ἀξίαν) on account of sensual desire, renounce their vow to God, and be a servant to sensual desire. Even if they repudiate the priesthood, their bodies that were once for all ordained will be prevented from being profaned by second marriages.[18]

From Balsamōn's viewpoint, the priest was unable to contract another marriage by virtue of his ordination, during which he renounced servitude to sensual desire. In this context, the renunciation of sensual desire referred to an additional union ("will not be profaned by the second marriage . . . who once for all renounced second marriage on account of being ordained") and, thus, was consistent with the long-established canonical text from St. Gregory the Theologian (329–ca. 390), commonly used in Byzantine legal collections regarding the remarriage of laity, which states that "the first marriage is legal, the second is a concession, the third is a transgression of law, and one beyond this, the life of a swine, which does not even have many examples of its evil."[19]

Widowed priest wives were unable to contract another marriage by virtue of their prior nuptial union, which was described as being "reckoned one body and one priestly flesh" with their priest husbands. The body or flesh of these wives had been "ordained so to speak" through union (συνάφεια) with their priest husbands. The marital union had an effect similar to that resulting from ordination.

The nature of marital union and its legal effects were further discussed in Balsamōn's treatise on the prohibition of consecutive marriage to two second cousins, mentioned earlier.[20] In this treatise, the canonist stated:

On account of the divine and saving voice of our Lord, God, and Savior Jesus Christ, who said to His disciples that had asked Him whether it was permissible for a man to dismiss his wife, and clearly taught the following, "Did you not read from the beginning He who created, made them male and female and on account of this a man will leave his father and mother and will cleave to his wife, and the two will become one flesh. So that they are no longer two, but one flesh (σὰρξ μία),"[21] we believe and confess that the spouses are on account of the marriage reckoned to be one humanity having more or less the same soul, which is perceived in two hypostases (ἕνα σχεδὸν ὁμόψυχον ἄνθρωπον ἐν δυσὶ θεωρούθμενον ὑποστάσεσι).[22]

Balsamōn was making an analogy between marriage and the Holy Trinity through the use of the word "hypostases." He continued, "I do not dare to say of the spouses that the flesh is of one or the other, even if I do contemplate them in two hypostases."[23]

In light of this statement, we see that the flesh or humanity was regarded as the commonly shared nature of husband and wife, the two hypostases in the marital union. The human nature could not be ascribed to only one of the hypostases. Just as the divinity in the Holy Trinity was equally spoken of with regard to the three hypostases, so also the humanity had to be ascribed to both spouses. Balsamōn then stated, "I discern that they are reckoned one flesh, and that the husband is bound by the same civil and canonical prescriptions as much with regard to the marital union, as also his wife is bound by them, just as vice versa is the case."[24] The canonist thus linked the "sharing of divine and human law," the final part of Herennius Modestinus's third-century definition of marriage often used in Byzantium, to the nature of the marital union as a sharing of one flesh or humanity by the spouses.[25]

Balsamōn then concluded that, for wives of priests, the sharing of one flesh with their husbands resulted in their common submission to regulations governing marriages:

> Therefore, looking toward the Leader of the faith and our most perfect Lord and God Jesus Christ, I say also again that since Paul the Great states, "The wife does not have authority over her own body, but the husband does. And likewise, also the husband does not have authority over his own body, but the wife does,"[26] the divine and sacred canons and decrees, which reckon as a digamist the one joined in a marital fashion after being widowed, do not permit him to enter into an ecclesiastical office, but do not even permit the wife of a deceased priest to marry a second time, completely on account of the identity of their bodies (διὰ τὴν ταυτότητα τῶν σωμάτων αὐτῶν), just as matters concerning this are described by chapters 31 and 32

of title 1 of book 3 of the *Basilika*, and canon 44 of Saint Basil who states near the end, "Therefore, we no longer permit the body of the deaconess as consecrated to be used sensually."[27]

Balsamōn regarded the identity of the spouses' bodies, the marital unity expressed in the *sharing of one flesh through nuptial relations*, to result in the *sharing of laws by the spouses*. The reality of this identity and its effects were emphasized to the extent that, *even in the case of widowhood*, the canons and laws governing clergy continued to be in effect for the wife of a priest.

Conclusion on the Prohibition of Remarriage

In summary, Cholij argues that the prohibition of remarriage of widowed priests should be interpreted as consistent with an earlier tradition, namely, that the priest renounced sexual relations in general, including those with his first wife, because of a "consecration" occurring through ordination. His argument that Trullo and Balsamōn innovated by permitting nuptial relations between priests and their wives is a *fundamental misunderstanding* of Byzantine canonical sources. Rather, these sources based this prohibition of remarriage on a well-established view that second marriage was *evidence of licentiousness*, which was renounced as "sensual desire" at ordination.[28] Consistent with this discipline, Balsamōn viewed *nuptial relations as the expression of marital unity* and the *sharing of one nature* by both persons.

From this standpoint, *wives literally shared in the ordained or consecrated nature of their priest husbands*, which resulted in their common submission to the same laws and canons governing the lives of the clergy. The notion of this sharing in a common nature was most likely the meaning of Balsamōn's expression "ordained so to speak," used in relation to spouses of priests.

As seen in the last previous writing discussed, the canonical effects of this union are viewed as affecting wives to such an extent that a second marriage was prohibited even in cases of widowhood. In this context, the prohibition of remarriage *presupposed prior nuptial relations* between the priest and his spouse rather than reflecting an earlier Byzantine canonical tradition of their renunciation.

Balsamōn on the Redemption of Marriage and Marital Relations

As outlined in Balsamōn's writings mentioned earlier, nuptial relations were the basis for the priest wife's sharing in the consecrated nature of her ordained husband. In his canonical treatise on the prohibition of consecutive marriage to two second cousins, mentioned earlier, Balsamōn also described the nature of this marital union (γαμικὴ συνάφεια), particularly with regard to the Fall and redemption:

> When the mixture of sinful union (τῆς γὰρ ἁμαρτητικῆς συναφείας . . . τὸ φύραμα) was imparted to all of humanity after the malice of the serpent and the transgression of God's commandment, and when evil advanced to other greater evils, the philanthropic God took thought for our regeneration and renewal. Accordingly, the Only-begotten Son of God who became man amongst us on our account, and who fulfilled every other economy, in order that we might receive the ancient beatitude, blessed also the marriage in Cana of Galilee, and changed the water of despair into the wine of the true knowledge of God. Thereupon, He fulfilled humanity in order that women no longer would give birth in pain and the one born from a marital union (ἐκ γαμικῆς συναφείας) might not say in accordance with the former, "In sins did my mother bear me."[29] But they who keep the commandments of God, just as the foreparents kept them before the transgression, will be deemed worthy of the same honor and glory, of which the foreparents were worthy before the disobedience. For a marriage is honorable that seeks after salvation, and the marriage bed undefiled.[30]

The existence of the marital union before the Fall was clearly ascribed to the foreparents and was characterized as possessing "honor and glory." The union was described as a creation of God, who made both female and male.[31]

After the "malice of the serpent" and the breaking of "God's commandment," these relations were described as a "mixture of sinful union." Christ's redemptive work included their purification and blessing. Specifically, marriage and marital relations were blessed through the miracle at Cana. The image of the "water of despair" being changed into the "wine of the true knowledge of God" signifies the restoration of marriage as well as the fulfillment of human nature as a whole and the bestowal of salvation by Christ.[32]

The restoration and redemption of marriage was linked to Christ's fulfillment of humanity. The union of human nature with the divine in Christ leads to the healing of the human race, which had been alienated from God by the sin of the foreparents.[33] The healing of this nature was discussed in terms of the restoration of nuptial relations, for Balsamōn described the fulfillment of humanity in Christ with the following words: "Thereupon, He fulfilled humanity in order that women no longer would give birth in pain and the one born from a marital union might not say in accordance with the former, 'In sins did my mother bear me.'"[34]

The transmission of the foreparents' sin occurred as a hereditary corruption from the "mixture of sinful union" after the "malice of the serpent."[35] Due to Christ's fulfillment of human nature, marital relations no longer took place in sin but *were chaste and undefiled by nature*. In this connection, Balsamōn cited Hebrews 13:4, which speaks of the chasteness of the marriage bed.[36] The redeemed marriage is worthy of the honor and glory that had been ascribed to that of the foreparents.

In summary, the canonist Theodōros Balsamōn drew a parallel between the marital union and the theology of the Holy Trinity. He stated, "The spouses are on account of the marriage reckoned to be one humanity having more or less the same soul, which is perceived in two hypostases." The flesh or humanity is the commonly shared nature of husband and wife, the two hypostases in the marital union.[37]

Balsamōn believed that the nuptial union was a divinely created image of the Holy Trinity that pre-existed the sin of the foreparents. He held that the sin of Adam and Eve was transmitted through marital relations and resulted in the hereditary corruption of human nature. By Christ's fulfillment of human nature, *redeemed marital relations* no longer took place in sin, but were chaste and not defiling by nature and thus had the potential to recover their original goodness.

Conclusion on the Distortion of the Church's Teachings

In this context, certain recent theological attempts in Catholicism to ascribe *perpetual continence* for a married couple as a canonical effect of ordination, such as the following by Cholij, also have implications regarding the nature of marriage and marital relations:

> The priesthood has always been seen, in ecclesiastical tradition, as the most sublime and exalted state possible within the Church. Consequently, theologians have not hesitated in demanding from the priest a holiness that surpasses even that of a religious. If a religious lived in a "consecrated" state, as did the virgins and widows of the early Church, is it conceivable that the priest, who rendered present in the community Christ Himself, could have been considered "less" consecrated and not have been required to live, once ordained, the counsel of perfect continence as a sign of his consecration?[38]

Such a viewpoint is founded on *a fundamental failure to appreciate the holiness of marital unity in the undefiled sharing of one human nature by the spouses*, whereby both share in consecration to God. This viewpoint is also based on *an unhealthy distortion of priestly consecration* by making ordination equivalent to, or even perhaps surpassing, monastic tonsure.

Within this context, the requirement of absolute continence between the spouses is an attempt *to prioritize celibacy as more identified with Christ than is marriage*. Consequently, the assertion that the obligation of "perfect continence," namely, perpetual abstinence from marital relations, must be imposed on husband and wife after ordination to the priesthood is, in effect, *a denial of marriage's holiness and redemption in Christ*.

Such a denial of the holiness and purity of marital relations both leads to a dangerous overemphasis on celibacy and denigrates the married lives of priests and their spouses. This approach, based on theological error, will continue contributing to distortions in ecclesiastical life and a failure to acknowledge the authenticity of married priesthood.

Modern Procedures Regarding Ordination in the Greek Orthodox Archdiocese of America

To provide some idea of contemporary Orthodox practice regarding married priesthood, the following is a brief overview of modern procedures for the ordination of married men in the Greek Orthodox Archdiocese of America. This canonical practice may provide a future model for

Catholic ordination of married candidates to the priesthood in both East and West.

The Greek Orthodox Archdiocese of America, being hierarchical, as an eparchy of the Ecumenical Throne, is governed by the Holy Scriptures, Sacred Tradition, the holy canons, the 2003 *Charter of the Greek Orthodox Archdiocese of America* (the *Charter*), the *Regulations of the Greek Orthodox Archdiocese of America* (the *Regulations*) promulgated pursuant to its *Charter*, and, as to canonical and ecclesiastical matters not provided for by these, by the decisions of the Holy and Sacred Synod of the Ecumenical Patriarchate.

Comprised of the archbishop as president and the metropolitans as members, the Archdiocesan Eparchial Synod is the ecclesiastical instrument of governance of the archdiocese. Each metropolitan "ordains . . . Clergy within his metropolis, by virtue of the authority of his office and in accordance with the holy canons, Charter and ecclesiastical procedures"[39] following "his submission of their candidacy to the Eparchial Synod and the Eparchial Synod's approval."[40]

The archbishop of America presides over the Holy Eparchial Synod and is the exarch of the Ecumenical Patriarchate in the United States of America. In his capacity as archbishop, as president of the Eparchial Synod, and as exarch of the Ecumenical Patriarchate, the archbishop "makes the initial placement of a clergyman in consultation with the Metropolitan in whose Metropolis the clergyman will be placed."[41]

The documents required for ordination consist of the following:

1. A letter from the applicant, including an autobiography, requesting ordination.
2. A letter of recommendation from the president of Holy Cross School of Theology or from the president of another Orthodox graduate school of theology.
3. A letter of recommendation from the applicant's metropolitan.
4. A *symmartyria* (testimonial) signed and submitted by the applicant's father-confessor.
5. A letter signed by the applicant affirming that he will faithfully observe the Ecclesiastical Order outlined in the *Typikon of the Great Church of Christ* (Patriarchate of Constantinople); follow the provisions of the Uniform Parish Regulations, the episcopal encyclicals, and the decisions of the Clergy-Laity Congresses; and be strictly

guided by the *Greek Orthodox Archdiocese Guide for Celebrants* (*The Priest's Handbook*).
6. If married, a signed letter written by the applicant's spouse indicating that she will fully support her husband in his vocation and that she will follow him wherever he may be assigned.
7. A copy of his baptismal (and, if applicable, chrismation) certificate or transcript and, if married, those of his wife.
8. If married, a copy of the certificate of marriage from the church where the sacrament was entered into or a transcript issued by the church. Civil certificates are not considered sufficient.
9. Copies of diplomas and degrees (including a master of divinity).
10. A current physician's certification that the applicant is in good health.
11. Two full-length photographs of applicant wearing a *rason* or an *anderi* [priestly garments].
12. A signed letter authorizing the Chancellor's Office to conduct a criminal background investigation of the applicant.
13. A signed letter stating that immediately upon ordination the applicant will become a member of the Clergy Pension Program of the Greek Orthodox Archdiocese of America and that he promises to remain active in his participation and current in his contributions for the duration of his ministry in the archdiocese.
14. A letter from the comptroller of the school of theology attended stating that the applicant does not have any debts or outstanding bills.
15. A psychological evaluation of the candidate and, if married, a psychological evaluation of the applicant's wife (optional for some metropolises) to be performed within six months of application.[42]

The Canonical Tradition and Modern Application in the Archdiocese

The *Charter* and *Regulations* refer to Sacred Tradition and to holy canons governing clergy and marriage. The ecclesiastical legislation may be briefly summarized based on the canonical sources.

In general, no male may be ordained who has married twice after baptism, although if remarriage occurs before the rites of initiation there does not appear to be a restriction on the reception of orders as long as he maintains only one union. The prohibition of ordination also includes one who has lived with a concubine after baptism. All clergy above the ranks of reader and chanter must marry prior to ordination. This restriction applies to subdeacons, deacons, and presbyters. Candidates for the priesthood are forbidden to marry certain categories of women, including widows, prostitutes, and others generally believed not to be chaste. Bishops are required to be celibate.

Candidates for the episcopacy, canonically married prior to ordination, are obliged to separate from their wives, who will be divorced on account of the monastic tonsure to which both the husband and his spouse submit. It is required that the wife consent to such a divorce in order for the consecration to proceed.

Once ordained, widowed or divorced presbyters are forbidden to remarry. With regard to readers, if they remarry prior to ordination and are subsequently discovered, they will be reduced to laity, but if united afterward, these minor clergy are allowed to retain their positions and are not advanced to higher ranks. Marital relations are permitted for married chanters, readers, subdeacons, deacons, and presbyters, but such clergy should refrain from nuptial relations prior to participating in sacramental rites, according to their own self-regulation.

A clergyman who engages in a sin such as adultery or another morally reprehensible act will be given a penance according to his sin. Certain canons stipulate that if repentant he will retain the honor of his seat, termed the clerical *schēma*, but will not be allowed to administer blessings or celebrate sacraments. Others make no distinction between unrepentant and repentant clergy, both of which will be reduced to laity. Minor excommunication, or suspension, is even stipulated. In general, the formation of a new marriage is forbidden after a clergyman is reduced to the laity. If the wife of a priest, deacon, or subdeacon engages in adultery, the clergyman who unknowingly has marital relations with the unfaithful spouse will retain only the honor of his position and will cease to be able to exercise sacerdotal functions. If he refuses to divorce his adulterous wife, the clergyman will be reduced to the laity. A clergyman who, in ignorance, prior to ordination contracted an illicit marriage, meaning one formed with a person whose kinship would prohibit matrimony, will be allowed to retain his office only if the union is dissolved.

In the application of the Church's canonical tradition within the Greek Orthodox Archdiocese of America, no male may be ordained as a subdeacon, deacon, or presbyter who has married twice after baptism.

The latter includes one who formed a new union after being widowed or divorced. The wives of candidates for ordination must be married only once. Both spouses are subject to these same canonical requirements regarding matrimony. Candidates may also be ordained celibate. In general, the anteriority of the matrimony to ordination is maintained, and no marriage is permitted after ordination. Bishops are chosen from celibate clergy, but may have been widowed. There is no instance within the archdiocese of a bishop consecrated following a divorce on account of monastic tonsure. Readers and chanters are subject to the same legislation as laity.

Instances exist of clergy who are permitted to continue in their ministry when divorced by their spouses or suffering widowhood, although such presbyters and deacons are generally not permitted remarriage.[43] There are also cases in which presbyters who were divorced from their spouses and defrocked are permitted remarriage in the Church. Such unions are understood as an exercise of *oikonomia*, since only one marriage for those ordained is permitted according to the principle of canonical strictness, even for the defrocked. On the other hand, the archdiocese's current canonical guidance and practice are silent regarding the remarriage of divorced or widowed priest wives.[44]

In addition, no formal guidance is currently articulated on the need for clergy or laity to abstain from marital relations in preparation for celebration or reception of the Eucharist or any other Mystery. Although such abstinence is clearly contained in the Byzantine canonical writings of the Church and was enjoined by certain councils and patristic texts, no modern guidance of the archdiocese exists regarding this form of fasting, and matters are left to the regulation of the couple.

Notes

This chapter was originally a paper delivered at the North American Orthodox-Catholic Theological Consultation. Portions of this chapter were developed from my previous research and my articles "Marital Relations in the Theology of the Byzantine Canonist Theodōros Balsamōn," *Ostkirchliche Studien* 39 (1990): 281–288, and "The Prohibition of Second Marriage for Women Married to Priests," *Orientalia Christiana Periodica* 66 (2000): 441–448.

    1. Christian Cochini, *The Apostolic Origins of Priestly Celibacy* (San Francisco: Ignatius Press, 1990); Alphons Maria Cardinal Stickler, *The Case for Clerical*

Celibacy: Its Historical Development and Theological Foundations (San Francisco, CA: Ignatius Press, 1995); and Roman Cholij, *Clerical Celibacy in East and West*, 2nd ed. (Madison, WI: Idea, 1989).

2. This chapter will focus on Cholij, *Clerical Celibacy in East and West*.

3. Most recently, on 8 February 2020, Cardinal Sarah stated in the *National Catholic Register*: "We are often victims of a profound historical ignorance on this subject. The Church had married priests during the first centuries. But as soon as they were ordained, they were required to abstain completely from sexual relations with their wives. Benedict XVI reminds us of this very clearly in this book. Everybody knows his deep historical culture and his perfect knowledge of the ancient tradition. This is a certain fact and is proven by the most recent historical research. There was no taboo in this requirement, no fear of sexuality. It was a matter of affirming that the priest is the exclusive spouse, body and soul, of the Church. From the historical point of view, things are very clear: from the year 305, the Council of Elvira recalls the law, 'received from the apostles,' the continence of priests. As the Church was just emerging from the age of martyrdom, one of her first concerns was to affirm that priests must abstain from sexual relations with their wives. Indeed, the Council states: 'It was unanimously agreed that bishops, priests and deacons, that is to say, all clerics constituted in the ministry, should abstain from their wives and should not bear children; whoever has done so [had sexual relations] should be declared to be deprived of the clerical office' (Canon 33). If this requirement had been an innovation, it would not have failed to provoke widespread protest among priests. On the whole, however, it was received peacefully. Christians were already aware that a priest who celebrates the Mass, that is, the renewal of Christ's sacrifice for the world, must also offer himself to God and to his whole Church, body and soul. He no longer belongs to himself. It was only much later, because of the corruption of the texts, that the East would evolve in its discipline, without ever renouncing the ontological link between priesthood and abstinence." https://www.ncregister.com/daily-news/cardinal-sarah-the-priesthood-today-is-in-mortal-danger.

4. For an overview of Balsamōn's life and work, see Patrick Viscuso, *Guide for a Church under Islām: The Sixty-Six Canonical Questions Attributed to Theodōros Balsamōn* (Brookline, MA: Holy Cross Orthodox Press, 2014).

5. Cholij, *Clerical Celibacy in East and West*, 28.

6. Γ.Α. Ῥάλλης and Μ. Ποτλής (henceforth cited as Rhallēs and Potlēs), *Σύνταγμα τῶν θείων καὶ ἱερῶν Κανόνων τῶν τε Ἁγίων καὶ Πανευφήμων Ἀποστόλων καὶ τῶν ἱερῶν Οἰκουμενικῶν καὶ τοπικῶν Συνόδων καὶ τῶν κατὰ μέρος Ἁγίων Πατέρων*, 6 vols. (Athens: Γ. Χαρτοφύλαξ, 1852–1859), 4:556–564.

7. Ibid., 2:419.

8. Ibid., 2:420.

9. Ibid.

10. Justinian I, *Novel* 123. 40; *Prochiron* 11. 4; J. Zepos and P. Zepos, eds., *Jus Graecoromanum*, 8 vols. (Athens, 1931; reprint, Darmstadt: Scientia Aalen, 1962), 2:146; *Basilika* 28. 7. 4; H. J. Scheltema, N. van der Wal, and D. Holwerda, eds., *Basilicorum libri LX*, Series A. Textus, 8 vols. (Groningen: J. B. Wolters, 1955–1988), 4:1363; *Nomokanon of Fourteen Titles* 13. 4 (Rhallēs and Potlēs, 1:297); Matthaios Blastarēs, *Alphabetical Collection* Γ.13 (Rhallēs and Potlēs, 6:178): "Indeed, the tonsure certainly occurs, even when the other spouse does not agree. And we say that the divorce takes place with good grace, and the remaining person is able to enter into another marriage."

11. Rhallēs and Potlēs, 2:422. Balsamōn's quotation is from St. John Chrysostom, *Homily 31 on Romans*, in J. P. Migne, ed., *Patrologia Graeca (PG)*, 167 vols. (Paris: J. P. Migne, Garnier Fratres, 1857–1912), 60:674.

12. Rhallēs and Potlēs, 5:321–323.

13. Rhallēs and Potlēs, 2:422. The word *schēma* denotes the outward appearance of a person and his or her status in life.

14. Justinian, *Novel* 22. 5; *Basilika* 28. 7. 4 (Scheltema et al., A4:1373); *Nomokanon of the Fourteen Titles* 13. 4 (Rhallēs and Potlēs, 1:297); Matthaios Blastarēs, *Alphabetical Collection* Γ.13 (Rhallēs and Potlēs, 6:178): "A marriage is also dissolved when one of the parties dedicates himself or herself to asceticism, traversing the road toward the better things and choosing the better life. Indeed, in this case, we prescribe that both the husband and wife who depart for better things be able to dissolve the cohabitation and retire with some small remaining consolation for the party left behind. Wherefore, the one contracting would fix by agreement a benefit to occur in case of the other's death. This benefit is necessary for the party left behind by the other (either husband or wife can establish it), since he that chooses one mode of life instead of another is thought to be dead for his spouse." For an overview of death in late Byzantine canon and civil law, see Patrick Viscuso, "Death in Late Byzantine Canon Law," *Ostkirchliche Studien* 51 (2002): 225–248.

15. Rhallēs and Potlēs, 4:191–192; Proverbs 26:11 (LXX); 2 Peter 2:22.

16. Rhallēs and Potlēs, 4:193.

17. Ibid. The term οἱ ἱερωμένοι in Balsamōn's commentaries generally refers to ordained subdeacons, deacons, priests, and bishops. Consequently, the term is translated here by the expression "those who are ordained." For a survey of the terminology used by Balsamōn to refer to clergy, see J. Darrouzès, *Recherches sur les ΟΦΦΙΚΙΑ de l'Église Byzantine* (Paris: Institut Français d'Études Byzantines, 1970), 86–91.

18. Rhallēs and Potlēs, 4:193.

19. St. Gregory the Theologian, *Homily 37*. 8; Claudio Moreschini, ed., and Paul Gallay, trans., *Grégoire Nazianze, Discours 32–37*, Sources Chrétiennes 318 (Paris: Les Éditions du Cerf, 1985), 287. See also the citation of this text in Matthaios Blastarēs, *Alphabetical Collection* Γ.4, Rhallēs and Potlēs, 6:158. The view of

second marriage as evidence of licentiousness is well established in Byzantine canonical thought; see Patrick Viscuso, "Canonical Aspects of Clerical Marriage during the Late Byzantine and Ottoman Periods," in *Vested in Grace: Priesthood and Marriage in the Christian East*, ed. Joseph J. Allen (Brookline, MA: Holy Cross Orthodox Press, 2001), 67–120, and also Patrick Viscuso, "Purity and Sexual Defilement in Late Byzantine Theology," *Orientalia Christiana Periodica* 57 (1991): 399–408.

20. Rhallēs and Potlēs, 4:556–564. For additional treatment of Balsamōn's treatise, see Patrick Viscuso, "Marital Relations in the Theology of the Byzantine Canonist Theodōros Balsamōn," *Ostkirchliche Studien* 39 (1990): 281–288.

21. Mark 10:6–8.

22. Rhallēs and Potlēs, 4:561.

23. Ibid., 4:562.

24. Ibid.

25. Theodor Mommsen and Paul Krueger, eds., and Alan Watson, trans., *The Digest of Justinian*, 4 vols. (Philadelphia: University of Pennsylvania Press, 1985), 2:657: "Nuptiae sunt coniunctio maris et feminæ et consortium omnis vitæ, divini et humani juris communicatio." The formula appeared in *Code* 9. 32. 4 and *Digest* 23. 2. 1. Compare also the definition contained in the *Institutes* 1. 9. 1: Paul Krüger, ed., Peter Birks and Grant McLeod, trans., *Justinian's Institutes* (Ithaca, NY: Cornell University Press, 1987), 42: "Nuptiæ autem sive matrimonium est viri et mulieris coniunctio, individuam consuetudinem vitæ continens." A Greek translation of Modestinus's formula appeared in *Basilika* 28. 4. 1, Scheltema et al., A4:1325: "Γάμος ἐστὶν ἀνδρὸς καὶ γυναικὸς συνάφεια καὶ συγκλήρωσις τοῦ βίου παντός, θείου τε καὶ ἀνθρωπίνου δικαίου κοινωνία" (Marriage is a union of a man and woman, a consortium for all of life, a sharing of divine and human law). For general coverage of the definition and its adoption by the Byzantine Church, see Patrick Viscuso, "The Theology of Marriage in the *Rudder* of Nikodemos the Hagiorite," *Ostkirchliche Studien* 41 (1992): 189–190, 204–206; cf. Matthaios Blastarēs (Rhallēs and Potlēs, 6:153), as well as Theodōros Balsamōn and Iōannēs Zonaras (Rhallēs and Potlēs, 2:472).

26. Mark 10:6–8.

27. Rhallēs and Potlēs, 4:563–564. In accordance with modern editions, the citations should be *Basilika* 3. 1. 24, 25 (Scheltema et al., A1:92). Balsamōn may have been using a different version of the *Basilika*. Translations of the texts in question are as follows: "We do not permit clergy to be ordained unless they are literate and have a correct faith as well as a seemly life, and neither have a concubine nor have or had natural children, but either live chastely or have, or have had, only one legal wife, and not a widow nor a woman separated from a husband nor one otherwise forbidden by the laws or the divine canons" (*Basilika* 3. 1. 24), and "We do not permit a man less than thirty years of age to become a presbyter, nor one less than twenty-five to become a deacon or subdeacon, nor less than eigh-

teen to be a reader. In the Holy Church, a deaconess is not ordained who is less than forty years of age or who entered into a second marriage" (*Basilika* 3. 1. 25). For the text of Basil, see Rhallēs and Potlēs, 4:563–564; Balsamōn's quotation of Canon 44 is exact.

28. Cholij, *Clerical Celibacy in East and West*, 25–30.

29. Psalm, 50:7 (LXX).

30. Rhallēs and Potlēs, 4:561–562; Hebrews 14:4.

31. Balsamōn affirmed his belief in the goodness of marriage's creation in his commentary on Canon 51 of the Holy Apostles (Rhallēs and Potlēs, 2:68).

32. Byzantine exegetes generally interpreted the miracle at Cana as representing the fulfillment of human nature as a whole. Euthymios Zigabēnos (early twelfth century) interpreted Christ's presence at the wedding at Cana as honoring marriage (*PG*, 129:1148). However, he offered an interpretation of the miracle in terms of the ethical life, viewing the six jars of water as corporal works of mercy that spiritually transformed the human νοῦς and soul. In this context, Christ was presented as the bridegroom who espoused the human νοῦς as a bride (*PG* 129:1149–1152). A second interpretation was given in which the empty jars represented human nature physically (water) and then spiritually (wine) changed through fulfillment by Christ (*PG* 129:1152). St. Theophylaktos of Ochrid (eleventh century) interpreted the wedding at Cana as the "union (συνάφεια) of God with our soul," viewing the six jars as representative of the five senses and the rational dimension of humanity, which Christ respectively cleansed of evil and filled with correct belief (*PG* 124:1191–1192).

33. The importance of this theological concept in Byzantine theology is traced by John Meyendorff in *Byzantine Theology* (New York: Fordham University Press, 1974), 151–167; cf. Vladimir Lossky, *Orthodox Theology: An Introduction* (Crestwood, NY: St. Vladimir's Seminary Press, 1978), 74–78, where there is a discussion of Christ's redemption of *eros* in patristic theology.

34. Psalm 50:7 (LXX); Rhallēs and Potlēs, 3:562.

35. An excellent analysis of this theological point in light of St. Gregory Palamas's *Homily 16* may be found in John Meyendorff, *Introduction á l'étude de Grégoire Palamas* (Paris: Éditions du Seuil), 224–226. A translation of the homily may be found in *Saint Gregory Palamas, The Homilies*, 2nd ed., trans. Christopher Veniamin (Dalton, PA: Mount Thabor Publications, 2016), 115–133.

36. It should be noted that Balsamōn changed the scripture by adding a condition for an honorable marriage to exist: "For a marriage is honorable *that seeks after salvation*, and the marriage bed undefiled."

37. If Balsamōn's thought is taken one step further, the hypostases of the married couple may be seen as differentiated by the particular mode in which the humanity of husband exists as male and the wife as female. The differences in their gender can be viewed as the properties particular to each hypostasis. These relations are complementary yet distinct. The hypostases of male and female after

the marital union manifest their continued existence by a difference of sexual roles and functions, different modes of existence for the same humanity; and yet are united by these very same functions through their marital unity in which they mutually partake of their common human nature.

38. Cholij, *Clerical Celibacy in East and West*, 201.

39. *Regulations*, article 10, section 2, § c.

40. *Charter*, article 7, § b, 2.

41. *Regulations*, article 3, section 1, § q. The archdiocese has its hierarchical seat (the cathedral of the archbishop) in New York City and is legally incorporated in the State of New York. The archdiocese is presently comprised of the direct archdiocesan district (New York City and Washington, DC), headed by the archbishop, and eight metropolises, each headed by a metropolitan. Each metropolis, which covers a large area of territory, is incorporated in the state or commonwealth in which its hierarchical seat (the cathedral of the metropolitan) is located, as follows: Atlanta (Georgia), Boston (Massachusetts), Chicago (Illinois), Denver (Colorado), Detroit (Michigan), Newark and Paterson (New Jersey), Pittsburgh (Pennsylvania), and San Francisco (California).

42. Greek Orthodox Archdiocese of America, Office of the Chancellor, *Documents Required for Ordination* (revised August 2011). The list of documents is cited precisely from the latter except for item fifteen (psychological evaluation), which is summarized for clarity.

43. Recently His All-Holiness Bartholomew announced that, by a decision of the Holy and Sacred Synod of the Ecumenical Patriarchate, the Great Church of Christ is able, by *oikonomia* and with due discretion—after a thorough synodal examination of the relevant cases submitted by hierarchs—to grant, separately and case by case, permission for a second marriage to those clergy in widowhood or in a blameless divorce. His All-Holiness expressed the view that any decision thus taken for a particular case would not be able to have universal applicability. A 16 October 2019 communiqué of the Holy Eparchial Synod of the Greek Orthodox Archdiocese of America stated that the latter "examined the petitions of three clergymen who have requested to enter into holy matrimony in the second instance and decided to formally extend a request to the Ecumenical Patriarchate" (accessed at https://www.goarch.org/news/releases/2019/-/asset _publisher/OZ7IjaVmjx7p/content/announcement-holy-eparchial-synod-fall -2019?_101_INSTANCE_OZ7IjaVmjx7p_languageId=en_US). At the time of this writing, no information is available regarding the disposition of these petitions.

44. However, the impediment to such remarriage was established in the historical legislation of the Ecumenical Patriarchate. For example, the following decisions were made as late as the nineteenth century by the Holy and Sacred Synod of the Ecumenical Patriarchate:

The Church taking under consideration both imperfection and difficulty, and no less also the spiritual and moral danger that threatens the wives of the priests in question, who were widowed from their deceased priest spouses, approved by synodal decree that permission be granted them to form new cohabitations. (Patriarchal and Synodal Letter, 12 May 1866)

The issuing of the letter of response that was commanded by His All-Holiness was approved in order firstly to give counsel to the widowed wife of the priest in question, to remain steadfast in widowhood, and in the opposite case to grant by condescension and economy the requested permission because during the ordination of her late husband, her condescension was not sought or acknowledged by the Spiritual Father in a canonical fashion. (Acts of the Holy Synod, 24 April 1867)

The Church by condescension occasionally permits *presbyteras* [priest wives] as well as monks to enter into a marriage which is thus legal. (Acts of the Holy Synod, 23 November 1874)

For these texts, see Μιχαὴλ Γ. Θεοτοκάς, *Νομολογία τοῦ Οἰκουμενικοῦ Πατριαρχείου ἤτοι τῆς Ἱερᾶς Συνόδου καὶ τοῦ Δ.Ε.Μ. Συμβουλίου ἐπὶ τοῦ ἀστικοῦ, κανονικοῦ καὶ δικονομικοῦ δικαίου ἀπὸ τοῦ ἔτους 1800 μέχρι τοῦ 1896, μετὰ σημειώσεων* (Constantinople: Νεολόγος, 1897), 173.

CHAPTER FIVE

Recent Papal Pronouncements on the Admission of Married Eastern Catholic Men to the Priesthood

An Ecumenical Issue

Alexander M. Laschuk

On 14 June 2014, Pope Francis approved a document permitting the expansion of the ordination of married Eastern Catholic men to the priesthood outside of their traditional territories. This is a move of great significance for Eastern Catholics in the diaspora. This document also has ecumenical implications for the dialogue with the Orthodox churches. This chapter has three sections: first, an overview of the history of married clergy in the Eastern Catholic Churches, including prohibitions; second, an overview of the recent papal document; and third, an analysis of the document, including its implications for ecumenical dialogue.

Married Clergy in the Catholic Eastern Churches

Following the earliest traditions of the Church, the Christian East admits married men to major orders. This practice is common to all the non-

Catholic churches of the Christian East. Further, the practice of ordaining married men generally continued for those Eastern communities that rejoined the Catholic communion. For example, the Ukrainian Greco-Catholic Church listed the preservation of married clergy among the thirty-three articles of the Union of Brest (1596).[1] Both Eastern Catholic and Orthodox churches continue to distinguish between a vocation to the priesthood and a vocation to celibacy. This was an uncontested practice among Eastern Catholics until the nineteenth century, when Eastern Christians began emigrating from their traditional territories into regions dominated by the Latin Church. It was during this period that large numbers of immigrants began entering the United States and Canada from the Austro-Hungarian Empire. Many of these immigrants were Eastern Catholics accustomed to the ministry of married presbyters.

In the United States, the first waves of Eastern Catholics settled primarily in the coal regions of Pennsylvania, while in Canada they settled on the Western Canadian prairies. These immigrant communities were joined by priests sent to minister to them by their ordinaries in Eastern Europe. However, married clerics were considered a grave scandal by Latin ordinaries. The first documented married Eastern Catholic clergyman, Fr. Ivan Volianskyi, arrived in the United States in 1884. After presenting himself to Fr. Ignatius Horstman, vicar general of the Archdiocese of Philadelphia, Fr. Ivan was informed that married priests were not welcome in America and that he would not be granted faculties. Fr. Volianskyj was recalled by his ordinary to Europe in 1889.[2] Another Ruthenian Catholic priest, Fr. Alexis Toth, visited the Latin archbishop of Saint Paul and Minneapolis, John Ireland, upon arriving in the United States. Archbishop Ireland, an advocate of the Americanization of Catholicism, refused to recognize Fr. Toth as a Catholic priest. Fr. Toth was a widower but did have his children with him. Archbishop Ireland expected Eastern Catholics to amalgamate into the Latin parishes. This dispute led to the eventual excommunication of Fr. Toth.[3] Knowing that being a priest requires a bishop's approval, Fr. Toth went to San Francisco, where he was received into the struggling Russian Orthodox mission in that city along with an estimated sixty-five parishes and 20,000 Ruthenians.[4] The Orthodox Church in America canonized Fr. Alexis as St. Alexis of Wilkes-Barre in 1994.

The question of married clergy is estimated to have resulted in several hundred thousand Eastern Catholics' becoming Orthodox, the majority from modern Ukraine and Sub-Carpathia. The numbers of Catholics entering Orthodoxy was so great that it eventually eliminated all Latin resistance to establishing Eastern Christian jurisdictions in Canada.[5] The Orthodox Church in America, the Ukrainian Orthodox Church of Canada, and the Ukrainian Orthodox Church of America were all established primarily by former Eastern Catholics.

The Holy See itself intervened in this situation and, while establishing hierarchies for these immigrant Eastern communities in the West, at the same time prohibited the activity of married priests. In 1890 the Sacred Congregation for the Propagation of the Faith issued a letter to Eastern Catholic bishops in Europe informing them that only celibates and widowers without their children were admissible to North America.[6] This letter was inspired by the Latin hierarchy of the United States, which felt that married priests injured ecclesiastical discipline and good morals.[7] Since celibate priests are generally a small fraction of priests in the Christian East, and of those celibates the majority are monastics, this prohibition had the practical result of leaving many Eastern faithful without proper ministers. This dearth of Eastern Catholic clergy was a factor that again contributed to the growth of Orthodoxy in North America.

Beginning in 1913, the Holy See clearly defined prohibitions of married clergy by means of legislative documents. This year the Sacred Congregation for the Propagation of the Faith issued *Fidelibus ruthenis*, which not only prohibited the ordination of married men in Canada to orders but also excluded the admission of already ordained married presbyters from other territories, excluding widowers without their children.[8] This prohibition was renewed in 1930 for ten years, when *Graeci-Rutheni ritus* was issued by the Sacred Congregation for the Eastern Churches.[9] The document provides norms for the administration of the Greco-Ruthenian ordinariate in Canada. *Graeci-Rutheni ritus* was itself extended in 1941 for an additional ten years.[10] The Sacred Congregation for the Eastern Churches issued *Cum data fuerit* in 1929, indefinitely prohibiting married clergy in the United States of America.[11] This same congregation issued *Qua sollerti* in 1929, prohibiting married clergy in South America and Australia while reemphasizing the existing prohibitions regarding North America.[12]

Thus married presbyters became *personae non gratae* throughout the Western world. The major exception to this rule existed in Eastern

Canada. First, after World War II numerous displaced married Ukrainian priests and seminarians were accepted for ministry with the hope that they would eventually be able to return to their territories. Later, clandestine ordinations were organized by Bishop Isidore Borecky, the Ukrainian Catholic bishop of Toronto: first with himself and his auxiliary, Bishop Michael Rusnak, in Canada, then in Rome with Josyf Cardinal Slipyj, and finally in the late 1980s with underground bishops in the USSR. This situation was unhindered by the Canadian episcopal conference, which indicated to the Holy See, in writing, their lack of opposition to any such ordinations. Despite these actions, the Holy See considered any ministry by these clandestinely ordained married presbyters illicit.[13]

A situation emerged in the Church in which the tradition of ordaining married men was recognized as part of the Christian East, but this practice was severely limited in its application. The Catholic Church recognizes the liceity of these ordinations, and the *Catechism of the Catholic Church* clearly states that "married men can be ordained as deacons and priests. This practice has long been considered legitimate; these priests exercise a fruitful ministry within their communities."[14] The 1990 *Code of Canons of the Eastern Churches* (*CCEO*) further recognizes the possibility of admitting married men to holy orders: "The state of married clerics, sanctioned in the practice of [the] primitive Church and in the Eastern Churches through the ages, is to be held in honor."[15]

In recent years several canonists have argued that these historical prohibitions were no longer in force. Motiuk argued that since the prohibition for Canada contained in *Graeci-Rutheni ritus* lapsed in 1951 and had not been renewed, and the prohibitions of both *Qua sollerti* and *Cum data fuerit* did not apply to Canada, it would seem that Canadian bishops could, in good conscience, ordain married candidates.[16] Others canonists argued that the promulgation of the *CCEO* had the result of abrogating this previous legislation globally.[17]

However, the 1990 Eastern Code not only provided for married clergy but also contains provisions for prohibitions concerning the ordination of married men in certain territories: "The particular law of each Church *sui iuris* or special norms established by the Apostolic See are to be followed in admitting married men to sacred orders."[18] In 2008, the Congregation for the Eastern Churches examined changing these prohibitions in consultation with the Congregation for the Doctrine of the

Faith. It was determined that the obligation of celibacy remained normative for candidates to the priesthood outside the traditional territories while admitting the possibility of the Holy See's granting dispensations in "a concrete and exceptional case."[19] This decision was approved by Pope Benedict XVI.[20] Following this decision, the prefect of the Congregation for the Eastern Churches reminded Eastern Catholic bishops in the United States that they should be "'embracing celibacy in respect of the ecclesial context' of the United States where mandatory celibacy is the general rule for priests."[21] This decision was received with uproar from Orthodox ecumenical partners.[22]

The Recent Papal Regulation on Married Eastern Clergy

Despite these prohibitions, the ordination of married men, considered illicit by the Holy See, continued in several jurisdictions. In Canada these ordinations have openly occurred since 1994.[23] In the United States, Melkite bishop Nicholas Samra announced his intention to study the ordination of married men on the day of his installation in 2011 as bishop of Newton, with offices in Boston and parishes across the United States.[24]

The significant moment, however, was in February 2014, when a married Maronite man was ordained to the priesthood in the United States; this ordination was organized not clandestinely but with the explicit permission of Pope Francis himself.[25] Unknown to the wider Church, Pope Francis had issued a decision on 23 December 2013 in which he rescinded any and all such bans. This was in response to a request for him to do so by the plenary membership of the Congregation for the Eastern Churches, which asked the Holy Father to allow the ministry of married Eastern presbyters.[26] This decision was not published until 14 June 2014 in the *Acta Apostolicae Sedis* (*AAS*). The pope's decision, the subject of the remainder of this chapter, is divided into two sections: first, an introductory note, and second, a decision approved by the Holy Father.

The first section, the introductory note, describes the history of the prohibition of the ordination of married men to the priesthood outside the traditional territories. The document notes that all Eastern Catholic churches except for the Syro-Malabar and Syro-Malankar ordain married deacons to the priesthood. The document enumerates the various bans that were considered in force by the Holy See, namely: *Cum data fuerit*, *Qua sollerti*, and *Gracei-Rutheni ritus*.[27] The document not only acknowledges that these decisions were motivated by the objections of the Latin hierarchy, who considered the presence of married clergy a "grave scandal" to the faithful, but also that, "deprived of the ministers of their proper rite, an estimated 200,000 Ruthenian faithful joined Orthodox Churches."[28]

The second part of this chapter contains the decision of Pope Francis. In November 2013 the Congregation for the Eastern Churches met in plenary session and reviewed the restrictions on the ordination of married men to the priesthood. At the end of this session, the members of the Congregation petitioned the pope to permit the ministry of married Eastern Catholic priests outside their traditional territories, and the pope granted this request in an audience with the pope on 23 December 2013, "anything to the contrary notwithstanding."[29] It is worth noting that the Eastern Congregation asked the pope to "give permission to the respective Church Authorities to *allow the ministry* of married Eastern clergy also outside the traditional Eastern territories."[30]

Three possibilities are provided in this decision. First, in *all* Eastern Catholic ecclesiastical jurisdictions (i.e., archeparchies, eparchies, and exarchates) the bishop is given the faculty to ordain married men in accord with the tradition of his particular church, with the obligation of informing the Latin bishop of the territory prior to the ordination in order to obtain his opinion.[31] Second, in ordinariates for Eastern Catholics that lack their own hierarchies (which exist in France, Argentina, and Brazil), the ordinary is also given this faculty; however, in these cases he must inform that nation's episcopal conference as well as the Congregation for the Eastern Churches. Finally, in territories where Eastern Catholics lack structures and are entrusted to the care of the local Latin bishop, the faculty is not provided to the Latin bishop but must be sought from the Congregation for the Eastern Churches, which will exercise it "in concrete and exceptional cases."[32]

Analysis of the Papal Regulation

This document is listed in the *AAS* as an act of the Congregation for the Eastern Churches, but it *did* receive papal approval, which is required by all dicasteries of the Holy See because they do not possess legislative power.³³ *Pastor Bonus* explains this: "Dicasteries cannot issue laws or general decrees having the force of law or derogate from the prescriptions of current universal law, unless in individual cases and with the specific approval of the Supreme Pontiff."³⁴ Since this document explicitly derogated from the legislative provisions of *Cum data fuerit*, *Qua sollerti*, and *Graeci-Rutheni ritus*, and congregations lack legislative power, the decision required the specific approval of Pope Francis to have any juridical effect. This is indicated in the document with the words "anything to the contrary notwithstanding."³⁵ This document eliminated the previous law and therefore is an act of the legislative power of governance of the bishop of Rome in his capacity as supreme pastor of the universal Church.

This document interestingly describes the ability of Eastern Catholic hierarchs to ordain married men as a "faculty." A faculty is, most generally speaking, a permission to perform an action.³⁶ This phrase reveals that the ability to ordain married men outside of the patriarchal territory is not understood by the Holy See to be within the rights of the individual Eastern Catholic bishop but is rather a delegated permission of the pope functioning as supreme judge of interchurch relations—despite the historical objections of some members of other churches *sui iuris*.³⁷ Among other reasons, John Huels postulates that this is termed a faculty to permit the included restrictions upon the admission of married men to the presbyterate.³⁸

This faculty is given to Eastern Catholic hierarchs and the ordinaries of ordinariates for Eastern Catholics, the latter having further restrictions than the former. This document addresses only the question of the ordination of married men to the priesthood and does not provide any direction on the presence of already ordained married presbyters in certain territories, which has also been a point of contention. For example, there are large numbers of migrant Ukrainian communities in Western Europe. While in some countries there are ecclesiastical circumscriptions for these faithful, this is not the case in all countries, such as Spain. In some of these countries, where the communities are subject to the local Latin hierarchy, only celibate presbyters are admitted to ministry.³⁹ This document provides no relief in these challenging situations.

Finally, it is important to consider the ecumenical context of this decree. The prohibition against married clergy resulted in hundreds of thousands of Eastern Catholics' becoming Orthodox, and the historical section of this document estimates the number as 200,000 Ruthenians alone.⁴⁰ The presence of married ministers has been central to the identity of many Eastern Christian communities and remains a sensitive issue. Excluding the ministry of married presbyters outside the traditional territories has been a warning for Eastern non-Catholic Christians that their rights would not be preserved should eucharistic communion ever be re-established. In this context it is understandable that the North American Orthodox/Catholic Theological Consultation condemned these prohibitions in 2014.⁴¹ Removing the prohibition against the ordination of married men certainly respects the traditions of the Christian East. However, describing the bishop's ability to ordain married men as a "faculty" given to him by the pope will remain problematic for many Eastern Christians.

There is one other ecumenical context for this decree: *Anglicanorum coetibus*. This 2009 apostolic constitution of Benedict XVI provided canonical structures for Anglicans who desired to enter the Catholic Church. This document held out the possibility of the ordination of married former Anglican clerics in the Latin Church.⁴² In some territories, such as the United States, it was licit for the Roman Catholic bishop to ordain a married Latin presbyter, while the Eastern Catholic bishop in the same territory could not. Interestingly, this provision was explicitly cited as a motivating factor in the regulation's introductory note.⁴³ The presence of married ministers in the Latin Church thus helped regularize this situation among Eastern Catholics.

Conclusions

In December 2013 Pope Francis rescinded the previous bans restricting the ordination of Eastern Catholic married men to the priesthood outside of their traditional territories. These prohibitions, officially promulgated in the early twentieth century, were a response to the concern of some Latin bishops that the presence of married ministers provided a great scandal to the faithful. Deprived of their ministers because of these bans, hundreds of thousands of Eastern Catholics entered Orthodoxy. Eastern Catholic bishops are now able to follow their ancestral traditions and ordain candidates, both celibate and married, for their particular churches. This is an application of the Second Vatican Council's decree on ecumenism: "Far from being an obstacle to the Church's unity, a certain diversity of customs and observances only adds to her splendor, and is of great help in carrying out her mission, as has already been stated."[44] The pope has decided to give precedence to the tradition of Eastern Catholics instead of the concerns of scandal expressed by some Latin ordinaries.

Unitatis redintegratio recognized that ecumenism can be achieved only if the diversity of customs and observances, especially those from the Christian East, are accepted: "The perfect observance of this traditional principle not always indeed carried out in practice, is one of the essential prerequisites for any restoration of unity."[45] The prohibition of married ministers has always demonstrated that, in terms of controversial and contradictory practices, especially the contested practice of clerical celibacy, the Latin discipline remains preeminent. This was not only a warning to non-Catholics as to the practical results of eucharistic communion but also a continued application of the old understanding of the preeminence of the Latin rite. The Second Vatican Council moved away from this concept, declaring the equality of all the rites.[46] Pope Francis has applied this principle in the Church's legislation, a welcome act toward Eastern Christians, both Catholic and non-Catholic. John Paul II indicated that, "In our ecumenical age, marked by the Second Vatican Council, the mission of the Bishop of Rome is particularly directed to recalling the need for full communion among Christ's disciples."[47] Francis has directed his ministry toward such a restoration, building up the splendor of the diversity of the Catholic churches in full communion with him.

Following is the text of the regulation on married Eastern clergy promulgated by Pope Francis.[48]

Text of the *Acts of the Congregation for the Eastern Churches*

Papal Regulation on Married Eastern Clergy

A) Introductory Note

Canon 758, §3 of the Code of Canons of the Eastern Churches prescribes: "Regarding the admission to Sacred Orders of married men, the Particular law of each Church *sui iuris* or special norms established by the Apostolic See are to be followed."

This allows each *sui iuris* Church to decide regarding the admission of married men to sacred orders.

At present, all the Eastern Catholic Churches, with the exception of the Syro-Malabar and Syro-Malankar Churches, can admit married men to the diaconate and to the presbyterate.

However, the canon foresees that the Apostolic See may issue special norms in this regard.

Pope Benedict XVI, in his post-synodal apostolic exhortation *Ecclesia in Medio Oriente* of 14 September 2012, after having affirmed that "priestly celibacy is an inestimable gift of God to His Church, [which] must be received with gratitude both in the East and the West, because it represents a prophetic sign that is always current," noted "the ministry of married priests, which represents an ancient part of the Eastern traditions." He further encouraged these priests, since, "with their families, they are called to holiness in the faithful exercise of their ministry and in often difficult life situations." The issue of the ministry of married priests ministering outside of their traditional Eastern territories goes back to the last decades of the 19th century, especially beginning in 1880, when thousands of Ruthenian Catholics emigrated to the United States from the Sub-Carpathian regions and also western Ukraine. The presence of these married missionaries elicited the protest of the Latin bishops, according to whom such a presence would cause a "grave scandal" among the Latin faithful. Thus the Congregation *De Propaganda Fide*, by a decree of 1 October 1890, prohibited married Ruthenian clergy from living in the USA.

In 1913 the Holy See decreed that, in Canada, only celibates could be ordained priests.

In 1929–1930 the (then) Congregation for the Eastern Church issued three decrees that prohibited married Eastern priests from carrying out their priestly ministry in certain regions:

1) the Decree *Cum data fuerit* of 1 March 1929, by which married Ruthenian clergy were forbidden to minister in North America;
2) the Decree *Qua sollerti* of 23 December 1929, by which the prohibition was extended to all married Eastern clergy who had emigrated to North and South America and Australia;
3) the Decree *Graeci-Rutheni* of 24 May 1930, by which it established that only celibate men could be admitted to the seminary and promoted to sacred orders.

Deprived of the ministers of their proper rite, an estimated 200,000 Ruthenian faithful joined Orthodox Churches.

The cited norms were extended to other territories not considered "Eastern regions," and exceptions were granted only after having consulted the local Episcopal Conference and after having received the authorization of the Holy See.

As the problem persisted, the Congregation of the Eastern Churches brought it to the attention of the Congregation for the Doctrine of the Faith. On 20 February 2008, the CDF reexamined the question in its Ordinary session and arrived at the following decision: "The current norms are to be maintained that bind Eastern priests in pastoral service to the faithful in diaspora to the obligation of celibacy, similarly to the Latin priests, foreseeing, in concrete and exceptional cases, the possibility of a dispensation from it, reserved to the Holy See." The above was approved by Pope Benedict XVI.

It should be noted that, recently, even in the West, with the *motu proprio Anglicanorum coetibus*, although not regarding the Eastern clergy, a discipline was adopted that was attentive to the concrete situation of those presbyters and their respective families who had embraced the Catholic Communion.

B) Decisions Approved by the Holy Father

In the Plenary Session of the Congregation for the Eastern Churches, held from 19 to 22 November 2013 at the [Vatican] Apostolic Palace, the question was thoroughly discussed and then the request was presented to the Holy Father to give permission to the respective Church Authorities to allow the ministry of married Eastern clergy also outside the traditional Eastern territories.

In the audience granted to the Prefect of the Congregation for the Eastern Churches, Cardinal Leonardo Sandri, on 23 December 2013, the Holy Father approved the request, *"anything to the contrary notwithstanding,"* in the following ways:

— in Eastern Administrative Constituencies (Metropolitan Churches, Eparchies, Exarchates) established outside of their traditional territories, this faculty is to be vested in the Eastern Hierarchs, who will exercise it according to the traditions of their respective Churches. Regarding ordinations of married candidates from these territories, this faculty includes the obligation to inform the resident Latin

bishop in writing and ahead of time, and to obtain his opinion, while providing all possible useful information;
— in Ordinariates for the Eastern Catholic faithful without a proper Hierarch, this faculty is to be vested in the Ordinaries, who will exercise it informing, in [each] concrete case, the respective Episcopal Conference and this Dicastery;
— in territories where Eastern Catholic faithful lack their own administrative structure and are entrusted to the [pastoral] care of the local Latin bishops, this faculty will continue to be reserved to the Congregation for the Eastern Churches, which will exercise it in concrete and exceptional cases after having sought the opinion of the respective Episcopal Conferences.

From the Seat of the Congregation for the Eastern Churches, 14 June 2014
LEONARDO Card. SANDRI
Prefect

Notes

1. For more on the Union of Brest, see Boris Gudziak, *Crisis and Reform: The Kyivan Metropolitanate, the Patriarchate of Constantinople, and the Genesis of the Union of Brest* (Cambridge, MA: Harvard University Press, 1998).

2. Victor J. Pospishil, *Ex occidente lex* (Carteret, NJ: St. Mary's Religious Action Fund, 1979), 23–24.

3. Ibid., 25–27.

4. John Binns, *An Introduction to the Christian Orthodox Churches* (Cambridge: Cambridge University Press, 2002), 157.

5. David Motiuk, *Eastern Christians in the New World* (Ottawa: Saint Paul University, 2005), 13–24.

6. Sacred Congregation for the Propagation of the Faith, *Alliquibis abhinc*, 1 October 1890, *Collecteana*, II, 357.

7. Motiuk, *Eastern Christians*, 124–125.

8. Sacred Congregation for the Propagation of the Faith, *Fidelibus ruthenis*, 18 August 1913: *AAS*, 5 (1913), 393–399, arts. 10–12.

9. Sacred Congregation for the Eastern Churches, *Graeci-Rutheni ritus*, 24 May 1930: *AAS*, 22 (1930), 346–354, arts. 12, 15.

10. Motiuk, *Eastern Christians*, 125.

11. Sacred Congregation for the Eastern Churches, *Cum data fuerit*, 1 March 1929: *AAS*, 21 (1929), 152–159.

12. Sacred Congregation for the Eastern Churches, *Qua sollerti*, 23 December 1929: *AAS*, 22 (1930), 99–105, arts. 6, 18.

13. Motiuk, *Eastern Christians*, 127–31.

14. *Catechism of the Catholic Church*, 1580.

15. *CCEO*, c. 373. All citations from the *CCEO* are taken from *Codex canonum Ecclesiarum orientalium auctoritate Ioannis Pauli PP.II promulgatus, fontium annotatione auctus*, Libreria editrice Vaticana, 1995, English translation *Code of Canons of the Eastern Churches: Latin-English Edition, New English Translation* (Washington, DC: Canon Law Society of America, 2001).

16. Motiuk, *Eastern Christians*, 131.

17. George Nedungatt, ed., *A Guide to the Eastern Code: A Commentary on the Code of Canons of the Eastern Churches* [*Kanonika*, no. 10] (Rome: Pontifical Oriental Institute, 2002), 303, 506; Roman Cholij, "An Eastern Catholic Married Clergy in North America: Recent Changes in Legal Status and Ecclesiological Perspective," *Studia Canonica* 31 (1997): 311–339.

18. *CCEO*, c. 758, §3.

19. Congregation for the Eastern Churches, *Pontificia praecepta de clero uxorato orientali*, 14 June 2014: *Acta Apostolica Sedis*, 106 (2014), 496–499, Introductory Note.

20. Ibid.

21. Cindy Wooden, "Eastern Catholics Have Much to Offer US Church, Cardinal Tells Bishops," *Catholic News Service*, http://www.catholicnews.com/data/stories/cns/1201976.htm.

22. See, for example, North American Orthodox/Catholic Theological Consultation, "Statement of the North American Orthodox/Catholic Theological Consultation on the Occasion of the Eighty-Fifth Anniversary of the Promulgation of the Decree *Cum data fuerit*," 6 June 2014, available at http://www.usccb.org/news/2014/14-099.cfm.

23. Motiuk, *Eastern Christians*, 130–131.

24. Cindy Wooden, "US Melkite Bishop Urges Study of Ordaining Married Men as Priests," *Catholic Review*, 19 November 2011, http://www.catholicreview.org/article/faith/canon-news/us-melkite-bishop-urges-study-of-ordaining-married-men-as-priests.

25. Jennifer Brinker, "First Married Man Ordained Priest for U.S. Maronite Church," *National Catholic Reporter*, 28 February 2014, http://ncronline.org/news/faith-parish/first-married-man-ordained-priest-us-maronite-catholic-church.

26. *Pontificia praecepta de clero uxorato orientali*, Introductory Note.

27. Ibid.

28. Ibid.

29. Ibid., Decisions.

30. Ibid. Emphasis added.

31. The document indicates that *hierarchs* are given this faculty, which would include the protosyncellus and the syncellus (*CCEO*, c. 984, §2). However, it is obvious that the document intends for this faculty to be restricted to the eparchial bishop, as it speaks of ordination. See John M. Huels, "Canonical Notes on the Pontifical Precepts on Married Eastern Clergy," *Studia Canonica*, 50 (2016): 149.

32. Ibid.

33. John Paul II, apostolic constitution *Pastor Bonus*, 28 June 1988, in *Acta Apostolica Sedis*, 80 (1988), English translation in *Code of Canons of the Eastern Churches: Latin-English Edition, New English Translation* (Washington, DC: Canon Law Society of America, 2001), art. 18, pp. 771–843.

34. Ibid., English translation in *Code of Canons of the Eastern Churches: Latin-English Edition*, 771–843.

35. *Pontificia praecepta de clero uxorato orientali*, Decisions.

36. On the juridic nature of faculties, see John M. Huels, *Empowerment for Ministry: A Complete Manual on Diocesan Faculties for Priests, Deacons, and Lay Ministers* (Mahwah, NJ: Paulist Press, 2003), esp. 3–37.

37. See *Orientalium Ecclesiarum* no. 4.

38. Huels, "Canonical Notes on the Pontifical Precepts on Married Eastern Clergy," 155.

39. Such restrictions may not be legislative in nature but more customary, such as the restriction of government stipends for Catholic clergy to celibate priests.

40. *Pontificia praecepta de clero uxorato orientali*, Introductory Note.

41. North American Orthodox/Catholic Theological Consultation, "Statement of the North American Orthodox/Catholic Theological Consultation on the Occasion of the Eighty-Fifth Anniversary of the Promulgation of the Decree *Cum data fuerit*," available at http://www.usccb.org/beliefs-and-teachings/ecumenical-and-interreligious/ecumenical/orthodox/on-the-occasion-of-the-eighty-fifth-anniversary-of-the-promulgation-of-the-decree-cum-data-fuerit.cfm.

42. Benedict XVI, apostolic constitution *Anglicanorum coetibus*, Complementary Norms, 4 November 2009: *AAS*, 101 (2009), 985–990, art. 6, §§1–2.

43. *Pontificia praecepta de clero uxorato orientali*, Introductory Note.

44. *Unitatis redintegratio* no. 16.

45. Ibid.

46. *Orientalium Ecclesiarum* no. 4.

47. John Paul II, *Ut unum sint*, no. 4.

48. Published as Congregation for the Oriental Churches, *Pontificia praecepta de clero uxorato orientali*, 14 June 2014, in *Acta Apostolica Sedis*, 106 (2014), 496–499. Translated from the Italian by the Rev. Dr. Athanasius McVay and edited by me.

PART III

Ecumenical Considerations

CHAPTER SIX

Married Clergy in the Anglican Tradition

John Hunwicke

When the Holy See gave St. John Henry Newman to the ordinariate in the British Isles as its patron, I wonder if it occurred to anyone to consider how suitable a model he would be for the considerable number of married clergy—and their wives!—who were enabled, by the generous provisions of *Anglicanorum coetibus*, to discharge a sacerdotal ministry in full communion with the See of Peter in the Latin Church. To be sure, the ordinariate is not the only source of married clergy in the English Catholic Church. Anglican clerical converts have for decades been granted dispensations from celibacy, and at any clerical meeting you will find a goodly number of married priests.

Newman's dislike of a culture of married clergy was, I think, visceral. In his semiautobiographical novel, *Loss and Gain*, the almost converted Charles Reding witnesses, in a Bath bookshop of religious works, a young clergyman called White, recently married. This gentleman had, earlier in the novel, been shown flirting with the lady to whom he is now married by means of titillating discussions about monks and nuns. Now Reding

> heard the shop-door open, and on looking round saw a familiar face. It was that of a young clergyman, with a very pretty girl on his arm, whom her dress pronounced to be a bride. Love was in their eyes, joy

in their voice, and affluence in their gait and bearing. Charles had a faintish feeling come over him; somewhat such as might beset a man on hearing a call for pork-chops when he was feeling sea-sick . . . a severe text of scripture rose on his mind, but he repressed the censorious or uncharitable feeling, and turned himself to the anxious duties which lay before him.[1]

Those duties were comprised of submission to the authority of the Catholic Church.

The many dialogues that enliven Newman's novel make it clear that, in Victorian Anglicanism, matrimony and celibacy were seen as distinguishing marks of, respectively, Anglicanism and Catholicism. One of Reding's Anglican interlocutors says, "If you look for types of our Church, can you find truer than the married excellence of Hooker the profound, Taylor the devotional, and Bull the polemical? The very first reformed primate is married; in Pole and Parker, the two systems, Roman and Anglican, come into strong contrast." This is well observed. Once the murderous Miles Coverdale has secured the See of Exeter, he demonstrates his own hermeneutic of rupture by sitting *with his wife* eating meat by royal dispensation *throughout Lent*. Newman's Carlton goes on to argue that

> the whole genius, structure, working of our Church goes the other way. For instance, we have no monasteries to relieve the poor; and, if we had, I suspect, as things are, a parson's wife would, in practical substantial usefulness, be indefinitely superior to all the monks that were ever shaven. I declare, I think the Bishop of Ipswich is almost justified in giving out that none but married men have chance of preferment with him; nay, the Bishop of Abingdon, who makes a rule of bestowing his best livings as marriage portions to the most virtuous young ladies in his diocese.

Newman adds that Carlton "spoke with more energy than was usual with him." Carlton was subsequently to marry Reding's sister.

Newman was not, I think, concerned to condemn the greater part of the Anglican clergy. He gives a moving description of Reding's own father: "He was a most respectable clergyman of the old school; pious in his sentiments, a gentleman in his feelings, exemplary in his social relations . . . his sermons were rarely doctrinal. They were sensible manly discourses on the moral duties. . . . He was incapable of anything harsh, or petty, or low, or uncourteous; and died esteemed by the great houses about him, and lamented by his parishioners." In this I detect none of the satirical waspishness that would have been clear to readers in the other passages already cited. But I am convinced that Newman *was* anxious to insinuate the reflection that the ministry of Mr. Reding senior was not a Catholic, sacerdotal ministry; it was a fine "natural" life but, in Newman's views, did not partake of the "supernatural." It is in the sacrificial, ascetic self-denial of the Latin Catholic priesthood that Newman discerns the difference between the two systems. Perhaps the key is in the descriptions of Mr. and Mrs. White as "affluent" and the insights we are given into the distribution of clerical patronage by the bishops of Ipswich and Abingdon.

It is difficult for us to imagine the centrality of upper-class money and status in the functioning of the Church of England before the twentieth century. We may sometimes wonder who was doing the clerical duty of Mr. Tilney while he conducted his *amours* in the society of Georgian Bath and amid the luxuries of Northanger Abbey, and we simply enjoy the contrast between the quiet indolence of Bishop Grantley of Barchester and the fierce party spirit of his son the archdeacon. But this was a church that functioned on the hopes of younger sons to be presented to lucrative benefices by members of their families or by influential patrons whose sympathy they had acquired. Central to its working were the universities of Oxford and Cambridge, in which every fellow of a college had to remain celibate until the acquisition of a living enabled him to marry his betrothed and, by the simple act of so doing, forfeit his fellowship. Among the upper classes, property descended by primogeniture; younger sons needed fat benefices or military commissions or heiresses.

Jeremy Gregory writes:

> Archbishops might also use the patronage at their disposal to reward or promote members of their own families or dependants. . . . Sixty per cent of clergy promoted to the 1st, 4th, and 6th stalls [at Canterbury] were related in some way or other to an archbishop: Sancroft, Tenison, Wake, Potter, Cornwallis, Moore, and Manners Sutton all advanced relations or former chaplains to Canterbury prebends. John Potter, the son of the archbishop, was presented to a Canterbury

stall, later becoming dean. Archbishop Moore promoted both his sons.... It was precisely this kind of nepotistic activity which the critics of the Church saw as the clearest testimony of corruption at the highest level, and early nineteenth-century pamphlets attacked Archbishops Moore and Manners Sutton on these grounds.... Hugh Percy, for example had received much preferment after marrying one of Archbishop Manners Sutton's daughters, becoming a prebendary in 1816 and dean in 1825.... James Croft, who was collated to a prebend by the archbishop and to the archdeaconry of Canterbury in 1825 ... [had] married another of his daughters.[2]

Dom Gregory Dix, an Anglican Benedictine, wrote about the eucharistic hunger of the first Wesleyans and asked, "When one contrasts this hunger for communion with the torpid rapacity of prelates like Archbishop Manners Sutton, who combined the See of Canterbury (then worth £40,000 a year) with sixty-three livings with cure of souls as well as other preferment, what can one say but that great as is the sin of schism, the sin of Amaziah the priest of Bethel may well be greater still?" (It may be added that Manners Sutton still managed to outspend his income.)

Curiously enough, this sort of consideration is bound up with the imposition of celibacy in the Latin Church in that period of its history with which the name of Hildebrand, Gregory VII (1073–1085), is associated. Of course this is not when celibacy was invented in the West. But in the eleventh century and later there was indeed a "deeper understanding of the sacred nature of priestly function in the celebration of the Eucharist, particularly in the thought of monastic proponents of asceticism and reform."[3] But it had been the fear of the alienation of Church property and the undesirability of hereditary benefices that had led to the onslaught on married clergy in the legislation of the Synod of Pavia (1022) and of the Council of Bourges (1031), and these "essentially practical concerns" still had a great deal of influence.[4] Relegation of the children of clerics to serf status, and prohibitions against anybody marrying the daughters of clergy, speak for themselves. Helen Parish is of the opinion that "the evidence is less than precise, but it still seems likely that many of clergy in the western church between the sixth and tenth centuries were married men ... and leading a life almost indistinguishable at first glance from that of their parishioners."[5]

It is against this model of clerical life, in which the priest functions as a cog in a society in which land, money, and inherited status, and not the gospel, prescribe his conduct, his motives, and his ambitions, that Newman, like the Hildebrandine reformers before him, was in reaction. It is hardly necessary to state that in the twenty-first century, the Church of England has found itself in a very different situation from that which so disgusted Newman. To put it crudely, nobody would seek a "career in the Church" out of a desire to feather their nest. On the contrary, a clerical life today is likely to mean a life of financial need accompanied by low status. Indeed, the typical Anglican clergyperson is increasingly likely to be middle-aged, female, and nonstipendiary but with the free use of a house and training in a part-time "ministerial training course." Today the "career parson," moving seamlessly from school to university to seminary to parish, is rapidly becoming a very rara avis.

But the Church of England does still have its rewards, although they are rewards of status rather than of money. It has a very much larger cohort of bishops than does the Catholic Church in England in order to service a broadly equivalent communicant body. And it has archdeacons and deans and the elite clerical bureaucrats of Church House. So the "career parsons," single-minded and professionally trained, may hope to advance, leaving behind them the part-time and nonstipendiary clergy, who thus form a sort of clerical *lumpenproletariat* not terribly dissimilar from the underclass of ill-paid clerics, such as Richardson's Parson Adams, who served as curates for the wealthy pluralists of earlier centuries. This culture of rewarding conformity with a mitre, it may be argued, is a source of corruption from which no other ecclesial body in Christendom suffers. The Eastern disciplines require a man to choose between domesticity and episcopacy. The Latin discipline requires of all the sacrifices that are involved in celibacy. Anglicanism offers the worst of both worlds.

However, it remains true that the pattern of a married clergy, as it has evolved in the Church of England, does provide pastoral advantages, although they are being narrowed by the financial state of the Church of England. When I was ordained to the priesthood in 1968, my "training rector" lived in a large Georgian house with his wife and four daughters. There, the kitchen was the center of the house, followed by the study for the more technical and private encounters. Any parishioner could drop in to the kitchen for tea, and very many did. There, the rector's wife presided, and the rector himself would drop in between his various encounters and excursions. The house was ripe for a ministry of dinner parties. Although there was no blurring of the gap between the rector and his parishioners (they would all, even those who thought of themselves as his intimates, address him as "Rector"), the warmth of the rectory and the ease of accessibility offered many pastoral opportunities. A parishioner did not need to seek an appointment. And, very often, the rector's wife would herself be able to deal with those who wished to raise particular topics.

Moreover, there did seem to be advantages in having a parish priest who, like most of his people, was married (I am far from denying that there are also advantages in celibacy, but that is not the subject of this chapter). Laypeople did not have to feel that there were areas of life that their priest did not really understand *ab intra*. He could not occupy the position of prescribing to others in fields in which he himself had no experience. To give a very simple workaday example: It is not easy to explain to a priest that you have been unable to get to church because you have two young children if the priest's own wife occupies, Sunday by Sunday, a pew in church with her own brood of four children beneath the age of six. And a priest's wife has an entrée into contexts from which a celibate male would necessarily be excluded, such as the melée of mums at the school gates.

The idyllic picture that I have painted has, I must confess, been eroded in the half-century since my ordination. For example, the Church Commissioners have sold off the large Georgian property that "my" rector occupied; new rectories are still decently sized houses, but they are always designed on the model of having a study, where the priest will meet people, just inside the front door and formally isolated from the rest of the house, including the kitchen. (My wife and I were very fortunate to have, in our last Anglican cure, a house in which the main entrance led into the kitchen.) And it is no longer safe to assume that a priest's wife will be prepared to forego a career of her own, as she would have done half a century ago. Besides, of the army of other women who once gathered around her, many have also vanished into other occupations, often driven by economic necessity. But it is my belief that there is still the possibility, in many social contexts, for a married couple to conduct a ministry much like the one that I have described.

There are definite disadvantages in a substantially married priesthood. Sometimes, when we used to spend our summers in Ireland, local

Catholics, as a sort of *captatio benevolentiae*, would say how much they would value a married priesthood. When I explained the financial implications of this with regard to clerical remuneration, they generally tended to become considerably more pensive. If it is possible to dislike an unmarried priest, whether fairly or unfairly, it is also certainly possible to dislike a married priest's wife (or husband). Having a spouse does not necessarily prevent a priest from having extramarital affairs. There have been high-profile and expensive court cases aiming to depose priests guilty of serial adultery. (The Church of England, in order to ensure a fair trial, has to pay the cleric's legal expenses as well as its own.) Because of these cases, the legal system has now been changed to make it easier to get rid of such men rather more quietly. A married priesthood also creates the possibility for the priest's spouse to have an affair, possibly then leaving the priest to bring up a young family single-handed. The presence of both men and women in the Anglican ministry creates opportunities, which have not always been ignored, for sexual relationships among the clergy.

So how about married priesthood within the ordinariate? It has to be said that these are early days. There are a few communities, but not many, in which a married priest and his wife are ministering to a locally situated group, geographically closely centered on the church and the clergy house in the way I described when writing about "my" rector. It may be that the English ordinariate will develop by having diocesan parishes and presbyteries, which local bishops are finding difficult to staff, handed over to it. In these circumstances, "ordinariate" Catholics and "diocesan" Catholics sharing a priest and church might well come to appreciate the sort of ministry that, in the Church of England, was integral to the culture of the married pastor.

It is no secret that, particularly in America, the twentieth century was marked by tensions between Eastern Catholics and local Latin hierarchies over the question of a married clergy. Sometimes there were actually attempts to force on the Eastern communities the Latin discipline of an unmarried clergy. I do not find it surprising that this led to serious schisms. Having a clergy in which married clergy form a large percentage is not an extraneous detail. It is integral to the religious culture of a group and deeply embedded in its centuries-old common experience. What the implications of this are for the ordinariates is a subject to which I shall return.

But it is worth considering what light the ordinariate experience can throw on the coexistence of a married clergy with a celibate clergy. Here the reader may recall my initial emphasis on the fact that, in the English Church, married clergy were already well established for some decades. Their numbers were increased in the 1990s when the Church of England resolved to admit women to its priesthood. The celebrated call of St. John Paul II for the English bishops to be "generous" in their reception of Anglican converts received a mixed response; the episcopal generation of that decade fiercely and successfully resisted the establishment of parishes composed of former Anglicans. But more generosity was shown (particularly by certain bishops) to individual priests, who were admitted to diocesan presbyterates after one or two years of "formation"; and English bishops did not discriminate against married clergy. They were, indeed, prepared to use the temporary faculties granted to them from Rome to grant the necessary permissions. This means that both Catholic bishops and their congregations have long since been familiar with married clergy. Since there are also married permanent deacons in many parishes, there is nothing strange about married men being styled "Reverend" and preaching and functioning liturgically in the sanctuary and wearing the *collare Romanum*.

There are, however, practical problems involved in the existence of married priests in Catholic dioceses. The main one is financial. A priest with a wife and family needs more money than a bachelor. One way in which Catholic bishops in England have commonly solved this problem is by easing them into chaplaincies, whether in prisons or hospitals, in which their remuneration falls upon the state. It is impossible to deny the difficulties that this might involve. It renders it less easy for a bishop to appoint whoever might seem most suitable for the post when he has a queue of former Anglicans with hungry families. And it may seem unfair to celibate clergy. The solution of having the Anglicans in a canonically distinct entity simply puts onto the shoulders of an unfortunate ordinary the problems of supporting many of his clergy out of very slight funds. Perhaps the ideal candidate for the presbyterate of an ordinariate may be a healthy Anglican priest of 65 years who was ordained in his midtwenties and can therefore live on the Anglican pension that has accrued for him year by year in accordance with the calculations of the Church of England's Pension Board. There remains the problem of housing, which could be addressed by making vacant diocesan churches and presbyteries (and stipends) available to the ordinariate in just the same way as members of particular religious orders, before the postconciliar slump in vocations, used to be responsible for particular parishes.

How acceptable are the clergy of my ordinariate (I am unwilling to speculate about the American and Australian ordinariates) to priests and people in the "mainstream" Church? A frank answer to this has to admit that two quite different reactions may be encountered. "Diocesan" clergy and congregations whose "churchmanship" was deeply marked by the decades immediately after Vatican II tend not to view an Anglican incursion with much favor. It seems to them that we are moving in a direction that is exactly opposite to the one in which they would themselves like to be moving. The former Anglicans do not favor the ordination of women or abortion or contraception; our liturgical tastes incline strongly to a style of Catholicism, particularly as expressed in worship, that we have long since convinced ourselves is obscurantist, reactionary, irreconcilable with something we consider Vatican II, which, this thinking runs, entitles us to be able to scrutinize a priest's face during Mass, having no desire to see the embroidery on the back of his chasuble. Such churchmen regard the ministry of extraordinary ministers of Holy Communion as one of the most important innovations that they think the Council introduced. Some of them may read the British Catholic magazine the *Tablet*.

I must make it clear that I have heard these things only anecdotally from fellow clergy in the ordinariate. My own experiences, both of clergy and of laity, have been universally good, indeed warm. I have been welcomed in England, in Ireland, in America, and in Europe. I have never sensed among brother priests any resentment arising from my married state, although in one parish in which I was briefly doing duty I was told that an old lady, hearing that I was "ordinariate," asked, "Is he married? I'm sure he can't be—he's so good." It has been my impression that the clergy with whom I have mixed have welcomed the strengthening of Catholic orthodoxy that the ordinariate has brought into the Catholic Church. They have shown a curiosity about how some of the practicalities work out, but never with the least hint of hostility or resentment. When giving talks or lectures about the ordinariate, which I consider it my duty to do whenever and wherever possible, I have found the same: curiosity, but friendliness.

We cannot leave this subject without considering the legal state of the Anglican tradition of a married clergy within the ordinariates. *Anglicanorum coetibus* VI 2 states: "The Ordinary, in full observance of the discipline of celibate clergy in the Latin Church, as a rule (*pro regula*) will admit only celibate men to the order of presbyter. He may also petition the Roman Pontiff, as a derogation from can. 277, §1, for the admission of married men to the order of presbyter on a case by case basis, according to objective criteria approved by the Holy See." This was inserted into the apostolic constitution, presumably to explicitly cover the case of married Anglican clergy seeking admission to the presbyterate of the ordinariate. *But it does not actually say that this provision applies only to those who are both ordained and married when they enter into full communion with the Catholic Church.* Of course, some such limitation may be included in the *obiectiva criteria* that were *ab Apostolica Sede comprobanda*. But at least it may be said that *Anglicanorum coetibus* itself does not prohibit the ordinary from seeking such derogation on behalf of married men whom he and his council may wish to promote to his presbyterate without their having previously been in Anglican orders.

What about the future? I have made it clear why I have not advocated the episcopal consecration of married men in the ordinariates. And I would not advocate permission for priests to get married. This would be contrary to the traditions both of the West and of the East. Additionally, I have memories of nice young unmarried curates arriving in their first parishes and finding that all the girls had set their caps at them. I never thought this was anything but monstrously unedifying.

But the admission to holy orders of married laymen is a different matter. It is strongly sanctioned by the culture and traditions of the Anglican patrimony and is not excluded by *Anglicanorum coetibus*. Ours, I suspect, is not the generation in which to press the matter. There are grounds for thinking that, had an attempt been made to incorporate such a suggestion in the apostolic constitution, such difficulties might very naturally and properly have been raised in Roman dicasteries that the entire project might have failed to get off the ground. But future generations may see it as a piece of unfinished business. For example, were the Holy See ever to sanction the presbyteral ordination of married *viri probati* who had served in the permanent diaconate, the question of the ordinariates' ordaining married laymen might look different, both in the corridors of Vatican power and in the English parishes.

Notes

1. John Henry Newman, *Loss and Gain*, Part III, chap. 2 (London: Longmans, Green, 1874).
2. Jeremy Gregory, *Restoration, Reformation, and Reform, 1660–1828: Archbishops of Canterbury and Their Diocese* (Cambridge: Oxford University Press, 2000), 36.
3. Helen Parish, *Clerical Celibacy in the West, 1100–1700* (London: Routledge, 2010), 95.
4. Ibid.
5. Ibid.

CHAPTER SEVEN

The Gift to the Church of Married Clergy

Edwin Barnes

In 2001 there was a farewell service in the cathedral in St. Albans when I retired after six years as an Anglican bishop and fifty years of ministry in the Church of England. My wife, Jane, was given a bouquet of flowers at the end of the Eucharist, and I asked if she would like to say a few words, expecting her simply to thank people for the flowers. She did indeed want to say something; and what she said was very moving.

As a provincial episcopal visitor—a "flying bishop"—my role had been unusual. Strictly speaking, I was a suffragan to the archbishop of Canterbury, with the responsibility of caring for traditionalist clergy in Canterbury Province. Three of us had been created in England after the Church of England decided to embark on the experiment of ordaining women to the priesthood. On my appointment, the archbishop had advised me that if I was going to a parish with a married incumbent, Jane should try to accompany me. We had gone to many different parishes, rural and urban, spread from the Channel Islands in the south up to the Humber and the boundary with Yorkshire in the north. We had stayed in rectories and vicarages, and sometimes in the homes of the laity.

Many of the clergy wives were very happy to talk to Jane while their husbands and I went about our business. It was of these women that Jane spoke at that farewell service. They often had to manage with very little money, sometimes even relying on a little state relief if they had several children in their families. Increasingly she had found that they were working women, holding down full-time jobs while also running the parsonages and their families. The expectations that the laity had of them were often unrealistic. In times past, some clergy wives had been the Ladies Bountiful of their parishes, doling out charity to the poor, visiting the sick in their homes, and presiding at meetings of the Mothers' Union. That was a time when the clergy often came from wealthy families, when many parishes were well endowed, and also when some stipends were more than generous (though others were disgracefully poor). We were living at a time when incomes had been levelled out, so that all clergy were meant to have adequate livings.

Despite this, there were and still are large discrepancies. Wealthier parishes provided the priests with benefits beyond their stipends, and in any case some vicarages were much easier to run than others. We ourselves had lived in a six-bedroom Victorian house with additional servants' accommodations on a second floor and central heating that was very expensive to run. Only forty years earlier the vicar had employed six live-in servants, and some parishioners supposed we still had the sort of means that he had enjoyed.

Jane told the congregation in St. Alban's Cathedral what a privilege it had been getting to know many clergy wives, hearing their stories, meeting their families, and learning how they coped with all sorts of problems and yet still found time to give support and encouragement to any who came to their doors. These included all sorts, from the wealthy woman who felt her life was useless to the gentleman of the road who wanted a cup of tea and something to eat. Jane had been impressed by the way such a range of clergy wives had coped with everything parish life threw their way.

These clergy wives were and are a huge gift to the Church. They support their husbands in every way, from ensuring that they eat properly to setting up and running groups for young wives or single mothers to doing whatever the parish seems most to need done. But not all women are able to bear such burdens, and we had been saddened by the failure of some clergy marriages and had given what support we could not only to the priests but also to the women who had left them, or the women they had left.

All this is meant as a preamble before we begin to consider what might be said to help the Catholic Church look at what clerical marriage might mean for it in principle, and in reality. Since my ordination as a Catholic priest six years ago, I have consistently heard laypeople say they are glad to have married priests among them and how they wish that *all* their priests might have the opportunity of marrying. Others have said that if the rules on clerical marriage were altered it would immediately resolve the problem of the shortage of priestly vocations. It would also, they thought, put an end to the scandal of clerical abuse of minors. Yet for many Catholic priests the prospect of changing the rules fills them with dread, and they suppose that a married priest would necessarily be less devoted, less fully committed, than they are to their congregations.

Perhaps what my wife said will dampen some of the unrealistic expectations of those Catholics who suppose that clergy marriage would solve all the Church's problems. There are many other important considerations to balance against any overenthusiasm for changing the rules. There are the financial implications of supporting the wife and family of a priest as well as the man himself. There is the matter of housing: What is appropriate for a celibate priest might be quite unworkable for a family. There are already difficulties for some Catholic priests who, appointed to parishes where previous priests have kept open houses, are finding the need to establish clear boundaries—which are doubly important when the presbytery is a family home.

Then there is the question of pensions. A retired married priest is unlikely to be content to be shunted off to look after aged nuns in an ancient convent. The pension must be adequate for himself and his wife, and there is also the matter of widows' pensions. These have particularly been a concern for the ordinariate in England and Wales. In the Church of England over the years, a stock of housing has been built up that is now rented out to retired clergy. How long would it take the Catholic Church to do anything similar?

Besides all this, there is the question of how the wives would be helped into the role of priests' wives. It used to be common in the Church of England for ordinands to be unmarried, to spend their first three years or so in a clergy house with other single curates, and only then, after obtaining the bishop's permission, to become engaged. That meant that the new bride at least knew that she was marrying a clergyman.

The situation for the Catholic Church would be entirely different. If there were to be a married priesthood, the candidates—it is assumed—would already be married and would undertake not to remarry if their wives should predecease them. But this in no way would guarantee a plentiful supply of priests; nor would it automatically prepare the wives for what would lie ahead of them.

Today in the Church of England, far fewer young men (and women) are offering themselves for ordination. Most candidates are already married, often with families. Frequently the complaint of clergy wives is "I did not marry a clergyman." That is, they had not expected to be thrown into the role of clergy wives and in some cases had not been in that role for many years as their husbands pursued their vocations in business or some other profession before taking holy orders relatively late. That said, it is remarkable how many wives do indeed adapt to the task, and take it on enthusiastically. At St. Stephen's House, when I worked there, my wife had given the ordinands' wives the opportunity to meet and talk about their hopes and fears as their husbands' ordinations approached.

The supposition that allowing clergy to marry would entirely resolve the problem of clerical abuse of minors is ill founded. I have visited Anglican clergy in prison, both married and single men, who were there for that very crime. It might be that the problem is less severe for a married priesthood—after all, St. Paul had advised us, "Better marry than burn"—but marriage does not remove the temptation or the propensity for abusing the young.

So far this seems to be dissuasive to the Catholic Church. The problems look far too difficult for anyone to want to change the system. Yet in fact I would still ask the Church to look once more at the possibility of ordaining married men. On ordination as Catholic priests in 2011, we former Anglicans were dispensed from clerical celibacy so long as our wives were alive. Should they predecease us, however, we would then remain unmarried, becoming, one might say, "potential celibates" so that the general rule of clerical celibacy was maintained. This same sort of dispensation applies to married deacons.

Now some would raise a question about this requirement, going so far as to suggest that allowing clergy to marry after ordination is not to denigrate celibacy. Quite the reverse: It is to say that celibacy, like marriage, is a vocation. It recognizes that a man, after ordination, might yet discover he also has a vocation to holy matrimony. From the number of men having to leave the Catholic ministry in order to marry, this certainly seems to be a reality that the Church needs to face.

Yes, there are married clergy who are less than totally committed to their parishioners. But is this not also true of some Catholic clergy? Far more important is the sympathy, the true fellow feeling, of a married priest for his married parishioners. No matter how an unmarried priest might try, the layman can always say, "Ah, but you don't understand." The married priest has been there. It is a difficult business, getting the demands of a wife and family and those of the parish into some sort of balance. But it is not greatly different from the problems facing men in other roles, in the Armed Forces, in industry, or in medicine or teaching. Some of the problems the Church faces are surely the product of overclericalism, of setting the priest too far apart from the people he is given to serve. The wife, and even more the children, of a married priest will prick the bubble of effortless superiority very quickly, to the great advantage of priest and parish alike. They will also tell him if his sermons are flying off into the realms of academic nonsense rather than being grounded in the everyday—the place from which Jesus spoke.

So what about the practicalities, particularly the financing of a married priesthood? This is a challenge, of course, but a challenge that the faithful will meet. In the Church of England, despite small worshipping congregations, parishes raise huge sums each year, far more than their Catholic counterparts. In the Church of England, for fifty years and more there has been an emphasis on stewardship, on giving a realistic proportion of one's income to the church. The rediscovery of tithing results in many congregations' paying fifty, sixty, or even a hundred thousand pounds a year to the church's central funds, which are devoted to paying for the clergy and their pensions, yet still raising enough to maintain expensive ancient buildings.

When all this is weighed and argued, still the real imperative for a married clergy is missed. It has been said that without the churches of the East, the Western Church was functioning on only one lung. It might equally be claimed that with only a celibate clergy, and without married priests, the Church is functioning only at half power. At present, since the establishment of the ordinariates in England, North America, and Australia, married clergy are to a greater or lesser degree tolerated. What my wife was saying to the congregation in St. Alban's was, "These women are a gift to the Church. Don't just put up with them. Value them." Anglicans generally do value their clergy wives. There are still a few Mrs. Proudies around, trying to dominate. The vast majority, though, are doing a great work for the Church, not least in the models they present of Christian wives and mothers, "not with braided hair or gold or pearls or costly attire but by good deeds as befits women who profess religion" (1 Tim. 2:9–10). They enable their husbands to do as St. Paul advised Timothy and the leaders in the Church of his day, to be "above reproach, married only once . . . managing his own household well, keeping his children submissive and respectful in every way—for if a man does not know how to manage his own household, how can he care for God's church?"

CHAPTER EIGHT

Official Catholic Pronouncements Regarding Presbyteral Celibacy

Their Fate and the Implications for Catholic-Orthodox Relations

Peter Galadza

Anyone familiar with the pronouncements of the Second Vatican Council and several other official Catholic statements regarding presbyteral celibacy may be surprised that the issue would even arise in the context of ecumenical discussions between Catholics and Orthodox. Documents from the Council and several subsequent documents clearly affirm the tradition of optional celibacy among Eastern Christians.[1] However, as historians know, affirmative assertions of this kind sometimes reveal more about the need to make them than about the fact that they are being honored.[2]

Let me begin, though, by noting that Pope Francis, while cardinal-archbishop of Buenos Aires, gave indications that for him, the Catholic Church's official pronouncements regarding presbyteral celibacy provide the inspiration and guidelines for his own approach to the question.[3] However, before summarizing these pronouncements as well as Cardinal Bergoglio's helpful thoughts on the topic, let me review what it is that has made this question a matter of concern in Catholic-Orthodox dialogue and why it is important to "put out the fire" before it becomes one more hindrance to East-West rapprochement.

Let me also immediately point out that the concern about developments within Catholicism surrounding this question do not derive from any desire—at least on my part—to see the Latin Church change its discipline. Rather, a certain concern is warranted because the developments summarized below can negatively affect Roman Catholic attitudes toward Orthodox (and Eastern Catholic) married priests—and thus their churches.

These developments relate to the fact that in the interests of presenting a positive theology of mandatory presbyteral celibacy, certain Catholic authors occasionally engage in detrimental totalizing. It is the totalizing, of course, that creates the problem, not the desire to provide an explanation of Roman Catholic practice. And it is a new wave of totalizing—verging at times on dogmatism—that makes this chapter necessary.

The *Lex Continentiae* as "Apostolic Practice"

In 1981 Christian Cochini published *Origines apostolique du célibat sacerdotal*.[4] The book's central thesis is that marital continence for the ordained "must have been" apostolic practice. The direct relevance to Orthodox-Catholic discussions is that Cochini's contention spawned not only a book that claimed that this was also the authentic *Eastern* tradition,[5] but also a series of articles by prominent Roman Catholic hierarchs and theologians repeating the claim.[6] In fact, within the last several years, for certain Roman Catholics the claim has become axiomatic.[7] The sometime prefect of the Vatican's Congregation for the Clergy, Cardinal Mauro Piacenza (in office 2010–2013), referred to celibacy as "the apostolic way of life." In the very first paragraph of his foreword to *Married Priests? 30 Crucial Questions about Celibacy*, the cardinal asserts that "ecclesiastical celibacy, *apostolica vivendi forma* [the apostolic way of life] should be reckoned as one of the greatest goods and most powerful vehicles of truth, one of the greatest gifts that the Lord left to his Church and continually reaffirms."[8] Again, the point is not to question the outstanding nature of this gift, but only to warn against univocal grounding in apostolic practice.

Cochini's scholarship[9]—and that of his Eastern Catholic disciple, Roman Cholij[10]—has been soundly critiqued by a phalanx of renowned Catholic academics.[11] Nonetheless, on the basis of Cochini's hypothesis[12] (and it can be nothing more than a hypothesis—and a flimsy one at that), prominent Roman Catholics have been implying—to put it most starkly—that countless numbers of children born to Orthodox married priests and their lawfully wedded wives throughout the centuries have been born in contravention of apostolic tradition. (There are children of Orthodox and Eastern Catholic priests still alive today who can recount stories of unedifying treatment at the hands of Catholic educators during the pre-Vatican II period.)

As proof that the Eastern Churches maintain a "vestige" of "apostolic practice," the proponents of this *lex continentiae* adduce the mandatory celibacy of Eastern Christian candidates to the *episcopate*. For them, the fact that the bishop possesses "the fullness of the priesthood" demonstrates that "even in the East" there is an appreciation for the desirable link between celibacy and the priesthood.[13] However, George Nedungatt critiques this approach thus:

> Pablo Gefaell (to quote the last writer on the topic to date), "Clerical Celibacy," *Folia Canonica* 4 (2001): 75–91, explains the obligation of celibacy on the part of bishops in the East as an exigency of the highest degree of priesthood and as expressive of their "spousal relationship with the Church" (p. 83). This is not only to invert history and theology but to ignore the best recent scholarship on the Council in Trullo, rescued from the debris of past Latin polemics. Unaware of it, he [Gefaell] writes: "The oriental discipline regarding celibate bishops, temporal continence and the matrimonial impediment of sacred Orders can be understood only under the light of the underlying theological basis of celibacy" (p. 90), and concludes viewing "the present praxis of the uxorate clergy as a permissive law of a situation less proper to the clerical state" (p. 91).[14]

Nedungatt later adds the following about the celibacy of Eastern bishops: "It is through the imperial legislation of Justinian that episcopal celibacy was introduced into the canons, as Pitsakis (n. 92) has shown. To see it as originating instead from 'the fullness of the priesthood' is the fantasy of *ahistorical* theology."[15] In other words, it was only after Justinian had introduced episcopal celibacy into "civil" law that the *Church of Byzantium*—more than a century later—made it part of canon law. And Justinian's main concern was to curtail abuses by wealthy bishops, who were inclined to transfer the Church's property to their children.

In certain circles, the notion of an apostolic source for the *lex continentiae* is now so entrenched that Stefan Heid, for example, could argue in 2012 for its possible reception by a new "ecumenical consensus":

> The Eastern interpretation [regarding Nicea I's refutation of the need for clerical continence] must therefore be rejected, because in historical terms it is untenable. The best Greek Fathers of the Church in the first centuries propagated clerical continence, and the highly esteemed Epiphanius of Salamis, to mention only the most prominent and widely recognized example, speaks unmistakably about indispensable clerical continence, whereby he means exactly the same discipline that prevailed at that time in the Latin West. Ecumenical dialogue today can start with these historical insights and perhaps arrive at a new consensus.[16]

Earlier in the same piece Heid writes: "Interestingly enough, the evidence for clerical continence in the first few centuries is even clearer in the East than in the West."[17] He goes on to insist that "the first tremors that weakened the unrestricted duty to practice continence came no doubt from the major schisms that the Church in the East experienced."[18] Heid has in mind Syrian and Coptic Christianity. "Schism" and "clerical nuptial relations" have now been linked.

Spousal Imagery and the Priesthood: From Metaphors to Metaphysics

The next significant development of a totalizing or potentially totalizing nature has occurred with the elaboration of Christological spousal imagery and its univocal application to the priesthood. A literature review confirms Basilio Petrà's observation that in some circles, "ordination has come to be understood not only as a consecration which *configures one ontologically to Christ as shepherd and head* . . . but also as a consecration which configures one to *Christ the Bridegroom.*"[19]

The following paragraphs from John Paul II's 1992 post-synodal apostolic exhortation *Pastores dabo vobis* sometimes provides inspiration for those who would like to create such an ontological configuration. However, as is obvious, there is no reason that one must interpret the pope's text in this manner. The most relevant paragraphs read as follows:

> The priest is called to be the living image of Jesus Christ, the spouse of the Church.... Of course, he will always remain a member of the community as a believer alongside his other brothers and sisters who have been called by the Spirit, but in virtue of his configuration to Christ, the head and shepherd, the priest stands in this spousal relationship with regard to the community. "Inasmuch as he represents Christ, the head, shepherd and spouse of the Church, the priest is placed not only in the Church but also in the forefront of the Church" [reference to proposal 7 of the synod]. In his spiritual life, therefore, he is called to live out Christ's spousal love toward the Church, his bride. Therefore, the priest's life ought to radiate this spousal character, which demands that he be a witness to Christ's spousal love and thus be capable of loving people with a heart which is new, generous and pure—with *genuine self-detachment* [emphasis added; see below], with full, constant and faithful dedication and at the same time with a kind of "divine jealousy" (cf. 2 Cor. 11:2) and even with a kind of maternal tenderness, capable of bearing "the pangs of birth" until "Christ be formed" in the faithful (cf. Gal. 4:19) (par. 22).
>
> ———
>
> But the will of the Church finds its ultimate motivation in the link between celibacy and sacred ordination, which configures the priest to Jesus Christ the head and spouse of the Church. The Church, as the spouse of Jesus Christ, wishes to be loved by the priest in the total and exclusive manner in which Jesus Christ her head and spouse loved her. Priestly celibacy, then, is the gift of self in and with Christ to his Church and expresses the priest's service to the Church in and with the Lord (par. 29).
>
> ———
>
> And so priestly celibacy should not be considered just as a legal norm or as a totally external condition for admission to ordination,

but rather as a value that is profoundly connected with ordination, whereby a man takes on the likeness of Jesus Christ, the good shepherd and spouse of the Church (par. 50).

John Paul II then continues in paragraph 72:

> The People of God should be able to say about the priest, who has increasingly matured in human sensitivity, something similar to what we read about Jesus in the letter to the Hebrews: "For we have not a high priest who is unable to sympathize with our weaknesses, but one who in every respect has been tempted as we are, yet without sinning" (Heb. 4:15).

Paradoxically, perhaps, this paragraph could be used precisely to develop a theology of married priesthood! The pope then continues to develop the themes of configuration to Christ, invoking "ontological" language more carefully than those who have come after him:

> The Spirit, by consecrating the priest and configuring him to Jesus Christ, head and shepherd, creates a bond which, located in the priest's very being, demands to be assimilated and lived out in a personal, free and conscious way through an ever richer communion of life and love and an ever broader and more radical sharing in the feelings and attitudes of Jesus Christ. In this bond between the Lord Jesus and the priest, an ontological and psychological bond, a sacramental and moral bond, is the foundation and likewise the power for that "life according to the Spirit" and that "radicalism of the Gospel" to which every priest is called today and which is fostered by ongoing formation in its spiritual aspect. This formation proves necessary also for the priestly ministry to be genuine and spiritually fruitful (par. 72).[20]

None of the above need be problematic for Orthodox-Catholic relations. Or rather, if read in the context of the Catholic Church's other—and more authoritative—pronouncements, it certainly need not be problematic. However, some of the recent literature on celibacy implies that a married man is simply incapable of such commitment to his flock.[21] Ironically, in recent memory alone, thousands of married Orthodox (and Eastern Catholic) priests in the former USSR and the Eastern bloc demonstrated "genuine self-detachment" during deportations and executions. The persecution sometimes included their wives and children.

But as just mentioned, if *Pastores dabo vobis* avoids totalizing the "spousal connection" between celibacy and the priesthood, certain Roman Catholic authorities are less careful in their own formulations. The following was written in 2011 by Cardinal Piacenza:

> Certainly one particularly important document dealing with all the themes concerned with priesthood and priestly formation was the apostolic exhortation *Pastores Dabo Vobis*, in which the *gift of celibacy is understood as part of the bond between Jesus and the priest, and for the first time, the psychological importance of this bond is mentioned also in a way that is not separate from the ontological importance* [emphasis added]. Indeed, we read in no. 72: "In this bond between the Lord Jesus and the priest, an ontological and psychological bond, a sacramental and moral bond, is the foundation and likewise the power for that 'life according to the Spirit' and that 'radicalism of the Gospel' to which every priest is called today and which is fostered by ongoing formation in its spiritual aspect."[22]

Note how Cardinal Piacenza identifies celibacy, on the one hand, and the priest's "life according to the Spirit" and evangelical radicalism, on the other. The cardinal has taken the liberty of suggesting that "the bond" with Christ, "located in the priest's very being," presumes celibacy. And the identification bears "ontological importance." A more precise reading of *Pastores dabo vobis* does not require such conclusions.

Later in the same article the cardinal writes:

> Although there are sometimes remarkably different emphases, more liturgical-sacral or more Christological-pastoral, the uninterrupted Magisterium of the aforementioned pontiffs is consistent in basing celibacy on the theological reality of the ministerial priesthood, on the ontological-sacramental configuration of the priest to Christ the Lord, on his participation in his Christ's unique priesthood and on the *imitatio Christi* that that implies.[23]

Cardinal Piacenza continues with the following appeal and assertion: "In light of the papal Magisterium that has been examined, the reduction of celibacy to a mere ecclesiastical law, which is so widespread in some circles, must be overcome. It is a law only because it is an intrinsic requirement of the priesthood [sic] and of the configuration to Christ intended by the sacrament of holy orders [sic]."[24] As we shall see below, the papal magisterium of Pope Francis, while cherishing celibacy, hardly shares this approach.

The views of the cardinal-prefect, nonetheless, find resonance among other Catholic authorities. The sometime secretary of the Vatican Congregation for the Clergy, Archbishop Crescenzio Sepe (in office 1992–2001), wrote the following in an article posted on the Vatican's website:

> It is on the strength of this essential, ontological and existential assimilation to Christ that the extreme congruity and relevance of priestly celibacy can and should be judged. The priest, inasmuch as he is an *alter Christus*, finds his true identity, his true *raison d'etre*, his true style, in his intimate, personal relationship with Christ. The force binding celibacy to the priesthood lies in the ontology of the priest.[25]

Archbishop Sepe's reflection includes the following remarks:

> Then again, the comparison with the married priests of some Oriental Churches does not seem to be a valid one, for here we have an ancient institution and not one established for reasons of expediency. It must also be said that, actually in those Churches, be they Catholic or Orthodox, the law of celibacy for the priesthood is recommended and held in high regard.[26]

Sepe's reference to "ancient institution" must be appreciated—especially as he has avoided suggesting that these priests "no doubt" were "originally" expected to curtail nuptial relations after ordination. And while it is not the case that among the Orthodox "the law of celibacy for the priesthood is recommended," there is indeed a high regard for those clergy living in this state. However, it is Sepe's following remark that especially deserves our attention:

This, for example is what a Russian Orthodox bishop of the Patriarchate of Moscow had to say on the subject in the immediate post-conciliar period: "For us Orthodox, the priesthood is a sacred function. For this reason we are convinced that you, Westerners, you Latins, are not on the right path where you allow the question of ecclesiastical celibacy to be debated in public, in the forum of public opinion. In our Oriental tradition, it has been possible to authorize the ordination of a handful of married men [sic], as in any case you have done and go on doing in certain regions. But take care: in the West, if you separate the priesthood from celibacy, a very swift decadence will set in. The West is not mystical enough to tolerate the marriage of its clergy without degenerating. The Church of Rome (and this is to her glory) has preserved this ecclesiastical ascesis for a whole millennium. Beware of compromising it."[27]

Unfortunately, Archbishop Sepe does not reveal the identity of this Russian bishop, nor does he provide a source for the quotation. Such information could have helped in determining what could possibly be meant by the Russian bishop's alleged reference to the fact that "in our Oriental tradition, it has been possible to authorize the ordination of a handful of married men."

In North America, a conference on clerical celibacy at the University of Notre Dame produced papers demonstrating far greater nuancing and acumen.[28] Most of the published lectures provide solid reflection on the topic and avoid the kind of totalizing referred to above. Among the instances, however, in which more precision would have been welcome is the following formulation. In "The Virginity of Jesus and the Celibacy of His Priests," Archbishop Allen Vigneron of Detroit writes: "Having considered the identity of gift and giver in the offering that establishes a nuptial covenant, we are now prepared to articulate the intrinsic connection between Jesus's virginity and his priesthood."[29] As legitimate as it might be to reflect on such a connection, one is surprised by a subsequent step in this articulation. I mention it here because it bears more directly on Orthodox-Catholic discussions. In a footnote devoted to the Eastern requirement of celibacy for bishops, Vigneron refers to Orthodox archbishop Peter L'Huillier's article on the topic[30] and writes: "L'Huillier sets as one of his goals 'to discover the reasons underlying this development,' that is, promoting only celibates to the episcopacy (p. 292). In working to that end he never mentions the virginity of Jesus; rather, he asserts that "the requirement of episcopal celibacy has no *dogmatic* significance" (p. 297). In view of the Church's belief in Jesus' virginity, this seems surprising."[31]

The precision I have in mind is the following: As legitimate as it may be to reflect on the dogmatic significance of Jesus's virginity, it is not legitimate to take the next step and suggest that dogmatic significance be ascribed to episcopal celibacy.

Earlier in the article Vigneron discusses one of the inspirations for his thought on this topic, and as is evident, the reference below to "the innermost of faith and revelation" brings us again to a kind of dogmatization of the celibacy question. He writes: "I am convinced that understanding the celibacy of priests as a participation in Jesus' virginity is the key to our being able to fulfill this part of our mission in the Church." This, of course, is unassailable. But the very next sentence reads: "In this I see myself as following in the path marked out by Hans Urs von Balthasar, when he wrote that 'the reasons for priestly celibacy [should be] presented as inseparably bound with the innermost of revelation and faith.'"[32]

The adjective "innermost" obviously functions here as a substantive. It presumably refers to the innermost "content" of revelation and faith. Von Balthasar's statement is significant by itself, and the attempt to determine its context, as well as the language of the original piece, led me to the actual article, which revealed similarly significant formulations. Von Balthasar's assertions deserve to be cited in full here for two reasons. First, without doubt the Swiss theologian was one of the most brilliant theologians of the twentieth century, one whose influence continued to grow after his death in 1988. Second, in our discussions of the growth of "totalizing" Latin theologies of mandatory celibacy, it is important to note that this trend is not confined to "curial theology." Even though von Balthasar was buried as a cardinal (having been named to the college but dying before the consistory at which he would have received his red hat), his theology is anything but formulaic or "institutional" as the following quotations from his article "The Meaning of Celibacy," published in English translation in 1976, show.[33] Taken individually, they might not warrant apprehension, but when read together they do. We begin with the paragraph that forms the context for the citation already adduced:

Dogma, exegesis, pastoral studies must be taught so that discernment is induced and is given a sound basis, which cannot be done in a broad study-plan but must be fostered by frequent and varied approaches. This would demand that professors, rectors, and spiritual directors work together and in the same spirit; that reasons for priestly celibacy be not merely hung on extraneously, in a superficial manner easily refuted by modern psychology and sociology, but that they be presented as inseparably bound with the innermost of revelation and faith.[34]

Note the reference to dogma; though, on the other hand, no one is suggesting that reflection on celibacy should remain "extraneous" or "superficial."

Then there are two citations of a more inspirational thrust: "The eucharistic sacrifice of Jesus on the cross is inseparably united with his celibacy."[35] And "Christian celibacy is often spoken of as 'an eschatological sign.' This is well and good, except for the article 'an.' Actually, it is 'the' sign, and as such it becomes indispensable."[36] Note that the context is a discussion of presbyteral celibacy. Thus, the "indispensability" relates to the latter.

Finally, we find two remarks bearing more directly on Eastern realities. "When St. Paul says: 'I wish all were like me,' unmarried, he does not imply one of two alternatives but unmistakably gives preference to one of the two, to a life thrown as a whole into the fire of Christ, ablaze like glowing iron. The *viri probati* are cold iron, no matter how zealous they might be personally. The unmarried shepherd is the glowing iron and he alone can communicate his radiance to others."[37]

Of course, in referring to *viri probati*, von Balthasar does not have in mind Eastern Catholic men per se, but that is the term used to describe some of the married candidates—or potential candidates—to the priesthood in North American Eastern Catholic eparchies. These are older men, usually with grown children. In any case, von Balthasar would consider them unacceptable. Squaring this with 1 Timothy 3:4–5 would be an interesting exercise in exegesis.

And then there is von Balthasar's direct reference to Eastern practice—both Orthodox and Catholic: "Among other things we would have to study the history of the separated churches and how their clergy fared, and would have to take to heart the experience of the eastern church in learning all about the pastoral, juridical, and financial problems of the eastern married clergy—which are so obviously complex that more than one uniate bishop does not use his authority to ordain married priests anymore."[38]

Certainly, throughout history there have been "uniate bishops" who were sincerely convinced that married candidates to the priesthood were undesirable. However, their "authority" to ordain them was rarely unconstrained. As for the "separated churches," in view of von Balthasar's presuppositions, both pastoral and theological, it is hard to imagine that any "study" would change his mind about married clergy. In any case, note how, as always, ad hominem and sociological arguments are permitted in the campaign for mandatory celibacy. Similar arguments marshaled in defense of optional celibacy generally evoke denunciation or even ecclesial ostracism.[39]

Ideas Bearing Consequences—and Presumably Fears of a "Very Swift Decadence"

There is writing that remains academic—in the pejorative sense—and then there is writing of consequence. One could probably ignore a fair amount of the literature cited above if not for the fact that it apparently provides the motivation for authoritative decisions by influential dicasteries in the Catholic Church, decisions that impact Catholic-Orthodox relations (not to mention "inter-ritual" relations within Catholicism). Let us then turn to some of these decisions.

There is enough literature regarding the ban on the ordination of married candidates to the priesthood in Eastern Catholic Churches to give a sense of how this question has harmed Orthodox-Catholic relations in the past.[40] This is not the place to review that literature. Allow me rather to focus on more recent events, which in any case provide the immediate motivation for the present research into the fate of Catholic pronouncements on celibacy.

George Nedungatt, in the volume already cited, reviews the prohibition on ordaining married Eastern Catholic candidates to the priesthood in the West (as well as the ban on "importing" married clergy from "home territories") and cites three Vatican decrees, *Cum data fuerit* (1929), *Graeci-Rutheni Ritus* (1929) and *Qua sollerti alacritate* (1930). He then states the following regarding the *present* situation: "Whether the above mentioned three decrees, which are cited in the sources of c. 758 § 3 [of the 1990 *CCEO*], are still in force has become a *quaestio disputata* after the Second Vatican Council and especially after the promulgation of the *CCEO* [the 1990 *Code of Canons of the Eastern Churches*], which has been interpreted by some as having effectively abolished the above mentioned Roman prohibition. But others doubt it. Questioned, COC [Congregation for the Oriental Churches] has replied that the prohibition is still in force."[41]

Nedungatt wrote this in 2002. According to reliable sources, in 2008 a Vatican dicastery repeated the ban. This would help explain why, to the present day in Italy, France, Spain, Portugal, and Ireland, married priests from Eastern Europe and the Middle East must separate from their wives—and children. With the influx of more than a million post-Soviet and Middle-Eastern emigrants flooding Western Europe, the number of such clergy ministering to them runs into the hundreds.[42]

Incidentally, canon 758 § 3 of the *CCEO*, referred to above by Nedungatt, reads as follows: "The particular law of each Church *sui iuris* or special norms established by the Apostolic See are to be followed in admitting married men to sacred orders." Obviously, for the United States the Apostolic See has established very restrictive norms. It is rumored that they are to become even more restrictive: Whereas during the past several years, Rome has insisted on vetting the case of each Byzantine-Ruthenian married candidate individually—in Rome—henceforth it may become policy for the vetting to be done also by (1) the papal nuncio, (2) the office of the president of the USCCB, and (3) the local *Latin-rite* ordinary of the Eastern Catholic ordinand's territory. (Note that all of the larger Eastern Catholic Churches in the United States have their own ordinaries, which, from an ecclesiological perspective, makes the last part of this proposal particularly odd.) It is also rumored that the Vatican has suggested that for any change to occur, the Latin-rite bishops of the United States would have to express their unanimous approval—as was the case in Canada. However, considering that even the age of confirmation cannot be agreed on by all the American bishops, unanimity on this issue would seem quite elusive.

In view of the aforementioned, there probably should have been little surprise when, in May of 2012, the then cardinal-prefect of the Congregation for the Eastern Churches told the Eastern Catholic bishops of the

United States during their *ad limina* visit that their priests should "embrace celibacy in respect of the ecclesial context."[43]

One should also not be entirely surprised by the story that appeared the following month, when newspapers carried information about the visitation of the Irish College in Rome. The cardinal-archbishop, charged by the Vatican with heading up the visitation, reported that "the presence of Orthodox students in the house, as well as of the Eastern Rite Catholic men not preparing for the celibate life," was an added complication [in addition to the apparently inadequate number of actual Irish at the College]. "The visitor's recommendation is that the college accept only seminarians from Ireland; if a seminarian is accepted from another country, it should be extraordinary; they should only enter at the start of the first-year and must demonstrate a facility in English. Eastern Rite and Orthodox students should not be accepted." The question of citizenship and language are, of course, separate matters. As regards the presence of Eastern Christians, however, even the four archbishops from Ireland who were also appointed to the visitation "found this element of the cardinal's report 'surprising.'"[44]

Conciliar, Canonical, and Catechetical Respect for the Married Presbyterate—and Bergoglio's Respect for Vatican II

We finally arrive at a review of the Catholic Church's most official teaching on celibacy. As noted above, this is codified in (1) the decree of a council considered ecumenical by the Church of Rome, (2) her *Catechism*—a very influential text[45]—and (3) the Eastern Catholic Code of Canons. As we proceed, it will become evident that if only Catholic authorities were able to adhere more directly to both the letter and the spirit of these pronouncements, many of the problems discussed above—both theoretical and practical—could be avoided.

Certainly the most authoritative modern text dealing with the issue at hand is *Presbyterorum ordinis*. As a decree of an ecumenical council promulgated by a pope, it obviously carries more weight than a papal encyclical, post-synodal exhortation, or apostolic letter. Within Catholicism, the only weightier documents are a dogmatic constitution, a (simple) constitution, and an actual (infallible) dogmatic pronouncement by the pope himself.

Paragraph 16 of *Presbyterorum ordinis* reads:

> Perfect and perpetual continence for the sake of the Kingdom of Heaven, commended by Christ the Lord and through the course of time as well as in our own days freely accepted and observed in a praiseworthy manner by many of the faithful, is held by the Church to be of great value in a special manner for the priestly life. It is at the same time a sign and a stimulus for pastoral charity and a special source of spiritual fecundity in the world. *Indeed, it is not demanded by the very nature of the priesthood* [emphasis added], as is apparent from the practice of the early Church and from *the traditions of the Eastern Churches* [emphasis added], where, besides those who with all the bishops, by a gift of grace, choose to observe celibacy, *there are also married priests of highest merit* [emphasis added]. This holy synod, while it commends ecclesiastical celibacy, *in no way intends to alter that different discipline which legitimately flourishes in the Eastern Churches* [emphasis added]. It permanently exhorts all those who have received the priesthood and marriage to persevere in their holy vocation so that they may fully and generously continue to expend themselves for the sake of the flock commended to them.[46]

Note that this conciliar decree not only does not insist on an intrinsic (or ontological!) connection between celibacy and the priesthood; it actually denies it. Then there is a reference to the fact that married priests, too, can be committed pastors. Finally, the council insists that it does not intend to change the tradition of optional celibacy for Eastern Catholics.

We now turn to par. 1580 of the *Catechism*. I cite it now even though it was promulgated after the Eastern Code, treated below, because the *Catechism* is intended to serve as an interpretive guide for the teachings of Vatican II. There we read:

> In the Eastern Churches a different discipline has been in force for many centuries: while bishops are chosen solely from among celibates, married men can be ordained as deacons and priests. This practice has long been considered legitimate; these priests exercise a fruitful ministry within their communities. Moreover, priestly celibacy is held in great honor in the Eastern Churches and many priests have freely chosen it for the sake of the Kingdom of God. In the East

as in the West a man who has already received the sacrament of Holy Orders can no longer marry.[47]

While this is not as affirming as the text in *Presbyteroum ordinis*, we still find recognition of the distinctive Eastern discipline and a reference to the married clergy's fruitful service. A skeptic could draw attention to the phrase: "This practice has long been considered legitimate," but even those hoping for a stronger formulation presumably need not fear that while "someone else" has considered optional celibacy "legitimate," Rome itself does not—or may not in the future.

As for canon 373 of the *Codex Canonum Ecclesiarum Orientalium*,[48] the text reads: "Clerical celibacy chosen for the sake of the kingdom of heaven and suited to the priesthood is to be greatly esteemed everywhere, as supported by the tradition of the whole Church; likewise, the hallowed practice of married clerics in the primitive Church and in the tradition of the Eastern Churches throughout the ages is to be held in honor."[49] While one notes the absence of the word "everywhere" after "is to be held in honor,"[50] Nedungatt is nonetheless correct when he asserts: "The canonical institution of the married clerics has been at best tolerated, when not vilified in the Catholic tradition generally. That trend has been redressed by Pope John Paul II with *CCEO* c. 373, which is indebted both to the conciliar revaluation of marriage in *Gaudium et spes* (*GS*) 47–52 and the traditional appreciation of clerical celibacy."[51]

Nedungatt's reference to Vatican II's revaluation of marriage in *GS* is, in my estimation, crucial. Part of the reason that clerical celibacy has become theologically more contentious is that it must now "compete" with the Council's declaration of this other "bonum." Basilio Petrà, in fact, develops a beautiful theology of married priesthood precisely by using such declarations.[52] (Before Vatican II there was a general tendency to underrate marriage in relation to virginity.)

As already noted, the present pontiff, while still archbishop of Buenos Aires, expressed himself in a way that indicates commitment to the three official formulations just cited. In a dialogue with Argentina's chief rabbi, Abraham Skorka, then Cardinal Bergoglio, in a chapter of their book headed "On the Disciples," expressed himself as follows: "I would like to make a clarification: a Catholic priest does not get married in the Western Tradition, but he can in the Eastern Tradition. There, priests can marry before being ordained, but if they have already been ordained, then they cannot get married." On the next page, Bergoglio continues:

In the Western rite, to which I belong, priests cannot marry like the Catholic Byzantine, Ukrainian, or Greek rites. In these Churches, the priests can get married; the bishops cannot, they have to remain celibate. They are very good priests. Sometimes I tease them, I tell them that they have a woman in their house, but that they do not realize that they also got themselves a mother-in-law. In Western Catholicism, the issue has been discussed by some organizations. For now, the Church remains firm on the discipline of celibacy. There are those who say, with a certain pragmatism, that we are missing out on more manpower. If, hypothetically, Western Catholicism would change on the issue of celibacy, I believe that it would be for cultural reasons (like in the Eastern Church), not as much as a universal option. For the time being, I am in favor of maintaining celibacy, with the pros and cons that it has, because it has been ten centuries of good experience more often than failure. What happens is that the scandals are immediately seen. But tradition has weight and validity. Catholic priests chose celibacy little by little. Until 1100, there were those who opted for it and those who did not. Later, in the Eastern Churches, they continued the non-celibacy tradition as a personal option, and in the West it was the other way. It is an issue of discipline, not of faith. It can be changed.[53]

For our purposes, the point is not to change the Latin discipline but to indicate that the present pope of Rome has recently expressed himself in a way that avoids all totalizing of the Latin discipline. He even refers to married Eastern Catholic clergy as "very good priests."[54]

Brief Texts and Large Contexts: What Can Be Expected?

The three texts just cited, along with the statement by Bergoglio, provide hope that Catholic and Orthodox can avoid moving further apart on an issue that should never be Church-dividing anyway. But without desiring to sound alarmist, I believe that vigilance is nonetheless called for. History teaches that some of the most acrimonious issues that eventually divided East and West percolated on the periphery centuries before "the center" took up the cause. In the case of the *Filioque*, for example, Rome itself resisted the insertion for centuries. By the eleventh century, however, Carolingian theology—from the "periphery"—eventually triumphed even there.

But having noted how many of the alarming theological opinions reviewed above are not enshrined in the most authoritative Catholic pronouncements on celibacy, it remains true that these sober assertions are easily lost in a mass of pronouncements and theologizing that by their sheer volume easily eclipse the restrained texts. If Eastern Catholics account for approximately one percent of Catholics worldwide, it is certainly not the case that anywhere near one percent of the discussion surrounding celibacy includes reference to Eastern practice.[55] In fact, we find a curious phenomenon. Frequently when papal statements do include such references, theologians bypass them in subsequent reflection. The papal text ends up suggesting a universality—a totalizing—never intended by the popes.

The following example is typical. The author, Allen Vigneron, the archbishop of Detroit, cites the following papal text (from Benedict XVI's *Sacramentum caritatis*): "The fact that Christ himself, the eternal priest, lived his mission even to the sacrifice of the Cross in the state of virginity constitutes the sure point of reference for understanding the meaning of the tradition of [priestly celibacy in] the Latin Church." The pope is careful to specify the Latin Church. The archbishop, however, immediately totalizes the text: "In this one rich formulation [the archbishop is referring to the text just cited], Pope Benedict, in his role as supreme pastor, testifies to three foundational convictions: first, the Lord Jesus lived his earthly life as a virgin; second, his virginity forms a unified whole with his priesthood; and third, the virginity of Christ the High Priest is the ground for the celibacy *of his priests* [emphasis added]." As frequently happens, the delimitation has been bypassed.[56]

One will notice that until now I have not made reference to two other Catholic documents pertaining to celibacy, the Vatican II decree on priestly training, *Optatam Totius*, promulgated by Pope Paul VI on 28 October 1965, and *Sacerdotalis Caelibatus*, Paul VI's encyclical on celibacy, issued on 24 June 1967.[57] I refer to them now to illustrate my point that the Catholic Church's actual teaching about celibacy is easily lost in a mass of pronouncements and theologizing that by their sheer volume obscure her comprehensive teaching.

Optatam Totius makes appropriate remarks about "different Rites" in paragraphs 1 and 10, and *Sacerdotalis Caelibatus* devotes paragraph 38 to married clergy:

> If the legislation of the Eastern Church is different in the matter of discipline with regard to clerical celibacy, as was finally established by the Council of Trullo held in the year 692, and which has been clearly recognized by the Second Vatican Council, this is due to the different historical background of that most noble part of the Church, a situation which the Holy Spirit has providentially and supernaturally influenced.
>
> ---
>
> We Ourselves take this opportunity to express Our esteem and Our respect for all the clergy of the Eastern Churches, and to recognize in them examples of fidelity and zeal which make them worthy of sincere veneration.[58]

But not only are the remarks in *Optatam Totius* simply inferences about a distinctiveness, but also the recognition of married Eastern priests in paragraph 38 of *Sacerdotalis Caelibatus* is immediately followed by paragraphs 39 and 40 of a different tonality:

> We find further comforting reasons for continuing to adhere to the observance of the discipline of clerical celibacy in the exaltation of virginity by the Eastern Fathers. We hear within Us, for example, the voice of St. Gregory of Nyssa, reminding us that "the life of virginity is the image of the blessedness that awaits us in the life to come." We are no less assured by St. John Chrysostom's treatise on the priesthood, which is still a fruitful subject for reflection. Intent on throwing light on the harmony which must exist between the private life of him who ministers at the altar and the dignity of the order to which his sacred duties belong, he affirmed: "It is becoming that he who accepts the priesthood be as pure as if he were in heaven."
>
> ---
>
> Further, it is by no means futile to observe that in the East only celibate priests are ordained bishops, and priests themselves cannot contract marriage after their ordination to the priesthood. This indicates that these venerable Churches also possess to a certain extent the principle of a celibate priesthood and even of the appropriateness of celibacy for the Christian priesthood, of which the bishops possess the summit and fullness.[59]

The tonality here—not to mention the copious and exclusively Latin-style reflections on mandatory celibacy—are what entirely dominate the discussion of the "Catholic" priesthood. Almost every Holy Thursday homily, papal allocution, and curial directive—not to mention diocesan instruction—simply presumes the Latin practice.

Of course, the point is not to suggest that Latin-rite Catholics diminish their promotion of celibacy. If anything, the present social climate may warrant the opposite. The point is rather for Roman authorities to take far greater pains in clarifying the limitations of such promotion.

Again, in view of the minoritarian status of Eastern Catholicism it may seem unrealistic to ask for a change in this approach. But Eastern Orthodoxy accounts for far more Christians, and making the distinction clearer would also provide an ecumenical service. In any case, the same frustration expressed here was articulated a half century ago by none other than Cardinal Augustine Bea. During the fifth revision of the decree that came to be *Presbyterorum ordinis*, Bea wrote the following to the 151st general congregation:

> That which is said in no. 14 (as it was in the fifth edition) about the motives, the nobility, the fruits of the celibate priesthood, is excellent and should be adopted in full without further discussion. Nevertheless, one notes correctly that celibacy is not required "of the priesthood by its very nature." But the things which follow are proposed in such an absolute manner that it seems celibacy follows from the very nature of the priesthood. In fact, of the mission of the priest in general, it says that it "is completely dedicated to the service of the new humanity" and concludes: "The priests *consequently* by means of celibacy . . . become a living symbol of that future world." What then of the married Eastern priests? Aren't they perhaps priests in the full sense? The schema indeed concedes that in the *Eastern* Church there are "married priests *optime meritos*," as if this could happen as an exception. If I am not mistaken our Ecumenical Council—*I say ecumenical*—should treat *both* priestly conditions: the condition of perfect continence of celibacy and the perfect (as I might have said "ideal") marriage of the married priest, *whose perfect example for the Eastern Church is of great importance*. It ought to be demonstrated how the one and the other should correctly be chosen, educated, and

molded for his own condition ... and *how each one may be able to learn in what way* he should be effectively protected against the incumbent dangers of the one and the other condition. Thus our Council would be greatly useful also to our dearest Eastern brothers.[60]

In view of Bea's strong commitment to ecumenism, it should be permissible to assume that his reference to "our dearest Eastern brothers" may have been intended to include the Orthodox—and possibly even denote them exclusively.

Finally, my reference above to vigilance also concerns the attitude of certain Catholics toward the pronouncements of Vatican II—and even the more Latin-oriented encyclical *Sacerdotalis Caelibatus*. Some of the very same theologians who would criticize authors developing the teachings of Vatican II in any expansive fashion insist that "Paul VI did not intend to say the last word on the subject, but rather to indicate authoritatively the direction for future efforts."[61] What they have in mind is the direction indicated by the "findings of new historical and theological research"[62] of authors like Cochini and Piacenza.

Notwithstanding the 2014 decree from the Oriental Congregation, which permits bishops in North America and many other parts of the world to ordain married men,[63] Eastern Catholics and their ecumenical partners in the East should not be lulled into complacency by the fact that the Latin discipline will presumably never come to dominate historic Eastern Christian lands. (It is very hard to imagine that the interwar situation, in which two of the three Greco-Catholic eparchies in Galicia adopted mandatory celibacy, could ever be revived.) The North American Orthodox-Catholic dialogue in which I serve is mandated to discuss Orthodox-Catholic issues, especially on this continent, where, as others have noted in this volume already, the largest schism in the history of American Catholicism occurred precisely over the issue of married priests, with the wounds still evident. Let us pray for no further wounds in the future and for the continued healing of the wounds from the past that harm us still.

Notes

1. *Presbyterorum Ordinis* [henceforth *PO*], par. 16; Pope Paul VI, *Sacerdotalis Caelibatus* [henceforth *SC*], 24 June 1967, pars. 38 and 44. In the present chapter,

all quotations from papal/conciliar documents will be from the official Vatican website. See also can. 373 of the 1990 *Codex Canonum Ecclesiarum Orientalium* [henceforth *CCEO*] and para. 1580 of the *Catechism of the Catholic Church*, 2nd rev. ed. (Vatican: Libreria Editrice Vaticana, 2000).

2. "If honour of celibacy was prescribed by *CS* 68 [*Cleri sanctitati*], for *CCEO* it is equally (if not more) important to prescribe honour due to the canonical state of married clerics." George Nedungatt, ed., *A Guide to the Eastern Code: A Commentary on the Code of Canons of the Eastern Churches* (Rome: Pontificio Istituto Orientale, 2002), 293. Later in the same volume, Nedungatt notes, referring to his work drafting the 1990 *Code*, "If at all there is need for a canon, it is rather to warn not to despise the married clergy" (293).

3. Jorge Mario Bergoglio and Abraham Skorka, "On the Disciples" in *On Heaven and Earth: Pope Francis on Faith, Family, and the Church in the Twenty-First Century*, trans. A. Bermudez and H. Goodman (New York: Image Books, 2013), 47–49.

4. Paris: Lethelieux/Namur: Culture et Verité, 1981. English translation, by Nelly Morans: *Apostolic Origins of Priestly Celibacy* (San Francisco: Ignatius Press, 1990).

5. Roman M. T. Cholij, *Clerical Celibacy in East and West* (Leominster, UK: Fowler Wright Books, 1989).

6. For example, "Recent historical research has been able to prove unmistakably the development from a unified practice throughout the Church to a relaxation of clerical continence in the Eastern churches." Stefan Heid, "Why Do the Eastern and the Western Churches Differ in the Matter of Priestly Celibacy?," in Arturo Cattaneo, ed., *Married Priests? 30 Crucial Questions about Celibacy* (San Francisco: Ignatius Press, 2012), 24. Such assertions are grounded in the following conviction: "From the time of the composition of the First Letter of Paul to Timothy and the Letter of Paul to Titus, bishops, priests, and deacons were expected to practice complete continence." Franco Manzi, "Is Priestly Celibacy a Discipline of the Latin Church, or Does It Have Biblical Origins?" in *Married Priests*, 15.

7. Emblematic of this is the fact that the Vatican has retained the following article by Roman Cholij on its website: "Priestly Celibacy in Patristics and in the History of the Church." Cholij begins the article thus: "It is clear from the New Testament (Mark 1:29–31; Matt. 8:14–15; Luke 4:38–39; 1 Tim. 3:2, 12; Tit. 1:6) that at least the Apostle Peter had been married, and that bishops, presbyters and deacons of the Primitive Church were often family men. It is also clear from epigraphy, the testimony of the Fathers, synodal legislation, papal decretals and other sources that in the following centuries, a married clergy, in greater or lesser numbers was a normal feature of the life of the Church. Even married popes are known to us. And yet, paradoxically, one has to desist, when faced with this incontrovertible fact, from assuming that this necessarily excluded

the co-existence of an obligatory [sic] celibacy discipline." See www.vatican.va/roman_curia/congregations/cclergy/documents/rc_con_cclergy_doc_01011993_chisto_en, accessed 31 May 2013. Without in any way trying to be unkind, I draw attention to the Vatican's continued display of this article by Cholij, who is listed as "Secretary of the Apostolic Exarch for Ukrainian Catholics in Great Britain," because Cholij left the priesthood—and eventually married—more than twenty years ago. To my knowledge, the Holy See does not usually promote the work of priests who have left the ministry. Thus the commitment to the Cochini-Cholij hypothesis seems resolute indeed.

8. Cattaneo, *Married Priests?*, xi.

9. The following is a partial list of critical reviews by Catholic scholars. All translations are mine.

Roger Balducelli, "*The Apostolic Origins of Clerical Continence*: A Critical Appraisal of a New Book," *Theological Studies* 43 (1982): 693–705. Balducelli writes: "[Cochini] seeks to contribute to that legitimation [of clerical continence] historically by contending that clerical continence is traceable to the teaching of the apostles. In my view, he does not manage to prove that it does. The commitment to a hybrid theological-historical methodology is in part responsible for this failure" (705).

Alexandre Faivre, *Revue d'Histoire et de philosophie religieuses* 63 (1983): 471–73. Faivre writes: "For the first three centuries, one is forced to admit that Cochini has not found a single document that one could invoke positively to support his thesis" (472). He concludes his review as follows: "Desiring to prove too much, this study, at times meticulous but always badly presented, will certainly lead the majority of readers who are non-specialists in this period to a demonstration of the opposite of what the book pretends to affirm" (473).

Roger Gryson, *Revue d'Histoire ecclésiastique* 78 (1983): 90–93. Gryson writes: "Constantly confusing the historical and the theological, [Cochini] reads into the texts that which he has decided to find there; or when it is really impossible to do so, he attempts to eliminate the texts from the debate by every means possible" (91). Gryson later asserts: "Even in the interests of [promoting] ecclesiastical celibacy it would have been better to avoid publishing this thesis" (92).

Adrian Hastings, "The Origins of Priestly Celibacy," *Heythrop Journal* 24 (1983): 171–177.

Charles Kannengiesser, *Recherches de Science religieuse* 70 (1982): 620–21. Kannengiesser is certainly the most damning: "Is it necessary to be precise and assert that this thesis gravely misleads one into error and falsifies the truth of history? During [Cochini's] doctoral defense at the Institut Catholique of Paris, in May 1969, the interdiction against having his dissertation appear [in print] was publicly made known to the author.... The author's ecclesiastical superiors and friends, all strangers to the Institut Catholique of Paris, who made possible the present publication, knew well enough that one is to receive the 'visa' of this Institute [to publish a dissertation]. They decided to prefer a pseudo-scholarly act with a strong odour of confessional obscurantism" (621).

Even in the following positive review we read: "As regards the apostolic origins, strictly speaking, of sacerdotal celibacy, the paucity of evidence is glaring for the first centuries." Charles Martin, *Nouvelle Revue Théologique* 105 (1983): 438.

10. The following is a partial list of critical reviews: Daniel Callam, *Journal of Theological Studies*, n.s. 41 (1990): 725–29; Peter L'Huillier, *Sobornost*, n.s. 12 (1990): 180–82, and the following review, which, though of a more popular nature, is very succinct in describing the issues: C. H. Lawrence, "Unconvincing Arguments against a Married Priesthood," *Tablet* 244 (6 January 1990): 14.

The following remarks by George Nedungatt seem to summarize a certain scholarly consensus: "With scarce knowledge of the Greek sources, but relying on Latin polemists of the past, [Cholij] charged the Council of Trullo with falsifying the canonical tradition. Cochini and Cholij won eminent Roman patronage and silent following, although their theses have generally been reviewed as critically inept and historically incompetent." *A Guide to the Eastern Code*, 291–92.

11. For an earlier critique of both Cochini's and Cholij's books, see J. Kevin Coyle's review essay elsewhere in this volume.

12. Among the few positive academic reviews of Cochini's work are the following: Henri Crouzel, "Une nouvelle étude sur les origines du célibat sacerdotal," *Bulletin de Littérature ecclésiastique* 83 (1982): 293–97; M. Trémeau, *Esprit et Vie* 92 (1982): 106–9; and Bertrand de Margerie, *Science et Esprit* 35 (1983): 260–61. However, these positive reviews either summarize the contents of Cochini's book or limit themselves to providing marginal technical corrections. Incidentally, Cochini's book has almost become part of a "canon" for apologists for celibacy—e.g., George Weigel, *Evangelical Catholicism: Deep Reform in the 21st-Century Church* (New York: Basic Books, 2013), 273.

13. See, e.g., Archbishop Allen Vigneron of Detroit, "The Virginity of Jesus and the Celibacy of His Priests," in John C. Cavadini, ed., *The Charism of Priestly Celibacy: Biblical, Theological, and Pastoral Reflections* (Notre Dame, IN: Ave Maria Press, 2012), 99.

14. *A Guide to the Eastern Code*, 289–90. Incidentally, Gefaell's reference to "permissive law" is crucial for understanding Rome's approach to the ordination of married Eastern Catholic men. It has frequently been the hope among certain Roman Catholic authorities that such ordinations will be a transitional concession.

15. Ibid., 298. Nedungatt's reference is to Constantin Pitsakis, "Clergé marié et célibat dans la législation du Concile in Trullo: Le point de vue oriental," in George Nedungatt and Michael Featherstone, eds., *The Council in Trullo Revisited*, Kanonika 6 (Rome, 1995), 263–306.

16. "Why Do the Eastern and the Western Churches Differ?," 24–25.

17. Ibid., 22.

18. Stefan Heid is also the author of the following book, significant for its opinions on Eastern practice: *Celibacy in the Early Church: The Beginnings of a Discipline of Obligatory Continence for Clerics in East and West* (San Francisco: Ignatius Press, 2000). The original German version appeared in 1997.

19. *Preti celibi e preti sposati: Due carismi della Chiesa cattolica* (Assisi: Cittadella, 2011), 32. Emphasis in the original.

20. http://www.vatican.va/holy_father/john_paul_ii/apost_exhortations/documents/hf_jp-ii_exh_25031992_pastores-dabo-vobis_en.html.

21. Cattaneo, *Married Priests?*, 82, 93, 103 *et passim*.

22. "Papal Teaching on the Subject from Pius XI to Benedict XVI," in *Married Priests*, 140.

23. Ibid., 148.

24. Ibid.

25. "The Relevance of Priestly Celibacy Today," www.vatican.va/roman_curia/congregations/cclergy/documents/rc_con_cclergy_doc_01011993_revel_en. The archbishop adds: "People who tend to call the connection between priesthood and celibacy into question cannot consequently deserve serious consideration." Of course, the point is not to question the connection, but to caution against attempts to make the connection intrinsic, inextricable, ontological.

26. Ibid.

27. Ibid.

28. Cavadini, *The Charism of Priestly Celibacy*.

29. Vigneron's text is published in *The Charism of Priestly Celibacy: Biblical, Theological, and Pastoral Reflections*, ed. J. Cavadini (Notre Dame, IN: Ave Maria Press, 2012), 85–108.

30. "Episcopal Celibacy in the Orthodox Tradition," *St. Vladimir's Theological Quarterly* 35 (1991): 271–300.

31. Vigneron in Cavadini, *The Charism of Priestly Celibacy*, 181. Emphasis added by Vigneron in the original.

32. Ibid., 88.

33. *Communio* 3 (1976): 318–29.

34. Ibid., 321–22.

35. Ibid., 324.

36. Ibid., 325.

37. Ibid., 320.

38. Ibid.

39. See Cattaneo, *Married Priests*, 31–32; 93–96; *et passim*.

40. For a brief overview, see Victor Pospishil's article elsewhere in this volume. See also Lawrence Barriger, *Good Victory* (Brookline, MA: Holy Cross Orthodox Press, 1985).

41. *A Guide to the Eastern Code*, 303. Nedungatt cites the following article: N. Rachford, "Norms of Particular Law for the Byzantine Metropolitan Church *sui iuris* of Pittsburgh, USA," *CLSA Proceedings* 62 (2000): 233–43.

42. For some historical background on this situation, see Antoine Fleyfel, "Quelques réflexions sur la presence en Occident de prêtres catholiques orientaux mariés," *Istina* 54 (2009): 409–25.

43. www.catholicnews.com/data/stories/cns/1201976.htm, accessed 31 May 2013.

44. http://www.irishtimes.com/news/call-for-substantial-reform-of-irish-college-1.1066614.

45. Ironically, the *Catechism* is considered "universal." How it can be "universal," that is, applicable to Eastern Catholics as well, when its doctrinal section consists of a reflection on the *Apostles'* Creed—a text unknown in the Eastern Churches—has always eluded me. Nonetheless, its reference to married Eastern clergy is appreciated, and in this case its "universal" status should be exploited.

46. This paragraph of *PO* includes four footnotes, which I have not included in my transcription. Another Vatican II decree that treats celibacy is *Optatam Totius* [henceforth *OT*], which I shall refer to below. For a helpful brief overview of the celibacy question at Vatican II and after, see J. A. Komonchak, "Celibacy and Tradition," *Chicago Studies* 20 (1981): 5–17.

47. *Catechism of the Catholic Church*, par. 1580.

48. "In Orthodoxy there is no need for a canon like *CCEO* c. 373, whose presence in the Eastern Catholic Code tells a whole story." George Nedungatt, *A Guide to the Eastern Code*, 300.

49. Can. 373, *CCEO*.

50. I mention this only because Nedungatt provides an actual schema to illustrate the parallelism between the canon's affirmation of celibacy on the one hand and married priesthood on the other. Nedungatt, *A Guide to the Eastern Code*, 288. The lack of a global, or worldwide, specification in the case of the latter diminishes the parallelism—and can be quite relevant in view of what we know about actual practice.

51. Nedungatt, *A Guide to the Eastern Code*, 291.

52. Petrà, *Preti celibi e preti sposati*, 88–98.

53. Bergoglio and Skorka, "On the Disciples," 47–49.

54. As happy as I am (as a married Eastern Catholic priest) to see that the pope has had such positive experiences, married clergy are frequently the first to insist that there is no warrant for romanticizing optional celibacy (no pun intended). Many of us are also the first to express anger when inane comparisons are made between celibate and married clergy, in favor of the latter. (Among Catholics, however, this is a relatively recent phenomenon.) In many Eastern Christian communities, married and celibate work side by side as committed friends without any of the competitiveness foisted upon the two "groups" in some Western contexts.

55. The suggestion that Eastern Catholics themselves should be writing more about this compels me to note the following. First, it is odd for us to be harping about "rights guaranteed by Vatican II" when far more basic evangelical,

liturgical, and catechetical issues cry out for attention in declining and suffering communities. Second, writing on the topic can still be perceived as "dissidence." In essence, then, the easiest way to deal with this problem would be for Eastern Catholic bishops to simply do what they are entitled to do: ordain qualified married candidates. In their support they certainly have the additional principle *lex dubia non obligat*. Ironically, the same Roman Cholij who previously argued for the apostolic origins of a *lex continentiae* among Eastern Christians subsequently wrote a lengthy *defense* of the right of Eastern Catholic bishops to ordain married candidates in Western countries: "An Eastern Catholic Married Clergy in North America: Recent Changes in Legal Status and Ecclesiological Perspective," *Eastern Churches Journal* 4 (1997): 23–58.

56. Vigneron, "The Virginity of Jesus," 85–86.

57. The totalizing I mentioned a moment ago is seen even in something as seemingly simple and perhaps even harmless as the opening salutation of Paul VI's encyclical on celibacy, which is addressed "To the Bishops, Priests and Faithful of the Whole [*sic*] Catholic World."

58. *Sacerdotalis Caelibatus*, par. 38.

59. Ibid.

60. Quoted in Petrà, *Preti celibi e preti sposati*, 69–70, emphasis in original.

61. Krzysztof Charamsa, "The Fundamental Magisterial Document on Priestly Celibacy Is the Encyclical by Paul VI," in Cattaneo, *Married Priests*, 46.

62. Ibid.

63. *Pontificia Praecepta de clero Uxorato Orientali*, published in the *Acta Apostolicae Sedes*, 106, no. 6 (6 June 2014), available at: http://www.vatican.va/archive/aas/documents/2014/acta-giugno2014.pdf, 496–99.

PART IV

Pastoral–Familial Life

CHAPTER NINE

Reflections on Two Vocations in Two Lungs of the One Church

David Meinzen

I have a varied background—as the son of a Lutheran pastor, sometime Lutheran (Missouri Synod) seminarian who finished seminary at St. Vladimir's Orthodox Seminary in New York and was ordained and served as a priest in the Orthodox Church of America for many years before becoming a Ukrainian Greco-Catholic priest serving bi-ritually in a Latin chaplaincy. I would define the continuity of my life by saying that I am a servant of Christ, a presbyter of His Church. I am a married priest of the Ukrainian Catholic Eparchy of St. Nicholas in Chicago, serving the Ukrainian Catholic mission parish of St. Andrew in Fort Wayne, Indiana, while also serving as the full-time chaplain of the VA hospital in the same city, where I function bi-ritually, offering Mass and other sacraments in the Latin Church with the permission of the Latin ordinary as well as my own. My dear wife, Elizabeth, and I have been married for more than a quarter century and have been blessed by our heavenly Father with three lovely, intelligent daughters to nurture in the faith of Christ Jesus by the grace of the Holy Spirit. Thus the Holy Trinity has called me to share in the priesthood of Christ both as a presbyter ("Father" in the spiritual family of His holy Catholic Church) and as the father of a biological family—the "domestic church," which has been entrusted to me in the image of His holy Church.

In a very real sense, my responsibility to Christ for the "domestic church" He has entrusted me with is *primary* to the responsibility He has entrusted me with for public ministry in His Church; in fact, the healthy exercise of the second is dependent on the healthy exercise of the first. I believe this point—which is almost never considered in discussions about a married presbyterate—to be so very important that it warrants deeper reflection. Following my patron, Irenaeus of Lyons, I would argue that care for one particular domestic church is an example of the "scandal of particularity" that is rarely faced in all these discussions about marriage and priesthood—still less in wider discussions of ecclesiology.

What do I mean when I say that my domestic vocation is primary to my pastoral-public one? Here I am thinking not just in terms of a personal material responsibility (i.e., to ensure my family has shelter, food, and so on), but also in terms of the highest spiritual responsibility before God and His whole Church for the eternal salvation of the souls over whom I have the most direct and immediate care—that is, my wife and children. Care for them is not secondary to care for those I minister to pastorally; serving them does not detract from my service to the wider Church. Serving them both enables my wider service to others and is simultaneously part of my wider service to the Church, for my family are just as much Christians and just as much a part of the Church as anyone else.

My assertion of the order of my responsibility may sound quite strange, if not borderline heretical, to many a Roman Catholic reader who entertains certain romanticized and fantastical notions of a celibate priesthood as being one endless sacrifice of self that makes the priest automatically ("ontologically," as some would dubiously assert) more holy and wholly dedicated to self-denying service to the Church, made easy by having neither spouse nor children. But such an idealized notion overlooks several important things. First, it ignores the sacrifices (chastity, in this context, chief among them) demanded by the Christian lives of *all* people, married and celibate alike. Second, it ignores the many sacrifices enjoined upon married priests by their own families, about which I will say more presently. Third, it fails to recognize that celibacy can be *easier* and can often be an *escape* from these very sacrifices that families regularly make; no celibate priest has to take his asthmatic son to the emergency room at 3 a.m. in a snowstorm or wonder if this week's paycheck can be stretched to buy his daughter's new school uniform or fund her band trip.

Fourth, in a world where people are increasingly refusing both sex and marriage, celibacy and continence are no longer invested with quite the same status of a culture-challenging "evangelical witness." As one precociously wise Latin seminarian, Samuel Bellafiore, has recently remarked, forgoing marriage today (celibacy) is no sacrifice in the eyes of much of the world, where the trend of not getting married in the first place is growing: "Sure, priests 'give up marriage'—but that is not much of a radical witness right now. Most people my age 'give up marriage' for all sorts of other goods. In the U.S. 51% even of people who get married eventually 'give up marriage,' often multiple times." Moreover, Bellafiore notes, even forgoing sex (continence) is not as strange and stark a sacrifice as it might once have seemed even a few short years ago, as we see increasing numbers of people in some cultures doing that also: "What if, as is happening in Japan, people stop having sex? On the anonymous social media app Whisper, a poll asked whether people would rather have sex or wifi—many preferred wifi. Joking or not, you can't fall in love unless you look at people and you can't look at people if you're looking at your phone. What does celibacy mean then?"[1]

Bellafiore's question—What, then, does celibacy mean today?—is an important one and clearly requires answers that go beyond the old idealized and now quite outdated notions, especially in a context in which, as Pope Francis regularly reminds us, there can be no shortage of sins among clerics ("clerical careerism" in the Vatican or, more simply and widely, "clericalism," are both regularly criticized by this pope) and celibates, not excluding the horrible sins of abuse against God's children that have come to light in recent decades as perpetrated by some who were *supposed to be* dedicated to "perfect continence."

But I am not writing this to chastise and correct erroneous popular assumptions among my Latin brothers and sisters, nor do I intend to hold them alone up to criticism, for we are all sinners. Rather than focusing on the varied degrees of sacrifice of celibate and married clergy, what I think we need to do now is to shift the discussion to one of wholeness and holiness *for everybody*. Here is where a new appreciation of chastity as *liberating self-control* and service to others as *joyful self-gift* becomes the unifying evangelical witness offered by all priests and indeed all Christians. Here is where chastity and service alike show us the way to overcome the fragmentation of our lives and to begin to find the healing integration necessary for all of us as a first step on the pathway to becoming "partakers of the divine nature," as 2 Peter famously puts it—for that is the goal of every station in life! And that goal can be and very often is undermined if the domestic church is neglected.

All this sounds and is quite abstract. To begin to illustrate what I mean in more concrete terms, let me recount some rather common background familiar to many Protestant and Eastern Orthodox readers, whose traditions have long allowed their pastors to be married. My point here is to illustrate that my initial claim of the priority and primacy of the domestic church is one that even Protestant and Orthodox Christians have often failed to appreciate, at great cost, losing many of their own children in the process.

While I cannot speak for the experience of all Protestant PKs ("preachers' kids"), I can speak from the experience that both my wife and I had growing up as children of Lutheran pastors; we also knew and observed other fellow Lutheran PKs in our youth. Our fathers were trained to think of their pastoral responsibilities as trumping their duties to their families—while not really being given the option to serve as celibates. In other words, the expectations they were schooled in put them in a "catch-22" situation: they were expected to be married and raise families, but also to give *all* their energies and attention to their congregations, pretending, in effect, that they were not husbands and fathers at all. The implied expectation was that they should neglect their families—yet God forbid it ever be stated in such a tactlessly blunt fashion! This observation from experience has also been confirmed by my father in recent conversations on this very subject. Even though this cultural expectation was not so explicitly stated, it was overwhelmingly implied in his seminary training and in peer and congregational expectations.

These expectations go back generations. My grandfather, also a Lutheran pastor, told me of his own seminary experience in the early twentieth century. He told me that in those "good old days," in order for young men to be considered viable candidates for Lutheran ordination, they had to be married, but they were not allowed to court a girl during their seminary training. In other words, as soon as they had graduated from seminary they were expected magically to pull a suitable wife out of a hat before they could be "called and ordained" to serve in a parish. In reality, they had to be secretly breaking the rules and courting while in seminary. Although that rule was relaxed over time, the general attitude of ranking care and consideration for wife and family secondary (yet, strangely, non-optional) to Church work remained the same.

And what is the legacy of these expectations? Here we encounter the legendary rebelliousness of many PKs against their Christian upbringing due to absentee fathers (absent because consumed by their work). This is not a dark secret confined just to certain parishes or families. It has long had standing in the popular cultural imaginations. One thinks here of movie portrayals going back decades of how pastors put their families beneath their "ministries" and of the resulting negative impact this had on spouses and children. Think, for example, of the 1947 movie *The Bishop's Wife* (with Cary Grant) or Kevin Bacon's *Footloose* from 1984. Or think of Patricia Lockwood's much more recent 2017 memoir, *Priestdaddy*, recounting her own rebellion from the Catholic Church as the daughter of a former Lutheran (Missouri Synod) pastor who became a married priest in the Latin Church.

Pop cultural portrayals aside, one has to wonder what part such pastoral examples have played in increasing the divorce rate among Christians in America over time. One must also wonder about the numbers of children estranged from the Church because they saw how it treated their fathers and families. What message about marriage has this sent to Christian people as a whole if so many leaders of Church communities have in this way acted no differently than their stereotypical lay counterparts in corporate and business vocations—putting family needs secondary to work "responsibilities"? This is a different type of "clerical careerism" than that condemned by Pope Francis, but it is no less deadly and destructive.

Such a downgrading of marriage is bad enough, though perhaps understandable, when "the world" does it. But what excuse do Christians have? Here suspect theological claims have been insidious and have made such worldly pressures even worse by dressing them up with spurious claims that they are "advancing the kingdom of God" or "building up the body of Christ" precisely at the expense of and often causing the real suffering of the members of that kingdom and that body who live under the same roof as the pastor. What we have, in other words, is worldly career and institutional advancement vested in pious clothing! How can God's kingdom really be advanced when one crucial outpost of that kingdom—one's own domestic church—is neglected and suffering, its members resentful and hurting from being so consistently neglected by their own husband and father and forgotten by the Church that he serves and of which they are also (supposedly) equal members as his parishioners?

All of this hints that perhaps the real issue is not "married" versus "celibate" states for clergy at all but actually lies elsewhere, in a more fundamental failure of all Christians to be true to our Lord's explicit Word (and hence will) that Christian marriage is, fundamentally, a revelation of the marriage feast of the Lamb—of the kingdom of God on earth! Whether it be married Protestant, Eastern Catholic, or Eastern Orthodox clergy neglecting their families "for the sake of the kingdom" or a celibate clerical monopoly in the Latin Church sometimes implying that marriage is not worthy of a man dedicated to the service of Christ's altar, the end result remains the same: a clear message that even among Christians, marriage is merely a lesser thing of this fallen world—despite what the Bible and the catechism say!

What we need today, then, is a thorough cleansing of the money-changers from the temple of our minds, for it is here that the idols of success and prosperity have taken up residence and continue to corrupt how we see marriage and family. Too many Christians, influenced by worldly concerns about advancing our careers and "growing" our institutions (which means, of course, developing bigger budgets), regard domestic service as a distraction from these larger, seemingly loftier, goals.

This is where I come back to my earlier statement: My responsibility to Christ for the "domestic church" He has entrusted me with is *primary* to the responsibility He has entrusted me with for public ministry in His Church, and the healthy exercise of the second is dependent on the healthy exercise of the first. I hold this to be true not just for myself but for *all* married clergy. And this is so because God "ordained" my wife and me to pursue His holy life together in the sacrament of Christian marriage *before* He ordained me to the holy sacrament of the priesthood. This conforms to the earliest apostolic tradition of both the "Greek" East *and* the "Latin" West, and it is still the canonical requirement in the Catholic (Eastern and Latin) churches today, as it is among the Orthodox. A man must have previously committed to being either celibate or married *before* being ordained as a priest, and his exercise of priestly vocation *in persona Christi* must include his first commitment to the Lord, whether it be to celibate or married life.

The last part of my statement, "The healthy exercise of the second is dependent on the healthy exercise of the first," is nothing other than the logical conclusion of the apostolic teaching given in both Ephesians 5 and, even more explicitly, in 1 Timothy 3:

> If anyone aspires to the office of bishop, he desires a noble task. Now a bishop must be above reproach, the husband of one wife, temperate, sensible, dignified, hospitable, an apt teacher, no drunkard, not violent but gentle, not quarrelsome, and no lover of money. He must manage his own household well, keeping his children submissive and respectful in every way; for if a man does not know how to manage his own household, how can he care for God's church? ... Deacons likewise must be serious, not double-tongued, not addicted to much wine, not greedy for gain; they must hold the mystery of the faith with a clear conscience. ... Let deacons be the husband of one wife, and let them manage their children and their households well; for those who serve well as deacons gain a good standing for themselves and also great confidence in the faith which is in Christ Jesus.

Note well: The "one wife" imagery here cannot be applied to the similitude of a priest's relationship to his parish! That is an analogy that has limits to its valid application and is not the primary meaning of the text written by St. Paul![2]

If the Latin Church today is beginning again to become acquainted, at least in small ways, with married priests, and if, as one regularly hears, this could be more widely developed under changes proposed by Pope Francis, this apostolic vision must be taken seriously in all respects. As the Latin Church begins anew to become aware of this long-standing tradition of married priests, it will also become aware again that none other than the first advocate for the celibate life himself, St. Paul, argued in 1 Corinthians 9:5 for the God-given right of no lesser figure than St. Peter himself (and the other apostles) to be married even while he, Paul, modeled and encouraged celibate service.

Just as God has given the celibate clergy the task of being living witnesses to the fact that the present form of this world is passing away, so has He given us married clergy the task of bearing witness through our marriages to what form this world is passing into—precisely the eternal kingdom of loving union with God our Father, which is coming upon us all in the man Jesus Christ. In the healthy union between a Christian husband and wife, marriage is supposed to be an *icon* for all to see, revealing salvation as the mystical union between Christ and His Church for all eternity. It is supposed to be an apocalyptic in-breaking here and now of the promised marriage feast of the Lamb of God and His bride the Church, yet to be fully manifest in the age to come.

But who is there to live out this manifestation, this living evangelical witness to God's kingdom already present to the world through His very family, the Church, when all too many Christian marriages are sadly just going the way of the fallen world? Who is there to lead Christian husbands to see again their primary role of manifesting Christ's priesthood in their households—to sacrifice themselves for their brides and their children in the "domestic church" of their family life? Who, I ask, if the only actual living examples given them are those of either a celibate clergy whose monopoly unintentionally conveys that marriage is somehow a worldly "condescension" to weakness or a married clergy who have themselves succumbed to a worldly emphasis on "career advancement"? In either case, the problem is exactly the same: a kind of self-seeking mentality when it comes to the ordained ministries of Christ Jesus crucified in the Church!

By contrast, in a proper understanding of married priesthood, there is no easy, materially cushy path for married clergy anymore. Here there is only the call to martyrdom! That is, here we find the path of bearing (unpopular!) witness to the inestimable truth that sacrifice and self-giving, even to the point of suffering, are the royal road to human beatitude in both home and Church. Married Eastern clergy often know this in very practical domestic and fiscal terms. The path of priesthood requires forgoing other "careers" in which much greater financial remuneration is possible. As a result, clerical families often live lives much closer to the poor than middle-class "professionals" usually do.

On this latter point, which is so often neglected in romantic notions of married priesthood by those with no practical experience of the same, let me note that we cannot escape some consideration of dollars and cents. Those advocating change in the Latin Church must ask themselves such questions as whether Latin dioceses are willing to tithe and donate more to support the families of married priests. Latin Catholics must grapple with basic issues such as the sizes of many of their parishes, which are *vastly* larger than any Eastern analogues—Catholic or Orthodox (indeed, some Roman Catholic *parishes* are larger than entire *dioceses* in some Eastern jurisdictions!). Given the sizes of such parishes, and therefore given their massive and unending workloads, there is a very real risk that a priest could easily lose himself in serving a huge parish to the utter detriment of his marriage—and where would the good be there? Surely the Lord would ask him—and perhaps also the parish and the bishop!—some variant of the question in Matthew 16:26: "What will it profit a man, if he gains the whole world [parish] and forfeits his [family] life?"

Yet, in the end, my family and I, along with those of other married Eastern clergy, are living proof that is not impossible to figure out such practical details. To be sure, some differences in administrative arrangements will be required, but these will by no means be impossible to manage if both celibate leaders (bishops) and married leaders (priests) are willing to work together to remind the faithful of just what we are all given in Christ so that they can begin again to live out their own baptismal share of Christ's self-sacrificial priesthood, bringing their tithes and other offerings of thanksgiving to His altar to give witness and worship to Him for the salvation of the world.

Notes

1. Samuel Bellafiore, "The Annunciation and Vocational Fear," *Church Life Journal* (April 9, 2018), http://churchlife.nd.edu/2018/04/09/the-annunciation-and-vocational-fear/.

2. That text, plainly, makes mention of the bishop and deacon; the development of the office of priest as we know it today has long been recognized as a later development tied, in part, to the expansion of Christianity after the Constantinian edict of toleration in 313 and to the erection of governing structures copied from comparable structural units (dioceses and metropolitical provinces) of the Roman Empire. As all three sacramental "orders" (another concept borrowed from imperial offices) developed, the married episcopate in both East and West would disappear under a barrage of often confusing canonical legislation well examined in Panagiotes I. Boumes, "Married Bishops (Agreement between Sacred Scripture and Holy Canons)," *Greek Orthodox Theological Review* 29 (1984): 81–93, and "The Possibility of Married Bishops Today," *Greek Orthodox Theological Review* 40 (1995): 221–27.

CHAPTER TEN

Growing Up in a Rectory

Using Oikonomia *to Answer the Tough Questions Posed by the Children of Priestly Families*

Julian Hayda

Many people, whether Christian or not, rely on their faith for some answers to the uncomfortable existential questions that keep them up at night—at least that is the comfort I seek from prayer when going through a tough time. These kinds of questions include: Why do bad things happen to good people? What approach should parents take to raising children? What are some of the moral issues one might encounter in secular Western society?

These are difficult questions, perhaps especially for the clergyman who may have entered seminary at the age of eighteen, or even twenty-two, and barreled through it with utopian blinders on, seeing only how members of a faith *should* behave without regard for extenuating factors or historical context.

Before you get too far into this chapter, permit me to add a word of background. I am not a formally trained theologian in the professional sense, nor am I a canon lawyer. I write as the son of a priest of the Ukrainian Greek-Catholic Church. My father, Pavlo Hayda (1964–2007), prided himself in taking a many-shades-of-gray approach, which contrasted with the frequently facile black-and-white answers offered by others. That approach was not easy. For some, a simple page-flip through a catechism might be thought to yield a quick and binding answer. But my father's approach was to draw on his human experience, gleaned from both his mistakes and his triumphs in raising four children.

For him, most of those aforementioned existential questions that keep people up at night arose through the simple and mundane experience of sending my brothers and me to school, observing us interact with our friends, helping us deal with bullies, and walking us through the realizations of death and sex. In this he helped us to engage in a process of deciphering what was healthy in the culture we children were surrounded by and wanted to participate in—and what was harmful to soul and body.

I believe that it was in this sense that my father exercised the ultimate manifestation of *oikonomia*, a term directly translated from Greek as "law of the house" or "home-rule." In standard Eastern Christian canonical practice, oikonomia usually refers to Church leaders' license, even *obligation*, mandated by Holy Tradition, to interpret the canons and to apply them in a unique way or at less than full measure in those singular situations in which full and strict application of the law would do more harm than good. Oikonomia is born of an implicit recognition that times *actually do* change, but the law may not have kept up. What was an important approach to Holy Tradition in, say, the Middle Ages might not be most appropriate for today's Christians.

Oikonomia, to be sure, is not a dismissal of the canons but merely a realignment of sorts—what might be roughly counted a "dispensation" in the Western tradition. We still uphold the general and fundamental principles but recognize, on a case-by-case basis, that some details of their application may need to be relaxed or altered somewhat.

For better or for worse, I believe that every Christian household tries to exercise its own "home-rule" in their spiritual lives. My father, in our household, was no different. But his application of oikonomia *was* different, at least from the expectations of many parishioners as to what constitutes "pious" or "proper" behavior for priest and child alike. Let me recount a few stories to illustrate the point.

The Fish Bowl

Not a day went by in the rectory as I was growing up when the watchful eye of the community didn't openly and bluntly judge our every move.

Perhaps this phenomenon is unique to the largely ethnic Ukrainian makeup of our parish, but I doubt it.

For the community, we were somewhat of a novelty. My father, though born in the United States and determined to serve in the United States, had to travel to Ukraine to be ordained at a time when Roman-imposed restrictions prevented him, a married man, from donning the priest's epitrachil (in the Western tradition, a stole) at any church this side of the prime meridian. When he returned to serve in the United States in 1992, just a month before I was born, he was part of a new generation of American-born priests serving in America who also had wives and children.[1]

Needless to say, the faithful didn't know exactly how to treat us when we settled in Chicago. Our family symbolized a transition from what was formerly a novelty to what is today the norm of having married clergy and their families assigned to serve Ukrainian Greek-Catholic parishes across North America.

What did this mean? It meant that what my father did with his family trumped whatever he said about family. It meant that my brothers and I were expected, sometimes irrationally, to be on our best behavior at all times—when we just wanted to be normal. Thankfully this kind of scrutiny never brought us to an all-out rebellion, as it could have.

It did, however, give rise to some frustrating situations. I recall one such situation when I was a nine-year-old at a Boy Scout camp in Michigan. Another camper and I were bullied for our funny hair or for whatever other reasons children get bullied. When we lashed out by shoving one of the bullies off our cabin's front stoop, the counselors, holding me to some higher expectation, sought to send me home. My accomplice, by contrast, only had to stand with his nose to the corner for an hour.

Despite the injustice I felt at the time, I found out many years later that the counselors actually debated for several hours as to who would be the unlucky one to tell the priest that his kid wasn't fit for camp, ultimately pulling straws to determine who'd be tasked with this unpleasantness.

Somehow, by virtue of *my father's* vocation, not only was his nine-year-old son expected to tolerate bullying, but he was supposed to have raised me to somehow not react in the same way any other bullied child would, regardless of whether it was right or wrong in hindsight. (For the record, I was wrong, and I did admit full responsibility and regret.)

At first, I had a difficult time wrapping my head around this; why would anybody be afraid to tell my father *anything*? He was one of the most understanding people I'd ever met—or at least *as* understanding as any other parent I'd ever met. While, on the one hand, they felt they had to hold up some sort of higher standard of discipline for me as a priest's son, on the other hand, they weren't exactly confident enough to confront him about it—perhaps because of the pedestal *all* clergy—married and celibate—are put on, at least in the minds of some of the faithful.

The counselors perceived my father somehow as untouchable—involved with some distant, ancient, and incomprehensible ritual meant to be observed from the family pew every Sunday morning. In a funny way, this incident of mine proved to them—and they'll admit it today—that clergy are indeed more accessible than they had been led to believe.

At the end of the day, I remember nine-year-old me wrongly thinking the counselors' standards for my behavior would be the same my father expected of me once I came home from camp. I was expecting some sort of extraneous punishment in what I can only believe was a bizarre projection of my counselors' personal relationship with a wrathful God onto my relationship with my father. When I wasn't further punished at home, not only was my relationship with my father made clear, but I think it also put my relationship with God into perspective.

Situations like these occurred from time to time, and I think my family and I quickly realized that I was no more nor less well behaved than the rest of my peers. Still, though, the community pointed their fingers and, as the old adage goes, "three fingers pointed right back."

A Parable of Baseball

Opinions vary widely over the merits of the 1990 *Code of Canons of the Eastern Churches*, with some seeing it as insufficiently respectful of Eastern traditions and practices while others view it as a positive step in the long-fought battle against Latinization in the *sui iuris* ("of their own law") Churches of the East. Regardless, I think there is one canon in particular, 375, that merits comment here. That canon reads, in part: "In leading family life and in educating children married clergy are to show an outstanding example to other Christian faithful."

When I first came across that canon, while casually perusing the *Code* in my father's library, I was somewhat taken aback. For me, it was that very sort of unfair assumption my camp counselors had made about me turned into a legal requirement. All I wanted to be—and to be treated as—was a normal American pre-teen boy, not some "outstanding example." Consciously or not, I wanted the freedom to break the same rules and do the same things that my peers did. This canon's seeming unfairness angered me.

As I grew older, I learned to read this canon more in the spirit of oikonomia. I pondered what it meant to show an "outstanding example to other Christian faithful." Is it to live up to a judgmental community's expectations of how an outstanding Christian should behave, or does it allow for a little more rebelliousness?

In all honesty, and even after careful consideration, I find that some of my father's decisions were occasionally not in strict adherence to what might be perceived as outstandingly Christian conduct. Whatever the moral gray area they may fall into, though, I do not have a doubt in the world that he made those decisions with the conviction that what he was doing was good for his family.

There was one time that my father instructed me to give my teachers a noted signed "Fr. Pavlo" to excuse me for a doctor's appointment, when its true purpose was to give us the opportunity to bond over a rare Chicago Cubs playoffs game at Wrigley Field. When I bragged to my classmates, and my teacher caught wind of our plan to play hooky, it ended up presenting an awfully embarrassing situation for both me and my father. The school's catechist/disciplinarian, Sr. Joan, a resentful old nun with a Nancy Reagan–like "Just say no" attitude to sin, even got involved.

Was my father's lying to get me out of an obligation an example of outstanding Christian behavior? Perhaps not. But was wanting to spend time with his sons in a wholesome and loving manner a Christian thing to do? I think yes—and I can only believe his risking his reputation for the sake of his family is outstandingly Christian.

Moments like these serve for me as almost modern parables of how our Western obsession with rules—"Don't do this, and don't do that"—fails to take into account the more noble motives someone has in mind when making a not-so-thought-out decision.

The expectation, a heavy and unhelpful one, is that priests somehow make for perfect parents, that they can somehow manage to have happy and healthy relationships with their children while toeing the presumed line of fearless, infallible leader who does no wrong. This is totally unrealistic.

The question here is whether a priest should be expected to hide his flaws as a parent or whether he may permit the world to see such flaws as a living parable of how parents, with the best of intentions, try as far as possible to raise outstanding Christian children. I don't have an answer to that question—but I can say that every situation along that path has the greatest potential to help other families feel confident in the decisions they make, knowing that even clergy can face the same pitfalls they do.

Being the Bee

While some instances of a priest's use of oikonomia in raising his family are easily understood by the faithful—sometimes as a simple demonstration of compassion and forgiveness and other times as not strictly applying the penalties that may be due because of extenuating circumstances—at yet other times his exercising oikonomia may be prone to causing deep rifts between the faithful, the priest, his family, and the secular society they are immersed in. What does one do in such circumstances?

The wisdom of St. Basil the Great reminds us that there is much in the secular world that can enrich our spiritual worldviews and as such should be engaged in:

> We shall receive gladly those [writings] in which [non-Christians] praise virtue or condemn vice. For just as bees know how to extract honey from flowers, which to men are agreeable only for their fragrance and color, even so here also those who look for something more than pleasure and enjoyment in such writers may derive profit for their souls. Now, then, altogether after the manner of bees must we use these writings, for the bees do not visit all the flowers without discrimination, nor indeed do they seek to carry away entire those upon which they light, but rather, having taken so much as is adapted to their needs, they let the rest go.[2]

St. John Chrysostom even expands on this allegory, saying that bees behave in a way that is beneficial to the community they belong to: "The bee is more honored than other animals," writes St. John, "not because she labors, but because she labors for others."³

I think that too often Christians feel compelled to believe that they cannot be like these bees, drawing sustenance from a wide diversity of sources, including the so-called secular world, which they must reject because, on certain readings of it—perhaps especially among those influenced by American Evangelical Christian culture—that secular culture is some sort of diabolical conspiracy to destroy Christianity. So culture must be shunned. But what if a priest and his wife do not agree with this reading in every detail? What if they see some good in a world that others reject *in toto*? What if their children are especially attracted to it? Clerical families are often faced with this dilemma, and their reaction to it may be unduly influenced by pressures exerted on them by their parishioners. Let me recall here two examples from my past.

When I was fourteen, I carved a drawing of my church building onto a pumpkin. Not too long after, its photo ended up on the internet as the target of incredible criticism. Indirectly alluding to the Halloween custom of carving jack-o'-lanterns, some of the faithful quickly began to condemn the practice as somehow demonic. One person actually commented, "I'm seriously beginning to question the judgment of the clergy to allow this kind of abomination."

My carving the pumpkin created an issue that I can't say was unforeseen. When I was a child, my father excitedly took me in my various costumes from door to door for Halloween candy. One time he let us decorate the rectory for Halloween with a giant garbage-bag spider, but we had to immediately take it down so as not to further upset some of the parishioners who stood vehemently against any expression of this children's holiday.

While this is not the place to debate Halloween and the spiritual dangers it may or may not pose to Christians, I think that instances like these ultimately create situations in which the faithful and the clergy have to have an honest conversation about what concerns them. Here both sides can walk away learning that the boundary between a priest's family and a priest's parish is sometimes necessarily a lot muddier than some may wish it to be.

A few years after the pumpkin-carving incident, my peers and I were invited to compete in a Ukrainian scholastic competition on the subject of Slavic paganism's influence on Ukrainian Christianity. In my opinion, this is a very important subject to teach young Christians so that they may have a deeper understanding of the reasons behind countless Christian customs and what those practices meant in pre-Christian times compared to today.

As the competition date drew closer, I kept learning that team after team was withdrawing from it, citing concerns that the organization spearheading this scholastic faceoff was somehow imposing an anti-Christian agenda rather than simply taking an innocent anthropological approach to teaching today's Ukrainian Christian customs. I later found out that it was the wife of a priest on the East Coast who had led the charge to withdraw all these teams from the competition. This struck me as odd since I figured a priest's wife, the mother of one of the competing students, would want her child to learn the most he or she could in a safe yet critical environment. And yet, as I concluded, not every priest and his wife would exercise oikonomia as my parents did. In the end—to return to our patristic analogy—I realized that my family in the Midwest had a beehive different from but no less valid than that of the other family on the East Coast. The end result for both of us was still honey.

Conclusion

It is easy for people supporting the institution of married clergy to glibly say, "Married clergy have the experience to substantiate their advice." Though I agree with this sentiment, I do not think that those who utter it are aware of how often a priest's experience may put him at odds with other parents and their experience—as I have tried to recount here. It's an important distinction for the faithful to realize so as to not expect perfect parenting and perfect children from a priest—but to expect only the best effort guided by love, caring, and prayer.

In many ways, married Eastern Catholic clergy and their families who live and minister in the West are the vanguard of the universal Church's understanding of family life. Much more than a celibate priest, or even one who was called to the priesthood after a long marriage followed by the death of his wife, a priest who ministers *while raising children* has a real-time perspective on the difficulties of growing up as a Christian engaged with and participating in Western secular society. Just seeing him and his family grappling with the questions of our time is worthwhile and profitable—it takes church teaching out of the realm of abstraction and into the messiness of daily life lived by families in community together.

At the same time, however, it also reminds families in the world that we all have a higher spiritual calling, and part of our task is to ensure that our children and generations yet to come do not forget it. The priest's dual vocation, as it were, is to remind families of the need to gather around both the ordinary dinner tables of their homes and the table of the Lord, a point that, curiously and perhaps ironically, is made in Pope Paul VI's 1967 encyclical on celibate priesthood (*Sacerdotalis caelibatus*, or *On Priestly Celibacy*), a document I believe can also be read to illustrate the benefit a priest's married life brings to both the altar and the pulpit: "The rest of a priest's life also acquires a greater richness of meaning and sanctifying power. In fact, his individual efforts at his own sanctification find new incentives in the ministry of grace and in the ministry of the Eucharist, in which 'the whole spiritual good of the Church is contained'" (*Sacerdotalis caelibatus*, no. 29).

Notes

1. The trailblazers ordained a decade or two before him were a small handful ordained in Rome by Patriarch Josyf Slipyj. But prior to those ordinations in the 1980s, earlier generations of married Eastern Catholic priests, as noted elsewhere in this volume (see Victor Pospishil's chapter in particular), took their marriages with them out the door to lay the groundwork for what we know today as the Orthodox Church in America and the Ukrainian Orthodox Church of the USA.

2. St. Basil, *Address to Young Men on the Right Use of Greek Literature*, IV.

3. Chrysostom is quoted in Tom Yeakley, *Growing Kingdom Character: Practical, Intentional Tools for Developing Leaders* (Carol Stream, IL: Tyndale House, 2014), 73.

CHAPTER ELEVEN

The Vocation of the *Presbytera*

*Icon of the Theotokos in the Midst of
the Ministerial Priesthood*

Irene Galadza

Much has been written on the vocation of woman in the Church, expressing deep insights into the mystery of her continuous role in the history of salvation, which she lives out by God's design in various ways. One such vocation is that of a priest's wife (the *presbytera*), unique in that, while it is entwined with her husband's ministry, it is, at the same time, a vocation in its own right. Rooted in Sacred Scripture and Tradition, this unique and apostolic calling (cf. 1 Cor. 9:5) developed within an ecclesial and cultural tradition that formed a woman for this specific role in the midst of the ministerial priesthood, preparing her to receive God's call and respond to it. The reflection in this chapter will focus on the Mother of God as the model for this ministry that poses so many challenges, both spiritual and pastoral.

Responding to God's Call

The dialogue between Mary and the archangel Gabriel in Luke reveals an important insight regarding God's call for humanity to participate in the work of salvation. Never forcing His will on His creatures, God waits for Mary's *fiat* before proceeding with His salvific plan for humanity. Her free choice to cooperate with God's plan is imperative. Unable to imagine how she is to become a mother without a man and what this role would demand of her, Mary, because of her faith and trust in Him, submits completely to God's will.

Mary's trusting *fiat* opened the door to her intimate involvement with God in the salvific events that followed. Similarly, the wife of a candidate for ordination to the priesthood must also give her *fiat* to open the door to her husband's ordination, agreeing to wholeheartedly support his ministry. This age-old tradition reflects the intimacy between the marital couple and God's call. Already members of the royal priesthood of all baptized believers, and having become one in the mystery of crowning, the call of the husband to the ministerial priesthood is simultaneously a call to his wife to intimately participate in this lofty vocation of spiritually parenting a Christian community. She is called not only to support her husband in his pastoral duties as spiritual father but to complement his ministry with her own God-given gifts, which are distinctly different from her husband's, the greatest of which is her maternal charism.

But Mary's *fiat* includes much more than an agreement to physically bear the Son of God. With it, she commits her entire life to doing God's will. "She hears the word of God and keeps it" (Luke 11:28) for the rest of her earthly life. Tradition teaches us that Mary grew up in a rich liturgical tradition in the Temple, where her love of God grew so intense that her whole being became open to the action of the Holy Spirit. Thus the "soil" of her heart was prepared to receive the Word and the gift of God's grace to bear the challenges and crosses that accompanied her *fiat*.

In just such a "Marian" fashion, the woman who has already made a marital commitment faces the challenge of lifting that commitment to a higher level with her promise to be a "spiritual life-giver" and bear the unknown crosses of her ministry as a *presbytera*. This demanding ministry alongside her priestly husband can bear fruit only if her heart is prepared to receive the grace needed to live this life of sacrificial service to God.

Roles and Relationships

Through the Incarnation, Mary becomes the *Theotokos*—the God-Bearer. Her life is now defined by her relationship with Christ, one that encompasses not only the mother-child relationship, but also that of Bride and Bridegroom—a spousal relationship. With her *fiat*, Mary becomes the Bride of God. As a symbol of the Church, she is the Bride of Christ the Bridegroom, who will come to wed the Church at the end of time. It is their spousal relationship that becomes a model for the common ministry of the presbyter and the *presbytera* and is mirrored so beautifully at the celebration of the Divine Liturgy. While the presbyter stands at the altar in the place of Christ the Bridegroom, his *presbytera* stands with the people—the Body of Christ, the Church, the Bride.

Mary's interaction with Christ at the wedding in Cana beautifully reveals the gift of complementarity in a spousal relationship. Typically, though not exclusively, it is the woman who intuitively perceives the needs of others. Mary senses the embarrassment the hosts will suffer for a lack of wine at their wedding. Her strength of character is evident when she brings this situation to Christ's attention and, in spite of His reluctance to take action, says to the servants, "Do whatever He tells you" (John 2:5). She is confident that He will act to avert the crisis because she knows from personal experience that "nothing is impossible for God" (Luke 1:37)—who is, of course, her very Son and responds accordingly. It is precisely out of her active receptivity that Mary intervenes and Jesus executes. She intercedes, and He acts. Indeed, her sensitivity toward the human needs of the wedding feast actively engages (even prompts) the initiative of Christ to meet them. Their mutual love and respect for each other, along with their complementary engagement of their inherent masculine and feminine gifts, form the foundation of a cooperative effort in ministering to others. This is a beautiful example for all couples involved in ministry. When the priest and his wife each acknowledge and respect the charismatic gifts of the other, they are able to work together for the spiritual benefit of the community.

"Do whatever He tells you." Nothing more of what Mary says is recorded in the Gospels, but her maternal presence throughout the events recorded "speaks" more than words. Luke specifically mentions Mary's presence in the upper room with the apostles as they prepared for the outpouring of the Holy Spirit at Pentecost. Mary, who *is* "full of grace" and the icon of its receptivity, teaches the apostles *how* to receive the anticipated grace. Following the example of Mary, the *presbytera*, in fulfilling her role as *icon of the Theotokos*, can be that maternal presence in her community, complementing the paternal and apostolic ministry of her husband.

So galvanizing was Mary's presence among the disciples that (according to Sacred Tradition) they came from all corners of the earth to be present at her holy dormition. The icon of this feast depicts faithless Athonios (a zealous priest of the Old Covenant), who was struck blind and whose hands were cut off by an angel when he attempted to throw to the ground the body of the Virgin being carried by the apostles. His faith was restored by a miracle of the Mother of God. Referring to this event, the Orthodox theologian Paul Evdokimov observes that "to woman belongs the task of correcting the masculine zeal that blunders so frequently, deeper and deeper, into a profanation of the mysteries, to the detriment of spiritual values."[1] This is a sobering thought for the *presbytera* and a reminder of the prophetic influence she has regarding her husband's pastoral ministry for good or ill.

Preparation and Discernment

A *presbytera* learns of that influence by watching others in the same role. This preparation was done very organically in past centuries and in cultures where married priests were the norm. A young woman who grew up in a priestly family was likely (and often expected) to marry the son of a priest, who would in many, if not most cases, be entering the priesthood. In her parents she observed firsthand the life of the priest and his wife and developed a clear understanding of what would be expected of her as a *presbytera*. Ideally she would have had a solid liturgical life, learned basic cantoring skills, and acquired the knowledge necessary to manage a household. Even knowledge of husbandry was essential for serving in a rural parish, where farming involved management of hired help and provided a living wage for the family, since the priest's stipends were rarely enough to live on. Thus, the preparation of a woman for her role as *presbytera* was passed from generation to generation in a kind of clerical subculture.

Though some remnants of that "clerical subculture" still exist, most women married to priests today do not come from clergy families. In many cases, the thought of being married to a priest comes to light only when a woman begins a relationship with a man studying for the priesthood. She has the opportunity of contemplating the vocation of a *presbytera* before she responds to his marriage proposal, an awesome responsibility in view of the fact that the bishop will require her *fiat* before ordaining her husband.

The wife of a "later vocation" does not have the advantage of forethought and faces a different challenge in her discernment. Her already established marital relationship will be profoundly affected by the inclusion of her husband's ministerial priesthood, and she must prayerfully discern whether she is called to participate in it. Her decision will determine whether he will be ordained. In either case, the woman's *fiat*, like our Lady's, must not be merely "for the moment" but rather all-encompassing and permanent: it must endure for her whole life and extend to its every aspect, for it involves nothing less than a commitment of her "whole life to Christ our God" (as we say in the Byzantine liturgy), who is the High Priest in whose service a *presbytera* participates in a daily and intimate way through *participation in* and *service of* her husband's ministerial priesthood.

The discernment of these women whose husbands have late vocations is significantly more complicated than that of a woman who grew up nurtured in her home for embracing the role of a *presbytera*. She had a fairly good understanding of the challenges she would face and likely had a network of relatives and friends to support her. Women today are not as fortunate. The challenges are not as clear and can differ greatly, depending on the husband's assignment. The women are less likely to have the same kind of support system. All of this means that a woman discerning the vocation of a *presbytera* must be a person of deep and uncompromising faith and trust in God, for only God's grace will enable her to respond confidently to the varying and ever-changing challenges in her life. This will be no easy task once she is faced with challenging circumstances that come to all who embrace the vocation of the *presbytera*. But her embrace of that vocation, and her deep faith and trust in God, do not mean that the *presbytera* must suffer alone. Seeking out others for help is a sign not of her weakness but of her wisdom and strength.

Embracing the Challenge

Challenges can be real or perceived and reasonable, unreasonable, or often a mixture of both. The new *presbytera* may feel (or be made to feel) that she must be involved in every aspect of parish life, providing leadership in activities and organizations and fulfilling the role of catechist, secretary, and social convener while tending to her primary role as wife and mother. Unable to fulfill these unreasonable expectations, whether they come from parishioners or she perceives them as such, she finds herself unduly stressed, most surely resulting in a loss of self-confidence and a feeling of inadequacy. The emotional and spiritual energy wasted on dealing with these kinds of delusions only weakens the *presbytera*'s ability to respond to the many real and unavoidable concerns she will face.

For one *presbytera*, the real challenge is dealing with the isolation of living in a remote parish far from her family and friends. For another, whose husband is assigned to a large, busy parish, it can be a different kind of isolation, as pastoral duties take him away from home at all times of the day and night, often with little notice. A *presbytera* may find herself very much alone in raising their children and managing the household. To be sure, today all these developments are not confined to those in parish ministry. The transient nature of today's world and the ever-changing demands of the economy mean that many people today find themselves uprooted from family, isolated, and overly busy. Many of these women struggle to raise their children on their own. The difference for the *presbytera* comes when she feels as if she is in competition with God for her husband's help and attention in facing these common socioeconomic challenges. Such an attitude can be fatal to their marital relationship if the husband and wife do not talk regularly about this issue and do not talk to God about it.

Thus we see that one important tool for surviving and even embracing these real challenges is prayer. Once again, our example is Mary. Her contemplative spirit is revealed in scripture with these words: "Mary kept all these things, pondering them in her heart" (Luke 2:19). Ironically, prayer is often the first thing to be "forgotten" when one is overwhelmed with responsibilities. Bitterness and emotional exhaustion follow, resulting in a dangerous descent into despair. Once the intimate link with God is ruptured, all other relationships (spousal, familial, and communal) suffer. It can even end in a crisis of identity for the *presbytera*, who can feel betrayed by the circumstances and abandoned by the Church, which offers her little to no help in pursuing her vocation as spiritual life-giver to her husband, children, and community. She cannot give what she does not have. Thus her own spiritual life must be her priority, and her first duty in regard to it is to seek the help of a spiritual father or mother. This is not an option but an absolute requirement if she is to grow in her vocation and experience the inexpressible joy it can bring.

So essential is experienced spiritual guidance for the *presbytera* that it cannot be overemphasized. Her husband, who may himself be overburdened with other people's difficulties or experiencing his own spiritual crisis, may not be able to help his wife with hers. Turning to other clergy in neighboring parishes can be awkward. Although it is healthy for parishioners to know that their priest and his family experience struggles similar to their own, sharing details of personal trials with parishioners can be very unwise, resulting in awkward parish relationships. A *presbytera* needs someone she trusts without hesitation, someone to whom she can open her heart and from whom she can receive the kind of guidance and encouragement that strengthens her spiritually. Ideally, but not necessarily, it might be a priest who can also be her confessor. The spiritual father (or mother) who knows the family and is familiar with their home and work environment can best help the *presbytera* stay on track with her prayer life and progress in it. He can help her recognize her God-given gifts and guide her discernment of when and how to apply them in response to the various demands made on her life. In personal matters involving faith, family, and marriage, he can be trusted to listen sympathetically and present an objective perspective on the issues at hand. Vulnerable to neglecting her need for spiritual renewal, the *presbytera* can depend on her spiritual father to remind her that she needs to take time to nurture her contemplative spirit, which enables her to maintain her intimacy with God and energizes her ministry. She must guard this peace and intimacy with God with all her might and respond quickly to recover it when she feels it slipping away, for this is the main source of her spiritual strength. With her own spiritual life in order, she is equipped to address her next-most-important responsibility: guarding the spiritual health of her husband and children.

Ministry in the Family

Women generally tend to be better at reaching out for help when needed. Men, on the other hand, perhaps fearing that such a request could be seen as a sign of weakness, tend to rely on their own devices. This can be very unwise when it comes to spiritual matters, especially for a priest, whose spiritual life needs to be in order if he is to pastor his flock effectively. With a full schedule of liturgical services to attend to, personal prayer is often neglected, especially during the very busy seasons of Great Lent and Pascha. The priest who diligently reminds his parishioners of their need for confession can easily forget his own need to avail himself of this healing sacrament. The *presbytera* is likely to be the first to notice the signs of spiritual burnout (impatience, depression, negativity) in her husband. With the sensitivity of Mary at the wedding feast in Cana, she brings to her husband's attention the urgent need to focus on a looming crisis: his own spiritual decline. A simple question posed lovingly ("When was the last time you went to confession or spoke to your spiritual father?") may be enough to initiate the first steps toward healing the soul. The *presbytera* who is married to a man tangled in the blunders of masculine zeal to which Evdokimov refers faces the difficult task of helping her husband recognize the dangerous spiritual battle he must wage. This is easier to accomplish in a healthy marital relationship with good communication, a relationship that needs to be nurtured with time alone as a couple away from the parish. The *presbytera*'s efforts in building a strong marriage are bound to bear fruit in the forms of her husband's spiritual well-being, effective pastoral ministry, and harmonious family life.

The same spiritual watchfulness the *presbytera* exercises over her husband must be extended to her children. One of the greatest pastoral challenges in a clergy family is raising spiritually and emotionally healthy children. Often unfairly placed on pedestals by parishioners and even teachers in schools, and still more often watching their father's time almost entirely consumed by the parish, the children—in fact, the whole family— are vulnerable to being judged and to judging: children on their behavior and parents on their parenting and pastoring style and degree of meeting parishioners' demands. Unlike children of doctors, teachers, or other professionals working with the public, children of priests live in their father's work environment. Therefore, they are often witnesses to much of the activity surrounding parish life, including both the triumphs and the struggles. They may, for example, be well within earshot of a disgruntled parishioner verbalizing his or her dissatisfaction with their pastor's performance. Children cannot distinguish between someone's founded or unfounded complaint against their father; they simply see that their dad is under attack, and by extension feel personally attacked as well. Even hearing another priest or his family being criticized can cause children anxiety, for they envision the same happening to their family. The emotional pain and insecurity children experience in such situations can stay with them for a very long time. If their woundedness is not dealt with, the effect on their emotional and spiritual lives can be devastating. It is no wonder that children of priests so often fall away from involvement in the Church and, in extreme cases, reject their faith altogether.

Protecting children from this kind of destructive experience is no easy task, especially if the parish residence is located adjacent to the church, but it must be done at all costs. Though this is the *mutual* responsibility of *both* parents, the *presbytera* is the one most often tending to her children when they need some protection. Seen as an intercessor by parishioners, she is frequently approached with questions and concerns of a controversial nature and must learn to steer such conversations in a different direction when her children are present. At the same time, she might gently educate parishioners on the appropriate time and place to voice their concerns. The *presbytera* and her husband must also remember never to conduct their own conversations about difficult situations and other people in the presence of their children. Greek archbishop Anargyros (of blessed memory), while socializing with a group of clergy families in Canada, emphatically warned against ever discussing church politics and controversies in the presence of children.

In spite of every effort to protect children from the traumas that accompany life in the midst of a parish community, there will always be situations that call for some damage control. Loving parental support and guidance combined with stress-relieving humor can turn such occasions into excellent learning experiences in communication, conflict resolution, and interpersonal dynamics. Children must be steered away from seeing themselves as martyrs, which can easily happen when they find themselves the only children in church along with, perhaps, the deacon's kids at Saturday Vespers or a weekday liturgy. Instilling in them the understanding that we come to worship on these occasions out of our love for God, not from obligation, is an ongoing process. With time, they may even come to recognize the special graces that come from their faithful participation in the liturgical life of the Church. A *presbytera*'s positive attitude toward worship and involvement in parish life is contagious to her young children. Helping older children discover their gifts and how to apply them to the service of God and community gives them a sense of belonging and accomplishment. Showing them appreciation for jobs well done with kind words and, when appropriate, with material rewards goes a long way toward neutralizing any negative episodes they may have experienced. Finally, taking family time away from the parish, whether a few hours or weeks, is essential for the kind of family bonding necessary to give children the sense of security they need to grow into spiritually and emotionally mature adults.

Reaching Out

The roles of the priest's wife examined thus far are foundational to her broader ministry. Other pastoral opportunities arise throughout her life. Some may present themselves in her work outside the parish, whether in her career, if God has led her to one, or in her involvement in the broader community. Often the respect she receives as the wife of a clergyman puts her in a good position to gently evangelize and give witness to her faith in a secular environment. When pastoral challenges in the parish emerge, the *presbytera* must carefully discern her readiness to respond, as she must not be distracted from her primary responsibilities. She, like her husband, is vulnerable to the kind of overzealousness that can be detrimental to her spiritual life and her pastoral ministry. She must wisely balance commitments to her husband and family with her desire to serve the community.

As her children grow toward independence, the *presbytera* may have more time and energy to offer her unique gifts in service to others: teaching, visiting the sick and elderly, ministering to young mothers, doing pro-life work, organizing retreats, leading marriage or baptismal preparation—the needs are many. Yet perhaps the most rewarding is the ministry that she experiences in her more mature years and grows out of being present to her community. Having reached a comfort level with their *presbytera*, women, especially, come to her with very personal struggles and pain: the loss of a child in the womb, the crumbling of a marriage, the pain of an abortion many years ago, the struggles with a spouse or child with mental illness, the news of terminal illness in oneself or a family member, the death of a dear friend. The list of crosses people bear is endless.

What a privilege it is for a *presbytera* to be trusted with such deeply personal experiences. In some cases, all that can be done is to listen and share tears, but in others a *presbytera* can lead the wounded souls to the person that can best help them through the process of healing. She can offer a grieving mother her own motherly embrace and arrange for prayers to be said over her. She can perhaps answer questions a woman is too embarrassed to ask her priest. She can encourage confession for someone burdened with sin. She can put a good book into the hands of a "seeker." She can connect individual parishioners with each other, forming a network for mutual support in their common struggles. This kind of one-to-one ministry is a blessing and a joy. It is worth patiently enduring all the annoyances that accompany ministry in a parish for the opportunity to share so intimately in people's lives and walk with them as they journey toward a deeper relationship with Christ.

The blessings of these ministries can come with a significant emotional toll as the *presbytera* shares the deep pain and sorrows of others. Remembering Mary's role in the paschal mystery is key. At the foot of the cross, we witness the fulfillment of Simeon's prophetic words to Mary: "a sword will pierce through your own soul also" (Luke 2:35). Mary patiently bears the travails and sorrows of these dark days of her Son's passion with complete faith in God's providence. With His Resurrection she no longer remembers her anguish. The heart-rending pain Mary experiences, which is common to all women in their maternal care of the suffering, does not embitter her or deter her from her mission, which continues to unfold after the Resurrection. It is her life of deep prayer and contemplation and her receptivity to the action of the Holy Spirit in her life that are the core of her apostolic dimension and the reasons she was able to maintain an unwavering commitment to the will of God all her life.

Dealing with people's complex and painful issues can be extremely demanding and intimidating. To the *presbytera* who may doubt her capacity to respond appropriately to the varied situations she encounters, Evdokimov offers these encouraging words: "The fact that a woman gave birth to God shows the power of every woman, when she is indeed a 'new creation,' to bring forth God in devastated souls. . . . Above all, woman possesses this natural charism to bring forth Christ in the souls of human beings."[2]

The *presbytera* need not doubt that she is capable of meeting the challenges of her vocation as icon of the Theotokos, for through baptism she became that "new creation" that she nurtures through her life of prayer, contemplation, and ascetic practice. Just as God provided Mary with all the necessary graces for her role in the salvation of the world, He will supplement the inherent maternal and spiritual gifts of the *presbytera* with the grace she needs to accomplish whatever tasks He sets before her. From her contemplative spirit flows the grace to adhere faithfully to the commitment of her *fiat* and to nurture the apostolic dimension of her husband's ministry. Thus the *presbytera* empowers the ministerial mission of her husband, the priest of God, and perfects her vocation as icon of the Theotokos—a journey that requires a life-long effort of struggle and prayer like this: "Open the ears of my soul, O Mother of God, for thou hast borne the Lord who once opened the ears of the deaf; enable us to hear the Word of God and keep it."[3]

Notes

1. Paul Evdokimov, *Woman and the Salvation of the World* (Crestwood, NY: St. Vladimir's Seminary Press, 1994), 223.

2. Ibid., 224.

3. The Theotokion of canticle four, second canon, for the second Sunday of Lent (as found in the *Lenten Triodion* from St. Tikhon's Seminary Press).

CHAPTER TWELVE

The Joys and Crosses of Clerical Families

Nicholas Denysenko

Since 2005, one by one, God has called members of my family home to eternal rest in his kingdom. It started that year with Dad, and then it was Grandpa (Fr. Nicholas) in 2011, Grandma (Matushka Margarita) in 2015, and Mom in 2017. Their departures from this world and entrance into the kingdom have given me an opportunity to reflect on our weird émigré family. The cliché "It takes a village" is repeated so often that it is often misused and misplaced. To the chagrin of my grandfather's parishioners, I would not claim that I was raised by a "village." My maternal grandparents, parents, and brother were the primary shapers of my life, infusing me with an identity from the very beginning.

The daily events that shaped who I would eventually become took place primarily in St. Paul, Minnesota, especially at Saints Volodymyr and Ol'ha Ukrainian Orthodox Church on Portland Avenue, where my grandfather served as pastor from 1974 to 1992. These events were not confined to the enormous building that provided a place of worship for a variety of communities throughout its history. Our journey as a "clerical family" was just as real and raw at the rectory next door, at my grandparents' cabin on Martin Lake in Anoka County, and at our house in Crystal, a northwest suburb of Minneapolis.

My testimony here leads me to the following hypothesis about the married priesthood and its impact on the priest's family: For better and worse, in joy and sorrow, the priest's wife and family close the separation between the priest and the parish community: The family is a part of that parish and thus lives within it, not outside of it. In our case, Fr. Nicholas's ministry delivered blessings and crosses. Ultimately, I chose to receive those crosses as blessings because they infused us with doses of authentic Christianity, which requires the disciple to take up his cross and follow Christ.

Managing Expectations

Orthodox parishes are not particularly large, so it can be difficult to remain anonymous or to live on the periphery of the parish without people noticing. It is typical for people to know one another, and this was the case in our smallish St. Paul parish of about a hundred families. The parish itself had a set of core values, and one of its priorities was to cultivate cultural identity in my generation. It did not suffice merely to be Orthodox; our parish also had a Saturday school that taught us the Ukrainian language as well as that country's history, geography, music, literature, and "religion." If a young person was absent from class, it was noticeable; if one of Fr. Nicholas's grandchildren was absent, it was scandalous.

For about twelve years, almost every weekend my parents drove us to this "Ukrainian" school on Saturdays. My brother and I occasionally protested: Surely Saturday mornings were made for cartoons, not school! Try explaining that one to your fellow kids in the neighborhood elementary school.

The bonus was that we got to spend the night at our grandparents' rectory. This meant an afternoon of watching *Grizzly Adams* and *Star Trek* on TV, helping Grandpa at Vespers (especially in the coveted task of holding the *kadylo*, or censer), and, if we were lucky, having a few minutes to play on the pool table in the parish hall. After spending the night, we would walk to liturgy the next morning and serve with Grandpa. Our parents would then take us home after liturgy.

Family Duty

An unavoidable reality of belonging to the priest's family is that you have to answer the call to duty. By this I do not mean merely mowing the lawn, raking leaves, or shoveling snow to help your grandparents, although we did those things, too. The priest's ministry threaded through the family. Obviously, we were expected to attend parish events. Frequent Sunday attendance was normal for us; showing up for commemorative events in the Ukrainian community was another story.

The Twin Cities area had three Ukrainian Orthodox parishes in my youth, and the three came together for each parish's patronal feast. When our parish hosted the feast, you knew you were in for an impossibly long afternoon following a lengthy liturgy. A dinner and program took place in the parish hall afterward, and in the émigré community, there were many official speeches delivered by diverse representatives of the community. We usually did not get home until 4 p.m. or so. It was a duty to be endured.

Both of my parents would complain bitterly, often to the point of fighting. My father would declare that he was finished with the political programs after church, and my mother would respond, "I know they're boring, but we have to stay because Dad is the priest!" Her role as the priest's daughter occasionally drove her to tears. The political positioning in the small parish choir made her feel singled out. She was so sensitive to the way parishioners perceived her that she would brush her teeth again after her last cigarette in the mornings before liturgy, because she knew that her father would be scandalized if people learned that his daughter had not quit smoking (she eventually quit in the mid-1980s).

The priest's grandchildren were not immune from the parish pressure. It began early, when my grandparents would host select parishioners for the Holy Supper (*sviata vechera*) at their home on Christmas Eve. We were the only children in attendance and sat quietly, trying to follow the adult discussion in Ukrainian and Russian while sampling strange foods and wishing we could sip the cognac Fr. Nicholas rolled out for his guests, all while our friends were watching football or playing video games. On Christmas Day (January 7 on the Julian calendar), our grandparents hosted the parish choir for a dinner after the liturgy. The choir would sing the favorite carols, and the family would assist with hosting, a tiring task, especially when certain parishioners wore out their welcome.

The rigor of this challenge increased when my grandparents were in their 80s and working in their second parish in the Twin Cities (St. George's in southeast Minneapolis). By then, my mother had assumed the role of host, and everyone felt her anxiety that everything had to be perfect for the grandparents. In all of those years, there was no family time on Old Calendar Christmas: after cleaning up, there was neither time nor energy for a family meal. The family shared in the pastoral duty of the priest to offer hospitality to the parish.

When my brother and I were young adults, in our mid- to late 20s, Fr. Nicholas was at St. George's, and macular degeneration made it hard for him to continue serving as a priest. My father drove him to and from church, and he carried out the liturgy by memory. On some special occasions, we read the gospel or special prayers for him. My brother assumed this duty for many Sundays over a few years, despite his nerves, which made him anxious that he had violated some canon or another when he chanted the special petitions for the blessing of waters on Theophany. We asked Fr. Nicholas, "Is there no parishioner who can do this competently?" And he responded, "Why should I ask them when I have you?"

There was no compensation for these duties, no reward, no certificate of recognition, no public thanks. The pressure to perform the duty could be heavy, and I was often frustrated by the lines separating "required" events from "optional" ones. Every year, the parish school would finish the year with a picnic (pronounced *peek-neek*), sometimes held jointly with the other parishes at a local lake. I despised these events because the weather was nice and I wanted to shoot baskets in my driveway, play baseball, or ride my bike—not sit through more stories about what life was like in Ukraine during the awful Stalin years. One year, my parents agreed that I did not have to go, so I stayed home. Immediately a phone call arrived from Fr. Nicholas. He insisted on speaking to me. After several complaints about how my absence humiliated him, he told me that I was a "bad Ukrainian." I cried and vowed to never again attend a *peek-neek*. There were other related episodes of conflict in which my absence resulted in humiliation.

I had no choice in belonging to a clerical family, and I learned that I had inherited a set of expectations that came with birth. Those expectations often translated into duties, and we were expected to comply. In many of these instances, perhaps a volunteer outside of the family could have offered the service. But we were following a family pattern: When you need help, calling a child or parent is often practical. It is safe; family is often more reliable than parishioners; and, in our case, we were part of the parish community. We knew we were not ourselves the priest, but we supported him as his family, just as children, grandchildren, and parents support their family members throughout the world.

A Grandfather with His Grandsons

Family relations extend beyond one's calling, so we knew Fr. Nicholas in ways that most parishioners never would. Back in the Portland rectory, I would spend hours sifting through the eccentric library of my grandfather's office. It had a distinct smell of old oak floors combined with the aftershave he always wore. Dusty copies of the *Ukrainian Orthodox Word* were stacked everywhere, along with a variety of liturgical books; Bibles; books in Ukrainian, Polish, and Russian; and his stack of handwritten sermons.

Sunday morning was a ritual: Fr. Nicholas arose early, and we never saw him before church, as he spent over an hour in that office, carefully reviewing his sermon notes, practicing his sermon aloud. It was a required ritual for him, and nothing could interrupt him. One Sunday when a mouse got in the house and was trapped by the dog, Fr. Nicholas refused to come down to take care of the mouse until he had finished his sermon preparation.

I was in awe of his liturgical presence. He was not an opera singer who uses his talents in a showy way. Fr. Nicholas did not call attention to himself at all; his liturgical sobriety was simple and quiet, yet real, and he had a commanding presence at the altar, as the young servers also feared his reprimands. I am not certain if his liturgical presence influenced his everyday posture, but it seems to have been the case. Car rides with my father included old music and advice, wanted and unwanted. A car ride with Fr. Nicholas was liturgical. Before he even started the car, he would make the sign of the cross and offer a simple prayer asking God to keep us safe, guarded as we were by the small cross on the dash. He barely spoke in the car; the only noises were his loud breathing through his nose. We could spend hours together without talking at all, sitting on the dock across the street from the cabin he shared with Matushka, catching one carp after another, which he then carefully cleaned and delivered for a delicious meal of fried fish and potatoes.

On one such occasion, I spent two weeks with him at the lake after leaving the local Ukrainian camp early. I had been the youngest person in my cabin at camp and could no longer endure the bullying, hazing, and overt Ukrainian nationalism imposed upon us by the counselors. I feared my grandfather's reprimand for embarrassing him for leaving camp early.

Over those two weeks we fished for hours in silence, and when we talked, he listened to my story. I learned then that he, too, had little patience for the nationalist politics of the Ukrainian émigré community and wished that their leaders would be more faithful to the Church, God, Christ, and his gospel. His acceptance of my explanation for leaving was like the removal of huge stones from my shoulders. I was grateful to have a real priest as my grandfather, not just an émigré patriot wearing vestments. I do not know this for certain, but perhaps he was grateful to have a young grandson who was actually interested in Church, willing to hear him out. My brother and I cherished those trips to the cabin. While Fr. Nicholas was present, we also saw another side of him, a man who enjoyed being with his boys. As a young adult, I fell in love with liturgical music and would begin singing hymns at the cabin that my brother joined, while my father asked us to "knock it off" with our piety outside of church. My father's wisecrack notwithstanding, I'm glad that my brother and I shared that with my grandfather. In other words, it was an aspect of church life that proved to be a source of joy in our family.

As I became an adult and attended seminary, I realized that Fr. Nicholas was an indefatigable source of knowledge about the Church and its people. I had an assignment to write an oral history of a Church figure, and I selected Patriarch Mstyslav (Skrypnyk), who had presided over the Ukrainian Orthodox Church in the USA since 1971 and was enthroned as patriarch of the reborn Ukrainian Autocephalous Orthodox Church in Ukraine from 1990 until his death in 1993. My sources for this history were Archbishop (now Metropolitan) Antony (Scharba), whom I interviewed in his office in New Jersey, and Fr. Nicholas.

When I arrived at my grandparents' St. Paul home for the interview, I delicately explained to my grandmother that this was being recorded and people might listen to it, so Fr. Nicholas and I needed privacy. I was nervous about her response, as we all revered her knowledge of languages and literature, but she cheerfully agreed to give us a few hours. Sure enough, an hour into the interview, Matushka padded into the kitchen in her slippers and began to fry *kutlyety* (meat patties with spices and onions). Due to my inability to stop the recording and remind her to give us space, she corrected my grandfather on some of his assertions and added her own two cents to the interview! To my surprise, he accepted her corrections without hesitation and seemed grateful that she was able to remind him about some details of important events and people. When

I listened to the recording later that day and several times afterward, I could hear the *kutlyety* frying in the background and realized that my grandmother knew all about the details of who, what, and when in Church history because she was part of the family.

Here I want to emphasize that she claimed no special role as Matushka—she baked the prosphora for the liturgy for as many years as her health permitted, but her heart problems often kept her at home from liturgy, so she was never a shadow rector. We had hundreds of discussions on clergy and their families, and Matushka Margarita surprised me when she told me, privately, that she wished that the Orthodox required clerical celibacy as the Roman Church does. I respectfully disagreed then and I do now, though I know she spoke from her own frustration at not being able to have a life that was not in the parish spotlight, keeping in mind that her health problems started when they lived in the rectory, so they were at the parish's mercy for family health insurance coverage.

What, then, is my final word on married priests? I have attempted to share a selection of my experiences as someone who had to manage expectations and tried to have a normal relationship with a grandparent. I will also disclose that I have much at stake, as I have been a deacon for seventeen years and continue to struggle to find suitable ways for my wife and daughter to participate in parish life without being buried by expectations.

First, one thing is obvious: I have no romanticized ideal of the priest's (or deacon's!) family as carrying out a special ministry that emanates from the ordination of a priest. When family members show up, endure the abuse that comes from parishioners and clergy, revel in the joy of ministry that comes into one's home, and perform unwanted duties in the parish, their performance is offered out of love, not in obedience to some implied ordination. Family pitches in, even when it is costly. Just as the spouses and children of doctors, engineers, teachers, and all workers bear the burdens brought home, the priest's family bears those particular burdens out of love and to fulfill God's command to honor one's father and mother.

That said, I think there is something theologically profound about a married priesthood and priests having spouses, children, and grandchildren. In the contemporary Byzantine rites of ordination and marriage, there is a prominent liturgical component in both rites. As the candidate for ordination is escorted around the altar table, three short hymns are sung in honor of the holy martyrs, recalling the joy (or dance) of Isaiah, and in praise of Christ. The same hymns are sung in a slightly different order as the bride and groom process around the table toward the end of the marriage rite. Theologians and pastors have reflected on the connection between ordination and marriage given this common circumambulation of the table, and usually one concludes that the relationship between the ordinand and the Church is similar to the marital bond of husband and wife. That the two rites share this common ritual is probably accidental, but I would like to offer a different take on the meaning of this procession around the table. The presence of the procession in both rites reminds us that marital and familial love and presbyteral ministry are neither mutually exclusive nor alien to one another, but rather they contribute to one another. The love of a spouse and family can contribute to presbyteral ministry, and the priest's service can enrich the life of a family.

A man is not defined solely by his ordination: Priests are also parents and grandparents, and this makes them like everyone else in the parish community. While one might wish to insulate family members from the ugliness that priests can bring home from working in the Lord's vineyard, these priests have someone who will help them bear this burden. Bearing the burden of another is not always sorrowful; it can be joyful, too, as I am claiming here. Personally, I cannot think of any downside to having a priest who is living the Christian life *with* his people instead of outside of them. I hope that my testimony might persuade the reader that married priests with families are positioned firmly within their communities, a place that is suitable for effective pastoral ministry.

CHAPTER THIRTEEN

Marriage and Ministry

An Eastern Orthodox Perspective

William C. Mills

I was a great dad—or tried.
—George Lucas, interview on CBS TV

If anyone aspires to the office of bishop, he desires a noble task. Now a bishop must be above reproach, the husband of one wife, temperate, sensible, dignified, hospitable, an apt teacher, no drunkard, not violent but gentle, not quarrelsome, and no lover of money. He must manage his own household well, keeping his children submissive and respectful in every way; for if a man does not know how to manage his own household, how can he care for God's Church?
—1 Timothy 3:1–7

It's already been a long day: making a series of pastoral visits, responding to emails, working on the Sunday bulletin, eating dinner on the run, and attending an evening parish council meeting. After all this there's nothing better than to come home to my family, especially my two daughters, Hannah and Emma, who run toward me quickly, all the while shouting,

"Daddy, Daddy, Daddy." The pains and problems from the day dissipate. I'm home, reunited with my family.

Many clergy, however, especially Roman Catholic priests, have a different experience. While many have similar schedules to mine, they come home to an empty rectory. If they are members of a religious order, they may come home to two or three other pastors who are also stressed out, anxious, and overworked. They may not have the energy to make their own supper, so they eat out at a local restaurant or diner. They may have little social interaction with friends, since so much of their time is taken up with parish work and diocesan meetings. They receive no social support or encouragement from immediate family. There are no spouses or children to listen to their problems or to encourage and comfort them in times of trouble. I cannot imagine serving in full-time parish ministry and being a single celibate priest.

In what follows, then, I take a deliberately personal approach to this series of reflections on life as a married priest in the Eastern Orthodox Church. The year 2017 marked our twentieth wedding anniversary, the eighteenth anniversary of my ordination, and my seventeenth anniversary in this parish. In this chapter I will discuss the choices and challenges, trials and tribulations, and joys and celebrations of being a husband, father, and full-time pastor.

"Goin' to the Chapel and We're Gonna Get Married"

Sunday, May 25, 1997, began with grey clouds and a drizzle. I was hoping that by mid-afternoon the clouds would pass and the sun would shine, but Mother Nature had other plans. During the Divine Liturgy the slight drizzle turned into a massive downpour. At 3 p.m. Taisia, my soon-to-be bride, would be escorted to the Three Hierarchs Chapel at St. Vladimir's Seminary, where I was a student. I was worried about our out-of-town guests: her parents from Florida, her elderly grandparents from Pennsylvania, and my family from New Jersey. As I was fretting over the wedding service the rain kept falling and falling and falling.

My mother-in-law always says that things work out the way they work out, and work out they did. Despite the rain, the wind, the loud clashes of thunder and lightning, we got married and all was well. Everyone got a little wet running to our cars, but in the end all was well.

Taisia and I first met in May 1995 while I was the summer intern at St. Stephen the Protomartyr Orthodox Church in Longwood, Florida. Taisia's dad, Fr. John Ealy, had a longstanding relationship with St. Vladimir's to accept summer interns for his congregation. I was their fourth intern. The internship program was established to assist young seminarians in finding their way in ministry, showing them the various aspects of parish life. My primary task would be to shadow Fr. John as he went about his daily activities, similar to medical students' shadowing residents. I helped organize summer church school, assisted with summer church camp, sang in the choir, delivered sermons, and taught a weekly adult education class. While I was helping Fr. John, Taisia was finishing up her degree in art at Stetson University.

It was not love at first sight for either of us. Later on in our relationship she admitted that I was too nerdy and liked books. She didn't like to read. I thought she was a bit different and came home with bits of clay and paint on her clothes. After all she was an artist, so of course she would be dirty.

I would not say we were opposites, but we were not exactly the same, which I later learned probably makes our marriage stronger. We both give one another freedom to be ourselves, yet we have a lot in common, too. We both enjoy the outdoors, exploring art museums, and traveling. We like to spend time at the beach and hike in the mountains. Even though she was from Florida and I was from New Jersey, we had similar faith formations: Both of us were raised in the Orthodox Church in America; we both attended summer church camps, attended high school and college winter retreats at St. Vladimir's Seminary, and experienced our annual home blessing in the Epiphany season. We had our Easter baskets blessed at Pascha, mounted paper icons on wood, sang in the choir, and read the epistle at the Divine Liturgy.

While we had our differences, we also had similarities and things in common that helped strengthen our bond. After our wedding, we spent the next three years in a small apartment in Weschester County, where Taisia was finishing her MFA degree in art while I was completing a second master's degree in theology. While we experienced the usual ups and downs of newlyweds, we eventually found a common rhythm of life that worked for us.

In June 2000 I was called to serve as the rector of the Nativity of the Holy Virgin Orthodox Church in Charlotte, North Carolina. We packed up our belongings in a small moving truck and headed south. This was going to be an adventure. In 2003 our first daughter, Hannah, was born, and then in 2006 Emma was born.

My Big Fat Happy Clergy Family

Being a pastor and having a family is a joy and a blessing. There is nothing better than to come home and hug my girls and receive great big bear hugs from them and talk about our daily activities. I've watched them grow up from being toddlers heading off to preschool to being teenagers and freshmen in high school. I've watched Hannah play soccer and basketball and have attended what seems like a thousand and one sports practices. I've chased them on the playground and made sand castles with them on the beach. We've laughed and cried, gotten into arguments and made up. I've seen both of them win and lose. Throughout the years Taisia and I have scrimped and saved so that the girls could attend educational and summer sports camps. I've read them bedtime stories and listened to their dreams and their fears, from being afraid of the boogeyman to getting braces. And we've watched countless Disney movies.

All of these parental experiences have greatly contributed to and influenced my pastoral ministry. My family has kept me human, humane, and humble. While every family has different social and cultural dynamics, I know what it's like to stay up till 2 a.m. for an infant's feeding or to stay home all day while nursing a sick child. I have waited for hours in doctors' offices and arranged for play dates and carpool pickups. These life challenges and choices are very real, and my parishioners deal with them on a daily basis, whether they have one child or ten. I know what it's like to be worried about paying for college and saving up for a used car.

Many of these wonderful child-rearing experiences have greatly influenced my preaching and pastoral care. Very often I will use a story from the playground or a scene from a Disney movie or a Dr. Seuss book in my sermons. People can easily identify with these stories since they have gone through similar experiences as well. Being married with children allows me to make social and cultural connections more quickly than I would otherwise. I always try to maintain good boundaries and never divulge anything particularly private or confidential about our family, but I will often mention family experiences in general or dumb things that I've done as a dad to show the faults and foibles of the human condition. I feel that these experiences have enhanced my general understanding of being a minister and have also increased my sensitivity to and compassion for those around me. Certainly a single celibate priest was a child once and may have siblings or even be an uncle. Yet a single celibate priest has never experienced marriage or child rearing. He does not know what it's like to stay up all hours of the night worrying whether his teen-aged son or daughter will come home safely from a party.

I wear many hats in life. I am a priest, husband, father, cook, gardener, baker, writer, and speaker; I am also a son and an uncle. I have many domestic duties: cleaning, paying bills, and doing countless errands. Among the most challenging parts of my life—but, at the same time, the most rewarding—are those of being a father and a husband. Spending seventeen years in parish ministry with Taisia has eased the burden. Sharing the pains, joys, and celebrations of my ministry with her is an amazing thing. She has been a soundboard for ideas of mine, as well as a voice of reason when needed. She has accompanied me through extremely difficult situations.

So, too, have my girls. I have watched Emma sing in the choir and Hannah lead an outreach ministry collecting socks to be used at a local homeless shelter. Our family is not perfect, and we have our own trials and tribulations, but they're minimal compared to the joys and celebrations that we have. Both Hannah and Emma like attending Sunday services, and if they have any complaints they keep them to themselves. It helps that Nativity is a family-friendly, vibrant community where families feel comfortable with children rolling on the floor and getting dirty on the playground. Taisia and I try to give both girls freedom in life so they can grow and become the persons that they are supposed to be. Once a journalist asked the famous *Star Wars* creator and director George Lucas about his life and legacy. After a slight pause, he said that on his tombstone he wanted the following: "I was a great dad—or tried." In 1981 Lucas and his wife divorced. He stepped down from directing movies for twenty years to raise his adopted children by himself. He told the journalist that of all the things in life that he did—his movies, his writing, his life's work—he wanted to be known as a great dad. For my tombstone I would just tweak what Lucas wants on his a bit: "I was a great dad *and husband*—or tried."

Roses Have Thorns

One may think that having married clergy is perfect for parish ministry. After all, the majority of parishioners on Sunday mornings are married or have been married, and many have both children and grandchildren. There are, however, some serious downsides, or at least major challenges, to being both ordained and married.

Being married with children, Taisia and I are constantly rearranging schedules. Taisia not only works as a full-time art teacher at a local charter school; she also coaches the middle school girls' soccer team. She often has at least one practice and two games per week during the fall and spring soccer seasons. My younger daughter, Emma, who is currently in fourth grade, has piano lessons once a week as well as tennis lessons four days a week.

My eldest daughter, Hannah, who is in eighth grade, has her regular school obligations such as homework, reading, and regular writing projects as well as playing on two soccer teams and a basketball team. In late January her winter basketball and spring soccer practices overlap for a three-week period, which means that our domestic life is rather harried.

Much of the school year is just shy of chaos. Taisia and I have to juggle trying to feed the girls as well as arranging carpool and my parish schedule. Thankfully I have a smaller parish, and I have more control over my schedule. Those clergy who have much larger parishes with pastoral staffs often have far less flexibility in their schedules and far more demands on their time.

When I'm home I can be more available to help out when needed. Most of my parish meetings are held on Sunday afternoons after the Divine Liturgy. However, there are several times a year when I have to leave for a few days for a clergy conference or diocesan meetings, which means that everything falls to Taisia—her own job, getting the girls fed and to school, and later getting them off to various practices and myriad other events. If I'm away for two days, life can be very hectic.

For clergy in larger parishes, one can see how life would be extremely challenging and difficult. It would not be uncommon to be out at least two or three evenings per week with either pastoral visits or church-related meetings. It's easy to see how difficult it would be for a clergy spouse to take care of two or three children (or more) while the clergy person is out on call. Resentment, jealousy, and anger can creep into a marriage, driving two very loving and compassionate people apart and often to divorce. Numerous studies have clearly shown that there is a high level of resentment and frustration in clergy families.[1]

    Being a pastor means that I have more flexibility during the week but have a tighter schedule on the weekends. While Taisia and the girls are often free on the weekends, I have to work, which of course is the common lot of all clergy. But for many Orthodox, that work is not confined to Sunday but begins Saturday evening with Vespers, which prepares us for the Sunday Divine Liturgy, often with sacramental confessions scheduled before and after. This time slot, of course, is very often one during which my daughters will be invited to a birthday party or other celebration—and parents are sometimes invited, too. Due to my busy weekend schedule, I cannot attend these social functions. I have turned down countless parties, dinners, and gatherings because of my work. This leaves me deeply troubled, because strong friendships and bonds are essential to human development, and since most of our friends work during the week and I work on the weekends, we don't get to have much social interaction, making the pastoral life often rather isolating even when—and often especially because of—being surrounded by people.

    Sunday mornings I leave the house at 7:30 a.m. and do not return until 2 p.m. After serving the Divine Liturgy, preaching, meeting new members, and spending time with parishioners, I am very tired and don't want to do much on Sunday afternoons. Taisia and the girls have weekends free, which means they can go camping or fishing or take a long weekend away. Due to my weekend activities, I must stay home. Numerous times throughout the year, they have weekend trips planned or visit friends out of town and I cannot go. This year Hannah had a club soccer weekend tournament in South Carolina, but I had to stay home so I could serve the liturgy. I do get vacation time, but the time is limited and I cannot simply leave the congregation. It is difficult for me to get a substitute priest to serve while I'm away. Thankfully Hannah understands the situation, and I do try to get to her games when I can, but you can see how over time this could make her angry and resentful. A few missed games in the season are fine, but when my absence becomes the standard, it is not good. Over the years I've built up enough social and emotional capital that it's not a problem, yet not all clergy can say the same. I have heard many stories from clergy children whose fathers missed many school and sports events, all in the name of God, the Church, and the parish. Whether the priest was absent because of a series of evening meetings or clergy retreats, children need to see their parents in the stands and need to see them take an interest in their lives.

Then there are the financial concerns of a married clergy. If our parish had a single celibate priest, there would be a smaller budget. Since I'm married and have children, they must pay a larger amount for my salary, pension, and health insurance. Over time, prices go up, and the parish must meet these challenges, too. Since the financial crisis in 2008, finances at the parish have been tight, which of course has caused personal concern. It's one thing to be concerned about just myself, but now I have a family to worry about. Even though the parish puts away funds in a church-sponsored pension plan I also put away extra money in an IRA as an extra layer of support for my retirement. I also have to provide funds for braces for Hannah and Emma, tuition for summer sports camps, funds for our yearly vacation, and money for college and all of the incidental costs that come with that—used cars, books, and spending money, among other things. Unlike some parishes, ours does not own a rectory: My wife and I have our own residence, which also means, of course, that we must pay for the vast array of the usual expenses familiar to middle-class families, none of which a single celibate priest would have to worry about. I confess that I have had a few—probably a few too many—sleepless nights. Yet I count myself lucky. I know of several married clergy with children who have had to survive on food stamps and Medicaid because their salaries were very low. This lack of funds, of course, builds up resentment and ill feelings in their spouses and children.[2]

Crowns of Martyrdom

Taisia and I have a small icon corner in our bedroom. Above the icons of St. Basil the Great, my patron saint, and St. Taisia of Egypt, my wife's patron saint, hang our wedding crowns.[3] Ours are made from small white artificial roses and are connected by a piece of white ribbon three feet long. While they have become slightly faded over time, they are constant reminders of our commitment to one another and to our girls.

During the marriage service in the Orthodox Church, the priest blesses the crowns and says:

Holy God, Who fashioned man from the dust, and from his rib fashioned woman, and joined her to him as a helpmate for him, for it was seemly unto Your Majesty for man not to be alone upon the earth, do You Yourself, O Sovereign Lord, stretch forth Your hand from Your holy dwelling place, and join together this Your servant (Name) and Your servant (Name), for by You is a wife joined to her husband. Join them together in oneness of mind; crown them with wedlock into one flesh; grant to them the fruit of the womb, and the gain of well favored children, for Yours is the dominion, and Yours is the Kingdom, and the Power, and the Glory: of the Father, and of the Son, and of the Holy Spirit, both now and ever, and to the ages of ages.

The marriage crowns symbolize martyrdom or witness to the couple's love for each other but, more importantly, to the sacrificial love of Christ. Married couples are called to have the same love, commitment, and devotion to one another and to their new family as Christ did for the Church. He lived his whole life to build up the Body of Christ, and married couples become witnesses to this sacrificial love. Marriage is wonderful and has many blessings and joys: the joy of watching one's spouse grow and develop as a person and the joy of watching one's own children grow and develop as people, too. I had the joy of watching the births of Hannah and Emma, as well as taking them to the park and to their art and music lessons, as well as spending countless hours at gymnastics, soccer, and tennis practices, games, and matches. I look forward to watching Hannah and Emma graduate high school, get married, and have children of their own. I look forward to pushing my grandchildren in a stroller, taking them to the park, baking brownies with them, and telling them bedtime stories. Being a husband and parent is an ongoing project, one that lasts a lifetime.

Being Hubby, Daddy, and Father

But so is being a priest. Serving in the same congregation for seventeen years has provided me with much joy, too. I have visited countless babies in the hospital the day after they were born, holding them in my arms and blessing them. I have baptized them and watched them grow into fine young adults; a few I have even seen grow up to have children of their own. I have watched adult parishioners take on greater responsibility in the parish, serving as parish council members, church school teachers, or leading various outreach ministries. I have married them and even buried a few.

In the Eastern Orthodox Church the priest is often referred to as "Father." I'm still not sure if I like that term or not, but it's the only title that we have so far, and it's what my parishioners call me. I'm not their biological father, but I am in some ways their spiritual father. I relate to them in that fatherly way the best that I can, yet not in a patronizing manner either; after all, they are adults. I am a fellow Christian like them, with the same temptations, choices, and challenges in life, and I, as Paul said to Timothy, am trying to work out my salvation in fear and trembling (Phil. 2:12). The Christian life is not an easy one. Following Jesus is not easy. Yet I follow him while walking alongside my wife and daughters, sharing my joys, pains, burdens, and sorrows with them. I cannot imagine doing all of this alone.

As a husband and father I can identify more intimately with my parishioners. Of course I cannot know exactly what they are going through, but, like them, I have to juggle my schedule with practices, games, mealtimes, grocery shopping, cooking, and cleaning. I, too, worry about paying bills, paying the mortgage, and saving money for college and other future things. I also know what it's like when children disobey us and don't want to do chores or homework. Yet this is what married life is like: It has good times and bad, both roses and thorns. In pastoral life there are also roses and thorns, but having a "helpmate" with whom to freely enjoy the roses and suffer the thorns makes all the difference.

Concluding Thoughts

There is ongoing debate within the Catholic Church about married clergy.[4] This is not a debate we have had in the East, where men are free to be both celibate and married priests—that freedom of choice is ours. My colleagues in the West do not have the freedom to choose. By limiting clergy's freedom and making celibacy a norm for them, the Church is neglecting a very large population of men who maybe have vocations to serve as parish priests *and* as husbands and fathers. Now, as the Church is experiencing great change—especially as bishops are closing parishes and seminaries are cutting back on staff—maybe it's time to take a long hard look at having married clergy in the West. For centuries a married priesthood has worked in the East—with many of the challenges I have detailed here. Surely it can work in the West as well.

Notes

1. https://journals.sagepub.com/doi/full/10.1177/1542305018762212.

2. https://www.christiancentury.org/article/critical-essay/what-pastors-get-paid-and-when-it-s-not-enough.

3. In the Eastern Orthodox Christian liturgical tradition, crowns—metal or metal-based or handmade—are used during the wedding service. The crowns are called *stephana* in Greek, which means "crowns" or "garlands" and is the origin or the proper names Stephen and Stephanie.

4. See Anthony Kowalski, *Married Catholic Priests: Their History, Their Journey, Their Reflections* (New York: Crossroad Publishing, 2005); Paul Sellin, *Keeping the Vow: The Untold Story of Married Catholic Priests* (London: Oxford University Press, 2015); Dom Arturo Cattaneo, *Married Priests? 30 Crucial Questions about Celibacy* (San Francisco: Ignatius Press, 2012).

CHAPTER FOURTEEN

"What Did You Expect?"
A Reflection on Married Clergy and Pastoral Ministry

Andrew Jarmus

I was once invited to give a talk at a local Roman Catholic parish, and my wife decided to join me at the event. I really do not remember the exact topic of my presentation that night. What I do remember is the reaction of the parishioners to seeing a "real live" married priest and his "real live" wife. The word "fascination" is not an overstatement. There is much about the married priesthood that remains a mystery to most people. Many are quite surprised to learn that priests and their families go out for fast food, stay home and watch movies, and engage in the pastimes of "normal" households.

Some people are even more surprised to discover that clergy families face the same issues and challenges of modern life as any other family. We struggle with paying the bills, juggling schedules to take children to extracurricular activities, and worrying about the perils of adolescent life—peer pressure, the struggle for identity, the lure of drugs and alcohol, the pain of teenage love. It is typical for clergy families to have pastoral assignments far from the communities where they grew up; therefore, like many families in our mobile modern culture, we often carry out day-to-day tasks without the help of extended family.

Clergy families also deal with a unique set of stressors related to the vocation of pastoral service. In August 2010, the *New York Times* published an article by Paul Vitello titled "Taking a Break from the Lord's Work." The article's subheading was "Evidence Grows of Problem of Clergy Burnout." This subheading is quite surprising because it suggests that it took to the end of the first decade of the twenty-first century to accumulate enough "evidence" to prove that clergy burnout is a concern among Christians. The reality is that clergy burnout has been well known as a phenomenon across confessional lines since the first half of the twentieth century.

It should not come as a surprise that pastoral ministry is a difficult calling. Shortly before his betrayal and crucifixion, Jesus tells his apostles, "Remember what I told you: 'A servant is not greater than his master.' If they persecuted me, they will persecute you also." Wounding the shepherd will also hurt the sheep.

Some of the better-known issues in ministry are the need for time management skills, coping mechanisms for stress, and ongoing vocational development and spiritual guidance. There is another challenge faced by priests on a daily basis that, although less obvious, has a profound impact on their ministry and their entire lives. This is the challenge of effectively addressing the multiple expectations they face. Expectations come from various sources, and their sheer number is formidable enough.[1]

A parish priest is a highly trained "generalist" who must have some degree of expertise, or at least experience, in numerous fields. As such, a priest faces multiple, sometimes conflicting, expectations in his parish work. In addition to those areas typically associated with seminary study—liturgy, music, preaching, teaching, counseling—a priest must also engage in human resource management (in particular with volunteers), office administration, mediation and negotiation, print and online communications, and not-for-profit administration. This is the short list.

Many of these expectations are quite legitimate, reflecting the authentic pastoral and administrative needs of the parish. A priest obviously cannot be in multiple places at the same time, and there is a limit to the amount of multitasking he will be able to do while still successfully carrying out the various tasks before him. To effectively meet these expectations, a priest must engage in an ongoing assessment and prioritization of wants and needs, roles and responsibilities.

A priest's hierarchy of expectations will vary to a degree from parish to parish. Furthermore, within a given parish they will change over the course of a year. For example, during Holy Week, when there are multiple services every day, a priest must focus more on what is expected of him as liturgical celebrant and preacher. During quieter times of the year, he can focus more on administrative or pedagogical tasks. These variances notwithstanding, the general principle holds.

A priest should not take on the task of assessing the multiple expectations related to his ministry alone. The Church's Holy Tradition is his primary guide in this work; chief among all his mandates, the priest must reflect the Good News of Christ in every aspect of his work, in actions as well as words. Directives of his diocesan bishop, as well as those of his local synod, provide the framework in which a priest will conduct his pastoral duties. Furthermore, cultivating a relationship with a spiritual father, a more experienced senior priest, or a peer in pastoral ministry (or all of the aforementioned) is invaluable in the work of discerning between expectations that are realistic and reasonable and those that are neither.

It can also be valuable for a priest to canvass parishioners, if only informally, to get a better understanding of their expectations of him as their pastor. The priest might not necessarily agree with all of these identified expectations, nor does he have to attempt to meet all of them. A priest is not required to cater to every need of every person who approaches him in ministry. The parish priest is the leader of his community and has the responsibility of setting a vision for his parish and guiding the faithful as they fulfill it, making changes as necessary along the way. Nevertheless, understanding the framework of pastoral expectations that his parishioners bring to church with them will help him understand how to develop and fulfill the mission of his parish.

Parish life presents another level of expectations that exists below the surface of the day-to-day work of a congregation. Christian communities define themselves as families. Priests and bishops are called "Father." Lay believers, both in monasteries and "in the world," identify themselves as "brothers" and "sisters." This language originates in the New Testament itself (cf. 1 Cor. 4:5).

Viewing the Church within the framework of family implies a level of intimacy, trust, and compassion that human beings need in order to thrive and that Christ himself clearly calls for among his disciples. Grounded in the Fatherhood of God, each believer is part of a family of faith. It is important to understand that spiritual families, just like biological families, have their own particular issues, challenges, and dysfunctions. A review of the content of St. Paul's letters to the Corinthian church will demonstrate that this is a phenomenon as old as the Church herself.

The reality of the fallen human condition means that families of all types are composed of broken individuals. In fact, broken individuals are to be expected in parish families, since people come to church seeking the healing that she offers. St. John Chrysostom is often quoted here as telling people, "Draw near to the Church, for she is not a court for criminals but a hospital for the infirm." Everyone involved in the life of a parish, including its clergy, brings with them their own particular dysfunctions (obsessions, compulsions, addictions—that is, "passions"). Through his Church, Christ offers all people a therapeutic regime "for the healing of soul and body" (Orthodox Pre-Communion Prayer).

Personal history plays a critical role in the types of expectations that one person will place on another. Many times these expectations act at an unconscious or preconscious level. It was one of several great discoveries of Freud, and has been confirmed by many psychologists since him, that in studying interpersonal relationships—whether in parishes, families, or a therapist's office—one often detects a phenomenon known as "transference." Robert Wicks, a contemporary pastoral counselor, explains transference as "projecting the dynamics of one significant relationship onto another, unrelated one."[2] A common experience of transference is when one immediately has a strong positive or negative emotional reaction to someone that one has met for the first time.

Given that an Orthodox priest is called "Father," the obvious example of transference in a pastoral relationship comes when parishioners project the dynamics of their relationships with their fathers onto their relationships with their priests. Transference can evoke either positive or negative psychodynamics in a relationship. People who have had negative experiences with their fathers can react to their priests in extremely negative ways—with distrust, defiance, and even aggression. Conversely, someone who felt starved for attention from his father might go out of his way to be the "model parishioner," attending every service, volunteering for every committee or ministry group, and offering his priest unquestioning support, thereby acting out his need for fatherly approval.

When transference results in a negative dynamic, it is perhaps easier to identify. However, positive transference reactions, although a much lighter load to bear, can also be disabling and unhealthy. In both cases, transference involves a set of unrealistic, potentially toxic expectations about the nature and purpose of the pastoral relationship.

In some respects, positive transference reactions can be more harmful than negative reactions. One possible problem is that the priest might, either inadvertently or consciously, enable the relationship, usually because of his own often unconscious needs to have an adoring "child" or disciple. But this relationship can be very fraught and can change swiftly and brutally if, for example, the parishioner deems the priest as not meeting his or her needs and as having become a "disappointment." This latter situation is the source of the pastoral axiom "The first person to invite you for lunch when you start a parish assignment will likely be the first one to have you for dinner."

The most unhealthy type of expectations are ones that are asserted without ever being clearly articulated, as in situations of transference. Transference, therefore, must be identified as soon as possible; once identified, clear steps must be taken to mitigate its impact on the pastoral relationship. Dealing forthrightly with transference dynamics might be met with resistance and negativity, but such dynamics, although uncomfortable, are far better than enabling potentially toxic interpersonal exchanges.

Priests must also be aware of how the significant relationships of their own personal histories affect their present interactions with people—what psychologists since Freud have called countertransference. In caregiving settings, caregivers (therapists, priests, and others) can project upon the people with whom they are working psychodynamics originating in important relationships in their early development. Like transference, countertransference can evoke either positive or negative reactions. Again, neither are healthy when neglected and allowed to develop. Vigilance and discernment are required in every pastoral relationship.

Returning again to the question of expectations, we can see that a priest not only faces multiple external expectations; many expectations are self-imposed. Thus, the first set of expectations a priest must deal with is his own. From his first days in seminary, the priest carries with him expectations of what his pastoral ministry will look like. Most of these subjective impressions are challenged (if not completely removed—at times unceremoniously) sometime in the first year of his first parish assignment. This is not necessarily a negative thing.

An ongoing source of inner tension for a priest can result from the discord between his impressions of what he should be doing in his parish assignment and the reality of what he actually can do. Every priest is a unique individual with his own particular strengths and weaknesses. For some priests, delivering a sermon comes more easily than for others. There are priests with very good singing voices, and there are ones who have difficulty carrying a tune. Some priests are very good in large groups of people, and others are more introverted. Any given priest must realistically accept his particular set of strengths and weaknesses. He must nurture his strengths and try to minimize his weaknesses where realistically possible. He also has to be willing to accept limitations that are beyond his control.

The late protopresbyter Thomas Hopko published a popular list called the "55 Maxims of the Christian Life." In the "55 Maxims," Fr. Thomas wrote, "Pray as you can, not as you think you must."[3] This principle provides sound advice for priests as they engage in pastoral ministry. Focusing on what they subjectively believe they should do, regardless of whether this is realistic for them and their particular setting, will eventually lead to frustration. Focusing instead on what they *can* do—depending on their particular aptitudes and parish situation—is a way of setting up healthy expectations for their work in that community.

What has been said on this point applies to all priests, both married and celibate. In addition to the various expectations associated with their pastoral ministry, married clergy face the expectations and responsibilities of their roles as husbands and fathers. They also carry a set of subjective expectations—realistic or not—of the behavior and attitudes of their wives and children as clergy families. In managing these varied expectations, conflicts are inevitable.

The nature of pastoral ministry requires priests to be "on" when their parishioners are "off"—typically evenings and weekends. This necessitates that the priests be out when the rest of their families are also enjoying their off time. Married priests face the constant need to balance their roles, sharing their time and energy with family and parishioners as needed. Both his parish and his family have legitimate claims to a priest's time and attention and legitimate expectations that he will actively engage in their respective lives. Inevitably, someone in that equation will feel slighted. Sacrifices must be made in both directions to keep a balance. The priest will have to be away from his wife and children at important family times, trusting that they will understand the need. This will be much easier if they also see their husband or father step away from his parish work in favor of his family at times, trusting that his parishioners will understand that need. Balancing parish and family needs is a delicate task requiring diplomacy, intuition, and attentiveness; the term "balance" is indeed fitting.

When a priest is facing difficulties in his parish, it is in some respects more stressful for his family than it is for him. What a priest can look upon philosophically, his family might have difficulty addressing, especially if a parishioner's behavior involves mistreatment of their husband or father. Since the priest is "on the ground" in such situations, he is directly aware of who is involved and of the general course the issue will take. The priest's family typically observes such issues one step removed from them. Often this means that the family is left "filling in the blanks" with their own assumptions and imaginings.

Furthermore, whether intentional or not, there are those who see the ministry of the priest as extending to his family, although it might be more accurate to say that they see his family as an extension of his pastoral ministry. Their pastoral expectations of the priest are to some degree placed upon his wife and children as well. This is particularly true for priests' wives. The spouse of anyone in a leadership position has to be ready to assume a certain level of leadership, too. An obvious example in the United States is the tradition of calling the wives of presidents "first ladies" and expecting them to support and perhaps even champion their husbands' policies—as well as initiatives of their own.

A similar dynamic plays out in the lives of married Orthodox priests, as evidenced by the fact that every Orthodox culture has its own particular term for a priest's wife (Greek: "Presbytera," Slavonic: "Matushka," Balkan: "Popadia," Arabic: "Khouria"). In the life of an Eastern Orthodox parish, the role of the priest's wife cannot be understated. Her particular perspective and position of authority are unlike those of any other layperson in the congregation. However, while a priest spends several years preparing for his ministry, there is little, if any, formal training for priests' wives and much that they have to learn solely from experience. Furthermore, no two people are the same, and thus each priest's wife has the task of discerning how she fits into the life of her parish, both as her own person, with a specific set of talents and experiences, and also as a part of the pastoral team that a clergy couple is.

Some priests' wives immerse themselves in the life of a parish, singing in the choir, teaching religious education, and taking part in other parish ministries and initiatives. The wives of other priests take less active roles in their parishes. The involvement of a priest's wife in her parish can change over time. A mother of small children will take a different role than a woman whose children are grown and out on their own. In a healthy parish situation, a priest's wife will have the freedom to engage in parish life as she feels called to do and is able. (Expectations that she will carry out her role in the exact same way that her predecessor[s] did are unrealistic and unhealthy.) That said, a priest's wife needs to accept that, regardless of how involved or disengaged she might wish to be, her role in parish life is unique and unavoidable.

The children of priests face unique experiences in parish life. On the one hand, a "priest's kid" (PK) tends to have a unique sense of ownership of the parish. Especially when they are younger, PKs spend a lot of family time at church; thus the church is very much a second home to them.

On the other hand, PKs face a degree and type of expectation unlike those of other children in the parish. The children of a priest were born into this role, with no say in it. Believing that all happens in the life of a Christian by the hand of God, one can find assurance in the fact that any children born into a priest's family are placed there by Providence, and therefore they belong in that family situation. However, explaining this to a PK, especially a teenaged one, may not be so easy.

The lasting impressions that people have of the Church come from their interactions with people of that faith. In the Gospel of John, Jesus tells his followers, "By this men will know that you are my disciples, if you have love for each other" (John 13:35). Although the term "martyr" popularly refers to someone who has died for his or her faith, the strict definition of the word, from the Greek μάρτυρός, means "witness." Thus every Christian, whether aware of it or not, is a witness to the faith. Children of clergy are particularly attuned to the witness of the people in their parish. Positive experiences in their parishes lead to positive impressions of the Church. Conversely, experiences of parishioners' poor treatment of their fathers (or themselves) can play a part in clergy children's abandoning the faith entirely.

Adolescent children of priests can experience an intense pressure as a result of their fathers' vocation. Adolescents possess a deep need to fit in with their peers—or, conversely, a need to not stand out. Given the small numbers of Orthodox Christians in North America, the odds are very high that a priest's son or daughter will be the only PK in their peer group, even at church. This unique family situation, combined with an increasing lack of awareness of Christianity and Church life, can make the children of priests feel very singled out. Many PKs react to this by going out of their way to prove that they are "normal" kids, which has led to the stereotype of clergy kids as the biggest troublemakers in a community.

As parents, the best thing that a priest and his wife can do for their children is to model authentic Christian behavior, always emphasizing that any expectations of their behavior and character exist because they are Christians, not specifically because their father is a priest. The most important impression that PKs need to get from their families is that they belong to a God who loves them, calls them to their own unique place in his Providence, and always offers them his healing and transforming grace.

Another key characteristic of adolescence is an inclination to separate one's identity from that of one's parents. In older cultures, certainly in the cultures of Orthodox "old countries," identity was always framed around the group. A person had to find his or her place within the framework of the collective identity of his or her people—where they came from, what they did, and where they were going.

Modern Western culture holds the identity of the individual self as the highest value. Furthermore, modernity asserts that an important step in becoming a fully actualized person is to step away from the nuclear family in terms of both geographic proximity and the rejection of its common identity and values. With the children of clergy seeing the church as their second home and parishioners as extended family, the implications of this cultural pressure for the family of a priest to "leave home" are obvious.

The various objective and subjective expectations outlined in this chapter relating to priests also apply to some degree to a married priest's wife and family as well. This is not always fair, but it is axiomatic nonetheless. The greatest advantage of married priests is that they are not alone in assessing and addressing these multiple layers of expectations that they face. A married priest's greatest ally in his pastoral ministry, and throughout every part of his life, is his wife. The perspective and counsel of one's wife is invaluable. When I was still fairly new to the priesthood, a senior priest shared with me a piece of advice that has consistently proven helpful throughout my ministry: "Listen to your wife."

As both a married priest and a PK, I have been intimately exposed to the lives of married clergy, quite literally, for my entire life. Although a priest's family has a unique set of struggles and issues, they are not insurmountable.

The ministry of a priest and his family life can be profound sources of blessing. Christ promises that whenever two or three gather in his name he is in their midst (Matt. 18:20). Christ the Good Shepherd can transform the life of the priest as he does the lives of those to whom the priest ministers.

When I was still fairly new in the priesthood, I was considering a possible change in pastoral assignment. I was very unsure of what path to take, and this was causing in me a great deal of turmoil. But I found peace in part by listening to the same priest who told me to always listen to my wife. He reminded me that, whatever decision I made, "God looks after those who serve him." This is an undeniable truth, attested to by countless clergy over the generations. His help is always on offer. From the very first moments of our ordination until the end of our lives, we receive "divine grace, which always heals that which is infirm and completes that which is lacking." These words from the Byzantine ordinal offer great consolation throughout a priest's ministry.

An important factor determining how a priest will experience his ministry is the degree to which he can discern and manage the subjective and objective expectations he faces in his pastoral ministry. Buddhism speaks of a phenomenon called the "monkey mind." When trying to focus on a thought, one finds that one's mind leaps from idea to idea like a monkey leaping from tree to tree. If a priest cannot manage the various expectations putting pressure on him, both legitimate and unrealistic, this is an apt way of describing how he will experience his ministry. He will leap from task to task, priority to priority, like a monkey leaping from tree to tree. This is unsustainable, and burnout is the inevitable result. A priest who can manage expectations will still feel their pressure from the various parts of his life. He will, however, be able to assess their urgency, priority, and, most importantly, their authenticity, with greater clarity.

The one set of expectations to which the priest must always attend is that of God, who called him to the ministries of priest, husband, and father. These expectations are discovered through prayer; through the good counsel of his spiritual father, his bishop, and his peers; and in his relationships with family and parishioners. Strengthening his own faith, the priest comes to trust that God will cover the gaps in his broken humanity, and he will discover that, both at church and at home, through him God can accomplish things both great and unexpected.

Notes

1. Before proceeding with this discussion, I offer one stylistic note: As this chapter focuses on Orthodox Christian married clergy, it will speak simply of "priests." This is purely for the sake of simplifying the discussion. To anyone involved in ministry, whether directly or indirectly—including bishops, deacons, and laypeople engaged in pastoral work—the issues faced by married priests and their families are not unfamiliar. Such issues are not unique to Eastern Orthodox clergy, either, or even to Christian clergy, for that matter.

2. R. Wicks, D. Parsons, and D. Capps, eds., *Clinical Handbook of Pastoral Counseling*, vol. 1 (Mahwah, NJ: Paulist Press, 1993).

3. These maxims have been published in various places online. See here: https://orthodoxtacoma.com/55maxims.

PART V

Theology

CHAPTER FIFTEEN

Celibacy and the Married Priesthood
Rediscovering the Spousal Mystery

Thomas J. Loya

I come from a long line of married priests on both sides of my family, which can be traced back for many generations. I am, however, a celibate priest, and there are other celibate priests and religious as well in my family.

During my first year as a seminarian, I had the occasion to attend an event at a parish where my paternal grandfather, Fr. John Loya, by then deceased, had been pastor for many years. As I was approaching the parish house, I could see that it was alive with the usual activity of clergy arriving for any significant parish event. Suddenly in that moment, I had an experience that I was not prepared for but that would be profoundly revelatory for me. In the same way that certain familiar smells can bring us back in time so as to make the past seem absolutely real and current, the sight of the clergy buzzing about the porch of this rectory suddenly transported me back in my mind and heart to my childhood, when I would come to visit "Grandpa" at this house, "his" house. This experience was more than just a memory. I was actually gripped by a profound feeling of the confusion and even anger of a child. The little Tommy deep within me was saying, "What are all these people doing in my Grandpa's house? This is *his* house! Where is my Grandpa?"

As I eventually came out of this moment, I was actually a bit shaken by it. I was even embarrassed at the poignancy of my inner child welling up in me although I was now a young adult. But over time, as I would reflect on this experience, I realized that it had revealed to me that the heritage of a priestly family allowed me to acquire a phenomenological understanding of what may well be the single greatest genius of Eastern Christian spirituality—living in the "both/and," in the very meaning of mystery.

Living in the Both/And

Church and family, while distinct, were at the same time one and the same for me. In my memory I was at a rectory that was simultaneously Grandpa's house. It was both/and, not either/or. Going to visit relatives for me meant going to a parish house. Dinner conversation was conversation about God and the Greek Catholic Church. My grandfather was married to one woman and yet, at the same time, in the essence of his priesthood he was espoused to all, to his mystical bride, the Church. There was *distinction* but not *dichotomy*, and this was my life's experience. It was perfectly normal to me, perfectly integrated. I was perfectly at home in the world of complementary realities, of paradox. This man was grandfather *and* priest, married but yet, by virtue of his priesthood, witnessing at the same time to the eschatological reality in which we shall "neither marry nor be given in marriage, but are like angels in heaven" (Matthew 22:30).

Growing up as a good "uniate" boy, I was also naturally completely familiar with the all-celibate Latin clergy. There was never even the slightest phenomenological difference for me between the priesthood of my married grandfather and that of a celibate priest of the Latin Church; my married grandfather was no less a priest to me than the celibate Latin priest who, equally, was no less a priest to me because he was celibate and not married like my grandfather. Such was my experience of the genuine catholicity of the Church.

Such catholicity today means that the discussion about the restoration or preservation of the practice of married clergy in the New World cannot simply be about a particular discipline of the Church. It cannot be treated compartmentally. Particularly in the New World, those Eastern

Catholic churches that have not yet begun to recover the tradition of ordaining married men cannot just start doing so without attending to some other issues.

I believe that the subject of a married priesthood and celibacy for the Eastern Catholic churches in the New World can be adequately approached only by rediscovering the genius that is particularly ours, the ability to live in the both/and rather than the either/or. Through the lens of the both/and we will see that a married priesthood (in fact, marriage itself) can be spoken of only in relation to celibacy, to monasticism. The two actually interpenetrate and subsist in each other. They are bound by the one, same reality; they are two complementary ways to be espoused. In the words of Pope John Paul II in his book on the theology of the body (which I had the privilege of hearing him deliver in Rome live and in person) "in particular the consciousness of the 'spousal' meaning of the body constitutes the fundamental component of human existence in the world."[1] If we call for and make an effort to restore the practice of a married priesthood in the New World without at the same time calling for the renewal of monasticism and a positive articulation of celibacy, our approach will be only superficially "Eastern" and not true to the real Eastern genius for integration. The results could be unfruitful, perhaps even disastrous.

This is really a call for an entire renewal of our understanding of theological anthropology, of the revelatory value of gender, and especially of the eschatological dimension inherent in marriage, priesthood, and celibacy and how all of this is lived out in the very liturgy of the Church. Approaching the subject of a married priesthood in an integrated way will help to protect the wider restoration of the practice among Eastern Catholic churches in the New World from being superficial, naïve, and awkward. It will also help to prevent a stubborn resistance to its restoration born of pragmatism, Latinization, Westernization, fear, a desire for control, or recycled Manicheanism. Furthermore, an integrated approach to this topic will also help to protect it from being co-opted into a so-called liberal or progressive agenda that simplistically sees a married clergy as a vaccination against clergy sex abuse and will further demand the ordination of women and the recognition of same-sex "marriage"—before indulging in an aversion to ascetical discipline and a fundamental narcissism. But, on an even larger scale, an integrated discussion of the restoration of a married priesthood engaged in through the consideration of the both/and and through the rediscovery of the spousal mystery can provide essential insights into the worlds of human sexuality, priesthood, pastoral ministry, and ecclesiology.

Leaving It to the Eastern Churches

The restoration of a married priesthood in those Eastern Catholic churches that have abandoned this tradition under Latinizing pressure must come about exclusively as a result of decisions internal to the respective Eastern Catholic churches themselves. Otherwise it will be, once again, Latinization, if in reverse this time. Other than, of course, respecting proper canonical considerations, there is no need for the Eastern Catholic churches to "check in" with Latin bishops (as Pope Francis, in late 2014, agreed),[2] nor to defer to the preferences of the Latin hierarchy on the issue of married priests in the Eastern Catholic churches. This issue is not the prerogative of the Latin Church, which remains merely one church (albeit, of course, the largest), *sui iuris*, alongside dozens of Eastern Catholic churches.

It is curious that usually when statements are put out, issues addressed, programs initiated, special theme days and days of prayer promoted, and even catechisms published by the United States Conference of Catholic Bishops (USCCB), the references and targeted audience for these things are entirely Latin Catholics. The Eastern Catholic churches are hardly players at all in most of these endeavors. The Eastern Catholic churches and their issues remain essentially invisible and inconsequential most of the time to most of the Latin Church. Yet from time to time the custom of having a married priesthood in the tiny Eastern Catholic churches suddenly moves front and center and somehow achieves an ostensible impact on the enormously larger Latin Church in America.

Confronting the Grave Injustice

When confronted with such an almost hysterical prospect, it is important to consider the recent history related to this issue. When the Latin hierarchy, in concert with Rome, stopped the practice and presence of married priests in the Eastern Catholic churches in the "New World," the grave injustice was not simply that one church encroached on a tradition of another. It was not that a bunch of men had their wives taken away from them. What was missed by the Latins and not even fully recognized by the Eastern Catholic churches themselves to this day was that a married priesthood was part of the very structure and character of the Eastern Catholic churches. Removing the custom of having married priests was like kicking one of the four legs of a table out from under it and still expecting that table to stand normally. The table at best will wobble, and indeed the Eastern Catholic churches have been wobbling ever since the 1929 *Cum Data Fuerit* debacle. But the worst part of the grave injustice was that after kicking the leg out from under the Eastern Catholic churches, the Latin Church *offered nothing to replace that leg*. The Eastern Catholic churches to this day have never really been given—nor have they themselves established and articulated—a suitable replacement for the missing leg. Mandatory celibacy is largely seen by Eastern Catholic seminarians and priests as ahistorical injustice simply to be endured, however faithfully.

The wife and family of an Eastern Catholic pastor served as a built-in sense of community and support for the pastor and most of the time contributed significantly to the life and community of the parish. There was a great fraternity among the married priests' families, as their children could play together, grow up together, form lasting bonds, and even, as in the case of my own patrimony, meet their future spouses. A priest's own family was often his "staff"—his altar servers, housekeepers, and go-to people. My grandfather's brother, Fr. Steven Loya, had fifteen children; he sired his own staff and practically his own parish! Since eleven of his children were boys, he was never without an altar server, usher, cantor, custodian, or general errand boy. Two of Fr. Steven's sons became priests. The custom of having a married priesthood in the Eastern Catholic churches was anything but a sign of tolerance or legitimate concession to concupiscence. It was not bigamy, as some skeptics have actually said to me. *The married priesthood was part of the very character and structure of the Eastern Catholic churches.*

When, in the New World, the support system for an Eastern Catholic pastor (which we continue to assert was also part of the structure of the Eastern Catholic parish) was removed and the foreign structure of a celibate pastor was imposed, it was done at the hands of a Latin Church that had already known celibacy and its accompanying support systems for centuries. The typical Latin parish had volunteer and paid staff, housekeepers, cooks, a community of priests living in the same rectory, and religious orders living on or near campus working in the parish schools. Their vastly larger numbers meant that they had many more people to draw from to fill these roles, and many more still whose donations could be used to fund them.

By contrast, the vastly smaller Eastern Catholic parishes were saddled with a celibate clergy but no staff, becoming a type of pastoral anomaly. These priests were not married, nor were they monastics or associated with monasteries (as Eastern wisdom very nearly insists on for unmarried clergy). There was no real sense or structure for the personal community so vital to any human being, let alone for a celibate pastor in a situation particular to an Eastern Catholic parish. Practically speaking, the Eastern Catholic priest in the post-married-priest era was an ordained bachelor, and many of them lived as such—instead of offering themselves as real fathers, biological *and* spiritual.

The Wobbling Table

With the removal of the married priesthood from Eastern Catholic parishes and with it the removal of part of the structure of these churches, the character of both churches and clergy began to change. The state of being married tended to ensure that an Eastern Catholic parish would be led by priests who were essentially integrated as men. They naturally had to possess the qualities of being a man, a spouse, and a father. Authentic manhood finds its very definition and essence in priesthood. A dynamic, fruitful priesthood demands the very qualities that are part of deep authentic paternity. Priests are male and are called "Father" for very profound reasons, which are in vital need of rediscovery and renewal today.

I knew personally many of the Ruthenian Greek Catholic clergy who were among the last generation of married priests in America. Although they also had to be responsible for wives and children, these priests had a drive, virility, and fruitfulness in their ministries the likes of which our church in America has not seen since. There have, of course, been many celibate Eastern Catholic priests with characteristically masculine drives, a true sense of fatherhood and fruitfulness in their priesthoods. However, with the marriage factor now gone, there is no longer the built-in structure that helped to ensure the predominance of the integrated male candidate for the priesthood, and the profile of the Eastern Catholic priest in the New World began to change. We now add to this the so-called sexual revolution of the 1960s.

The fallout of that ghastly revolution brings to this discussion the proverbial "elephant in the room": the influx into seminaries, monasteries, the priesthood, and even the episcopacy in the New World of the sexually disintegrated and often gender-confused candidate. Many of the Eastern Catholic churches in the New World today find themselves in a struggle for survival. While there are flashes of brilliance to be sure, essentially we have become impotent and infertile. For the most part, the Eastern Catholic churches today are without the positive and dynamic, masculine, fatherly qualities of vision, initiative, courage, and zeal that once marked the leadership of these churches during the days of their married pastors. This is one important factor—alongside other, broader socioeconomic changes—leading us to no longer "put out in the deep" as we once did. Rarely today are we establishing new parishes, schools, and missions; rare is the growing parish today; and rare is the attempt to face these problems with creative, evangelical solutions.

Furthermore, like our Latin brethren, the Eastern churches were hit with the clergy sex abuse scandal. But it is worth noting that the two independent studies on clergy sexual abuse authorized by the American bishops revealed that the sex abuse scandal in America was not a phenomenon of pedophilia per se, but rather, more precisely, of *pederasty*, which is a subset of homosexual behavior.[3] I am suggesting here not that every priest who may have struggled with a sexually interpreted attraction to the same sex (homosexuality) committed acts of pederasty, but simply that the preponderance of sexual molestation cases themselves were homosexual in nature. Nor am I implying the naïve and simplistic solution of secular progressives that if we would just allow priests to be married, there would not be a sexual abuse problem. I am only illustrating that with the unjust removal of the married priesthood from the Eastern Catholic churches in America, the profile of the Eastern Catholic priesthood and parish was profoundly changed, rarely for the better. In a number of ways, a wound was opened in the Eastern churches, and, absent any real remedy, most of what rushed into that wound was not restorative and healing.

Restoring the Table Leg and the Spousal Mystery

The restoration of the table leg for Eastern Catholics in the New World cannot be a matter of just trying to retrieve the old leg. Too much has changed in our culture, and we have been away from the married priesthood for a long time. The women who might become wives of Eastern Catholic priests are not themselves likely to come from priestly families, as was the norm years ago and in the countries of origin of that tradition. And not just any woman will do as the wife of a priest. The trend of a career woman who just happens to be married to an Eastern Catholic priest is not going to adequately replace the missing table leg.

Simply ordaining married men to the priesthood will not ensure a priesthood of integrated men, as it once did. Vocations come from the soil of the culture, and the soil in the New World today has become "pornified" and polluted by the sexual revolution, secularism, and a growing moral relativism. Few candidates for either the celibate or the married priesthood today are untouched by this pollution. Something more is needed today: the renewal of monasticism. The entire question of a married priesthood and celibacy for the Eastern Catholic churches in the New World will go by way of the renewal of monasticism. In this we now return to that genius of the East that we referred to at the beginning of the chapter, that genius of living in the both/and.

The current consideration of the issue of a married priesthood for the Eastern Catholic churches tends to be fundamentally pragmatic: "Can we afford married priests and their families? What about the possibilities of divorce? It is not as easy to transfer a married pastor as it is a celibate one." In light of such pragmatism, monasticism is essentially regarded as nonessential. Yet the barometer of the health of a church, especially an Eastern church, is its monasticism.

Monasticism is the reservoir out of which this renewal (of marriage *and* priesthood) can spring. If we turn our attention to monasticism, the question of a married priesthood and even of the plentitude of vocations to the priesthood and religious life is likely to take care of itself. This is because monasticism takes the question of a married priesthood out of the constraints of the either/or. Monasticism, and with it a positive and adequate articulation of celibacy, raises the choice of being a celibate priest to the level of being perhaps as attractive as being a married priest. Instead of celibacy by default and injustice, as opposed to marriage with all of its attributes, which are naturally so much more desirable, both options become the same choice but in different ways. Each choice affirms the integrity of the other. They become two different choices as to how to live one and the same spousal mystery, mindful of the inescapable dimension of the eschatological. With this approach, the candidate for priestly celibacy, and of course for monasticism, must be every bit a man, spouse, and father as a married priest. Conversely, the married priest and his wife are reminded of the eschatological (monastic) dimension of their marriage and of his priesthood: although sacramentally married to one woman, he is at the same time the mystical spouse of the Church. This point becomes particularly critical in the New World, where the potential candidates for priestly wives do not come from a culture that knew and supported the married priest system in the past.

The celibate has to be a good "husband and father." This is the only thing that makes sense of his celibacy. Celibacy is not just a discipline of the Church. It is a way to live fully as a man, and as mystical father and spouse. Conversely, the married priest and his wife must ultimately be good "monks." This theological reality is something that as a boy I witnessed in my grandfather and in that entire marvelous fraternity of married priests that formed the character of my church years ago.

In his book *The Sacrament of Love*, Paul Evdokimov writes:

> Thus marriage includes within itself the monastic state.... The two converge as complementary aspects of the same virginal reality of the human spirit. The ancient Russian tradition viewed the time of engagement as a monastic novitiate. After the ceremony, a retreat in a monastery was prescribed for the newly married to prepare for entrance into their "nuptial priesthood." Monastic holiness and married holiness are the two faces of Tabor ... the two ways, contrary to human reason, are found to be inwardly united in the end, mysteriously identical. It is sufficiently clear by now that the best, and perhaps the only, method to fashion the value proper to matrimony is by comprehending the greatness of the meaning of monasticism. One will better understand the vocation of marriage in the light and school of monasticism.[4]

In his apostolic letter of 1995, *Orientale Lumen*, John Paul II said that "monasticism is the reference point for all of the baptized." In his monumental work on marriage and celibacy, known as the theology of the body, he further writes:

> Perfect conjugal love must be marked by the faithfulness and the gift to the one and only Bridegroom (and also by the faithfulness of the one Bridegroom to the one and only Bride) on which religious profession and priestly celibacy are based. In sum, the nature of the one as well as the other is "spousal," that is, expressed through the complete gift of self. The one as well as the other love tends to express that spousal meaning of the body, which has been inscribed "from the beginning" in the personal structure of man and woman.[5]

Our Latin brethren, who often have difficulty accepting that a priest can be sacramentally and mystically married at the same time, need look no further than the Byzantine liturgy. It is there that the spousal mystery is played out. From the vesting prayers to the design of classic Byzantine (and Western!) architecture to the *ad orientem* posture of the celebrant, the priest takes on the persona of both bride and bridegroom. Liturgy is the quintessential experience of living in the genius of the both/and. Liturgy gives us an experience of the eschatological, of the convergence of monasticism and marriage.

Seminary formation must focus on helping the candidate come to a deep understanding of the spousal meaning of his manhood. This will take the entire question of the married priesthood out of the realm of the either/or because the celibate priesthood and the married priesthood will become two very natural and attractive choices that coexist, interpenetrate each other, and mutually support each other. This will also require the reassessment of the current lives of celibate pastors and perhaps the creation of quasi-monastic communities or some type of structure that brings the lives of celibate Eastern clergy into closer conformity to the wisdom of the East on such matters. All of this, in turn, will be a sign of a truly integrated, renewed, and mature Church. Then the leg of the table will have been restored.

Conclusion

Bishop John Kudrick, recently retired from the Eparchy of Parma in the United States, has been the only Ruthenian bishop thus far to ordain a married man and to invite several married priests to serve in his eparchy. At the same time, Bishop Kudrick established a new women's monastery that specifically took the name Christ the Bridegroom Monastery because these female monastics are committed to living and modeling the spousal mystery and the interdependency of marriage and monasticism. As a priest of the Eparchy of Parma, I can testify that two of the most fruitful and dynamic forces in our eparchy are those emanating from the presence of these married priests and that of the young, vibrant women at Christ the Bridegroom Monastery.

In regard to the healing and resolution of the issue of married priests for the Eastern Catholic churches in the New World, it is time for these churches to ask Rome and our Latin brethren to wait outside as we close our doors for a while and take care of family business. Inside those doors we must reach into the depths of our own genius and be thoroughly rather than superficially Eastern in our ethos. Thus we need to live the liturgy deeply and to renew monasticism profoundly; in so doing we will discover a wellspring from which will come much wider renewal of every aspect of our lives. If the Eastern Catholic churches can seriously and authentically tend to their own family business, when they emerge from behind those closed doors they will be able to offer to our Latin brethren—indeed to the whole Church and to the whole world—an immense and long-awaited gift.

Notes

1. Pope John Paul II, *Man and Woman He Created Them: A Theology of the Body*, trans. Michael Waldstein (Boston: Pauline Books, 2006), 189.
2. See the editor's introduction to this volume for details, along with the chapter by the canonist Alexander Laschuk.
3. On this see Patrick Guinan, *After Asceticism: Sex, Prayer, and Deviant Priests* (Palos Park, IL: Linacre Institute, 2006).
4. Paul Evdokimov, *The Sacrament of Love* (Crestwood, NY: St. Vladimir's Seminary Press, 2011), 72–73.
5. John Paul II, *Man and Woman He Created Them*, 78:4.

CHAPTER SIXTEEN

Married Priests

At the Heart of Tradition

Lawrence Cross and Basilio Petrà

Many people are surprised to learn that the Church has had married priests from the time of the apostles. In fact, married clergy were common even in the West until the changes introduced by the Gregorian reforms to the papacy in the eleventh century. Against such a historical background, in this chapter we seek to demonstrate that both the married and the celibate priesthood stand on the very same theological foundations and are expressions of one and the same mystery in different vocational contexts within the life of the Church.

In a recent local publication, Bishop Cesare Bonivento of Vanimo in Papua New Guinea, recently retired, argued that years ago the Second Council of Trullo (691) became "the ridge of separation between the Eastern and Western Churches in the question of priestly continence."[1] We should note, first of all, that the "ridge of separation" is to be located in the eleventh century, not the seventh. Theological and magisterial insistence on the connection between celibacy and the ordained priesthood flows from the era of the so-called Gregorian reformation. Following the Gregorian epoch, the Latin Church worked on the principle that the "ordained priesthood" automatically demanded celibacy. Such a demand not only survived the Second Vatican Council but also came to be even more strongly emphasized in the years following it.

The Council had, in fact, given an ecclesial and theological dignity to the married clergy. It held that married clergy had gained a greatly esteemed place in the history of the Church and should be honored as an authentic priesthood. Like the celibate priesthood, it arises from a divine call and from an ecclesial inspiration. The Council also recognized that celibacy has its own special theological significance and remains an ecclesiastical law. More recent statements, however, moved into a more restrictive position.

In the apostolic exhortation *Pastores dabo vobis* (*PDV*), which appeared in 1992, John Paul II formally affirmed that there is an objectively founded link between celibacy and priesthood. He does not speak, in historical terms, in reference to the legal requirement of celibacy for Latin priests in accordance with its particular traditional theological, pastoral, spiritual, and practical principles. In *PDV* he takes a different tack by arguing for celibacy from the very meaning of ordination itself: sacramental ordination configures the priest ontologically to Christ, the head, shepherd, and bridegroom of the Church. This ontological characterization finds its proper expression in celibacy.[2] By implication, the married priesthood must appear as abnormal or a lesser form of priestly life in that it lacks its proper celibate expression.

Before Vatican II, few theologians would have ventured to assert such an opinion. When the principal author of this chapter alerted the Jesuit priest Ivan Fucek, who was then secretary of the commission for the Eastern code—a great canonist, a person of great humanity and science, and secretary of the Pontifical Council for the Interpretation of Legislative Texts—to the novelty of *PDV* in this respect, he registered surprise and disbelief. The same reaction was found in others who clearly remembered centuries of theological manuals according to which the requirement of priestly celibacy is clearly stated to be part of ecclesiastical law. In contrast, the post-conciliar position of *PDV* is quite novel. It surfaces again in *Tota ecclesia* (1994), the Congregation for the Clergy's Directory for the Ministry and the Life of Priests. It is extended in other ways, for example, in courses conducted by means of monthly video conferences such as the forty-sixth world video conference on the theme Celibacy and the Paternity of the Priest that was organized for 5 April 2005 by the Congregation for the Clergy; this gathering brought together theologians from Rome,

New York, Moscow, Bogotà, Madrid, Taiwan, Sydney, Manila, Johannesburg, and Regensburg.³

Two months prior to the video conference, the then-prefect of the Congregation for the Clergy, Cardinal Darío Castrillón Hoyos, gave an interview that subsequently appeared in *Dossier on the Clergy*, a publication of the agency *Fides*. The prefect's reply to the first two questions raised in the interview is revealing. He was asked if priestly celibacy was only a question of ecclesiastical discipline, and therefore modifiable, or whether there was a special bond between priesthood and celibacy. The cardinal emphatically answered by saying that "celibacy was always considered by the Church as a fitting companion to the priestly life. There exists in fact a strict bond between celibacy and priestly ordination, a sacrament that ontologically configures the priest to Jesus Christ, head and bridegroom of his Church."⁴ The cardinal, however, did admit the existence of "the difficulties and the objections raised from many sides and throughout the centuries about understanding and embracing this gift," but he claimed that "the teaching of the Church, even after the last Council, has reiterated that there exist theological reasons...which manifest the intimate link of celibacy to the ordained ministry." He agreed that priestly celibacy is indeed an ecclesiastical law, not "an arbitrary imposition of the Church." Rather, "the ecclesiastical law of celibacy has its roots in the mystery of Christ and his Church."

Asked about the theological reasons for priestly celibacy, the cardinal enumerated what he called "three principles of a biblical-theological nature," naming them as Christological, ecclesiological, and eschatological principles: Christological, because Jesus "lived a celibate life, asked his apostles to imitate him and to follow him with an undivided heart"; ecclesiological, because "the priest as sacred minister of Christ is called upon to love the Church in the all-embracing and exclusive manner whereby Christ, head and bridegroom, has loved her"; and eschatological, because "the priest prefigures and anticipates in this world the communion and the total and final gift of Christ to his Church in eternity." The cardinal rounded this off with a citation from John Paul II's *Rise, Let Us Be on Our Way* and introduced the theme of what John Paul II calls spiritual paternity.⁵ The cardinal considers the link between celibacy and spiritual paternity particularly appropriate and beautiful: "Celibacy, in fact, provides the fullest opportunity to live out this type of fatherhood: chaste and totally dedicated to Christ and to his Virgin Mother. Unconstrained by any personal solicitude for a family, a priest can dedicate himself with his whole heart to his pastoral responsibilities" (140–141). The claim for an objectively founded connection between celibacy and priesthood is linked to and reinforced by the claim to ontological change in the being of the person at ordination. But the use of the terms "ontological" and "ontologically" is novel and misleading.[6] The fathers of Nicaea in 325 agonized over the use of ομοουσιος (consubstantial) in the creed. They realized that it was a risk to introduce a philosophical term with no biblical or theological pedigree into the deliberations on the question of the identity of being in the Holy Trinity. But the term was eventually employed since no other expression could be found to express the orthodox faith within the problematic context that had emerged. Now, a similar degree of caution should be exercised before using the term "ontological change." Strictly speaking, it denotes a change in being resulting in a new reality or mode of being in the world. Admittedly, "ontological" is often used very loosely and in areas other than theology. It suggests "different"—often paired with "ontological" in a kind of tautology.

An example of how this word is generally understood in theological circles occurred during the first visit to the United States of the Ecumenical Patriarch Bartholomew of Constantinople in 1991. In a speech at Georgetown University, he said that the separation between the Eastern and Western churches was not merely one of geography, structure, or religious law. Rather, he declared, "the manner in which we exist has become ontologically different." Ecumenical panic ensued on both sides. The patriarch later declared he did not intend this literally. He meant something like "very different." But that is not the use current in the papal and curial documents referred to.

The deepest theological objection to the novel assertion that an ontological change takes place in a man at ordination is that it runs counter to an orthodox understanding of the Incarnation itself; that it is insipiently *monophysite* in minimizing and distorting the place and function of the sacred humanity of Christ in the work of redemption.[7] The Divine Word received his humanity from Mary, the virgin of Nazareth. The humanity offered to God through Mary is not a minimized or spiritualized humanity, not something other than the humanity of Adam. The whole wonder of the Incarnation is that God did not choose to redeem mankind through an act of pure divine power. Rather, the instrument by which the human race is redeemed is our very human nature itself assumed by the

Son of God. Following the pattern of the Incarnation, the sacraments of the Church, through which the grace of the Holy Spirit flows to heal and deify humanity, are also founded upon the things of earth and of the creation. In contrast to this, the proponents of ontological change would find little amiss with the insipiently monophysite stance of no less a person than the popular pre–Vatican II writer Abbot Vonier, who wrote: "The world of the sacraments is a new world, created by God entirely apart from the natural and even from the spiritual world.... Neither in heaven nor on earth is there anything like the sacraments.... They have their own form of existence, their own psychology, their own grace.... We must understand that the idea of the sacraments is something entirely 'sui generis.'"[8] The Eastern approach to the matter, always liturgical in nature, following the principle of *lex orandi, lex credendi*, clarifies what a priest is and what occurs at ordination. At the great entrance in the Byzantine Divine Liturgy, the priest or bishop prays, "By the power of the Holy Spirit, make me worthy—since I am clothed with the grace of the priesthood—to stand before your holy altar and consecrate your sacred and immaculate body and precious blood." An ontologically changed being is not speaking here, but *your sinful and unprofitable servant* to whom the Holy Spirit is faithful because of the grace bestowed by that same Holy Spirit at ordination. The ordination prayers say this clearly. The Christian priest is no shaman, which the use of *ontological change* can imply. Rather, "divine Grace, which always heals that which is infirm, and completes that which is wanting, elevates, through the laying-on of hands, the most devout [Subdeacon to Deacon, Deacon to Priest, etc.]. Wherefore, let us pray for him, that the Grace of the All-Holy Spirit may come upon him." The second prayer at ordination makes it even clearer: "Do you, the same Lord, fill with the gift of your Holy Spirit this man whom it has pleased you to advance to the degree of Priest, that he may be worthy to stand in innocence before your Altar, to proclaim the Gospel of your Kingdom, to minister the word of your truth, to offer you spiritual gifts and sacrifices, to renew your people through the bath of regeneration?"

Clearly it is the Holy Spirit who will make up in a real way (that is to say, in the ontology of the spirit's action that is not merely a logical or imputative consideration) whatever is lacking in this unworthy candidate.

It is not only the liturgy that contradicts the assertion that there is an essential link between ordained priesthood and celibacy. The scriptures and the developing tradition also provide no support for ontological change. The biblical references to ordination speak only of a special grace conferred by the laying on of hands: "Do not neglect the spiritual gift (charisma) given you when the elders ... laid their hands on you" (1 Tim. 4:14), and "Stir into flame the gift from God which is in you through the laying on of my hands" (2 Tim. 1:6). Clearly a special gift comes upon the person at ordination, but not a change in his being.

The developing tradition confirms this. The *Decretum pro Armenis* (*DH* 1326) declares: "Effectus (scil. ordinis) augmentum gratiae, ut quis sit idoneus minister." The Council of Trent (*DH* 1766) says: "Cum Scripturae testimonio, apostolica traditione et Patrum unanimi consensus perspicuum sit, per sacrum ordinationem, quae verbis et signis exterioribus perficitur, gratiam conferri." Vatican II writings likewise speak of the full power bestowed on the presbyter, not of a change in his being: "Sacra ordinis potestate pollerent Sacrificium offerendi et peccata remittendi" (*Presb. Ordinis* 2). The "*indelebis*" character has as an effect "ut in persona Christi Capitis agere valeant" (*Presb. Ordinis* 2), but not that they are transformed into something different: "Presbyteri Novi Testamenti, vocatione quidem et ordinatione sua quodam modo in sinu Populi Dei segregantur, non tamen ut separentur" (*Presb. Ordinis* 3). Even the most famous statement of the Second Vatican Council on the presbyterate affirms that "it differs in essence not in grade only from the priesthood of the faithful" and finishes with the remark that they are referred one to the other: "Sacerdotium autem commune fidelium et sacerdotium ministeriale seu hierarchicum, licet essentia et non gradu tantum differant, ad invicem tamen ordinantur" (*Lumen gentium* 10). Finally, as to celibacy, the Council provides the most important statement, which is in direct opposition to ontologists: "Perfecta et perpetua propter Regnum caelorum continentia ... non exigitur quidem a sacerdotio suapte natura" (*Presb. Ordinis* 16), a statement that Pope John Paul II repeated in his general audience of 17 July 1993, that "celibacy is not required by the very nature of priesthood" (Documentation catholique, 19.9.1993, pp. 760f).

However, all this was sidelined by the world video conference and the interview with the cardinal-prefect noted above. Both show the extent to which Rome's theology of celibacy has changed. The unqualified assertion of an essential link between priesthood and celibacy necessarily places the Eastern tradition of married clergy on the outside. It cannot imagine that the real or ontological meaning of ordination is diminished by married life.

While the Roman congregations proceeded peacefully to propagate the new approach of *Pastores dabo vobis*, the Eastern Catholic churches, and in particular the Congregation for the Eastern Churches, did nothing to affirm the reality, theological and historical, of the married priesthood. It, too, like the celibate priesthood, originates from the direct will of God and constitutes a life of fidelity to the Lord.

Canonical regulations dealing with the remarriage of priests and the celibacy required of bishops do indeed indicate a certain emphasis on celibacy even in the East. But there is a further consideration: Does the very persistence of a married clergy—always strenuously defended—lack any positive theological significance as a genuine realization of the ordained priesthood and an authentic ecclesial vocation?

Understanding the Theological Foundation of the Married Presbyterate

The first thing to consider is that the Eastern tradition has maintained a married priesthood in fidelity to the apostolic mandate in the pastoral letters of the Pauline corpus, 1 Timothy 3:2 and Titus 1:6. Consequently, the analogy between management of the home and management of the church, highlighted in the pastoral letters, has always been clearly kept in mind. If one can be a good spouse and parent, this is a solid indication of one's ability to manage the ecclesial family as well. The logic of the pastoral letters indicates that the married priesthood reveals the family character of the ecclesial community. Consequently, the criterion for discerning the suitability of candidates for the priesthood is precisely their ability to be good husbands and fathers. While this is to be understood within the strengths and limitations of first-century family culture, it is still the template for understanding the meaning of the married clergy in the unfolding of tradition.

The pastoral letters presume a married priesthood. The meaning of the priestly ministry is analogically related to a husband's care for his spouse and to a father's responsibility for his children. A priest's family life, by being a shining example of Christian life, models, as it were, the presbyter's relationship to the ecclesial community. The canons governing the admission of married men to the clergy and the remarriage of widowed priests reinforce the connection between family life and priestly ordination. They have little to do with celibacy. Both Orthodox and Eastern Catholic authorities are unanimous on this matter.

For instance, Metropolitan Stephanos Charalambidis of Nazianzus, speaking about the married priesthood in Orthodoxy, makes it clear that "all the canonical norms concerning married priests which are in force in the Orthodox Church to this day, fully agree with the Christian ideal of an absolute monogamy. For priests this becomes a formal necessity."[9] Philotheos Pharos, a Greek theologian, psychologist, and celibate priest, sums up the traditional exemplary role of the married priest from the point of view of family management and parental role as follows: "A priest is bound to have a notably exemplary family life because, according to the Apostle Paul in 1 Tim. 3:5, if one does not know how to control his family, how can he look after God's people?"[10] St. John Chrysostom adds to this: "For he who cannot be the instructor of his own children, how could he be a teacher to others?"[11] He continues,

> He must see that his children are obedient and always respectful (1 Tim. 3:4). Good example has to be exhibited in his house. For who would believe that he who had not his own son in control, would keep a stranger under command? Church leaders must be in control of their own families (1 Tim. 3:4). Even pagans say this, that he who is a good steward of a house will be a good leader. For the Church is, as it were, a small household, and as in a house there are children and a wife and domestics, and the man has rule over them all, just so in the Church there are women, children, and servants. And as he who presides in the Church has partners in his powers, so in his house has the man a partner, that is, his wife.[12]

We should not be surprised that the *Code of Canons of the Eastern Churches* adopts precisely this point of view, particularly canons 374–375, which focus on how the exemplary character of the married clergy is underlined and how it should be understood in the context of the Catholic teaching on conjugal love.

Canon 374 thus states: "Clerics, celibate as well as married, should shine forth with the splendor of chastity; it is for particular law to establish suitable means to attain this end."[13] Chastity is the virtue that makes love possible. It is an essential virtue for any person, as *PDV* pointed out. This virtue truly fulfills itself in the various states of life. Conjugal chastity in particular safeguards the truth and the fullness of conjugal love.[14] The necessity of the exemplary character of conjugal love mentioned by canon 374 is restated in an even clearer manner by canon 375: "Married clerics are to offer an outstanding example to other Christian faithful in conducting their family life and in educating their children."

To be a united couple and good parents, to build a family based on love and capable of radiating and manifesting love, according to the program of life outlined in the apostolic exhortation *Familiaris Consortio*,[15] is not a moral obligation simply for the priestly couple. It is a moral obligation for all Christian couples. It also becomes an ethical duty that is intimately connected with the priest's ecclesial role. Indeed, it is connected to the very meaning of the priestly ministry. According to the *Corpus Canonum Ecclesiarum Orientalium* (*CCEO*), the life of a minister is, by its very nature (namely, by virtue of ordination) a call to live the exemplary condition of his very state of life, both celibate and married.[16]

This priestly witness is meant to be a clear witness to all believers, and even to those who do not belong to the fold of believers. This is because the priest and his spouse and family inevitably become, in an institutional mode, the representative or emblematic image of the Christian couple and family.

So far we have spoken only of what is traditionally required of the married clergy. We have not yet considered what could appropriately be called the "theological meaning" of clerical marriage. This development needs explanation.

The Theological Significance of Married Clergy: Difficulties in the Latin Approach

The theological meaning of the married priesthood is not to be confused with other merely contingent factors, such as economical, educational, disciplinary, practical, devotional, moral, or generally religious considerations. Nor is theological meaning to be confused with theological convenience, which indicates only a degree of correlation between theological values but does not indicate an intrinsic connection between them.[17] The development of the Roman theology of celibacy is a good example of the confusion of the essential and the contingent.

Can it not be argued that the married priest and his wife are also a sign of the relationship of Christ to the Church? In the newly restricted view we have outlined, however, the married priest is the sign of Christ the spouse of the Church inasmuch as he is spouse and father of a family, and yet it does not seem to follow that he is a sign of Christ in his capacity as shepherd and head of his community in the celebration of the Eucharist and in service to the community. This is clearly anomalous, since factually he is truly a shepherd, head, and priest for his community, just as much as any celibate priest.

Here, in order to identify the theological value of the married clergy, we must begin from a permanent key element of the Eastern tradition: Those who are called to the married priesthood are in reality called to a spiritual path that, in the first place, is characterized by a conjugal, family form of life. It is upon the solidity and continuity of such form that they receive the priestly mandate.

In the Eastern tradition, it is a permanent practice that marriage precedes ordination. Moreover, ordination does not change the matrimonial/family way of life. Rather, it configures it according to the pastoral needs of the priestly mandate in the community. Therefore, married priesthood and Christian marriage are not mutually exclusive but converge in that the sacramental character of marriage blends with the sacramental character of the priesthood without contradiction or loss to either. They are sacramentally complementary. Indeed, as each subsequent sacrament is also a continuation and further development of previous elements, marriage and married priesthood are able to complement and develop each other. Perhaps, in the past, this complementarity was not as discernible as it can be today: With the development of the theology of marriage, Catholic sacramental theology is aware of elements not previously clearly perceived or appreciated. In other words, today we are capable of better understanding the relationship between marriage and priesthood in the way they have been maintained in the Eastern tradition.

In contemporary Church teaching, marriage is not viewed simply as a natural contract that is blessed and elevated to the level of a sacrament to bind a man and woman for the purpose of procreation and the education of offspring. Tradition has retrieved its understanding of marriage as a covenant-communion of life and conjugal love between a man and woman which, celebrated as it is in the Church, is elevated to signify the very communion between God and man, that between Christ and his Church, and, according to some, even the Trinitarian communion itself.

In its own way, marriage becomes a manifestation of the Church. In his apostolic exhortation of 1981, *Familiaris Consortio* 49, Pope John Paul II declares that "the Christian family as a 'Church in miniature' is in its own way a living image and historical representation of the mystery of the Church." Two further aspects of this need to be considered and stressed. The first concerns the kind of union that originates between the spouses by virtue of their total self-giving in matrimonial love. It is a deep and intimate union that can be called a kind of "one-in-two."[18] The second aspect is that the marriage sacrament and the family that issues from it, in the light of modern theology, is not simply a reality in the Church but rather a reality that *is* the Church, namely, its actuation and symbol.

This latter aspect was particularly developed and expressed in *Familiaris Consortio* 49. There, citing Vatican II's *Lumen Gentium*, John Paul II declares:

> The Christian family is grafted into the mystery of the Church to such a degree as to become a sharer, in its own way, in the saving mission proper to the Church. By virtue of the sacrament, Christian married couples and parents "in their state and way of life have their own special gift among the people of God" (*Lumen Gentium*, 11). For this reason they not only *receive* the love of Christ and become a *saved* community, but they are also called upon to *communicate* Christ's love to their brethren, thus becoming a *saving* community. In this way, while the Christian family is a fruit and sign of the supernatural fecundity of the Church, it stands also as a symbol, witness and participation of the Church's motherhood (*Lumen Gentium*, 41). (emphasis added)

Therefore, the Christian family communion shares the Church's mission in its particular capacity to serve the kingdom of God (*Familiaris Consortio*, 50) by fulfilling the threefold ministry of Christ as prophet, priest, and king.

For this reason the Christian family must be a "believing and evangelizing community." Within and outside the family environs, the spouses have a mission of spreading the gospel and catechizing. Indeed, they are endowed with a universal missionary task. Therefore, "just as in the dawn of Christianity, so also today the Church shows forth her perennial newness and fruitfulness by the presence of Christian couples and families who dedicate at least a part of their lives to working in mission territories, proclaiming the Gospel and doing service to their fellowmen in the love of Jesus Christ" (*Familiaris Consortio*, 54). The Christian family must be also a "domestic church," or the "little church" in Eastern terms, a place of sanctification that originates from the sacrament of matrimony and from the presence of Christ in the life of the couple (*Lumen Gentium*, 48). The spouses are called on to be holy in fidelity to their conjugal love: "Christian spouses and parents are included in the universal call to sanctity.... [Christian marriage] is in itself a liturgical action glorifying God in Jesus Christ and in the Church. By celebrating it, Christian spouses profess their gratitude to God for the sublime gift bestowed on them of being able to live in their married and family lives the very love of God for people and the love of the Lord Jesus for the Church, his bride" (*Familiaris Consortio*, 56).

At the center of Christian marriage there is a God-given love embodied in human love. It is precisely for this reason that the Eucharist is the very source of matrimony. Indeed, it is "in this sacrifice of the New and Eternal Covenant that Christian spouses encounter the source from which their own marriage originates, is interiorly structured and continuously renewed" (*Familiaris Consortio*, 57). By acting out the commandment of charity as acceptance, respect, and service to everyone, the Christian family is a community at the service of human society (*Familiaris Consortio*, 63). This is realized in the microcosm of the domestic community and then in the macrocosm of the Church, "in the wider circle of the ecclesial community of which the Christian family is a part. Thanks to love in the family, the Church can and ought to take on a more homelike or family dimension, developing a more human and fraternal style of relationship.... In each individual, especially in the poor, the weak and those who suffer or are unjustly treated, love knows how to discover the face of Christ, and discover a fellow human being to be loved and served" (*Familiaris Consortio*, 64).[19] Therefore, marriage and Christian family are ordered, of themselves, toward a prophetic, priestly, and kingly service of the Church and the world. Some families can open themselves only in a limited way (such as when there are sick people in the home, people in financial difficulties, or those with other personal constraints). Other families have amazing capabilities of acceptance, service, and availability to the mission of the Church. All of this must be considered in the ambience of God's providence over the world and the Church. It is he who distributes gifts and charisms, who facilitates or makes things harder, who has one way of calling or another. Just as the Lord may call some couples to the task of evangelizing families, one of the spouses to ecclesial ministry or to a deacon's service, some children to a monastic or eremitical life, so, too, he may call a husband to the priestly ministry and his wife and family to participate in it.

Such theological views of marriage and the family are already a Catholic heritage. They did not develop in relation to the question of a contemporary married priesthood. However, they do throw light on the authenticity of the Eastern practice because they help manifest their deep significance in relation to the economy of salvation.

For a Christian to move from marriage to the sacrament of orders can be seen as a process of growth that makes the connections explicit. Marriage and family life are not in contradiction to priestly ministry; on the contrary, they find in it one valid way to completely fulfill the Christian meaning of marriage and the family in a vocation to ministry in the service of the Church and for the salvation of the world.

We can say that the married priest—namely, a man called to accept and live his presbyterate *in* marriage—receives a call that includes his marriage and his family, his wife and his children, in its horizon. It is a call that is in continuity with the sacramental meaning of matrimony, namely, to be a sign of and participate in the love of God and his Church. We can now pinpoint the theological significance of the married presbyterate, or the meaning whereby the married priest—precisely because he is married—has a direct relation to the mystery of salvation in Christ. The spouse who is called to the presbyterate, by way of his conjugal call (that is, following the path of his call), by becoming a presbyter with the consent and sharing of his wife (and children), presents concretely and historically a full image of the ecclesial meaning of the very conjugal vocation itself. The conjugal vocation is in fact a call to build the Church through the one-in-two quality of marriage and to widen its boundaries.

The husband, by becoming a priest, unites two sacraments, and in sharing both with his wife, is called to love more, not less, and in particular to widen his capacity to love. The boundaries of his family are widened: He acquires sons and daughters; his paternity is widened; his family becomes the community, and the community becomes his family.

The love that binds the man to his wife and his wife to him in the one-in-two reality—a love that, by virtue of the sacrament of matrimony, is in both man and wife a participation in the very spousal love (charity) of Christ—acquires a still deeper strength and can love "to the end" by loving one another in marriage.

This clear reference to John 13:1 is not cited casually. Pope John Paul II sounds this theme in his letter to Christian families of 1994, *Gratissimam sane*, where he comments on Ephesians 5:32:

> The Church cannot be understood as the mystical body of Christ, as the sign of man's covenant with God in Christ, or as the universal sacrament of salvation, unless we keep in mind the "great mystery" involved in the creation of man as male and female and the vocation of both to conjugal love, to fatherhood and motherhood. The "great mystery" that is the Church and humanity in Christ does not exist apart from the "great mystery" expressed in "one flesh," that is, in the reality of marriage and family. The family itself is the great mystery of God. As the "domestic church," it is the bride of Christ. The universal Church, and every particular Church in her, is most immediately revealed as the bride of Christ in the domestic church, and in its experience of love: conjugal love, paternal and maternal love, fraternal love, the love of a community of persons and of generations. Could we even imagine human love without the Bridegroom and the love with which He first loved "to the end"? Only if husbands and wives share in that love and in that great mystery can they love "to the end." Unless they share in it, they do not know "to the end" what love truly is and how radical are its demands. (*Gratissimam sane*, 19)

Thus, John Paul II forcefully underlines, in fact, the theological meaning of the married clergy. It accords with the 2,000-year-old practice of the Church. In its conjugal and priestly existence, the ecclesial community becomes the living image of the deep unity of the great mystery, both as the domestic church and as its larger congregations. Again the pope says, "There is no 'great mystery,' which is the Church and the humanity of Christ, without the 'great mystery' expressed in the 'one flesh' (Gen. 2:24; Eph. 5:31–32), that exists in the reality of marriage and the family." Following the thought of the pope, we can say that one sacrament is the symbol of the other. Each manifests the other. Thus the married presbyterate blends in a personal way the two "great mysteries." It symbolizes the one Church manifested in two homologous and concentric forms. The conjugal love of the one "who is called to the priesthood of the one-in-two" is called to be the living image of that love of the bridegroom who gives his life for his church. This is a particular realization of that Christ-like love "to the end" to which every Christian is called in baptism.

However, caution must be exercised when using spousal-bridegroom language in the context of priesthood. *PDV* does not exercise the caution that should apply when speaking of a priest as the bridegroom of the community, irrespective of whether he is celibate or married. There is only one Bridegroom of the Church, and that is Christ (Eph. 5:23 and Rev. 19:7–9). The presbyter is to be understood to represent Christ iconically, certainly not ontologically. The presbyter belongs to the body of Christ; he is not the Head. He indeed may be the "right hand" of Christ when he consecrates the holy gifts, but in the *epiklesis* he asks the Father to send the Holy Spirit upon the gifts. It is the Spirit who consecrates, while it is the priest who offers the Father the perfect sacrifice "in the name of the whole Church" (*Presbyterorum Ordinis* 2). Thus he may never darken the image of Christ as the only Bridegroom of the Church. "He who has the bride is the bridegroom; the friend of the bridegroom, who stands by and listens to him, rejoices in hearing the voice of the bridegroom" (John 3:29). The priest-presbyter is ever the servant of the Bridegroom, Christ.

Finally, for Eastern priests the married state is a reality with a full right to exist in the Catholic Church. It has its own theological meaning, which is neither superior nor inferior to that of ecclesiastical celibacy. Holy Scripture and the early Church regarded the married state as the norm. Matthew 19:12, on the other hand, while having everything to do with radical discipleship, has nothing to do with ministry or priesthood directly. The ecclesiastical law of celibacy comes from other sources. The two modes of exercising the presbyterate are different, but altogether in harmony and compatible. The married clergy, by its very existence, manifests the full ecclesial vocation of every Christian marriage and the deep unity of the manifestations of the great mystery.

In conclusion we turn to the response received from the secretariat of state by the married priest of the Byzantine tradition mentioned in the following chapter. We note that the Lord can make use of even official replies to serious questions to achieve his own unforeseen purposes (cf.

Num. 22:28). This particular one tells us something germane to the married priesthood. It recognizes that the married priest is truly a priest and performs a priestly mission. It exhorts him to continue such priestly mission in joy by "making of [his] life a constant offering to God, to [his] family and to the community entrusted to [his] care." In the final analysis he is invited to manifest that marriage and priesthood can exist in mutual continuity and unity, in full harmony and in fidelity to the will of God.

Grounded firmly in Holy Scripture and constantly expressed and defended in the tradition of the Christian East, the married priesthood is a true vocation and a genuine realization of the priestly ministry, a precious gift in and to the Catholic Church.

Notes

1. C. Bonivento, *Priestly Celibacy: Ecclesiastical Institution or Apostolic Tradition?* (Sydney, Australia, 2006).

2. According to *PDV*, 29, priestly ordination makes of the priest the sacramental sign—ontologically configured not only to Christ, the head and shepherd of his people, but also to Christ, the Bridegroom of the Church, to the extent that only the "celibate" priest is the full and true expression of the priestly ordination. "It is especially important that the priest understand the theological motivation of the Church's law on celibacy. Inasmuch as it is a law, it expresses the Church's will, even before the will of the subject expressed by his acceptance. But the will of the Church finds its ultimate motivation in the link between celibacy and sacred ordination, which configures the priest to Jesus Christ, the head and spouse of the Church. The Church, as the bride of Jesus Christ, wished to be loved by the priest in the total and exclusive manner in which Jesus Christ her head and spouse loved her. Priestly celibacy, then, is the gift of self in and with Christ to his Church and expresses the priest's service to the Church in and with the Lord." So saying, *Pastores dabo vobis* has accomplished this apart not only from the sacramental tradition, which has always linked the sign of Christ as spouse to matrimony, but also from the existence of the Eastern tradition and from the overall respect for the Latin practice, which, as is well known, does have married priests.

3. The list of topics for this video conference is interesting and revealing:
- Priestly celibacy "propter regnum caelorum"
- The apostolic origin of priestly celibacy
- The sign of celibacy and priestly fatherhood
- Virginity of the body and of the spirit

- How to respond to the objection of why the priests of the Latin Church must be celibate
- Celibacy and Holy Mass: The eucharistic sacrifice and the sacrifice of life
- How to live and to witness celibacy before a secularized world
- What factors threaten the correct understanding of celibacy?
- Celibacy as a sign of total dedication to Christ and his Church
- Brotherhood among the priests as a help to better live their celibacy
- Celibacy and the Blessed Mother.

4. Here the cardinal interprets *Presbyterorum ordinis* as if it had the same perspective as *Pastores dabo vobis*, from which this last sentence is taken. This presumption is unfounded.

5. By John Paul II and Walter Ziemba (Montgomery, IL: Warner Books, 2004).

6. The most extravagant insistence on ontological change has to be the late John Cardinal O'Connor's address given in Fatima on 18 June 1996, "The Necessity of Continuing Formation for the Priest." The cardinal uses the word "ontological" five times in almost as many sentences. Why there was no reaction from his hearers to this absurd claim, particularly the use of the eucharistic analogy, is another question in itself. He said: "Above all, formation, the Pontiff tells us, must be rooted in 'awareness of the *specific ontological bond* which unites the priesthood to Christ the High Priest and Good Shepherd' [n 11]. In my judgment, this concept of the ontological nature of the priesthood, is critical. We don't just put on vestments; we don't just receive an assignment. Neither makes us priests. We *become* priests at ordination. There is an 'ontological change' in our spiritual nature. Such is a profound mystery. Is it too bold an analogy to compare the change to Christ the Son of God's retaining His Divinity while becoming a man? Or to observe that after bread becomes the Sacred Body of Christ, it still tastes like bread and feels like bread, but is now the Body of Christ? There has been an ontological change. A cup of wine still smells like wine and tastes like it, but it is now the Blood of Christ. At ordination an *ontological* change takes place."

7. H.E.W. Turner, *The Pattern of Christian Truth*, the Bampton Lectures of 1954 (London: Mowbray, 1954), 489–492.

8. Cited in A. Schmemann, *Eucharist: Sacrament of the Kingdom* (NY: St. Vladimir's Press, 1987), 32.

9. S. Charalambidis, *Ministry and Charismas in the Orthodox Church* (in Italian) (Milan, 1994), 98.

10. P. Pharos, *The Clergy. The Unfulfilled Promise of Paternity* (in Greek) (Nea Smyrni, 1992), 243–245.

11. Homily II on Titus, *Patrologia Graeca* (*PG*) 62:679.

12. Homily X on 1 Timothy, *PG* 62:549–550.

13. The term "chastity" is used in its general sense, applicable both to celibates and to noncelibates. Both celibate clerics and married ones are called to chastity. The *Catechism of the Catholic Church*, no. 2349, has these words, and adds: "Married persons are called to live a conjugal chastity, the others to practice chastity in continence."

14. See *Familiaris Consortio*, 33: "According to the Christian outlook, chastity does not at all mean either a refusal or a lack of esteem for human sexuality; rather it means a spiritual energy that is able to defend love from the dangers of selfishness and of aggressiveness and can foster it towards its complete fulfillment." See also *PDV*, 29: "[Even] in *virginity* and *celibacy*, chastity maintains its original meaning, namely a human sexuality lived out as an authentic manifestation and precious service of love, communion and interpersonal self-giving."

15. *Familiaris Consortio*, 17: "For this reason, the family is given *the mission to guard, reveal and communicate love* [emphasis added], and this is a living reflection of and real sharing in God's love for man and the love of Christ the Lord to the Church his bride. Every particular task of the family is an expression and concrete actuation of that fundamental mission."

16. This is explicitly contained in canon 368: "Clerics are bound, in a special manner, to the perfection which Christ proposes to his disciples, since they are consecrated to God in a new way by sacred ordination, to become more suitable instruments of Christ, the eternal priest, in the service of God's people and, at the same time, to be an exemplary model to the faithful." We should note that the reference to 1 Peter 5:3 is a new element in contrast to can. 276, § 1, of the (Latin) *Code of Canon Law*, which applies only to the Catholic Church of the Latin rite.

17. For a fuller discussion see Basilio Petrà, *Married Priests According to the Will of God? An Essay on a Church with Two Lungs* (in Italian) (Bologna: EDB, 2004).

18. John Paul II thus writes in his *Letter to Women* (29 June 1995), which he addresses "To each of you, to the women of the entire world": "In their fruitful relationship as husband and wife, in their common task of exercising dominion over the earth, man and woman are marked neither by a static and undifferentiated equality, nor by an irreconcilable and inexorably conflictive difference. Their most natural relationship, which corresponds to the plan of God, is the 'unity-of-the-two,' namely a 'one-in-two' relationship as a gift which enriches and which confers responsibility" (no. 8).

19. In the same no. 64, *FC* recalls a point of the *Sixth Synod of Bishops' Message to Christian Families in the Modern World* (24 October 1980): "Another task for the family is to form persons in love and also to practice love in all its relationships, so that it does not live closed in on itself, but remains open to the community, moved by a sense of justice and concern for others, as well as by a consciousness of its responsibility toward society as a whole."

CHAPTER SEVENTEEN

Married Priesthood

Some Theological "Resonances"

Basilio Petrà

As far as we know, this is the first time in history that a Catholic eparchy has held a conference, with the participation of bishop, priests, deacons, monastics, and laypeople, on the subject of married clergy (*status clericorum matrimonio iunctorum*) viewed in its own terms and in terms of its value for the whole Church.[1] We would dare to say that it is the very first time that a conference was held about the theological and ecclesial significance of the married clergy.

There have, of course, been married priests for two thousand years; but contemporary writers lead us to think that nothing of the kind had been tried before. It is only natural to ask why this has taken place. All we must say at this point is that in the Western Church, since the eleventh century, there has been an extremely long list of theological and magisterial—as well as disciplinary, canonical, and spiritual—publications that defend the connection between celibacy and the ordained priesthood.[2] This literature directly rejects or, in any case, contradicts the practice and, even more so, the theological meaning of the married clergy. In fact, in the Latin Church—in great measure—there came into being the implicit axiom that the *priesthood automatically entails celibacy*. Such an axiom is so widespread that it not only has survived the Second Vatican Council but has become even more deep-rooted and more strongly propounded after it.

Post-Conciliar Changes in the Roman Theology of Celibacy

It seems incredible, but it is true. Precisely after the Council, which had given an ecclesial and theological dignity to the practice of having a married clergy, which for century after century had been merely a tolerated and provisional practice, eventually to be eliminated, many have gone so far, on the relationship between priesthood and celibacy, as to utter statements that no one had dared make beforehand. The Council had stated clearly that the married clergy had gained a greatly esteemed place in the history of the Church and hence should be honored; that it is an authentic priesthood and arises from a divine call and from an ecclesial inspiration, just as does the celibate priesthood; that it is a gift, namely a charism from God, just like the celibate priesthood; and that celibacy has special reasons for its theological significance and remains an ecclesiastical law. After all this, we saw the appearance in 1992 of the apostolic exhortation *PDV*, which formally affirms the objectively founded link between celibacy and the priesthood. I want to stress this point: According to *PDV*, the Catholic Church, by imposing celibacy on the Latin Church, does not simply establish a law that has several motivations (of a practical and theological nature), but also adopts a norm based on the very meaning of ordination itself, which configures one ontologically to Christ, the head, shepherd, and bridegroom of the Church, and finds in celibacy its adequate parallel. In other words, the married priesthood has become either an abnormal priesthood (in the sense that it does not correspond to what priestly ordination signifies ontologically speaking), and therefore is simply tolerated, or is a different kind of priesthood than the celibate priesthood. Before Vatican II, no one had dared say as much.

I remember that when I pointed out this idea of *PDV* to the then-secretary of the Pontifical Council for the Interpretation of Legislative Texts, he was extremely surprised and could not believe it himself. I found the same reaction in many others who clearly remembered centuries of theological manuals according to which the law of celibacy is merely an *ecclesiastical law*. And yet such texts as *PDV* strongly suggest that a change in Latin theology proves it unmistakably, and the documents of the Roman congregations confirm it repeatedly.

The Congregation for the Clergy has reiterated this point in its "Directory for the Ministry and the Life of the Priests," *Tota ecclesia* (1994), and has proceeded along these lines in its activities of formation, both those put into practice through internal courses as well as those propounded by means of monthly video conferences.

On 5 April 2005, for instance, the congregation organized a global video conference on the theme Celibacy and Paternity of the Priest, assembling through modern communication technologies theologian professors from Rome, New York, Moscow, Bogotà, Madrid, Taiwan, Sydney, Manila, Johannesburg, and Regensburg. It is interesting to go down the list of theologian professors and their topics: Antonio Miralles (Rome), Priestly Celibacy "Propter regnum *caelorum*"; Alfonso Carrasco (Madrid), The Apostolic Origin of Priestly Celibacy; Gary Devery (Sydney), The Sign of Celibacy and Priestly Fatherhood; Igor Kowalewsky (Moscow), Virginity of the Body and of the Spirit; Michael Hull (New York), How to Respond to the Objection of Why the Priests of the Latin Church Must Be Celibate; Louis Aldrich (Taiwan), Celibacy and Holy Mass: The Eucharistic Sacrifice and the Sacrifice of Life; José Vidamor (Manila), How to Live and to Witness Celibacy before a Secularized World; Gehrhard Müller (Regensburg), What Factors Threaten the Correct Understanding of Celibacy?; Rodney Moss (Johannesburg), Celibacy as a Sign of Total Dedication to Christ and His Church; Silvio Cajiao (Bogotà), Brotherhood among the Priests as a Help to Better Live Their Celibacy; and Paolo Scarafoni (Rome), Celibacy and the Blessed Mother.

Two months prior to this conference, on 16 February 2005, the cardinal-prefect of the Congregation for the Clergy at the time, Darío Castrillón Hoyos, issued an interview, later published in a *Dossier on the Clergy*, prepared by the agency *Fides*. We think that the replies he gives to the first two questions he was asked is quite interesting:

1. **Question:** *Priestly celibacy, some people say, is only a question of ecclesiastical discipline and legislation, which could eventually be modified. Is this true, or is there a special bond between vocation to the priesthood and celibacy?*
Cardinal: This question gives me the opportunity to clarify that for believers celibacy is not merely a "question," as if celibacy were a prob-

lem to be solved or a simple theory; it is instead a gift of the merciful love of God which the Church continuously receives and wishes to treasure, convinced as she is that it is a supreme good for herself and the entire world. This has been propounded by the teaching of the Church since apostolic times and was reiterated more than once by the Vatican Council and in particular by the constitution *Lumen Gentium* (*LG*) where we find the following statement: "this precious gift of divine grace stands out, given by the Father to some (Mt. 19:11; 1 Cor. 7:7) to give themselves to God more freely and with undivided heart (1 Cor. 7:32–34) in virginity and in celibacy (no. 42).

With special reference to priestly celibacy, the conciliar decree *Presbyterorum Ordinis* (*PO*) states: "Perfect and perpetual continence for the sake of the Kingdom of Heaven, commended by Christ the Lord . . . and through the course of time as well as in our own days freely accepted and observed in a praiseworthy manner by many of the faithful, is held by the Church to be of great value in a special manner for the priestly life" (no. 16). There exists in fact a strict bond between celibacy and priestly ordination, a sacrament that ontologically configures the priest to Jesus Christ, head and bridegroom of his Church.

I must add at this point that priestly celibacy is indeed an ecclesiastical law; however, the canonical injunction must not be understood as an arbitrary imposition of the Church, as if it were an external command imposed on the priest to pay, as it were, a kind of fee to God for becoming an ordained minister. The ecclesiastical law of celibacy has its roots in the mystery of Christ and his Church. Moreover, we cannot forget that the entire ecclesiastical legislation is founded on the saving will of God the Father, fulfilled in Christ through the Holy Spirit. Canonical law guides the Church in the mission which Christ has entrusted to her, to be the universal sacrament of salvation.

Confronted with the difficulties and the objections raised from many sides and throughout the centuries about understanding and embracing this gift, the teaching of the Church, even after the last council, has reiterated that there exist theological reasons of a Christological, ecclesiological and eschatological nature which manifest the intimate link of celibacy to the ordained ministry in its dual dimension of relationship to Christ and his Church.

2. **Question:** *Can you tell us something about these reasons?*
Cardinal: I will sum them up by way of three principles of a biblical-theological nature.

The first principle is of *Christological* nature. Christ, who has lived a celibate life, asked his apostles to imitate him and to follow him with an undivided heart and to leave everything in order to bring to the entire humanity the salvation won by him on the cross, to the ends of the earth while waiting his final coming.

The second principle is of an *ecclesiological* nature. The priest as sacred minister of Christ is called upon to love the Church in the all-embracing and exclusive manner whereby Christ, head and bridegroom, has loved her, namely with His total self, body and soul, thus witnessing Christ's spousal love to the Church, His bride, and receiving in exchange a wide spiritual paternity in Christ.

The third principle is of an *eschatological nature.* Through his full communion and personal gift of himself to Christ and his Church, the priest prefigures and anticipates in this world the communion and the total and final gift of Christ to His Church in eternity, thus becoming a living sign of the future world.

In this light, it becomes easier to understand the reasons for the long-standing option of the Latin Church, which she still maintains "to confer sacramental ordination only to men who have given proof of having been called by God to the gift of chastity in absolute and perpetual celibacy," as the apostolic exhortation *PDV* clearly states.

What John Paul II wrote in his autobiographical book *Rise, Let Us Be on Our Way* about the link between celibacy and spiritual paternity is particularly appropriate and beautiful: "Celibacy, in fact, provides the fullest opportunity to live out this type of fatherhood: chaste and totally dedicated to Christ and to his Virgin Mother. Unconstrained by any personal solicitude for a family, a priest can dedicate himself *with his whole heart* to his pastoral responsibilities. One can therefore understand the tenacity with which the Latin Church has defended the tradition of celibacy for its priests, resisting the pressures that have arisen from time to time throughout history. This tradition is clearly demanding, but it has yielded particularly rich spiritual results." (pp. 140–41)

Both the program of the video conference and the interview by the then-prefect show the extent of the change undergone, in Roman quarters, by the theology of celibacy: It is not, however, solely the Congregation for the Clergy that proceeds along this line, thus practically isolating the Eastern tradition into a kind of ecclesial reserve (not unlike an Indian reservation). Other Roman congregations also embrace the same perspective. As a confirmation, let me quote the *Instruction Concerning the Criteria for the Discernment of Vocations with Regard to Persons with Homosexual Tendencies in View of Their Admission to the Seminary and to Sacred Orders* (Congregation for Catholic Education, 4 November 2005), which begins:

> According to the constant Tradition of the Church, only a baptized person of the male sex validly receives sacred Ordination. By means of the Sacrament of Orders, the Holy Spirit configures the candidate to Jesus Christ in a new and specific way: the priest, in fact, sacramentally, represents Christ, the head, shepherd and spouse of the Church. Because of this configuration to Christ, the entire life of the sacred minister must be animated by the gift of his whole person to the Church and by an authentic pastoral charity. (no. 1)

It needs to be added that, while the Roman congregations proceeded with these changes in Latin theology, the Eastern Catholic churches—in particular the Congregation for the Eastern Churches—did not do much to point out that the married clergy is not an archaic reality, a discipline tolerated for practical reasons but lacking theological meaning, a practice to be rather kept hidden away. Rather, it has a theological significance, since it was born from the direct will of God and it constitutes an act of fidelity to the Lord on a par with the call to the celibate priesthood.

The same cardinal-prefect interviewed and quoted above, when questioned on the Eastern churches, could only reply in the following manner:

3. **Question:** *Does not the discipline of the Eastern Churches contradict the position of the Latin Church?*
   Cardinal: Absolutely not. There is no contradiction. I reply with the words of the Directory for the Ministry and the Life of the priest of January 31, 1994: "The discipline of the Eastern Churches which admit the married clergy in not opposed to the discipline of the Latin Church. In fact the Eastern Churches themselves demand celibacy for their bishops. Moreover, they do not allow the marriage of already

ordained priests and do not allow a second marriage for widowed priests" (no. 60). This means that in the East as well as in the West it is never allowed for a priest to marry and that only celibate priests can become bishops. Therefore I reiterate that priestly celibacy is intimately linked to the priesthood. The celibate priest imitates Christ and lives like the apostles. Celibacy is always a free choice and a joyous acceptance of a specific calling of love of God and of others, and it is not at all fruit of an empty spirituality or contempt for human sexuality by the candidates to the priesthood.

This is indeed a strange reply: The practice of a married clergy is an imitation of the apostles? In the final analysis, the suggestion prevails that even in the East the true priesthood, the one considered in its fullness, can be only the celibate priesthood, and the married priesthood is merely tolerated even in the East.

All of this raises a series of substantial questions we must take up presently: Does the persistence of a married clergy—strenuously defended—lack any positive significance? Does it lack a theological value? Is it not a true priesthood? Is it not the result of a call from God? And is the *Code of Canons of the Eastern Churches* (*CCEO*) perhaps the child of a lesser god?

The Theological Significance of Married Clergy in the East

Looking at the origins of the Eastern tradition, it is easy to perceive that, in maintaining a married priesthood, the value of fidelity to the apostolic mandate has always been preserved, as attested by the pastoral letters of the Pauline corpus (1 Tim. 3:2; Titus 1:6). As a consequence, the analogy between management of the home and management of the church highlighted by the pastoral letters was clearly kept in mind. The ability to be a good spouse and a good parent is a solid indication of the ability to manage the ecclesial community as well. In a way, the logic of the pastoral letters seems to indicate that the married priesthood reveals the family character of the ecclesial community, so much so that a discerning criterion of the managing ability of the candidate to the priesthood is precisely his ability to be a good husband and a good father, albeit within the limitations of the family culture of the first century after Christ.

It is therefore inevitable that the pastoral letters outline a concept of the married priesthood as linked to an exemplary realization of a priestly family both in the relationship between man and woman and in the relationship between father and children. This necessity of the exemplary quality of the priestly family can explain why the monogamy of the priests and of their wives is conceived as absolute, at least in principle, and why the life of a priestly family must be in perfect keeping with an exemplary Christian life. On this, both Orthodox and Eastern Catholic authors completely agree. For instance, Stephanos Charalambidis, bishop of Nazianzus, speaking about the married priesthood in Orthodoxy, clearly states: "All the canonical norms concerning married priests which are in force in the Orthodox Church to this day, fully agree with the Christian ideal of an absolute monogamy. For priests this becomes a formal necessity."[3]

Philotheos Pharos, a Greek theologian and psychologist and himself a celibate priest, sums up the traditional exemplary role of the married priest from the point of view of family management and parental role in this way:

> A priest is bound to have a notably exemplary family life because, according to the Apostle Paul, "If one does not know how to control his family, how can he look after God's people?" (1 Tim. 3:5). And John Chrysostom adds: "For he who cannot be the instructor of his own children, how could he be a teacher to others?" (Homily II on Titus, *PG* 62: 679); and elsewhere he continues: "He must see that his children are obedient and always respectful" (1 Tim. 3:4). Good example has to be exhibited in his house. For who would believe that he who had not his own son in control, would keep a stranger under command? "Church leaders must be in control of their own families" (1 Tim. 3:4). Even pagans say this, that he who is a good steward of a house will be a good leader. For the Church is, as it were, a small household, and as in a house there are children and a wife and domestics, and the man has rule over them all, just so in the Church there are women, children, and servants. And as he who presides in the Church has partners in his powers, so in his house has the man a partner, that is, his wife." (Homily X on 1 Tim., *PG* 62: 549–550)[4]

It is particularly interesting how the Eastern Code adopts similar points of view (see canons 374–375 of the *CCEO*). I limit myself to underlining how the exemplary character of the married clergy should be understood in the context of the Catholic doctrine of conjugal love.

Canon 374 thus states: "Clerics, celibate as well as married, should shine forth with the splendor of chastity; it is for particular law to establish suitable means to attain this end."[5] Chastity is the virtue that allows love—an essential virtue for any person, as the apostolic exhortation *PDV* points out (7)—to fulfill itself in truth in the various states of life; conjugal chastity in particular safeguards the truth and the fullness of conjugal love.[6]

The necessity of the exemplary character of conjugal love mentioned by canon 374 is restated in a still clearer manner by canon 375: "Married clerics are to offer an outstanding example to other Christian faithful in conducting their family life and in educating their children."

To be a united couple and good parents, to build a family based on love and capable of radiating and manifesting love, is not simply a moral obligation for the priestly couple, as it is for all Christian couples. It also becomes intimately connected with the priest's ecclesial role, indeed connected with the very meaning of the priestly ministry, because for the *CCEO* the life of a minister is by its very nature (through ordination) a call toward the exemplary condition of his very state of life, both celibate and married.[7] This priestly witness is meant to be a clear example to all believers, and also, in a way, to those who do not belong to the fold of believers, because the priestly couple becomes inevitably the *representative image* of the Christian couple and family, as it were, in an *institutional manner*.

Up to this point, I have spoken of the married clergy and of what is traditionally required of them. However, we have not yet considered what could appropriately be called the *theological meaning* of the married clergy. This development needs a brief explanation.

The Theological Significance of the Married Clergy and the Contradictions in the Latin Church

As I have argued in my book *Married Priests According to the Will of God? An Essay on a Church with Two Lungs* (in Italian) (Bologna, 2004), the Roman theology of celibacy has undergone changes in the past century. Before the Second Vatican Council, Catholic theology in general talked about the functional, pastoral, spiritual, devotional, disciplinary, and practical value of celibacy. It also spoke of its theological expediency in the sense that the celibate state appeared particularly suited in view of the totality of the service required from the ministerial priesthood and the exercise of representing Christ, head and good shepherd of His Church. However, this did not alter the fact that celibacy was merely an ecclesiastical law, subject to change and dispensation by the authority of the Church, and that, as a consequence, celibacy was basically something added to the priesthood, not something required by it.

With the recent developments (covered in Alexander Laschuk's chapter), a great step forward was accomplished, albeit deviating from the Council: Now the Church teaches that celibacy is based on the very ontological meaning of ordination. Theologically speaking, this means that ordination objectively demands the state of celibacy. This necessity is based on the idea that the priest, in addition to everything else, is configured in his ordination to Christ as spouse of the Church. Christ was a male and a celibate, and His characteristic of being a spouse was totally directed to the Church. Therefore, considering the way Latin theology has developed, the true theological significance of the priesthood resides totally in celibacy, since the Christ-configuring ordination consists totally in celibacy. In this view, there is no theological reason for the married condition of the priesthood. Only its historical existence is acknowledged, because in Latin circles the principles expounded by the three main apologists for celibacy—Christian Cochini, Alfons Stickler, and Roman Cholij—were accepted without leaving any room for the true theological value of a married clergy.

Roman theology has accomplished a master stroke: It has transformed the spousal character of Christ, which could have been the best way to theologically validate married clergy, into the very foundation for priestly celibacy. In fact, the celibate priest becomes the "true" sign of Christ the spouse. In such a context, where does the married priest fit?

In Latin theology, since he is not celibate, the married priest *could not* be the sign of Christ, spouse of the Church, precisely because he is not celibate. In fact, however, being married, he, together with his wife, is the sign of the relationship of Christ to the Church. Thus, in the new Roman view, he *is* the sign of Christ-spouse inasmuch as he is spouse and father of a family, but not the sign of Christ-spouse in his capacity as shepherd and head of his community in the celebration of the Eucharist and service to the community. And yet he is truly shepherd, head, and priest of his community, just as much as a celibate priest.

This is a strange and absurd situation, the result of a theology that seems to have little interest in being "catholic" (that is, universal), namely capable of integrating all the truths of the Catholic tradition, and is more interested in extolling the value of ecclesiastical celibacy.

Consider a second example of this confusing situation, where all the theological motivations seem to favor celibacy. On the occasion of World Mission Day (23 October 2005), the Roman pontiff uttered these words: "On the mystery of the Eucharist, celebrated and venerated, is founded the celibacy which priests have received as a priceless gift and a sign of the undivided love to God and to neighbor." In response, a married priest of the Byzantine tradition wrote to him, asking in substance this question: "If these words apply also to married priests, I do not know how to behave. Must I celebrate the Eucharist or not?" The question was very direct: If ecclesiastical celibacy is the existential sign required by a true and proper celebration/adoration of the eucharistic mystery and is a gift of God to priests, then where do married priests stand?

He received the following reply from the Vatican's secretariat of state: "Reverend Father, recently you have sent to the Holy Father a letter where you speak of your personal experience as a priest in the Catholic Church of the Eastern rite. As I'm grateful to you for your letter, I urge you to continue living joyously your priestly mission, making of your life a constant offering to God, to your family and to the community entrusted to your care."

This is a bureaucratic masterpiece! The question becomes a personal witness, and the response does not reply directly. It thanks with courtesy and offers an exhortation instead. At times, however, the Lord makes use even of bureaucracy to tell us interesting truths. I will return to this note at the end of the chapter; but let us now return to the problem, which is precisely this: Is there a theological meaning to the married clergy, or is it just a simple practice based on tradition but devoid of any theological value, whether Christological or ecclesial or eschatological (which Roman theology attributes to celibacy)? And from where must we begin our research in order to discover such possible theological value?

I believe that in order to identify the theological value of the married clergy we must begin from a key and permanent element of the Eastern tradition: Those who are called to the married priesthood are in reality called to a spiritual path that, in the first place, is characterized by a conjugal/family form of life, and upon *the solidity and continuity* of such form, they receive the priestly mandate.

In the Eastern tradition it is a permanent practice for marriage to precede ordination. Moreover, marriage or ordination does not change the matrimonial/family way of life but rather configures it according to the pastoral needs of the priestly mandate in the community. Therefore, a married priesthood and Christian marriage are not mutually exclusive but have aspects of such continuity that the sacramental character of marriage can merge into the sacramental character of the priesthood without either contradicting the another or losing anything; indeed they find the fulfillment of an already present element. As each subsequent sacrament is at once a continuation and further development of previous elements, so also do marriage and the married priesthood complement each other and develop into each other.

We can comprehend this point today as never before since we possess a theology of marriage that has brought to Catholic awareness elements not clearly perceived previously. In other words, *today we are capable of better understanding the relationship between marriage and priesthood in the Eastern tradition because we have a theological awareness of marriage much deeper than we had in the past.*

In fact, in the present-day teaching of the Church, marriage is not simply a natural contract—which is blessed and elevated to the level of sacrament—binding man and woman for the purpose of procreation and education of their offspring. It is much more: It is a covenant/communion of life and conjugal love between a man and a woman that, celebrated as it is in the Church, is elevated to signify the very communion between God and man, the communion between Christ and His Church, and, according to some, even the Trinitarian communion. Marriage becomes in a way a manifestation of the Church, and Christian spouses are a church that is fulfilled in their conjugal and family communion. As Pope John Paul II wrote, "The Christian family as a 'Church in miniature' is in its own way a living image and historical representation of the mystery of the Church" (*FC*, 49).[8] Two aspects in particular need to be considered and stressed.

The first aspect concerns the kind of union that originates between the spouses by virtue of their total self-giving in matrimonial love. It is a deep and intimate union that can be called a kind of "one-in-two."[9] The second aspect is that the marriage sacrament and the family that issues from it, in the light of modern theology, are not simply a reality in the Church but rather a reality "which is Church," namely, its actuation and symbol. This aspect was particularly developed and expressed in *FC*, to which we turn now at some length.

In paragraph 49, the pope writes:

> The Christian family is grafted into the mystery of the Church to such a degree as to become a sharer, in its own way, in the saving mission proper to the Church. By virtue of the sacrament, Christian married couples and parents "in their state and way of life have their own special gift among the people of God" (*LG*, 11). For this reason they not only *receive* the love of Christ and become a *saved* community, but they are also called upon to *communicate* Christ's love to their brethren, thus becoming a *saving* community. In this way, while the Christian family is a fruit and sign of the supernatural fecundity of the Church, it stands also as a symbol, witness and participation of the Church's motherhood (*LG*, 41).

For this reason the Christian family must be a "believing and evangelizing community." Within and outside the family, the spouses have a mission of spreading the gospel and catechizing. Indeed, they are endowed with a universal missionary task. Therefore, "just as in the dawn of Christianity, so also today the Church shows forth her perennial newness and fruitfulness by the presence of Christian couples and families who dedicate at least a part of their lives to working in mission territories, proclaiming the Gospel and doing service to their fellowmen in the love of Jesus Christ" (*FC*, 54).

The Christian family must be also a "domestic church," a place of sanctification that originates from the sacrament of matrimony and from the presence of Christ in the life of the couple (see *LG*, 48). The spouses are called on to be holy and faithful to their conjugal love, as *FC* makes clear:

> Christian spouses and parents are included in the universal call to sanctity.... [Christian marriage] is in itself a liturgical action glorifying God in Jesus Christ and in the Church. By celebrating it, Christian spouses profess their gratitude to God for the sublime gift bestowed on them of being able to live in their married and family lives the very love of God for people and the love of the Lord Jesus for the Church, his bride. (*FC*, 56)

Precisely because in the center of Christian marriage there is a God-given love that becomes human love, the Eucharist is the very source of matrimony (*FC*, 57). *FC* says, "In this sacrifice of the New and Eternal Covenant, Christian spouses encounter the source from which their own marriage originates, is interiorly structured and continuously renewed" (*FC*, 57).

Marriage and the Christian family are ordained by themselves toward a prophetic, priestly, and kingly service of the Church and the world, beginning from the domestic dimension without becoming closed in it. Some families can open themselves only in a limited way. Other families, instead, have amazing capabilities of acceptance, service, and availability to the mission of the Church. All of this must be considered within the ambience of God's providence over the world and the Church. It is he who distributes gifts and charisms, who facilitates or makes things harder, who has one way of calling or another.

Such theological outlooks on marriage and the family are already a Catholic heritage. They did not originate, nor were they developed, in relation to the question of a contemporary married priesthood. However, we must say that they greatly illustrate the Eastern practice because they help manifest their deep significance in relation to the economy of salvation.

Marriage and family life are not in contradiction to priestly ministry; on the contrary, *they find in it a way (though not the only one) to completely fulfill the Christian meaning of marriage and the family,* a marriage lived out as a ministry in the service of the Church and for the salvation of the world. According to this point of view, we may state that the married priest—namely, a man called to accept or live his priesthood *in* marriage—receives a call that includes between its horizons his marriage and his family, his wife and his children. It is a call that is in continuity with the sacramental meaning of matrimony—namely, to be a sign of and participant in the love of God and His Church.

Perhaps at this point we come to perceive what, in my opinion, may be called the theological significance of the married priesthood, namely, the meaning whereby the married priest—precisely because he *is* married—has a direct relation to the mystery of salvation in Christ. The spouse who is called to the priesthood, by way of his conjugal call (that is, following the path of his call), by becoming a priest with the consent/sharing of his wife (and children), concretely and historically *presents a full image of the ecclesial meaning of the very conjugal vocation*. The conjugal vocation is, in fact, a call to build the Church through the one-in-two quality and to widen its boundaries. The husband, by becoming a priest, is called—within the one-in-two dimension, hence in sharing with his wife—to love more, not less, to widen his capacity to love. The boundaries of his family are widened, he acquires sons and daughters, and his paternity is widened; his family becomes the community, and the community becomes his family. In the end, they acquire a still deeper strength and can love "to the end" by loving one another in marriage and their parent-child relationships.

These last words, which are a clear reference to John 13:1, are not quoted off-handedly. I take them from Pope John Paul II's letter to Christian families of 1994, *Gratissimam sane*, where the pope comments on Ephesians 5:32:

> The Church cannot therefore be understood as the Mystical Body of Christ, as the sign of man's Covenant with God in Christ, or as the universal sacrament of salvation, unless we keep in mind the "great mystery" involved in the creation of man as male and female and the vocation of both to conjugal love, to fatherhood and to motherhood. The "great mystery," which is the Church and humanity in Christ, does not exist apart from the "great mystery" expressed in the "one flesh" (cf. Gen. 2:24; Eph. 5:31–32), that is, in the reality of marriage and the family.
>
> The family itself is the great mystery of God. As the "domestic church" it is the *bride of Christ*. The universal Church, and every particular Church in her, is most immediately revealed as the bride of Christ in the "domestic church" and in its experience of love: conjugal love, paternal and maternal love, fraternal love, the love of a community of persons and of generations. Could we even imagine human love without the Bridegroom and the love with which he first loved to the end? Only if husbands and wives share in that love and in that "great mystery" can they love "to the end." Unless they share in it, they do not know "to the end" what love truly is and how radical are its demands.[10]

John Paul II says here forcefully what I have tried to state previously: The theological meaning of a married clergy is that it seeks to become, by its conjugal and priestly existence, the living image of the deep unity of the "great mystery," both as domestic church and as community church. "There is no 'great mystery,' which is the Church and the humanity of Christ, without the 'great mystery' expressed in the 'one flesh' (Gen. 2:24; Eph. 5:31–32), that exists in the reality of marriage and the family." Such are the words of the pope. According to his words, the one is the symbol of the other; one manifests the other. Thus the married priesthood, because of the "personal" coinciding of the two "great mysteries," manifests that the two are in reality symbols of one another; they are the only church that is manifested in two homologous and concentric forms. The conjugal love of the one *who is called to the priesthood of the one-in-two* is called to be the living image of that love of the bridegroom who gives His life for His Church, a special and adequate realization of that Christlike love "to the end" to which every Christian is called from the moment he is taken from the baptismal font.

Conclusion

Now, to conclude this chapter of mine, let me go back for a moment to the bureaucratic note received by the married priest of the Byzantine tradition, which I mentioned before. I said then that the Lord at times makes use of bureaucracy for His own unforeseen purposes. That reply, which was intended to be evasive, perhaps tells us something that brings us back to the married priesthood. In fact, it recognizes that the married priest is truly a priest and that he performs a priestly mission; it exhorts him to continue that priestly mission in joy by "making of [his] life a constant gift to God, to [his] family and to the community entrusted to [his] cares." In the final analysis, he is invited to show that marriage and priesthood can exist in mutual continuity and unity, in full fidelity to the will of God—and this is not something to be taken lightly!

Thus does one finally come to see, albeit indirectly, a new and more theologically substantiated defense (if, perhaps, an unwitting or unintentional defense) of the married condition of Eastern priests as a reality with full right of existence in the Catholic Church; it has its own theological meaning, which is neither superior nor inferior to that of ecclesiastical celibacy. It is simply different, but altogether in harmony and compatibility with recent magisterial teaching on marriage itself. The married clergy, by its very existence, manifests the full ecclesial vocation of every Christian marriage and the deep unity of this "great mystery."

Notes

1. I presented the original Italian version of this chapter at a conference held by the Eparchy of Piana degli Albanesi in Sicily. Professor George Gallaro of the Byzantine Catholic Seminary of SS. Cyril and Methodius in Pittsburgh kindly arranged a translation, which I submitted to *Logos: A Journal of Eastern Christian Studies*, which published it in vol. 50 (2009), nos. 3–4, pp. 459–479.

2. Perhaps the greatest recent example of this is Pope John Paul's postsynodal apostolic exhortation *Pastores dabo vobis* (*PDV*, trans. *I Will Give You Shepherds*), where we are told that priestly ordination makes of the priest a sacramental sign, ontologically configured not only to Christ, the head and shepherd of His people, but also to Christ as bridegroom of the Church, to the extent that only the celibate priest is the full and true expression of the priestly ordination. Indeed, the following words must be brought to mind:

> It is especially important that the priest understand the theological motivation of the Church's law on celibacy. Inasmuch as it is a law, it expresses the Church's will, even before the will of the subject expressed by his acceptance. But the will of the Church finds its ultimate motivation in the link between celibacy and sacred ordination, which configures the priest to Jesus Christ, the head and spouse of the Church. The Church, as the bride of Jesus Christ, wished to be loved by the priest in the total and exclusive manner in which Jesus Christ, her head and spouse, loved her. Priestly celibacy, then, is the gift of self in and with Christ to his Church and expresses the priest's service to the Church in and with the Lord. (*PDV*, no. 29)

PDV has accomplished this apart from not only the sacramental tradition that has always linked the sign of Christ the spouse to matrimony but also apart from the existence of the Eastern tradition. *PDV*, moreover, glosses over the fact that the Latin tradition has had, and today in fact has, some married priests. The example of Eastern Catholics could be a corrective *aide memoire* to their Latin brothers here, but the former have failed to speak up—and when they do speak, even very highly placed authorities, they seem to prefer to complain about married priests and to express their preference for the celibate clergy for reasons that are practical, albeit not just practical.

3. S. Charalambidis, *Ministry and Charisms in the Orthodox Church* (in Italian) (Milan, 1994), 98.

4. P. Pharos, *The Clergy: The Unfulfilled Promise of Paternity* (in Greek) (Nea Smyrne, 1992), 243–245.

5. The term "chastity" is used in its general sense, applicable both to celibates and to noncelibates. Both celibate clerics and married ones are called to chastity. The *Catechism of the Catholic Church* notes that "married persons are called to live a conjugal chastity, the others to practice chastity in continence" (no. 2349).

6. See also *Familiaris Consortio*: "According to the Christian outlook, chastity does not at all mean either a refusal or a lack of esteem for human sexuality; rather it means a spiritual energy that is able to defend love from the dangers of selfishness and of aggressiveness and can foster it towards its complete fulfillment" (no. 33). See also *PDV*: "Even in *virginity* and *celibacy*, chastity maintains its original meaning, namely a human sexuality lived out as an authentic manifestation and precious service of love, communion and interpersonal self-giving" (no. 29).

7. This is explicitly contained in canon 368: "Clerics are bound, in a special manner, to the perfection which Christ proposes to his disciples, since they are consecrated to God in a new way by sacred ordination, to become more suitable instruments of Christ, the eternal priest, in the service of God's people and, at the same time, to be an exemplary model to the faithful."

8. Here and following, I refer to two Church documents: *FC*, *Familiaris Consortio*, The Christian Family in the Modern World, Pope John Paul II, 1981, and *LG*, *Lumen Gentium*, Dogmatic Constitution on the Church, Vatican II, 1962–1965.

9. John Paul II thus writes in his 1995 *Letter to Women*: "In their fruitful relationship as husband and wife, in their common task of exercising dominion over the earth, man and woman are marked neither by a static and undifferentiated equality, nor by an irreconcilable and inexorably conflictive difference. Their most natural relationship, which corresponds to the plan of God, is the 'unity-of-the-two', namely a 'one-in-two' relationship as a gift which enriches and which confers responsibility" (no. 8).

10. *Gratissimam sane*, Letter to Families, 1994, Year of the Family, 19.

Conclusion

Toward a Theology of Married Priesthood

Adam A. J. DeVille

Two words in my title—"toward" and "theology"—are both encountered far too often in too much academic writing today. The former seems forever to be promising yet greater insights into some matter already discussed at enormous length—but not now, as though all of life were one continuous intellectual IOU. The latter phrasing, "theology of" this, that, and the other thing, is perhaps even more widely abused—a theology of youth ministry, a theology of potluck suppers, a theology of recycling and trash bins—until the words come to mean almost everything and therefore nothing. Yet both are appropriate here because we have not yet tied together all the necessary strands, including many from contributors to this volume (Thomas Loya, Irene Galadza, and especially Lawrence Cross and Basilio Petrá) that might give us, indeed, a theology of married priesthood. Why is such a thing necessary?

It is important to stress the theology of this tradition for at least two reasons: first, so that it is no longer dismissed merely as a "discipline" that can be changed on a whim without any deeper consequences. Peter Galadza's chapter in this volume cautiously expresses some hope that we are now beyond a time in the Catholic Church when enforced celibacy could be reintroduced, and I am generally inclined to agree with this hope; but the risk does remain as long as popes and curialists feel themselves empowered to try to change things, a risk that seems forever present, even in attenuated form in this Franciscan era, as long as Eastern Catholics remain numerically tiny and financially dependent on Roman institutions and as long as the Roman papacy itself remains in its current heavily centralized form, able to insert itself into the lives of otherwise supposedly self-governing (*sui iuris*) churches.[1]

Second, it is necessary to develop a theology of married priesthood to push back against those theologizing in the opposite direction: those, that is, who are trying to suggest an "ontological" link between celibacy and priesthood to the total exclusion of married priesthood or, at least, to a rather unsubtle denigration of it through such questions (which I have repeatedly heard over the years from self-identified "traditional" Roman Catholics) as "Can a married priest, whose hands have touched a woman, 'validly' confect the Eucharist?" (the question posed, in only slightly less vulgar form, as recently as March 2018 by Bishop Robert Barron, as I discussed in my introduction to this volume). The chapters by Lawrence Cross and Basilio Petrá in this volume go some way toward resisting this language of "ontology," as does our opening contribution by David Hunter. But sweeping the house and securing it (cf. Matt. 12:43–45) against dubious concepts and language is not enough: We must also replace them with something healthier. Thus, in the second and final part of this chapter, I will turn, appropriately, to a voice from the East, Paul Evdokimov, and draw on his *The Sacrament of Love*.

But I will begin, more appropriately still, with the internal voice of the Catholic Church herself as expressed authoritatively in various papal and magisterial documents in order, inter alia, to counter this pejorative idea that married priesthood is merely and only a "discipline" lacking theological substance and support—while celibacy "should not be considered just as a legal norm or as a totally external condition for admission to ordination, but rather as a value that is profoundly connected with ordination."[2] Some of that substance and support has been indicated by others in this book—see Thomas Loya's chapter focusing on the late pope John Paul II's "theology of the body"—while here I want to focus on his 1981 apostolic exhortation, *Familiaris Consortio* (*FC*), which presents a beautiful and compelling theology not just of marriage, but indeed of all the sacraments in an ecclesiology of communion. Even *FC*, however, hesitates in places, and so I will move on to what some (happily, and others bitterly) see as the "successor" document to *FC*, Pope Francis's *Amoris Laetitia* (The Joy of Love, 2015), which advances the discussion in one particularly surprising and helpful way.

Familiaris Consortio: Sacramental Communion

FC was the final document ("postsynodal apostolic exhortation") of a gathering in Rome of select Catholic bishops on the theme of marriage and family. Since 1965, when Pope Paul VI set up purely consultative "synods" (i.e., without any electoral or legislative power), they have met on a regular basis to deal with a variety of topics. An October 1980 synod dealt with marriage and family, but not in isolation. Interestingly enough, the pope himself, seemingly without realizing it, has drawn a brief and most likely unintentional connection at the outset of the document when he notes that the 1980 synod on the family "is logically connected in some way as well with that on the *ministerial priesthood*" (no. 2, my emphasis).[3] The connection between marriage and priesthood would surface again later, as we shall see—but always rather tacitly and without much development, which I shall supply here.

After this introduction, the pope begins by noting the challenges to marriage and family life today. In such a context, he urges families to discover a theology of communion at the heart of who they are and how they live. This theme of communion is arguably *the* central theological recovery of the twentieth century,[4] a product in large part of the ecumenical-ecclesiological work begun by the *ressourcement* movement[5] and leading to the ecclesiological "charter" of Vatican II—*Lumen gentium*—with many spillover effects in other texts and traditions.[6] Today it is almost a commonplace to think of the Church in terms of communion and to conceive of the "domestic church," the family, in those terms also.[7] Indeed, *FC* makes the connection between communion in ecclesial and domestic terms in several places. For example, in paragraph 50 the pope writes: "The Christian family is called upon to take part actively and responsibly in the mission of the Church in a way that is original and specific, by placing itself, in what it is and what it does as an 'intimate community of life and love,' at the service of the Church and of society." In serving Church and society, the "Christian family also builds up the Kingdom of God," largely through "the love between husband and wife and between the members of the family—a love lived out in all its extraordinary richness of values and demands: totality, oneness, fidelity and fruitfulness" (no. 50). Such a loving community ensures "the Christian family's participation in the prophetic, priestly and kingly mission of Jesus Christ and of His Church" (no. 50).

This theme of loving communion is invoked repeatedly throughout *FC*, tying together various diverse sections and reflections therein. Moreover, the pope explicitly linked this theme of communion to other sacraments, especially baptism (nos. 13, 15, 51, 52, 54–57), confirmation (nos. 54, 60), reconciliation (nos. 21, 58), and the Eucharist (no. 57).[8]

The pope also links marriage and a fifth sacrament—holy orders—in quoting a compelling passage from Aquinas:

> The sacrament of marriage gives to the educational role the dignity and vocation of being really and truly a "ministry" of the Church at the service of the building up of her members. So great and splendid is the educational ministry of Christian parents that Saint Thomas has no hesitation in comparing it with the ministry of priests: "Some propagate and guard spiritual life by a spiritual ministry: this is the role of the sacrament of Orders; others do this for both corporal and spiritual life, and this is brought about by the sacrament of marriage, by which a man and a woman join in order to beget offspring and bring them up to worship God." (no. 38)

Later on, the pope, invoking the famous distinction between the "baptismal" and "sacerdotal" priesthood, says: "The Church prays for the Christian family and educates the family to live in generous accord with the priestly gift and role received from Christ the High Priest. In effect, the baptismal priesthood of the faithful, exercised in the sacrament of marriage, constitutes the basis of a priestly vocation and mission for the spouses and family by which their daily lives are transformed into 'spiritual sacrifices acceptable to God through Jesus Christ'" (no. 59). What is striking in these references and every other to the sacraments is that there is never the slightest hesitation or suggestion that marriage in any way undermines, "taints," or otherwise calls into question the holiness of the couple or the "validity" of any of the sacraments. Indeed, the entire document, in both tone and contents, contains not the slightest skepticism about marriage and family: there is no "two-tier" approach to sacraments, no triumphalist or at least apologetic treatment—as one saw in earlier Latin sacramental theology—that would seem to suggest that marriage is a "lower" sacrament for those baser beings unable to attain to the "evangelical perfection" of celibacy.[9]

From this, then, one must conclude that any fear of marriage somehow undermining any of the sacraments, calling into question the holiness of the couple, or being on a lower level than the other sacraments—including especially, of course, holy orders—or even in opposition to one of them (orders), as has so commonly been assumed, at least at the popular level, is officially—*magisterially*—rejected. In other words, *nothing* the pope says can be taken as assuming any opposition between the sacraments of marriage and ordination (both of which, incidentally, are grouped together in the 1992 catechism under the heading "sacraments at the service of communion"). Put differently still, everything the pope and synod fathers said throughout *FC* applies equally and unequivocally to married couples, *including married priests*. The rich and hearty theology of marriage presented here can no longer be gainsaid.[10] If, then, one wishes to somehow elevate celibacy above marriage at least insofar as the question of priestly ordination is concerned, one will have to look to quite other sources than *FC* and additional synodal and papal documents[11]—including the universal catechism of 1992—from which to draw such pejorative reflections.[12] In sum, then, *FC*, using, as it were, both kataphatic and apophatic methods, presents us with two major milestones: first, a positive and lasting theology of marriage and family, and second, no comment or even hint that marriage is on a lower level than any other sacrament.

Though themselves celibate, of course, the late pope John Paul II and the synod fathers did not indulge in romanticism about the family in *FC*. Indeed, there are many welcome notes of realism about the struggles of family life today, thanks both to external pressures and to the internal pressures of sin and conflict.[13] (Such awareness of the struggles would be deepened and magnified by another postsynodal apostolic exhortation a quarter-century later, *Amoris Laetitia*.) One of the most common themes in the document is that of the many and constant *sacrifices* necessary to live a Christian life in families today. Again and again the bishops write that "sacrifice cannot be removed from family life, but must in fact be wholeheartedly accepted if the love between husband and wife is to be deepened and become a source of intimate joy" (no. 34). Sacrifice is linked to the ability to preserve the communion discussed earlier: "Family communion can only be preserved and perfected through a great spirit of sacrifice. It requires, in fact, a ready and generous openness of each and all to understanding, to forbearance, to pardon, to reconciliation. There is no family that does not know how selfishness, discord, tension and conflict violently attack and at times mortally wound its own communion" (no. 21). Nevertheless, the family's recognition of these attacks of sinfulness by the family against itself are not used by the synod fathers to prove a point, as though celibacy somehow is a reservation magically kept free from such invaders and attackers. Indeed, in a surprising passage in a later document, the synod fathers of 2015 candidly recognize that celibacy can too often be a convenient way to *avoid* sacrifice: "Celibacy can risk becoming a comfortable single life that provides the freedom to be independent, to move from one residence, work or option to another, to spend money as one sees fit and to spend time with others as one wants." What is an antidote to this? In a surprisingly generous recognition, the fathers immediately write that "in such cases, the witness of married people becomes especially eloquent. Those called to virginity can encounter in some marriages a clear sign of God's generous and steadfast fidelity to his covenant, and this can move them to a more concrete and generous availability to others" (*Amoris Laetitia*, no. 162). This bearing of sacrifices, this concrete and generous serving of others, comes about precisely as a result of the sacramental grace and gift given by marriage, which takes sacrificial moments and allows them to become occasions of joy: "Just as husbands and wives receive from the sacrament the gift and responsibility of translating into daily living the sanctification bestowed on them, so the same sacrament confers on them the grace and moral obligation of transforming their whole lives into a 'spiritual sacrifice.' What the Second Vatican Council says of the laity also applies to Christian spouses and parents, especially with regard to the earthly and temporal realities that characterize their lives: 'As worshippers leading holy lives in every place, the laity consecrate the world itself to God'" (no. 56).[14]

Paul Evdokimov on Sacrifice, Askesis, and Universal-Ontological Monasticism

These themes of sacrifice, of liturgy and laity in the world, are given much richer and more ample reflection in the work of the Orthodox theologian Paul Evdokimov, who died in 1970. His book *The Sacrament of Love* (*SL*) remains one of the richest such works to reflect on marriage,[15] especially insofar as Evdokimov very explicitly and unhesitatingly aims to destroy any vestiges of opposition not only between men and women[16] but also between marriage and monasticism. Evdokimov, a contemporary of Pope John Paul II, lived in some ways a life, especially an intellectual life, that bears a striking resemblance to that of the pope, particularly in their commitment to a personalist-phenomenological approach to moral and spiritual questions.

In turning to *The Sacrament of Love* (*SL*), a book of several parts written in a somewhat diffuse style, it is striking to see how Evdokimov, from the outset, makes large and strong claims for marriage, as though anticipating pushback from more "traditionalist" approaches in both East and West alike, where some have been inclined to see marriage as a second-tier sacrament. What is especially interesting is that Evdokimov also uses language we have already encountered in the apologetics of some trying to justify priestly celibacy, writing that, since the coming of the Messiah, "the nuptial marriage-priesthood is *ontological*, the new creation that saturates human time with eternity. Like monasticism, marriage is eschatological; it is the mystery of the 'eighth day' and the prophetic figure of the Kingdom."[17] What links marriage and monasticism is the fact that both are comprehensible only through a shared commitment to asceticism.

SL develops the theme of asceticism in a rich and very original way. Evdokimov begins in a classically Eastern mode—apophaticism—by telling us what asceticism is not: "asceticism ... is never against the flesh but against the perversions of the flesh, against unlawful concupiscence that is *against nature*."[18] Such asceticism is the same for those who are married and those who are monastic, that is, celibate.[19] Such is the position of one of the great fathers of the Church, St. John Chrysostom,[20] according to Evdokimov: "'The perfect spouses are not inferior to monks,' and indeed 'they can manifest greater virtues than monastics.'"[21] But from here Evdokimov blurs the boundaries further, arguing that "marriage includes within itself the monastic state and that is why the latter is not a sacrament."[22] Evdokimov is explicit about why he takes this step, arguing that "the time has come to assert the fullness of matrimony, its state of grace, and to free the married conscience from the complexes imposed upon it. The true monk will rejoice in this, for he, more than anyone else, is able to discern the real value of marriage. Its path is narrow, perhaps the most narrow of all, since there are two that walk upon it." And then, in two of the most moving and psychologically profound passages in the entire book, Evdokimov continues this theme: "In order to be loved by the other, one must renounce oneself completely. It is a deep and unceasing ascetic practice. The crowns of the betrothed refer to martyrdom.[23] ... It is possible that the most ascetic act is not renunciation of self, but total self-acceptance."[24]

He continues to assert the connections between marriage and monasticism a little later, using language similar to Vatican II's "universal call to holiness" when he writes that "since its advent, monasticism has been an integral part of the Church because it expresses a spiritual norm that is *universal*, a normative value for *every* believer."[25] And every believer is called on to be not only monastic but sacerdotal as we move from linking marriage and monasticism to linking them both to the priesthood: "Every layperson is the priest of his existence," set apart as such and anointed for such via the sacrament of chrismation, a sacrament given to all believers and thereby creating a "perfect equality [from which] some are chosen and installed as bishops and priests, always by a divine act." Those who are, by divine act, chosen for ordained ministry in the Church always are without in any way being elevated over others: "There is a difference of ministries within the priestly body. The ministry of the priest is *functional*; there is *no ontological* difference between clerics and laypeople."[26]

This latter point is an important one that has largely been ignored by both East and West, where one still finds deeply entrenched cultures of clericalism. The priest, whether married or celibate, is no higher than or different from other people. His sole function is sacramental service in very particular ways. His being is no different in that regard from that of any other Christian also called to service. Thus, for the second time, Evdokimov has turned the language of ontology on its head, using it in a way quite different from its more recent usage at the hands of apologists for celibacy.

Finally, Evdokimov continues his vigorous and unapologetic campaign to extirpate unhelpful and unhealthy psychotheological complexes about marriage and sexuality when he asserts that "under the grace of the sacrament, the sexual life is lived without causing the slightest decline of the inner life."[27] If this latter point is true—and everything in *SL*, as in *FC* before it,[28] would have us believe it is—there are no grounds for assuming any incompatibility in the simultaneous exercise of both the sacrament of marriage and the sacrament of orders by certain men called by God to the ordained presbyterate.

In concluding, then, we can be confident that the arguments against a married priesthood have no force: historically, as our opening chapter by David Hunter showed, and as the literature review by Kevin Coyle confirmed, the idea that a celibate priesthood is somehow more "apostolic" or reflects "original" practice cannot be sustained. Theologically, the Church—in both East and West—has moved past her previous suspicions ("complexes" in Evdokimov's terminology) about marriage and sexuality as mere "disciplinary" concessions to human weakness ("concupiscence") to offer today, as we saw in Pope John Paul II's *Familiaris Consortio* (and before that in his "theology of the body," which Thomas Loya briefly touched on), a full-throated and robust defense of marriage in all its aspects. Gone is the Tridentine legacy of seeing marriage as a lesser sacrament, a mere concession to human weakness. Gone is any suspicion that marriage is in any way an impediment to the pursuit of holiness. In fact, marriage has never been elevated so high theologically as it has been in the last half-century, when it has become common to link it directly (following Chrysostom's lead, now recovered) to the Trinity, of which it is seen as an icon. Marriage is, indeed, for most people today the primary context in which they "work out their salvation in fear and trembling."

If marriage has such a status today in a renewed sacramental theology, there is nothing in that theology to suggest for a moment that marriage and ordination cannot be lived together. There is nothing "ontological" about celibacy—a very recent and dubious opinion advanced by some careless apologists slyly trying to extend Latin theological claims about the ontological status of the priestly character conferred by ordination (see, e.g., *Lumen Gentium* no. 10.2 and *Catechism of the Catholic Church* nos. 1546–1547 and 1581–1582) to cover optional celibacy as well. There are no longer any intellectually coherent or theologically defensible reasons why celibacy should be "privileged" in the Catholic Church to the exclusion or denigration of a married priesthood. With the existence of the Eastern Catholic churches and their married clergy (and beyond them, with the hope of unity with the entire Orthodox East), and increasingly with the existence of married Latin-rite clergy today coming from Anglicanism and Lutheranism (inter alia), we are now living in an era when apologies for celibacy are increasingly out of date both pastorally and theologically—to say nothing of their often dubious historical argumentation. We no longer need such apologetic treatments of celibacy; the era in which the "lay faithful" were supposedly "scandalized" by married priests is over, just as the era of triumphalistic apologetics—in which the West tried to demonstrate its superior "apostolicity" over the East, and vice versa—is over (at least at the official and highest levels of the Church).

Moving forward, then, Eastern and Western Christians should expect that both disciplines will continue to be respected without the latter's discipline attempting to undermine the former's, as has happened with such dolorous and destructive consequences. If the ecumenical declarations and advances of the past half-century and more mean anything, especially those emanating from Rome, both East and West have a right to expect that this issue will simply, quietly disappear into the background of Christian history, no longer a flashpoint of controversy, division, and schism. Such a disappearance, to assure justly nervous Orthodox observers only too aware of the treatment of Eastern Catholics,[29] may well require canonical and other manifestly kenotic self-limitations on the part of Rome to prevent the resurgence of her longstanding imperialistic tendencies, which lurk, neither dead nor forgotten, in the ecclesial consciousness of her past.[30]

Notes

1. About the reform of the Roman papacy see my *Orthodoxy and the Roman Papacy: Ut Unum Sint and the Prospects of East-West Unity* (Notre Dame, IN: University of Notre Dame Press, 2011).

2. Pope John Paul II, *Pastores dabo vobis* (*PDV*), apostolic exhortation, 1992, no. 50.

3. The 1971 synod was on the themes of both ministerial priesthood and justice in the world.

4. Arguably the most widely influential book in this recovery of communion remains John Zizioulas's landmark work, *Being as Communion* (Crestwood, NY: St. Vladimir's Seminary Press, 1985). Cf., inter alia, Joseph Ratzinger, *Called to Communion: Understanding the Church Today* (San Francisco: Ignatius Press, 1986), and Catherine Clifford, ed., *For the Communion of the Churches: The Contribution of the Groupe des Dombes* (Grand Rapids, MI: Eerdmans, 2010).

5. See my chapter "Orientalium Ecclesiarum" in Matthew Levering and Matthew Lamb, eds., *The Reception of Vatican II* (Oxford: Oxford University Press, 2017), 324–346. On the *ressourcement* movement, see Gabriel Flynn and Paul Murray, eds., *Ressourcement: A Movement for Renewal in Twentieth-Century Catholic Theology* (Oxford: Oxford University Press, 2014).

6. On the widespread, ecumenically far-reaching changes, see Paul D. Murray, ed., *Receptive Ecumenism and the Call to Catholic Learning: Exploring a Way for Contemporary Ecumenism* (Oxford: Oxford University Press, 2010).

7. See, for example, Stephen F. Brett, *The Law of Love: From Autonomy to Communion* (Scranton, PA: University of Scranton Press, 2010), and then two studies in the "Ressourcement" series from Eerdmans: Angelo Cardinal Scola, *The Nuptial Mystery*, trans. M. K. Borras (Grand Rapids, MI: Eerdmans, 2005),

and Marc Cardinal Ouellet, *Divine Likeness: Toward a Trinitarian Anthropology of the Family* (Eerdmans, 2006).

8. For a fuller reflection on orders in the whole sacramental economy, see my "The Sacrament of Orders Dogmatically Understood," in H. Boersma and M. Lamb, eds., *The Oxford Handbook of Sacramental Theology* (Oxford: Oxford University Press, 2015), 531–544.

9. Cf., for example, the Catechism of the Council of Trent, which lists marriage as the last of the seven sacraments, coming after holy orders, saying of those in orders that "no nobler function than theirs can be imagined. Justly, therefore, are they called not only Angels, but even gods, because of the fact that they exercise in our midst the power and prerogatives of the immortal God."

10. The stout defense of marriage and family was a hallmark of John Paul's papacy, as seen in numerous documents and interventions, including the 1983 "Charter of the Rights of the Family," available here: http://www.vatican.va/roman_curia/pontifical_councils/family/documents/rc_pc_family_doc_19831022_family-rights_en.html.

11. Cf., for example, the pope's 1994 "Letter to Families," available here: http://www.vatican.va/holy_father/john_paul_ii/letters/documents/hf_jp-ii_let_02021994_families_en.html.

12. Such a movement would be heavy with irony insofar as apologists for celibacy often cloak themselves in the bright raiment of Catholic "traditionalism" and claim merely to be "following the Magisterium"—to which one is tempted to reply with Alasdair MacIntyre's famous interrogatory formula: Whose magisterium? Which tradition?

13. Jessica Millard Hartman, "Clerical Marriage from a Wife's Viewpoint," in Peter M. J. Stravinskas, ed., *Priestly Celibacy: The Scriptural, Historical, Spiritual, and Psychological Roots* (Mt. Pocono, PA: Newman House Press, 2001), 95–106, documents the breakdown of her marriage in a parish and the cost to her children.

14. The internal reference is to *Lumen Gentium* no. 34. For more on sacrifice, see John Haas, "Marriage and the Priesthood," in Stravinskas, *Priestly Celibacy*, 64–85. Haas was an Episcopalian cleric who converted and opted not to get ordained because of the demands on his family.

15. Paul Evdokimov, *The Sacrament of Love* (Crestwood, NY: St. Vladimir's Seminary Press, 1985).

16. On this point, see Evdokimov's posthumously published *Woman and the Salvation of the World*, trans. A. P. Gythiel (Crestwood, NY: St. Vladimir's Seminary Press, 1994).

17. *SL*, 47; emphasis in the original.

18. Ibid., 60; emphasis in original.

19. Celibacy outside monastic communities is not common in the East and is in fact usually looked upon askance. Almost always, parish priests are married;

celibate pastors living on their own are very rare. The Byzantine Catholic hieromonk Maximos Davies' article "Celibacy in Context" helpfully explains why: http://www.firstthings.com/article/2002/12/celibacy-in-context.

20. "Marriage is a mysterious icon of the Church," according to Chrysostom in J. P. Migne, ed., *Patrologia Graeca* (*PG*) (Paris, 1867–1866), 62:387. See further Josiah B. Trenham, *Marriage and Virginity According to St. John Chrysostom* (Platina, CA: St. Herman of Alaska Press, 2013).

21. *SL*, 164, quoting Chrysostom's Homily XX as recorded in *PG* 62:147.

22. *SL*, 68.

23. In the Byzantine marriage liturgy, the couple wear crowns on their heads, symbolic of the crown of thorns of Christ at Calvary and so making clear that marriage, from the very beginning, can survive only through self-sacrifice.

24. *SL*, 70 and 100.

25. Ibid., 81; emphasis in original.

26. Ibid., 85–86; emphasis in original. Cf., for example, *Lumen Gentium* no. 10.2 and *Catechism of the Catholic Church* nos. 1546–1547 and 1581–1582.

27. *SL*, 171.

28. And indeed, written not only in *FC*, but elsewhere in documents of the pontificate of Pope John Paul II—a man who, let us remember, even before becoming pope had reflected intelligently, uniquely, and significantly on the gift of human sexuality—and whose desire to canonize or beatify married saints was well known.

29. See, for example, the many blunt observations by the late Ukrainian Orthodox archbishop Vsevelod of Chicago, especially his "Toward Reconciliation of the Catholic Church and the Orthodox Church," in his *We Are All Brothers*, 3 vols. (Fairfax, VA: Eastern Christian Publications, 1999), I: 145–162, in which he discusses the question of celibacy and other issues that Orthodox regard with "apprehension" upon seeing the fate of Eastern Catholics since the Union of Brest.

30. A number of recent studies have looked at the intersection of imperialism and the rise of the papacy after the collapse of the Roman Empire in the West. See in particular Susan Wessel, *Leo the Great and the Spiritual Rebuilding of a Universal Rome* (Leiden, Netherlands: Brill, 2008).

APPENDIX ONE

The Toronto Tempest

Victor Pospishil

Edited by Adam A. J. DeVille

September 7, 1975, was a Sunday on which Christians gathered in the Church of the Nativity of the Blessed Virgin Mary, a Byzantine Catholic parish in the Eparchy of Toronto, Canada, where liturgy that day would be celebrated by Bishop Michael Rusnak, a member of the Slovak-Byzantine province of the Redemptorist Fathers. Rusnak, ordained a priest in 1949 and bishop in 1965, was auxiliary to the Ukrainian Catholic bishop of Toronto with responsibility for Byzantine-rite Slovak Catholics in Canada. Rusnak on this day, by delegation of Bishop Isidore Borecky, was to ordain three men as priests: John Gihirny, Andrew Kormanik, and Terence Lozynsky.[1]

These three deacons as well as their wives were all full-time employees of the public or semi-public (separate) school system of Ontario[2] and could therefore be classified as auxiliary or part-time clergy. One should not, however, put them into the category of "weekend" ecclesiastical workers, as their daily existence was intimately interwoven with the lives of the congregations to which they had been assigned as deacons. They certainly were not "mercenaries" in the service of the Church, as they were making their livelihoods on the outside. We can in sincere sympathy understand the overwhelming joy which they experienced on the occasion of finally reaching the priesthood.

We may also understand—though the prudence of the serpent which Christians ought to possess in this vale of tears should have held them back—that they gave vent to their feelings of jubilation and shouted their exultation in a paean of publicity from the rooftops of Toronto. The press picked up the news greedily, saying that three married (!) men had been ordained Catholic (!) priests, and strong gusts of a tempest began to blow.

It appears that two Latin bishops brought the matter at once to the attention of Pro-Nuncio Guido Del Mestri in Ottawa,[3] already set to depart for another assignment.[4] The [Latin] bishop of Hamilton forbade the Catholic school system in his diocese to regard, treat, or address Fr. Andrew Kormanik as a priest and suggested to the latter that he resign his teaching position.[5]

There is also the suspicion that a certain ambitious priest of the eparchy attempted to ingratiate himself with the expectation of future reward, perhaps even an episcopal mitre,[6] and denounced the two bishops to the pro-nuncio, stating, namely that they had acted against the latest prohibition of ordaining married men priests, issued on January 14, 1971 (N.344/70),[7] as the will of the pope himself: "*ex audientia SSmi.*" However, no proof whatsoever has been offered for such a suspicion of an act which others would regard as despicable treason, and all such speculation ought to be suspended.

Bishop Rusnak received a request from the pro-nuncio to come to Ottawa. Then he received a letter of the pro-nuncio of September 18, 1975, in which their oral discussion was summarized, and the bishop issued an order "to inform the three priests in question that, until the Holy Father decides otherwise, they are prohibited to exercise their priestly function." Rusnak complied with this command at once. The three priests, utterly dazed and confused, continued to exercise their ministries as presbyters, supported morally by their consciences and the nearly unanimous displeasure of the clergy and of the faithful.[8] They thought that in order to deserve suspension—a serious and grave canonical punishment—a cleric must have committed a crime according to external signs. Can one judge as sinful the ordination of married men to the priesthood in a church which had received and practiced this apostolic norm since the time of entering Christendom? How shall such a man, who had served as a deacon for some time in the same church, and had begun to celebrate liturgies alone and hear confession, now refuse these presbyterial services when the dearth of priests is so great that Bishop Rusnak himself usually has to celebrate on a weekend six liturgies in several places? Can he cease to function as a priest without causing great scandal and without engendering a deep hatred and contempt for the supreme authority in the Church and for the entire ecclesiastical structure? Indeed, a hard nut to crack!

Everything seemed to quiet down, and the whole affair seemed to have been really only an isolated one soon to be forgotten: such was the prayer of the pious. But what stood behind a renewed interest in Rome is difficult to say. It could be that the new publicity that was started with sensational statements in the press, which had to be corrected by the Ukrainian clergy with the explanation of the differences between the Eastern and Latin churches, blew up a new flame from the cooling embers. Sometimes these rejoinders were done with rancor, in a rage that should have been absent. Whatever caused it, the letter of the new pro-nuncio, Archbishop Angelo Palmas,[9] of February 19, 1976, transmitted the text of a letter of the Congregation for the Oriental Churches in which the prohibition was repeated and the bishop was requested to consider justifying himself in person in Rome. In addition to being married, it was insinuated that the three priests had not studied in a seminary and that they possessed an inadequate education—an assumption which was erroneous since the three had better academic preparation than the average Catholic priest.

Rome relented later from the demand to see the bishop in person for unrelated reasons.[10] Metropolitan Maxim Hermaniuk[11] then submitted, on 3 May 1976, a petition to Pope Paul VI requesting that the ban on the ordination of married men to the presbyterate be rescinded. I shall express further below some thoughts on the likelihood that this wish would fall on benevolent ears. Looking at the past history of the problem in the Americas, *Roma locuta, causa finita*, will be true only if the Holy See finally decides to relent in the opposition to the ordination of married men in the Eastern churches.

Consuetudo contra legem: The History of the Celibacy Legislation for the Eastern Catholics in the Americas

1. The Roman Prohibition

Byzantine Catholics from the Austro-Hungarian monarchy started to arrive in large numbers in North America in the 1880s. The Holy See, at the insistence of the Latin hierarchy, who not only opposed a married

Eastern priesthood but demanded the suppression of the Eastern Catholics in the United States, established a rule that only celibate or widowed priests—if the latter came without their children—could emigrate to the New World. This idea was contained in the letter of the Sacred Congregation for the Propagation of the Faith of May 2, 1890, to the archbishop of Paris[12] and was repeated in a letter of Propaganda on October 1, 1890, to the Ukrainian and Ruthenian hierarchy in Austro-Hungary and in a letter of the same dicastery to Cardinal James Gibbons, archbishop of Baltimore, of May 10, 1892. The same principle was applied to the United States by a decree of the Propaganda [Congregation] of October 1, 1890: "Priests of the Greek-Ruthenian Rite who desire to immigrate to and remain in the United States of America must be celibate." A decree of the same congregation of May 1, 1897, instructs the local Latin ordinaries to grant faculties only to that Ruthenian priest who is praiseworthy in his "celibacy and suitability" and if such were lacking, the Latin bishop was directed to send a Latin priest to minister to these Eastern communities in his diocese. It was not said how that could be done considering the difference of language and rite.

In *Ea Semper*, the bull of Pius X of June 14, 1907, with which he accompanied the appointment of Bishop Soter Stephen Ortynsky as ecclesiastical "superior" for the Byzantine Catholics, without ordinary jurisdiction but only with delegated jurisdiction to be received from each individual Latin bishop, it was stipulated that the Ruthenian priest "must be celibate or a widower without children, of upright life."

This rule was wholly unrealistic. There were at that time no religious priests in the Byzantine-rite dioceses whence these people came, and the few celibate secular priests were needed at home for such positions as the episcopacy, seminary professorships, canons of cathedral chapters, etc.

The same norm was repeated in subsequent papal documents. The last forceful re-affirmation of celibacy occurred under Pius XI in the decree *Cum Data Fuerit* of March 1, 1929 (and the identical decree *Graeci-Rutheni Ritus* of May 24, 1930, for Canada). Art. 12 declares: "Again, as already many times before it was decreed, priests of the Greek-Ruthenian Rite who desire to immigrate to the United States of North America [*sic*] and stay there must be celibate." The forcible re-introduction of the celibacy rule under Bishop Basil Takach—whose apprehensions Pius XI is said to have brushed aside with the peremptory command "per forza"—led to the defection from the Ruthenian jurisdiction of some 100,000 to the Eastern Orthodox Church, of which more below.[13]

In spite of this continuous iteration of the exclusion of a married Eastern clergy from the Americas, the law was never in reality observed as the following facts show:

2. A Contrary Legal Custom?

i) There was never a time when married priests did not come to minister to the Ukrainians, Ruthenians, Slovaks, Croats, and Romanians of the Byzantine rite in the United States and Canada. At no time in the past as well as the present did the celibate priests—including the religious—constitute the majority of clergy.[14]

ii) In order to stem at least partially the inroads of the Orthodox ecclesiastical structure among the Catholics, Bishop Soter Ortynsky, ordinary of the Byzantine-rite Ruthenian-Ukrainian Catholics in the United States between 1907 and 1916, ordained a number of married cantors (*diaks*) after they had received a perfunctory formation within one year.

iii) From 1912 until his recall to Europe in 1927, Bishop Nicetas Budka,[15] the ordinary for the Ukrainian Catholics in Canada and the only bishop between 1916 and 1925 on the North American continent of his rite, ordained numerous candidates from Canada and the United States who were married, of whom a number are still alive. That this was done unbeknownst to Rome was later acknowledged in a letter of Cardinal Luigi Sincero of July 23, 1934, acknowledging the "indulgent attitude of the Holy See."[16]

iv) At various times married priests, ordained by Orthodox bishops, were received into Byzantine-rite dioceses, always with the permission of the Holy See, and not rarely after being recommended by it, nay, even by applying some pressure.

v) Catholic men, not rarely former seminarians, joined the Orthodox churches in order to be able to be ordained as married candidates. The majority repented later and were received back into the Catholic Church with the permission of the Holy See.

vi) Before World War II, bishops were sometimes forced to tolerate even priests who had married after ordination to the priesthood by a Catholic bishop, as the late metropolitan Constantine Bohachevsky in Philadelphia had to do,[17] a situation which was reported also to the Holy See.

vii) In the wake of World War II, the Holy See permitted married priests who had fled before the Communists to be accepted in the dioceses of Canada and the United States (1947). This extended also to former seminarians from Western Ukraine who had been in preparation for the married priesthood when the occupation by the Soviet Union forced them to flee to Western Europe. The Holy See permitted the Ukrainian Catholic bishops of North America to accept and ordain such married men to the priesthood. These priests were accompanied by their faithful, and they constituted the majority of the clergy in both countries.

viii) Because of the extreme dearth of priests, at the suggestion of the late Eugene Cardinal Tisserant, prefect of the Congregation for the Oriental Churches for many years, married candidates were sent to bishops in Europe, ordained there, and then returned to Canada.

ix) Josyf Cardinal Slipyj, ordained in Rome and elsewhere since 1963,[18] married candidates for Canada and other parts of the world, of which the Holy See was cognizant.

x) Several married candidates were ordained in Canada also by the bishop of Toronto and by the metropolitan of Winnipeg.

xi) During all these years, other Eastern Catholic churches sent married priests to the United States and Canada—e.g., the Romanian Church and the Melkite Church. Since the number of various religious institutes in the Near East is large, most priests of these areas on the North American continent were celibates. But there were always also married ones, and some have been ordained as such quite recently.

When one surveys these "exceptions" from the rule established by the Holy See, it is clear that the "law" was never considered truly obligatory. It had been enacted at the insistence of the Latin hierarchy at a time when the Eastern Catholic churches were regarded as second-class structures in the Church, to be faded out everywhere except perhaps the Near East. Since it is inconceivable that the Holy See could have been ignorant of the true situation on the North American continent, and because one assumed that the popes must have had the welfare of these Catholics on their minds, the principle applies that *Qui tacet consentire videtur* and that silence and tolerance are equivalent to approval, though perhaps a reluctant one.

The reason for this apparent disregard of the demand of the Holy See is clear: it was not wanton disrespect for the Roman pontiff but the factual crying need for priests: *salus animarum suprema lex*.[19] Second, the sincere conviction of bishops, priests, and faithful that they were following a tradition in force since their forefathers accepted Christianity and to which Eastern Christendom had adhered since apostolic times. Third, the sincere and justified belief that in ordaining some married candidates the true will of the Holy See was being fulfilled; the popes could not be imagined as willing the destruction of the Byzantine-rite Church.

It is true that for some twenty years between the two world wars, two dioceses in Galicia[20] (Stanislawiw since 1920 and Peremyshl since 1925) had accepted compulsory celibacy, but the Servant of God Andrey Sheptytsky, metropolitan of Lviv, rejected this risky and shortsighted experiment. The results were disappointing. Because of the lack of celibate candidates, parishes could not be provided with priests, and several Protestant sects established themselves in various parts of these dioceses. This was the time when Eastern Orthodoxy, for other reasons, gained a large following in the Subcarpathian region then under Czechoslovakia. Those priests who had been ordained as celibates under these circumstances, a condition which they had accepted often reluctantly, were among the first who joined the Orthodox Church when the union was abolished by force under the Communists,[21] since they were now permitted to enter marriage.

3. The Problem of Celibacy in the Universal Catholic Church

Voices are being heard in the Church, even of patriarchs, cardinals, and bishops, especially from mission countries, suggesting that the Catholic Church freely ordain married men. Such demands were peremptorily suppressed at Vatican II when Pope Paul VI forbade the discussion of this topic, and also at subsequent synods of bishops, including one in 1974.

It has been speculated that church authorities may gravely sin when they prevent married candidates from entering the priesthood. This must not mean that the pope has no right to render such a decision, but rather he may cause great damage to the Church of God by the exclusion of a married clergy in a situation such as exists today, especially if his decision is not supported by other members of the Church. A decision of such a magnitude, when rendered after a deliberate exclusion of his fellow bishops from a discussion of the problem—that, after all, is not in the area in which he enjoys infallibility—with the full awareness that the Eastern churches and all the ancient churches had a married clergy, must be regarded with apprehension.

4. An Ancient Issue

The Church of the first centuries had to contend with the problem caused by the demand of the Roman Church to make celibacy compulsory. It is well known that the Synod of Trullo (692) had been assembled to complement by appropriate disciplinary canons the Fifth (553) and the Sixth (681) Ecumenical Councils since they had concentrated exclusively on doctrinal matters. Canon 13 of Trullo rejected compulsory celibacy for deacons and presbyters but sanctioned it for bishops. I think it is worthwhile to quote this canon, which was not recognized, of course, by the West, in its entirety:

> Since we know it to be handed down as a rule of the Roman Church that those who are deemed worthy to be advanced to the diaconate or presbyterate should promise no longer to cohabit with their wives, we, preserving the ancient rule and apostolic perfection and order, will that the lawful marriages of men who are in holy orders be from this time forward firm, by no means dissolving their union with their wives nor depriving them of their mutual intercourse at a convenient time. Wherefore, if anyone shall have been found worthy to be ordained subdeacon, or deacon, or presbyter, he is by no means to be prohibited from admittance to such a rank, even if he shall live with a lawful wife. Nor shall it be demanded of him at the time of his ordination that he promise to abstain from lawful intercourse with his wife: Lest we should affect injuriously marriage constituted by God and blessed by his presence, as the Gospel says, "What God has joined together let no man put asunder" and the Apostle said, "Marriage is honorable and the bed undefiled"; and again, "Are you bound to a wife? Seek not to be loosed." But we know, as they who assembled at Carthage (with a care for the honest life of the clergy) said, that subdeacons, who handle the Holy Mysteries, and deacons, and presbyters should abstain from their consorts according to their own course of service. So that what has been handed down through the Apostles and preserved by ancient custom, we too likewise maintain, knowing that there is a time for all things and especially for fasting

and prayer. For it is meet that they who assist at the divine altar should be absolutely continent when they are handling holy things, in order that they may be able to obtain from God what they ask in sincerity.

If therefore anyone shall have dared, contrary to the Apostolic Canons, to deprive any of those who are in holy orders, presbyter, or deacon, or subdeacon of cohabitation and intercourse with his lawful wife, let him be deposed. In like manner also if any presbyter or deacon on pretense of piety has dismissed his wife, let him be excluded from communion; and if he persevere in this let him be deposed.[22]

Canon XII forbids the same thing, which was permitted the presbyters and deacons, to bishops after ordination.

In discussing the opposition of Trullo to compulsory celibacy, Catholic authors attempt to brush it aside as having been dictated by bitterness at the refusal of the West to submit politically and culturally to the primacy of the East. However, even a cursory reader of can. 13 will be astonished by its deeply pastoral tenor, full of compassion and human understanding.

The Great Apostasy

The Roman Curia must *nolens volens* own up to the dubious merit of having presided over the creation of several Eastern Orthodox churches in North America from Catholics who left the Church because of the refusal by Rome to permit the ordination of married priests.

The Russian Orthodox Church had established a mission in Alaska in 1794, later erected into a diocese. After Alaska had been sold to the United States in 1867, the bishop found it more practical to transfer his residence to San Francisco (1872). The future of the Russian Orthodox Church in the United States would have remained quite unglamorous but for one new and unexpected development. In the 1880s a new wave of immigration started coming from the Austro-Hungarian monarchy, especially from the economically underdeveloped region of the Carpathian mountains. A majority of the new settlers were so-called Greek Catholics, that is Uniates or Catholics of the Slavic-Byzantine rite. Their national consciousness had not yet clearly evolved in the mind of this simple people, and their ecclesiastical affiliation was the most significant characteristic for them. They called themselves "Russki," Little Russians, or Carpatho-Russians, sometimes also Russines or Ruthenians, and a few may have foreshadowed their present national names, Ukrainian and Slovak. In order to understand the cool, nay even hostile reception in the United States by their Catholic brethren, we must take cognizance of the situation of the Catholic Church at that time in this country.

The Catholics in the United States had for a long time been represented by the Irish, largely third-grade citizens, exploited in the mines of Pennsylvania or at the construction of the Erie Canal or the new railroads which began to crisscross the country around the middle of the 19th century. Finally, more and more of them were able slowly to advance upward into that class which has some political clout, at least on the local scene. Of course, they had the advantage of speaking the language of the ruling majority, English. Farsighted Catholic leaders, such as John Ireland (1838–1918), archbishop of St. Paul, Minnesota, worked toward the integration of the Catholic immigrant into the life of the nation because otherwise Catholicism would remain but a foreign intrusion and could never expect to become a factor in the political and cultural life of the nation.

The prospects for achieving this aim were rather dim. The numerous German Catholic immigration was well organized and seemed near its goal of attaining ecclesiastical separation and independence by obtaining from Rome their own hierarchy, disconnected from the other bishops of the United States. The thousands, nay millions, of Italians, Poles, Slovaks, Lithuanians, Croats, and other European Catholics who flooded the cities of the North-East and Middle-West closed themselves up into their ethnic ghettos, apparently impervious to those cultural influences which could enable them to become active citizens of their new country.

We can understand the utter dismay of Archbishop Ireland when in his diocese appeared the first Byzantine Catholics. Not only were they of a foreign tongue, but they were not even Catholic in the "true" sense of the word. There was simply no hope of ever assimilating them in the American Catholic Church, let alone the possibility of making them Americans. His disappointment exceeded everything conceivable when their priest, a Catholic priest in good standing, was discovered to be a formerly married man, married according to the laws of God and the Catholic Church, who had brought with him his orphaned children. Archbishop Ireland could not have been ignorant of the married clergy of the Eastern churches, and he was certainly a farsighted liberal man, but such an anomaly could not fit in his plans for the future of the American Church.

It was therefore not long afterward that Father Alexis Toth was suspended from his priestly functions.[23] Since the Roman Curia did not wish to support him, Toth ended up excommunicated for his refusal to send his children back to Europe or to abandon his flock and return home himself. Toth, utterly disappointed by the attitude of Rome toward his faithful, could not conceive of a church or a priest without a bishop, and he therefore approached the Russian Orthodox bishop in San Francisco. He and his flock were cordially received in 1892 into the Russian Orthodox Church. This fateful step developed into a stampede of Uniates into Russian Orthodoxy. It shall suffice to say that historically some 90% of the members of the Orthodox Church of America were former Catholics or their offspring.

It is necessary to ask for the causes of such a colossal apostasy. It is not prejudice to assert that it was the fault of the Roman Curia. The movement away from the Catholic Church could not have been engineered better by an avowed enemy of Catholicism. Here are a few reasons for this judgment.

In order to satisfy the American bishops, the Holy See forbade that the emigrants be accompanied by married priests, and even widowers were to be permitted only if they left their children back in Europe. The nearly total absence of celibate priests in the home country had the result that the prohibition deprived the faithful of priests of their own rite, although a certain number of married priests immigrated against the Roman veto. Neither did the people have much to expect from the ministrations of other Catholic priests, whose rite was foreign to them and whose languages they did not understand.

The Russian Orthodox hierarchy showed themselves more practical. They ordained any candidate able to perform the liturgical services. True, these men were often not far above illiteracy, and not rarely defective in their morals, not to mention their nonprofessional conduct, but they satisfied the simple need of a faithful who themselves were in the majority either illiterate or semiliterate, but otherwise deeply devoted to their own form of Christianity. The growth of the Russian Orthodox Church in the American East suggested to the Holy Synod that it transfer the center to New York (1905), and soon there was a net of Russian bishops all over the United States.

The flight from the Catholic Church was several times repeated. The last occasion was in the 1930s, when Rome attempted to enforce the celibacy rule, which had been silently disregarded since 1916. The Holy See succeeded as far as the dwindling Catholic minority is concerned, but in the meantime one Ruthenian Orthodox and two Ukrainian Orthodox churches were formed, their numerous priests and some 200,000 faithful being former Catholics. The end result was that some 1.3 million former Catholics are members of the Orthodox Church, and only 400,000 are left still united with Rome. Probably twice as many joined the Latin Church or Protestant churches in order to escape the internal dissensions.

The Demand for a Married Priesthood: Obstinancy or Pastoral Solicitude?

1. The Reality

The Ukrainian Catholic Church in Canada comprises now five dioceses with some 300,000 faithful and 280 secular and religious priests, counting the retired ones too. This proportion between clergy and people appears quite encouraging until one is made aware that there are 530 communities of these Ukrainians, Slovaks, and Magyars of the Byzantine rite with their own churches, distant from each other by tens and hundreds of miles, which expect pastoral care on Sundays and holy days. The Canadian census of 1971, which contained also a question concerning religious affiliation, discovered some 80,000 Ukrainian Catholics more than the bishops had on their books. These were people who had remained outside the reach of the Church because of the lack of priests. This led to the erection of the fifth diocese of New Westminster in British Columbia.

These statistical facts explain much, especially the alarm of the bishops, and the consequent desire to ordain married candidates. It is true that the ordination of such men was opposed by the Holy Father, and any wish expressed by the Roman pontiff cannot be treated lightly. However, it is another matter whether it is necessary to regard it as canon law, especially if it is opposed to a canonical norm of apostolic origin. The request of the pope to cease with ordinations of married candidates ought to be understood *rebus sic stantibus*.[24] Considering the repeated assurances of all popes, and also of the present one, that they desired that there should be no interference with the canonical discipline of the Eastern churches, such a demand could have been only the result of insistent moral pressure, to the point of extortion, on the part of Latin-rite bishops or of misguided curial dignitaries, who are still unable to see the damage which they thereby inflict upon the credibility of the Church and of the Holy See. Could the bishops therefore not consider the demand of 1971 as having lost its legislative *raison d'etre*? A legal norm which produces an effect contrary to that envisioned by an enlightened legislator ceases to be reasonable and prudent and thereby stops to be law in accordance with basic principles well established in canon law and moral theology.

2. A Change of Attitude in the Offing?

The ecclesiastical situation in Canada appears to be now changing. Not only have the circumstances of an extreme dearth of priests been a cause of grave alarm among the Byzantine Catholics; so also the Latin hierarchy of Canada has largely recognized what harm can result, especially in a country where Catholics are a minority, for the good name of the Church when the Eastern Catholics are prevented from following their own canonical discipline, while the Eastern Orthodox, composed chiefly of former Catholics and their offspring, have no fear of any interference from anybody.

A different state of mind has manifested itself in a part of the Latin hierarchy of Canada as it appears in a statement of the board of the Canadian Catholic Conference of March 1974: "The CCC Administrative Board indicates that it sees no difficulty in ... the Latin Rite ... accepting married men as candidates for the priesthood in the Oriental Rites in Canada in accordance with their laws and traditions." This generous and understanding attitude was repulsed in a letter of the Oriental Congregation of October 1974 to the president of the CCC, Archbishop Jean-Marie Fortier of Sherbrooke. In the accompanying "Note," we find a statement that is difficult to explain because it is so obviously erroneous to a student of canon law. It insinuates that the Ukrainians, Melkites, and Maronites (and by analogous extension other Eastern Catholics) have become new rites (?) in which married candidates cannot be ordained priests: "This prohibition is confirmed in the M. P. 'Episcopalis potestatis,' VII, I, 2: 'In ritibus in quibus non admittuntur clerici coniugati, a prohibitione exercendi ordinem presbyteratus facta coniugatis, qui eundem ordinem sine dispensatione Apostolicae Sedis receperunt.' Thus, dispensation from the prohibition is expressly reserved to the Holy Father." It was recently reported that the archbishop of Toronto, who, though Latin, is the ordinary of those Eastern Catholics who have no ordinary of their own, has requested that Rome permit the ordination of a married Maronite as a priest for his community.

3. A Changed People

While it is certainly true that the Ukrainians, Slovaks, and Hungarians are still dedicated to the Catholic Church, they have difficulties in accepting an order that must necessarily appear to them unjustified, even preposterous and suicidal, in view of the unbroken tradition of a married pastoral clergy since the beginning of Christianity among them. To not a few it appears that there must be persons in authority in the Church who are unaware of the changes of the times that have occurred during the last decade. These Catholics are living in Canada, in a country of liberty for every citizen, even the lowliest one, each of whom has learned to raise high his head, a situation so different from that out of which the officials of the Curia operate. These new Canadians are ready to submit to demands that can be justified by reference to law, but their longing for liberty, which made them flee their homelands and come to the free air of their new country, boils up again when there is a threat to their ancient rights and traditions for the safekeeping of which they left their home country. The fierce determination of these Ukrainians, Slovaks, and Hungarians to defend their traditions and the heritage of their fathers will not humble itself before the admonitions of the bishops to obey Rome in this suppression of a perpetual tradition. The possibility of manipulating the faithful and the clergy has passed here and also in Europe, and it will never return.

4. An Apostolic Tradition

It may sound trite and superfluous to speak of the apostolic origin of the married clergy. Latin Catholics may not give a thought to this truth, but it is different with Eastern Catholics, who were always provided with pastoral care by married priests. The Ukrainian Catholics, having in their midst also a numerous, conspicuous, zealous regular clergy (Basilians, Redemptorists, Salesians), and living among a numerous Latin celibate clergy, have become conscious that their custom is different, not some privilege or indult, nay, not even mere canon law or a creation of the Church, but that it is the ordinance of the apostles themselves.

Opposition to the institution of a married clergy must necessarily appear to the faithful at large anti-apostolic, anti-Catholic, a disavowal of the perpetual tradition of all the Eastern churches. A canonical institution which goes back to the beginning of the Church, which is the normal way of life for all the Eastern Orthodox in Canada and in the United States, cannot be abolished or discontinued without grave suspicions being aroused among the people of God, justified or not, namely, that those who attempt to subvert the ancient order are disguised enemies of God and of His Church.

5. Why Not Follow the Latin-Rite Example?

It was the policy of the North American Byzantine Catholic bishops to give preference to celibate vocations from among their faithful. These men were actually the normal, official candidates to the priesthood. Only in exceptional cases have some married been selected and ordained as priests. The majority of the clergy were always married, but they had come from Europe. In order not to discourage celibate vocations, married candidates had to possess some unusual attainments, especially academic ones, had to have demonstrated zeal and dedication to the goals of the Church, and had to have been tested for a number of years. These requirements, if applied in the future, the years of waiting for ordination, and the fact that sometimes they will have to earn a living outside the Church, would not easily divert those candidates who have a vocation to the celibate priesthood.

However, the question to be answered here is: why can the Byzantine and other Eastern churches not follow the example of the Latin Church and rely solely on celibate candidates to the priesthood? By phrasing the question in this form, the assumption is made that a vocation to the priesthood is dependent solely on the candidate himself and that the social climate and familial circumstances in which he grows up have no influence on the vocation. This view is mistaken. The Ukrainian and Slovak Catholics left their homes in Europe with determination to preserve in the New World all those religious and spiritual treasures which a theistic

Communism has decided to extirpate in the home country. Right or wrong, they wish to carry on also the tradition of a married pastoral clergy. While a priestly vocation begins in the heart of a boy or young man, it will develop and be preserved only with the support and approval of the parents. These people knew a married pastoral clergy ever since they accepted Christianity, and they were well aware that this is in continuation of an apostolic tradition. Consequently, they are disinclined to favor a celibate vocation for their sons, except perhaps in a monastic community. The recent vehement discussions and the numerous defections from the priesthood in the Latin Church could only confirm them in their resolve against a celibate vocation for their sons.

This reluctance of the faithful to accept celibacy for their sons—except in religious orders—fortified by the experience of the last decades, cannot be overcome by a fiat of the bishops. The spirit of democratic freedom has never more prefaced the minds of immigrants to the New World than in our own time, and we will never again see obedient sheep docilely following their shepherds wherever they lead them.

6. The Possibility of Negative Repercussions?

The fear that the ordination of married men to the presbyterate could influence Latin Catholics in the Americas has no basis in reality. Those who are acquainted with life in the United States and Canada are aware that each of the numerous religious and ethnic groups leads an existence separate from others, with its own churches, newspapers, grocery stores, lawyers, physicians, etc. What each group does rarely comes to the attention of other communities.[25]

In addition, Latin Catholics at large are cognizant that there are married Catholic priests even in Canada since such priests lived among them for nearly a century. They generally assume that the respective Eastern churches replenish their number, celibate or married, either by ordination or by immigration from abroad.

Also the possibility that the ordination of some married candidates may adversely affect the vocations to the religious priesthood is not justified. The reform of the Basilian Order in Galicia since the 1880s was opposed by a large segment of the clergy and the laity of Western Ukraine but enjoyed great success. Similarly, the introduction of the Redemptorists from Belgium resulted in numerous vocations, and, like the Basilian Fathers, they were able to establish several provinces. This was true in

Galicia, in Subcarpathia, and in Romania. (This would have happened also to the Salesians had World War II not intervened.) Even today, in Canada, the Basilians and the Redemptorists attract more vocations than the secular clergy. From the experience of Eastern Europe and the Near East, where a numerous married pastoral clergy was working side by side with a numerous celibate religious clergy, it can be asserted that those who have a celibate vocation will, in the Eastern churches, gravitate to the religious life. This was and is the case also in the Melkite, Maronite, and other churches.

7. The Bishops as Ethnarchs (Guardians of Heritage)

The bishops of the Ukrainian, Slovak, Hungarian, and other churches outside their homelands also have the duty to function as ethnarchs for their respective people. After their compatriots lost their homes to the Communists, these bishops have seen it as their sacred duty to preserve their national heritage as much as possible in their new home countries, which liberally grant them full freedom in that pursuit.[26] Because their national life had developed in close affiliation with the Church, which is also the explanation of why they could not submit to atheism and Communism, they see their bishops not as political but as national leaders. They expect their bishops and priests to keep alive all the respective national and religio-cultural treasures which the patrimony of their people has accumulated, including, of course, a married priesthood.

The greatest peril menacing their national communities is the dispersal of the people due to the lack of churches and priests. No ethnic group was able to maintain itself in the Americas except if it identified entirely with a religious institution. If there are no priests, there can be no religious communities, and then the entire fabric of that national group falls apart and disappears. What will history say about bishops who bear responsibility for the collapse of one of the few remaining remnants of an otherwise captive and subjugated nation?

How to Explain Rome

It is natural that the question is raised as to why Rome does what it does, since these measures must be judged self-defeating by those who take the Church by her words when she claims to care for the welfare of the Eastern Churches, not only the Catholic but also the Orthodox. Why does the Curia not listen to the pleading of the bishops and permit the ordination of married candidates in the Americas? Do we have to assume lack of information or, even worse, of human feeling and understanding on the part of the officials of the Curia? Not necessarily!

The most obvious reason for this lack of attention is simple inertia. As with all bureaucracies, solutions that have become routine, even if they had no effect, are carried along irrespective of whether they are good or bad. Rome has maintained this stance at least since the coming of the Eastern Catholics to the Americas, and only a cataclysmic event or the appearance of such a charismatic person as Pope John XXIII could effect a change. The personnel of the Congregation for the Eastern Churches, especially the secretary, are well acquainted with the problems, and they are inclined to understand the viewpoint of the Eastern bishops.

However, they are powerless, first because there is nobody in the Curia entitled to make decisions on public policy except Pope Paul VI, who sees it as his specific task to stem the tide against compulsory celibacy in the entire Church. Secondly, since the rearrangement of the Curia in 1967, all policy matters are to be decided by the secretary of state, who is now the only true minister of the papal government.[27] Thus the protest of two Latin bishops in Canada against the Toronto ordinations is sufficient to push the problem into the category of political decisions where pastoral considerations of a particular group have to take a backseat.

Another explanation may be the connection between the demand of the Eastern hierarchy to follow their perpetual tradition in the Americas and the question of whether the pope should continue to claim exclusive patriarchal jurisdiction everywhere outside the Near East and Eastern Europe. The Eastern hierarchies, being now set up by the Eastern Catholic Churches in Western Europe, North and South America, and Australia, do not form integral parts of the respective Eastern Catholic Churches but are, it is claimed, a part of the patriarchate of the West and thereby directly subject to the pope. Their patriarchs and synods have no jurisdiction over them, except in purely liturgical matters. The only concession made was the decree of May 25, 1970,[28] which permitted such heads of dioceses and apostolic exarchies to participate as full members in the synods of their patriarchates but excluded the synods from exercising any authority over these parts of their rite, except that they may submit to the pope a list of at least three candidates whenever the eparchy or exarchy becomes vacant. It is said that this position shall be in force "during the interim until the Eastern canon law discipline is organically revised."

Thus the revocation of the papal prohibition of ordaining married candidates to the presbyterate at the insistence of the Eastern Churches, which wish to follow their own canonical system, could be construed as tantamount to an admission that the papal claims to direct and immediate jurisdiction had been abandoned. Because of this tacit conclusion from such a step, no solution can be expected at this time.

The exclusion of the Eastern patriarchal jurisdiction in the New World over their own faithful has been challenged as being opposed to an express stipulation of Vatican II. The *Motu proprio* of June 1957, *Cleri Sanctitati*, had stated that a patriarch "presides [over] his own patriarchate or (*seu*) Rite as father and head with the most ample powers." Since the conjunction *seu* could be understood as equating rite with patriarchate or the territory of the patriarchate, Vatican II's decree *Orientalium Ecclesiarum*, repeating the definition of a patriarch, used the conjunction *vel*: "By the name of Eastern patriarch is meant a bishop who possesses jurisdiction over all bishops, not excepting metropolitans, the clergy and the faithful of his own territory or (*vel*) Rite," which is to say that territory and rite are not identical. Thus the Oriental patriarch has jurisdiction in a certain territory and, in addition, also outside over members and structures of his rite (art. 7). Since major archbishops are in general equated with patriarchs (art. 10), the same is asserted also in respect to the Ukrainians.[29]

This problem of jurisdiction in the New World exists also within the Eastern Orthodox Church, where canon 28 of Chalcedon (451) gave to the patriarch of Constantinople the authority to take care of the bishops of the churches *en tois barbarois* [among the barbarians]. Whether this applies to the Americas or not, and whether it means that the Ecumenical Patriarch can claim exclusive, pre-eminent, or solely concurrent jurisdiction in the New World, or if other autocephalous churches can establish themselves on their own, is now hotly disputed within the Eastern Orthodox Churches, especially since the Moscow Patriarchate has unilaterally granted autocephaly to the Orthodox Church in America.[30]

The Problem in Ecumenical Perspective

Pope Paul VI performed in March 1976 an act of humility which will forever be remembered in the annals of history, when he knelt down in front of the representative of the Eastern Orthodox Church, a metropolitan of the Ecumenical Patriarchate, present in the Sistine Chapel, and kissed his foot.[31] Was it not the meaning of this inspiring, symbolic gesture of such sublime significance that the Roman pontiff is ready in case of a re-union to recognize the inviolability at least of the different Eastern canonical discipline? The Roman Curia cannot be unaware that interference with the apostolic practice of ordaining married men in the Eastern Church must by necessity be seen by any onlooker as an example wholly contrary to the words and gestures of the Holy Father, as he demonstrated on the mentioned occasion. By this example of obstruction of the Eastern practice, is not all credibility being taken away from the Catholic Church and the popes?

Here we must ask, What is the true aim of the ecumenical movement of our days? Is it really what it is claimed to be, a joyful discovery in brotherly love of the identity existing, especially between the Roman Catholic and the Eastern Churches, under the presidency of the Roman pontiff ? At the peril of shocking the professional ecumenists, the answer is negative. The only conclusion that can be drawn is that the Roman pontiff is an absolute monarch, though he may not always behave as such.

It is naïve to mention the promises made by one pope at the time, for example, of the Union of Brest (1596) and point to the fact that the Roman Curia blithely ignored them.[32] The bishops of Brest submitted to Pope Clement VIII an Act of Reunion dated June 11, 1595, in which article 9 expressly stipulated that "Matrimonia sacerdotalia ut integra constent" [Let priestly marriages remain intact]. The pope accepted this condition in the constitution *Magnus Dominus* of December 23, 1595. Later, the provincial synod of Lviv in 1891, under the presidency of a papal legate, confirmed again this discipline. However, what one pope has promised does not bind him, and even less his successors. The party of the second part, the specific Eastern Catholic Church, relinquishes at the time of "union" or, more correctly, submission, any and all rights except those which are graciously granted by the pope in office.

Thus, the Congregation for the Eastern Churches under the signature of Cardinal Luigi Sincero did not have to blush at all when it asserted in a letter of July 23, 1934, to Bishop Basil Takach, the apostolic exarch for the Ruthenians in the United States:

> When the Holy See recognized the particularities of the Greek Ruthenian Church and guaranteed them, it intended principally—as is

evident from the Decree of Union of 1596, during the Pontificate of Clement VIII, and from the Brief of Paul V of 1615—to recognize and guarantee the ritual traditions of the Ruthenians. As regards their particular canonical discipline, the Holy See could not have affirmed its integral application at all times and in all places without taking into account the different exigencies and circumstances. Thus one well understands how a married clergy, permitted in those places where the Greek Ruthenian Rite originated and constitutes a predominant element, could hardly seem advisable in places where the same Rite has been imported and finds an environment and a mentality altogether different.

And let it not be imagined that this attitude has undergone a change in these decades after Vatican II! A layman in Toronto wrote recently to remonstrate with his friend, now a cardinal in Rome, about the Roman conduct in the affair of the three priests. The cardinal, himself apparently disinterested in the problem, wrote him back, after having made some inquiries, that the Curia does not consider that the promises made at the time of the Union of Brest or Mukachevo apply to regions outside of Europe. Thus, the Ukrainians, Slovaks and other Eastern Catholics had been permitted to delude themselves for such a long time with unrealistic dreams.

Contacts with the Orthodox

But what about the repercussions which the prohibition of ordaining married candidates in the Americas must have on the official and unofficial contacts with the Eastern Orthodox? Will the latter not become alarmed at what Rome is preparing for them? This is an enigma in respect to both partners, though a hypothesis of explanation shall be offered here. Why would Rome apparently woo the Orthodox while acting in such a way as to put them to flight? And why would the Orthodox continue their overtures in spite of clear indications that their position would never be acceptable in Rome?

We are again in the same political circumstances as those preceding the Council of Ferrara-Florence (1437–1438). "*Turci ante portas*" [The Turks are at the door] is the cry heard in Constantinople. The Turkish government seeks an excuse to expel the Ecumenical Patriarchate from Istanbul and thereby end once and for all this last relic of the Eastern Roman Empire. This is the sole reason why the emissaries of Constantinople flock to the Vatican, gratefully pleading for any sign of recognition in the international arena and thereby also before the Turks. As at the time of Florence, so also now, these endeavors do not have the moral support of the Greek nation. Only the senior bishops dependent on Constantinople joined in the ecumenical initiative, namely, those in Western Europe and in the United States, Archbishop Iakovos. The Churches of Greece and Mount Athos have moved away from all ecumenism with the Roman Church or have condemned it. They have been joined by the Serbian Patriarchate of Yugoslavia and other minor Orthodox Churches.

For political considerations of a different nature, the Russian Patriarchate of Moscow and the Romanian Patriarchate have also entered into ecumenical contacts, possibly in order to render Rome incapable of protesting against the forceful suppression and liquidation of the Union in the two nations. In reality, concessions were made only by Catholics, while the Orthodox cannot move away from the teaching of the majority of their theologians that Roman Catholicism is a heresy and that not even the most innocent *communicatio in sacris* with Catholics can be permitted.

Rome is, of course, aware of the political motivation on the part of the Patriarchates of Constantinople, Moscow, and Bucharest in seeking ecumenical meetings. While burying for the time the hope for union in the next century, Rome expects to create good will for the more distant future by the moral and sometimes also material aid extended to the Orthodox, and probably also by having through silence virtually extradited the Uniates in the Soviet Union and in Romania into the hands of the Orthodox.

However, the same situation suggests also that there is no need to treat the Eastern Catholics with some special consideration, since what is done to them will not affect the relationship with the Eastern Orthodox. On the contrary, quite a few observers have suggested that any measures adopted by Rome that lead to the liquidation of the Uniates will ultimately benefit the ecumenical endeavors in the distant future. The prohibition of ordaining married candidates in the Americas and Australia is one of the more efficient steps toward this goal. As for the rest, the Uniate churches in Eastern Europe and in the Near East, Communism, and pressure from the Islamic world will take care of them.

The Judgment of History and the Credibility of the Papacy and the Church

The separation between the Christian East and the West occurred for a number of reasons, but outstanding was the increasing abandonment by the Western or Roman Church of some apostolic traditions, a change certainly justified by the special needs of that epoch in Western Europe. At the same time the Christian East continued to maintain the way of life of the ancient Church as faithfully as possible. The ensuing difference was mirrored at the Synod of Trullo (692) when the East condemned certain practices which had crept into the Church, among others also compulsory celibacy. It was coincidental that these innovations had arisen in the Western Church.

When some members of the Eastern Churches decided to re-unite themselves with the Roman Church, as the Ukrainians and the Slovaks did in the 16th and 17th centuries, they were moved by an increasing awareness of the clear tradition of the ancient Church, which assigned to the Roman bishop supreme leadership in Christendom. They desired to re-establish the same order which had been that of the holy Fathers. They declared their submission to the Roman pontiff and acceptance of all doctrinal differences should such exist. They never considered abandoning their own canon law, if for no other reason than because they knew that they had always maintained an apostolic tradition. And nobody demanded it at that time.

In this resolve they were confirmed by the words of the popes who solemnly promised them that they would be able to continue undisturbed with their own genuine system of law and worship; nay, they even repeatedly commanded them most severely not to make any changes which would disagree with the ecclesiastical order of their own tradition. Vatican II reminded all Eastern Catholics and the entire Church of the obligation that all Eastern Catholic Churches continue and even reestablish their own traditions and customs which they had perhaps abandoned: "For this reason it solemnly declares that the Churches of the East as much as those of the West possess the right and are bound by duty to rule themselves each in accordance with its own discipline" (*Orientalium Ecclesiarum* 5).

The Ukrainian, Slovak, Melkite, Maronite and other Eastern Catholic faithful have a right to see the question which we treat here also within the framework of their national survival. The Ukrainian and the Slovak bishops are also part of the leadership of their nations, as is the case in other Catholic nations around the world. Their Churches are subjected to merciless annihilation in their homelands by the Communists. Similarly the Arabic Christians of the Near East are fighting for their lives. Should not their bishops be considered derelict in the fulfillment of their duty toward the fate of their nations if they should refuse to provide their faithful with priests according to their genuine tradition by ordaining also married candidates? Who would otherwise absolve them from the indictment of having contributed to the dispersal and loss of their compatriots in the free world, a modern kind of treason?

As members of the Body of Christ, the Church, as sons of their respective nations and of the Church, they have always thought that it is the will of God and the wish, nay, even command, of the Church that they uphold the genuine tradition of the Eastern Church, especially when it is of apostolic origin. It is their sworn duty to resist the encroachments from the traditions of other Churches, especially from Latin canon law. Nothing has done greater damage to the credibility of the Roman See than the tendencies of Latinization, introduced into the Uniate Churches, usually without, and even against, the expressed intention of the popes.

Let us not forget the judgment of history. How often have we wished, in reading about the past actions and omissions in the Church, that certain mistakes in centuries past could be undone today? But to no avail such wishes now. However, here we have an opportunity to avoid a repetition of errors in judgment which a future generation will regret.

A Look toward the Future

1. A Compromise Solution

To ask Rome to reverse itself and to permit now in a written document something which was resisted in repeated prohibitions by the Curia for many decades cannot be expected without the intervention of such a miraculous event as would be the coming of another John XXIII. It should also be said that not all Ukrainian or all Eastern Catholic bishops support this request for reasons about which we can only speculate.

This is why I dare to submit a compromise solution, namely, that the Eastern bishops be permitted to ordain married candidates to the presbyterate who will function as auxiliary priests. The normal candidate to the priesthood will be a celibate man, and exceptionally a widower. The bishops will do everything to promote such vocations, and they will give preference to celibate priests in appointments. Vocations to the religious state, especially the male institutes of priests, will be encouraged and promoted by the bishops and the clergy. It has been recognized that true pastoral goals cannot be achieved without the assistance of the clergy belonging to religious institutes.

Married candidates for the permanent diaconate may be ordained within the guidelines issued by the Holy See in respect to their general educational and theological preparation. Married candidates will be ordained to the presbyterate only as long as there is not available an adequate number of celibate candidates of the secular and the regular clergy, a situation which will continue for a long time. Such married priests will exercise an auxiliary function, which could refer to one of several such possible employments: weekend or part-time priests, earning a livelihood in a suitable nonecclesiastical employment, such as, for example, teaching or social work, or in medicine, as one such priest does in the Melkite Exarchate. They will be available on weekends, at vacation time, in evenings, etc.

Others would be assigned as assistant priests, full-time or part-time, in the larger parishes of the diocese, or they would be placed in charge of pastoral mission stations as part-time priests whenever such units cannot support a regular pastor.

Such candidates would have proven themselves in life. They would not be ordained as a rule to the presbyterate before their thirty-fifth year of age, would have had to receive a superior education and theological preparation equivalent to that available in a seminary curriculum, and would have received an ecclesiastical training as deacons for at least five years. In addition, they would have to be recommended for ordination by a diocesan board of examiners.

This answer to the problem would be clearly unique to the Eastern Catholic Churches and would not extend itself to the Latin Church because of the different situation. It has been tested already as feasible with a number of individuals in Canada and the United States. The end result could perhaps lead to a relative diminution of secular celibate vocations, but this will favor then religious vocations. The example of Western Ukraine and the Near East shows that there was always a sufficient number of secular celibate priests who dedicated themselves entirely to the

Church and therefore were called to occupy higher positions in the hierarchy and in church administration.

2. Auxiliary Priests

First-generation Eastern Christians, Catholic or Orthodox, in North America have nearly exclusively lived in cities, residing as closely as possible to their own churches. It is different with their children, who, on account of the opportunity for social mobility, have often acquired a professional education which carries them to all parts of the country. This is true, of course, also of Roman Catholics, but they will today find in any place where they settle or in its vicinity a Catholic church, while Eastern Christians will encounter others of their kind only in small groups, not numerous enough to start at once a parish of their own. Eastern Orthodox Christians either maintain a loose connection with the nearest church of their affiliation, possibly hundreds of miles away, or visit it perhaps once or twice annually. Eastern Catholics have been trained not to let a Sunday pass without the Eucharist in a Catholic church, and so they start going to a Latin-rite church and soon become absorbed by that rite.

Not rarely Eastern Christians find themselves in a small group in a suburb of some metropolitan center. The Orthodox may then receive from their bishop a married man who earns his main livelihood in secular employment and gives his free time to the organization of a parish, which will marginally augment his earnings. Celibate priests, if they were available, would not accept non-ecclesiastical employment, and nobody would suggest it. An auxiliary priest, married to a wife who usually herself has a career, would be the ideal solution for making it possible for the respective Eastern Catholic Churches to retain their faithful. Without the employment of an auxiliary or part-time clergy, as a rule married and making a living in secular occupations, this goal cannot be attained. After studying this phenomenon for over a quarter-century, I cannot see another solution but to employ dedicated part-time or married priests in an auxiliary capacity.

3. Seminary Preparation

In discussing the ordination to the presbyterate of married candidates, it has been tacitly assumed that education within the walls of a seminary is a universal condition for future Catholic priests, and such candidates would not receive it because they are married. Seminary education is certainly desirable for future celibate priests, and useful also for married candidates before their marriage, but it is not indispensable, especially if the candidates have lived under surveillance and instruction of the bishop and his clergy for a number of years.

The judgment of whether a candidate is sufficiently theologically prepared is, according to canon law, to be left to the informed opinion of the bishops, who are to follow the custom of the country, but with the possibility to dispense with some requirements normally prescribed. There are numerous examples in Latin dioceses around the world today, as there were in the past, of the fact that bishops ordain candidates who are deficient in some parts of their preparation if they compensate for this by zeal, maturity, and practical intelligence.

Not only in the Americas but in Rome itself, the theological course of four years has been recently reduced to three years, and much of the theoretical studies has been replaced by practical training in the parishes. This has been the case also with the married candidates in Canada, who have been employed first as pastoral assistants and then as deacons alongside the more experienced and active pastors before ordination. Constant discussion and teaching within their assignments during these years are the most effective preparation for a future Catholic pastor.

There are a number of priests employed in the Ukrainian eparchies of Canada and the United States who were ordained by Orthodox bishops. Not a few were accepted upon the recommendation, nay, insistence, of Rome, though these priests usually had no theological or seminary studies or training whatsoever. Most of them have shown maturity of common sense, judgment, zeal in performing their priestly duties and eagerness to learn from association with other priests what they had not acquired in a school.

The situation of the married candidates recently ordained in Canada is entirely different, since they had not only a superior scholastic and professional preparation and several years of experience with teaching sacred doctrine in Catholic schools but were also often scholars who in their academic attainment excel by far the average Catholic priest. In addition, the candidates had been recommended to the bishop by respected priests of superior standing who had known them well for a number of years from daily contact and had had opportunities to acquaint themselves with their learning, priestly zeal, and dedication.

4. Not a Panacea

In advocating the ordination of married candidates to the presbyterate, it would be a mistake to imply that this would put an end to the problem of priestly vocations, wishfully creating a stampede toward the altar. Careers which entail work with people are always a second choice. What it would do is to overcome the reluctance of parents who are unable to envision a celibate career for their sons. As is well known, the Eastern Churches permit ordination of married candidates, but a second marriage after ordination is excluded even for a widower.[33] If canon law would permit a priest to marry at any time he chooses, the number of candidates who would accept ordination unmarried would be relatively large, and those who later would not marry at all because they would be absorbed by their vocation could be expected to be considerable.[34]

This caution, not to expect miracles from the possibility of a married priesthood, must be stated here because one hears not rarely from those who oppose the ordination of married men that the Eastern Orthodox Churches also have difficulties in recruiting clergy though they permit them to be married. The reasons for the scarcity of priestly vocations among the Orthodox are of a different nature. The Ukrainian and Russian Orthodox parishes are often small in number of members and short on funds. Consequently, the remuneration they can offer to their priests is far below that offered to professional men. The authority of the bishop over the priest and the parish council is weak, and pastors are therefore entirely dependent on the council, which treats them not rarely in a humiliating manner. The social background of the membership is lower-middle-class, people who have not yet learned how to conduct themselves with an employee who has a professional education. This is the continual complaint of all Eastern Orthodox priests in North America, that their parish councils interfere even in purely spiritual matters, as, for example, whether the pastor may grant a funeral to a repentant Orthodox who has not been a regular member of the parish.

Another aspect of the vocational problem in Orthodox Churches is the relative youth of many candidates, who have only the equivalent of a college education and not the graduate education of the Roman Catholic or Protestant clergy. In the Americas such candidates find it difficult to meet a woman suitable for the special requirements of a priest's wife, but they can accept meantime secular employment with which they later stay since it remunerates them so much better than the priesthood.

In other Eastern Orthodox Churches, as was the case in Yugoslavia, a candidate terminated his seminary studies when he was 20 to 22 years old. He could not be ordained before marriage, nor was there a possibility for any kind of other gainful employment. He was anxious to marry and to earn a living. Yet he could not give enough time judiciously to choose a girl capable of being a priest's wife. A bride was often selected because of the dowry she brought into the marriage. The result of such abrupt decisions was a considerable number of unhappy marriages. This was my observation many years ago, and the situation still persists, as is witnessed by Cedomir Draskovic, professor of the Patriarchal School of Theology in Belgrade:

> The candidates to the priesthood would be in a much more satisfactory situation if they could solve the question of their marriage at a time which would be most appropriate for them, and if they were not forced—entirely unprepared—to decide the question of marriage immediately after leaving school, without any experience and without means, since they thereby find themselves unnecessarily in a very serious situation, in which they resolve the question of their marriage in a manner which does not insure the conditions that are required for a normal and happy marriage.[35]

The possibility of ordination of married candidates will retain a number of excellent men, capable and dedicated to their calling, who otherwise would be lost because they are conscientious enough not to attempt a celibate life when they see how many have failed in it. With compulsory celibacy one result is assured: all those who are incapable of making a living in the outside world will be retained. They become later a nuisance for the Church when they form part of a disgruntled clergy who perform their duties only perfunctorily.

A hearing should be accorded to the proposals coming from missionaries in the depths of Africa or Indonesia to ordain as a priest perhaps the headman of his village after his people have accepted Christianity. Such a priest would not be much different from the priests of the first centuries of Christian history, who were rich on faith and fervor and short on theology and general education.

5. Epilogue

It has been said that the Council of Trent was first ignored by the Church at large and promoted by Rome, while Vatican II has not only been enthusiastically received by Catholics around the world but also has attracted the respect and admiration even of non-Catholics. At the same time, however, the Curia behaves as if the Council had not happened at all. Vatican II explicitly endorsed an Eastern married priesthood in the Decree on the Ministry and Life of Priests when it speaks of celibacy and states: "It is not, indeed, demanded by the very nature of the priesthood, as is evident from the practice of the primitive Church and from the tradition of the Eastern Churches.... While this most sacred Synod recommends ecclesiastical celibacy, it in no way intends to change that different discipline which lawfully prevails in Eastern Churches. It exhorts all those who have received the priesthood after marriage to persevere in their sacred vocation, and to continue to spend their lives fully and generously for the flock committed to them" (n. 16). Even the most extensive legalistic interpretation could not discover here a restriction of priestly marriage to the Near East.

Could we not return to the more generous evaluation, as in the past, of differences in discipline among the churches? Even Photius, so maligned by Catholic writers,[36] had criticized in his encyclical letter of 867 several liturgical and canonical practices introduced by Frankish missionaries in Bulgaria, among others also opposition to a married priesthood.[37] "But his criticism was directed at the fact that the missionaries were requiring from the newly baptized Bulgarians complete abandonment of Greek usages. He did not yet consider diversity in practice and discipline as an obstacle to Church unity."[38] And the same Photius could demonstrate true Christian magnanimity by asserting in his letter to Pope Nicholas I: "When faith remains inviolate, the common and catholic decisions are also safe; a sensible man respects the practices and law of others; he considers that it is neither wrong to observe them nor illegal to violate them."[39]

Could we not persuade the Roman See to let the Eastern Christians in the Americas live their own life, organize their own existence, and solve their own problems not more and not less than their Eastern Orthodox brothers do in the same countries and in the same circumstances?

A Question: Are the Walls Tumbling Down?

The demands of various factors in the Church to change the policy of not ordaining married candidates to the presbyterate continue to be heard in the world.

Patriarch Maximos V Hakim, the head of the Melkite Patriarchate of Antioch, Alexandria, and Jerusalem, was the first to respond to the reports of the press that the Vatican had repeated the prohibition to ordain Eastern Catholic married candidates to the priesthood in the United States and in Canada. The official statement issued by His Beatitude says:

> The Second Vatican Council settled once and for all the question of church law for the Eastern Churches. Paul VI and all the Fathers of the Council explicitly declared, "to remove any shadow of doubt, that the Churches of the East, keeping in mind the necessary unity of the whole Church, have the power to govern themselves according to their own discipline." No distinctions were made to exclude the Western Church's special law of priestly celibacy from this sweeping and deliberate affirmation, nor was there any restriction imposed upon Eastern Church faithful and clergy who live in the Western hemisphere.
>
> The bishops of the Second Vatican Council were well aware of the different traditions and practices, and they clearly intended to respect the older, more venerable usages of the Eastern Churches—including the right, and the exercise of the right, to admit married men to the order of priests. In recommending ecclesiastical celibacy for the sake of the Kingdom of God, as the Eastern Churches themselves do, the Council was explicit that it did not intend "in any way to change the discipline which lawfully prevails in the Eastern Churches. It lovingly exhorts all those who have received priesthood after marriage to persevere in their second vocation and to continue to spend their lives fully and generously for the flock committed to them."
>
> I am completely satisfied that Pope Paul, who headed the Council, would not repudiate its sacred declarations and decisions. It is all

the more tragic that lesser officials of the Roman Curia take positions contrary to the Council. It is gravely offensive to Catholic and Orthodox Christians alike when, by reason of its majority status, the Western or Latin Church attempts to impose its usage upon us. It is an example of Latinization of a minority by the majority. It is disrespectful of the thousands of married priests, both Catholic and Orthodox, who lead their communities with just as great devotion and dedication to the gospel as do celibate priests.

If it is ever necessary, in those regions where the numbers of Eastern Church members predominate, to have Latin bishops and priests to serve the Western Catholics in our midst, we would not think of requiring that they observe the Eastern discipline. The anonymous "high Vatican source" has been quoted as saying that the question of ordaining Eastern married men in the United States will concern "among others, the local bishops' conference, and, of course, the Holy See." I am assured by Archbishop Tawil, who is a voting member of the National Conference of Catholic Bishops, that the three hundred members of that conference have not in fact taken any action contrary to our Eastern practice of a married clergy. In fact, the New England bishops participating in a conference on April 27–29, 1971, dealing with the question of priestly celibacy, explicitly disclaimed any intention to interfere with the customary practices of the Eastern Churches in this regard. I hope that the Catholic bishops of the United States will publicly affirm the Council's decree and respect the traditional rights of the Eastern Catholics and Orthodox of this country.[40]

The issue of married priests is a topic of discussion also in the Western Church. The bishops of France had a consultation on priestly celibacy and the possible re-admission to sacerdotal functioning of those priests who had married at their meeting held in Lourdes, October 23–30, 1976. The catastrophic dearth of (celibate) priests and the rapidly progressing re-paganization of the "oldest daughter of Rome" draws the attention of conscientious shepherds to the absurdity that thousands of capable men are prevented from offering their services as priests because they have received an additional sacrament, that of holy matrimony.

The apostolic delegate to the United States, Archbishop Jean Jadot, a Belgian, and a late acquisition to the Vatican diplomacy, spoke to the fall conference of U.S. bishops in Washington, D.C., on November 9, 1976.⁴¹ Such an address of the apostolic delegate has become a standard feature of all such episcopal meetings, and great importance is attributed to its contents because what the apostolic delegate has to say is presumed to be the most recent directive from the Vatican, a message from the mouth of the Holy Father himself. And indeed, Archbishop Jadot had just returned a few days earlier from a visit of several weeks in Rome.

The archbishop spoke briefly. He had only three items to discuss, and the first was the extreme shortage of priests. He suggested as remedies that the bishops should be willing to share more pastoral responsibilities with the laity, both men and women. Further he would like to see a more effective use of permanent deacons and of extraordinary ministers who are not deacons. And he added a proposal which gave rise to a lively discussion among the bishops. He urged them to "search for new avenues of pastoral care." Since he had exhaustively enumerated all the usual possibilities, what could he have meant to say in this phrase? Many bishops present at the talk thought that he must have referred to the ordination of married candidates not only to the diaconate but also to the presbyterate, and also to the re-admission of those priests who had to leave the clergy when they married. It could be that the bishops were also influenced by what two weeks earlier the Bi-Centennial Catholic Consultation, gathered in Detroit and composed of bishops, priests, and lay representatives, largely appointed by the bishops themselves, had by majority vote endorsed, namely, married priests in the Latin Church. The bishops, or a goodly number of them, asked during the next days of the Conference for more information on the subject from the Eastern bishops and priests present.

Whether the meager words of Archbishop Jadot actually referred to this possibility or not is less significant than the interpretation it received in the minds of at least some U.S. bishops. They were not the only ones looking in this direction. Archbishop Joseph Aurele Plourde of Ottawa said recently in an interview that the next decade will bring many changes, and he feels that married men will be ordained priests by 1987. He warns, unless ordination is opened to married men, there may be no priests at all, as in Ottawa, where the average age of the 350 priests is 60, with only two men in training to replace them for the 260,000 Catholics.⁴²

The situation is even more desperate in the Latin-American nations. Bishops from the Dominican Republic mentioned in conversation that they had begun ordaining so-called presidents of parishes to the priesthood, as yet only unmarried—celibates or widowers—candidates. Because of the extreme dearth of priests, many parishes in Central and South America are under the care of lay presidents, who perform as many priestly functions as can be delegated to them. These parish presidents, who were ordained priests (presbyters), had not received any seminary or other professional preparation whatsoever. The bishops expressed the hope that these men will function so well as priests that in a not too distant future they will receive permission to ordain also the married ones among the presidents, who constitute the great majority.

Considering the recent publication of the declaration of the Congregation for the Doctrine of the Faith that precludes permanently the ordination of women to the presbyterate, it is odd to find several hundred parishes in South America administered by nuns in place of priests. A priest leaves behind, on his occasional visits, consecrated hosts with which the nuns distribute communion, in addition to administering baptisms, preparing the faithful for death, teaching catechism, presiding at prayer liturgies, etc.

The various endeavors to bring the Catholic Church and the Church of England closer together suggest the possibility that the latter may one day re-join the Church of Rome as a body and retain within the Catholic Church its separate autonomous status as a new "Anglican rite," with its own liturgy and canon law.[43] Bishop Christopher Butler, an auxiliary of the Roman Catholic archbishops of Westminster and a member of the Anglican-Roman Catholic International Commission, argued recently that the statement on authority issued by the commission contains the conditions for a future union of the two churches, which, he suggested, would allow Anglicans to retain their own customs and autonomy just as the Ukrainians of the Byzantine rite do.

However, a reader replied that "for fear of difficulty with the Latins, the Ukrainians in the West are forbidden their tradition of a married clergy.... Will the unfortunate Ukrainians have to wait for reunion between Rome and Canterbury to shame the Vatican into restoring their immemorial rights?" How can the non-Catholics, the Western, as the Anglicans, or the Eastern, as the Orthodox, ever believe the promises of Rome when those given solemnly in the past are so flagrantly broken?

A turn to a greater understanding by the officials of the Roman Curia is never impossible. Such a change occurred just before World War I, when the decree *Cum Episcopo* (1914) omitted any mention of the demand that priests in the United States be only celibates or widowers without children. The mass apostasy of so many Ruthenians to Russian Orthodoxy in order to secure for themselves priests must have made some impression upon someone in power in Rome. The lack of a repetition of that standard demand was understood as it only could be understood in the given circumstances, namely, that henceforth married men could be ordained priests. And this was then done over the years, especially after the death of Bishop Ortynsky (1916). The two administrators sent candidates who were married to Bishop Budka in Canada for ordination.

Then an astonishing reverse occurred with the decree *Cum data fuerit* (1929), which stipulated in art. 1, 2: "As has already several times been decreed, priests of the Greek-Ruthenian Rite who wish to go to the United States of North America and stay there, must be celibates." How can we explain this reversal? We really cannot without access to the archives of the Congregation. Could it be that this was the result of the change which had occurred in Galicia, where the bishops of Peremyshl and of Stanislaviv had decided after World War II henceforth to ordain only celibates, although Metropolitan Andrew Sheptyts'kyi of Lviv continued to ordain married men, and the Carpathian dioceses, those of Hungary and Croatia, did not either introduce compulsory celibacy. The application of this return to the Latin-rite discipline led to the apostasy of some 100,000 faithful to the Orthodox Church under the leadership of Fr. Orestes Chornock (1936).

What will be the future for the Eastern Catholics on the North American continent? It is certain that the continued prohibition of ordaining married men will lead to their accelerated disappearance. It is an example of ethnocide, which, it is true, does not result in the physical killing of people but "only" in the loss of their ethnic souls. It is of little consolation to know that this may not have been intended by the Roman authorities; the result is the same.

Notes

Editor's note: As I mentioned in the preface, this is a lightly edited version of a pamphlet that circulated privately in Canada in the late 1970s. I have cleaned up a number of typographical errors, eliminated a very few and very short passages no longer relevant, and introduced a few notes to clarify historically obscure or recondite references. Otherwise the text remains as it was published more than forty years ago now.

1. *Editor's note*: Bishop Borecky was the first bishop of the new Ukrainian Catholic Eparchy of Toronto and Eastern Canada, established in 1948; he held this office until 1998 and died in 2003. John Gihirny was 35 years old at the time; a deacon since March 1976; married for seven years; holder of a PhD from McMaster University in Hamilton, Ontario; and active in Catholic education at local and provincial levels. He was supposed to serve Hungarians (Magyars) of the Byzantine rite. Andrew Kormanik was 30 years old at the time; a deacon since April 1975; married for three years; a teacher of religion by profession who had studied at seminaries in Pittsburgh and Toronto; and was active in catechetical instruction. He was to serve Slovak Catholics of the Byzantine rite. Lozynsky was 31 years old at the time; a deacon since February 1973; married for six years; educated in theology at St. Paul University in Ottawa, the University of Toronto, and the John XXIII Institute in New York, holding master's degrees as a result. He was to serve at the same Ukrainian parish where he had been a deacon.

2. *Editor's note*: Until the mid-1980s, Catholic schools in Ontario were "separate," that is, not public, receiving only partial public funding—a situation that changed in 1985, when Catholic schools became fully publicly funded; they remain so, on the same level as "public" schools.

3. *Editor's note*: Del Mestri was pro-nuncio in Ottawa from June 1970 to August 1975; nuncio in Germany thereafter until retirement in 1984; made a cardinal in 1991; and died in 1993.

4. *Editor's note*: He had been appointed apostolic nuncio to West Germany effective August 12, 1975. His replacement, Archbishop Angelo Palmas, would not, at least on paper, take up his appointment in Ottawa until September 2, 1975. See http://www.nuntiatura.ca/history_en.html.

5. *Editor's note*: Paul Francis Reding, previously auxiliary bishop from 1966 to 1973, was that year named bishop of Hamilton and remained so until his death in 1983.

6. *Editor's note*: There is a likelihood that the priest referred to here is Roman Danylak, who would indeed be rewarded with a mitre on his episcopal appointment in 1992, an event that caused enormous damage and massive division in and to the Toronto eparchy and eventually caused Danylak's removal to some obscure sinecure in Rome under the age-old principle of *promoveatur ut amoveatur* (promote [in order] to remove).

7. *Editor's note*: Imposing this number on official Roman documents is a standard protocol, but the author does not tell us more about it.

8. *Editor's note*: Presumably displeasure at Roman intervention!

9. *Editor's note*: Palmas was ordained bishop in 1964 and served as pronuncio to Canada from 1975 until his retirement in 1990; he died in 2003.

10. Josyf Cardinal Slipyj, the major archbishop and patriarch-designate of the Ukrainian Catholic Church, called a meeting of the permanent synod of the Ukrainian bishops in Rome for the first days of May 1976. The Holy See forbade the bishops to take part in it, not so much because the cardinal had proclaimed the establishment of a Ukrainian Catholic patriarchate against the prohibition of the pope as because the latter recognized assemblies of the Ukrainian bishops not as legislative synods but only as simple episcopal conferences.

11. *Editor's note*: Hermaniuk was the metropolitan of Winnipeg and, during the first session of Vatican II, the leader of the largest Ukrainian "diaspora" community. He emerged as the de facto leader, according to some, of the entire Church, while the actual hierarchy in Ukraine was in the Gulag. Some of Hermaniuk's diaries for the post-conciliar period have been recently published, shedding light on this fascinating and little-known period and its controversies. See J. Z. Skira, trans., *The Second Vatican Council Diaries of Met. Maxim Hermaniuk, C.Ss.R. (1960–1965)* (Leuven, Belgium: Peeters, 2012).

12. *Acta Sanctae Sedis*, vol. 1891/92, p. 390.

13. Cf. my article "Clerical Celibacy in the Eastern Rite Catholic Dioceses of the United States and Canada," *Diakonia* 2 (1967): 137–155.

14. Cf. Walter Paska, *Sources of Particular Law for the Ukrainian Catholic Church in the United States* (Washington, DC: Catholic University of America, 1975), passim.

15. *Editor's note*: Budka is the subject of a new biography, by a properly trained historian: Athanasius McVay, *God's Martyr, History's Witness: Blessed Nykyta Budka, the First Ukrainian Catholic Bishop in Canada* (Ottawa and Edmonton: Sheptytsky Institute, 2014).

16. Cf. my "Clerical Celibacy," p. 144.

17. *Editor's note*: A biography of Bohachevsky has been recently published: Martha Bohachevsky-Chomiak, *Ukrainian Bishop, American Church: Constantine Bohachevsky and the Ukrainian Catholic Church* (Washington, DC: Catholic University of America Press, 2018).

18. *Editor's note*: Slipyj, along with the rest of the Ukrainian Catholic hierarchy in Ukraine, was arrested on direct orders of Stalin at the end of the war and sent to the Gulag. A sham synod, the so-called Lviv Sobor, was held in early 1946 at which a bishop-less Ukrainian Catholic Church "voted" to "rejoin" the Russian Orthodox Church. (Under both Catholic and Orthodox canon law and ecclesiology, no synod can validly vote on anything without bishops present.) The Soviets had coerced, using lethal threats, several Ukrainian Catholic priests to take part and vote the "right" way. Thus the entire church disappeared officially, though it continued a vibrant and astonishingly widespread underground existence until 1989. Slipyj was released in 1963 on the condition that he be permanently exiled and never permitted to return to the Soviet Union. He found himself in the "gilded cage" of the Vatican on his release and thus joined the Second Vatican

Council at a crucial moment, defying all expectations by living until 1984. A staunch defender of the rights of the Ukrainian Catholic Church against both Russian and Roman imperialism, he ordained married men even in Rome itself (at one point in the papal summer residence of Castelgandalfo!) in defiance of the Vatican ban on such ordinations. One of the priests thus ordained in 1981 is a contributor to this volume: Peter Galadza. See Jaroslav Pelikan, *Confessor between East and West: A Portrait of Ukrainian Cardinal Josyf Slipyj* (Grand Rapids, MI: Eerdmans, 1990).

19. *Editor's note*: This is a venerable canonical maxim that "the salvation of souls is the supreme law."

20. *Editor's note*: Here Galicia (not to be confused with a territory of the same name in Spain) was a province of the Habsburg Empire stretching roughly from Warsaw in the West to Lviv (Lvov/Lwow/Lemberg) in the East. It was the homeland of the Ukrainian Catholic Church, and her primate was based there until he was moved to Kyiv in the early years of the twenty-first century.

21. *Editor's note*: See B. R. Bociurkiw, *The Ukrainian Catholic Church and the Soviet State (1939–1950)* (Edmonton/Toronto: Canadian Institute of Ukrainian Studies Press, 1996); Ivan Bilas, "The Moscow Patriarchate, the Penal Organs of the USSR, and the Attempted Destruction of the Ukrainian Greco-Catholic Church during the 1940s," *Logos: A Journal of Eastern Christian Studies* 38 (1997): 41–92; and Robert Taft, "The Problem of 'Uniatism' and the 'Healing of Memories': Anamnesis, not Amnesia," *Logos: A Journal of Eastern Christian Studies* 41–42 (2000–2001): 168–170 especially.

22. Henry R. Percival, ed., *The Seven Ecumenical Councils of the Undivided Church: Their Canons and Dogmatic Decrees* (Grand Rapids, MI: Eerdmans, 1971), 371. *Editor's note*: There has been more recent scholarship on Trullo, some of which is described and summed up in Patrick Viscuso's contribution to this volume.

23. *Editor's note*: The best treatment of Toth is found in D. O. Herbel's book, details of which he references in his chapter elsewhere in this volume.

24. *Editor's note*: "In these circumstances alone," that is, the papal request should not be interpreted widely to cover other cases.

25. *Editor's note*: In addition to the reasons Pospishil enumerates here, it must also be noted that, even at their height (from which, alas, we have long ago descended sharply), the sum total of Eastern Catholics in the entire world—a few million—was completely dwarfed by the hundreds of millions (today, over 1 billion) of Latin Catholics, the overwhelming majority of whom have no clue about the existence of Eastern Catholics.

26. *Editor's note*: It was often said of Ukrainian Catholics in Canada—especially in southwestern Ontario, where I grew up—that during the Soviet period, the Ukrainian Catholic Church functioned as a "surrogate state" since the Ukrainian state did not exist as an independent body until 1991.

27. *Regimini Ecclesiae universae*, apostolic constitution, August 15, 1967 (*AAS* 1967, 59–88). The secretariat of state or papal secretariate has the function of giving the most immediate help to the pope both in the care of the universal Church and in his dealings with the departments of the Curia. Bishops have, in matters that are not routine, automatic application of law to approach the Holy See through the nuncios or delegates, who again direct themselves to the secretariat of state, and only then may the problem reach the competent congregation.

28. *L'Osservatore Romano*, April 23, 1970.

29. *Editor's note*: Following his release in 1963, Slipyj and many other Ukrainian Catholics began insisting that he be treated as a patriarch, which is how many Ukrainian parishes styled him. Pope Paul VI, under his policy of *Ostpolitik*, refused to concede such a title (whether it is his to concede in the first place is a matter of no small, and still unresolved, debate), fearing it would upset the Russian Orthodox Church. Instead, an entirely new title was conjured up: "major archbishop," which, canonically, was virtually equivalent to a patriarch save for the fact he had to have his election by the Ukrainian Catholic synod confirmed by the Roman pontiff, whereas a patriarch does not, instead merely sending word of his election to the pope for the latter simply to accept.

30. See the special issue on autocephaly of *St. Vladimir's Theological Quarterly* 15 (1971); see also P. N. Trempelas, *The Autocephaly of the Metropolia in America* (Brookline, MA: Holy Cross, 1973).

31. *Editor's note*: For more on this deeply affecting embrace, see the short book by Athanasios Papas, *Rome and Constantinople: Pope Paul VI and Metropolitan Meliton of Chalcedon*, trans. G. D. Dragas (New Hampshire: Orthodox Research Institute, 2006).

32. "The Union of the Ruthenians was not formally an agreement between two churches, as the Union of Florence had been. It was a unilateral acceptance by the Holy See. The bishops had not gained a formal promise that the conditions of union as expressed in the 'Articles' would be met": Joseph Macha, *Ecclesiastical Unification* (Rome: Pontificio Istituto Orientale, 1974), 193.

Editor's note: Since Pospishil wrote this, scholarship on the Union of Brest has been aided immeasurably by two landmark scholarly books: Boris Gudziak, *Crisis and Reform: The Kyivan Metropolitanate, the Patriarchate of Constantinople, and the Genesis of the Union of Brest* (Cambridge, MA: Harvard University Press, 1999); and B. Groen et al., *Four Hundred Years: Union of Brest (1596–1996): A Critical Reevaluation* (Leuven, Belgium: Peeters, 1998).

33. Three changes in Orthodox canon law have been proposed on many occasions in this respect: (1) To let priests enter marriage at any time, even after ordination. (2) To permit married priests to become bishops. These two suggestions could be enacted in law by an ecumenical or pan-Orthodox council. (3) To permit widowed priests to remarry and stay in the clergy. Since Orthodoxy had

experienced divorce and remarriage, this would include the possibility to marry a divorced woman and for a divorced priest to marry again, perhaps even twice. Some theologians have excluded this last possibility entirely because it is opposed to an apostolic ordinance (1 Tim. 3:2; Titus 1:6). Cf. John Meyendorff, *Marriage: An Orthodox Perspective* (Crestwood, NY: St. Vladimir's Seminary Press, 1970), 52ff, and Demetrios J. Constantelos, *Marriage, Sexuality, and Celibacy: A Greek Orthodox Perspective* (Minneapolis, MN: Light and Life, 1975), 83ff.

Editor's note: Since Pospishil wrote this, one of these scenarios infamously erupted in North America: Fr. Joseph Allen, an Orthodox priest, remarried after the death of his wife, as he recounts in his book *Widowed Priest* (Minneapolis, MN: Light and Life, 1994). This event created great furor among North American Orthodox and led, inter alia, to Allen's removal from lecturing at St. Vladimir's Seminary and his being treated as a *persona non grata* by other Orthodox. But his bishop, the late metropolitan Philip Saliba of the Antiochian Orthodox archdiocese, supported him. For more on this topic, see a scholarly collection of articles also edited by Allen, *Vested in Grace: Priesthood and Marriage in the Christian East* (Brookline, MA: Holy Cross Press, 2001).

34. *Editor's note*: Since Pospishil wrote, many professional societies—physicians, including especially psychiatrists; psychologists and other therapists; lawyers; teachers—have all written into their professional codes prohibitions against practitioners dating their patients or clients because of perceived power imbalances and vulnerabilities on the part of patients and clients. Some of these factors were alleged to have been at work in the Joseph Allen situation discussed in the note above, and for these reasons it would seem imperative that the requirement of priests' marrying before ordination be maintained. As I put it to my students who regularly inquire about this, you do not want a priest on the prowl in the parish because it creates all sorts of questionable dynamics, and not merely for the women who attract his attention. Fr. John Hunwicke's chapter, elsewhere in this volume, also touches on the problems created by such situations in the Church of England, whose clerics are permitted marriage even after ordination.

35. Cedomir Draskovic, *Bogoslovlje* (Belgrade, 1962), 2.

36. *Editor's note*: In 1948, Photius was subjected to a dramatic and far-reaching re-evaluation precisely by Catholic scholars. See the historian Francis Dvornik's study *The Photian Schism: History and Legend* (Cambridge: Cambridge University Press, 1948), which rehabilitated Photius in Catholic and even some Orthodox eyes and in the past seven decades has remained the seminal treatment of this controversial and difficult figure.

37. Photius, *Letter to the Eastern Patriarchs*, encyclical, 897.

38. John Meyendorff, *Byzantine Theology: Historical Trends and Doctrinal Themes* (New York: Fordham University Press, 1974), 94.

39. Ibid., 60.

40. Issued during the Forty-First International Eucharistic Congress in Philadelphia (August 1–8, 1976) and published in *Diakonia* 11 (1976): 298–299.

41. *Editor's note*: Jadot was made a bishop in 1968 and served as the apostolic delegate to the United States from 1973 to 1980 before being assigned to the United Nations. He died in 2009.

42. *Ontario English Catholic Teachers Association Reporter* (Toronto), February 1977, 49.

43. *Editor's note*: Pospishil was clearly prescient here, predicting more than thirty years in advance more or less the arrangement that emerged under Pope Benedict XVI in 2009 in *Anglicanorum Coetibus*, whose details are here: http://www.vatican.va/holy_father/benedict_xvi/apost_constitutions/documents/hf_ben-xvi_apc_20091104_anglicanorum-coetibus_en.html.

APPENDIX TWO

Recent Views on the Origins of Clerical Celibacy
A Review of the Literature from 1980 to 1991

J. Kevin Coyle

Edited by Adam A. J. DeVille

The requirement that priests of the Roman Catholic Church observe perpetual celibacy (a requirement also imposed in certain Eastern Catholic jurisdictions) continues to elicit discussion by historians, theologians, Vatican authorities, and the media. The interest is currently fueled by concerns over a shortage of priests in the Latin Church,[1] as well as by shifts in views on ecclesiology, ministry, and sexuality. Nor ought one to overlook the many depressing reports of sexual scandals involving Catholic clergy in North America[2] or, for that matter, sociological studies of clerical and religious life,[3] including studies and research by theologians on the Catholic clergy in general and celibacy in particular.[4]

The present article does not presume to discuss the merits of clerical celibacy itself but to review recent discussion by scholars of the origins of the current discipline for clergy in Roman Catholicism. I will pay special attention to the two works primarily responsible for keeping the issue alive. In 1980, Roger Gryson examined works of the preceding decade on the same issue,[5] which was a follow-up to his famous book of 1970 in which he had argued that there is no historical evidence from earlier than the late fourth century to support the present-day Roman Catholic requirement of perpetual clerical celibacy.[6] Much of the literature Gryson reviewed at the time had, of course, appeared in response to his own writings. Since then, discussion has orbited around the 1981 work of Christian Cochini (translated into English in 1991) and the subsequent publications of Roman Cholij.[7]

This article, then, will focus primarily on these two authors in an effort to extend Gryson's overview of 1980 to literature that has appeared on the same subject.[8] I will do this in the first two sections through a discussion of the thesis of Cochini and Cholij by other commentators as well as by me, paying close attention to the main sources in Christian antiquity invoked by Cochini and Cholij. In a third section I will look briefly at other authors who have entered the debate to some extent. The references to these two will appear parenthetically in the text itself; where there is no such attribution the views are my own.

Throughout, I will maintain a distinction (made by Cochini and Cholij)[9] between "celibacy," in the sense of being unmarried as a *sine qua non* for receiving major orders (diaconate, presbyterate, or episcopate)—the current discipline in Roman Catholicism (and some Eastern Catholic eparchies)—and the terms "chastity" and "continence." "Chastity" means the virtue that regulates the sexual appetite, regardless of one's state in life; in Western canonical terms, however, it has come to mean the practice of continence within a consecrated (religious) state. "Continence," which means the voluntary abstention from sexual activity within marriage, can be temporary or perpetual; when it is the latter, it means celibacy in the wide sense, or *lex continentiae*.[10]

I. Christian Cochini

a. His Thesis

Cochini's volume, originally a doctoral dissertation defended in 1969 at the Institut Catholique (Paris) and translated into English, drew attention by reorienting the whole debate through an elaborate defense of what he views as an undeviating *sensus Ecclesiae* of the Catholic tradition of the first centuries (p. 469), even as seen in the light of a history broadly defined as "the memory of humanity" (p. 39).[11] Cochini's fundamental thesis is therefore a simple one: as Gryson had shown, from the fourth century on we have had clear legislation prohibiting major clerics, married or not, from sexual relations once they received orders (pp. 70–71).[12] However, Cochini parts company with Gryson over what the lack of pre-fourth-century ecclesiastical legislation on this issue signifies. Whereas Gryson concluded that there had simply never been any, Cochini infers that such legislation existed from apostolic times, regarding not celibacy of the type known in Roman Catholicism today but instead continence. This would have constituted an unwritten law of the whole Church until the fourth century, when the need for and possibility of written legislation, in the light of Christianity's new-found freedom, had emerged: "Concluons que l'obligation faite aux diacres, aux prêtres, et aux évêques maries de garder la continence parfait avec leur épouse n'est pas dans l'Eglise le fruit d'une elaboration tardive, mais est au contraire, dans toute l'acceptation du terme, une *tradition non-écrite d'origine apostolique* qui, â notre connaissance, trouva sa première expression canonique au 4e siècle."[13]

Cochini infers the corollary of a consistent idea running through the parallel traditions of the early Christian churches, namely, that continence is required of ministers employed in the "service of the altar" because they exercise a unique intercessory and mediating function between God and humanity (26–27 and 278–281). The object of this rule, he says, was to forbid sexual relations between spouses without casting aspersions on their marriage or suggesting that marriage is incompatible with ordination (275). Thus the focus of the study has virtually nothing to do with the transformation of this rule into the law of celibacy known today. Rather, it looks backward in order to vindicate the claim that a law of continence enacted at the regional Council of Carthage in 390 was in keeping with a practice derived from the origins of Christianity—from the teaching of the apostles and from ancient custom.

Cochini considers the lack of clear textual evidence prior to the "violent crisis" reflected in fourth-century legislation to be supportive of his claim that a practice of clerical continence existed and had gone without serious challenge up to that time. In his view, the severity of Roman legislative measures and the vigor of Christian apologetics reflect opposition to what was perceived as a challenge to a traditional discipline and to the principles on which it rested (278). But elsewhere (86–87) Cochini defends the same lack of positive evidence for his theory with the claim that documents that would sustain the theory must have been lost during the persecutions of the first three centuries!

b. Critique

i. *The Thesis in General*

Tempting though it is, a full examination of the premise of earlier missing documentation is out of the question here—except for two observations. First, the premise evades an equally plausible conjecture: Such materials (if they ever existed) might have represented a single side of a polemic raging in those same centuries over an issue far from decided. Second, one could also, and with no less plausibility, envisage the willful destruction of *opposing* documentation with the objective of creating the illusion of a single, unbroken tradition regarding the continence discipline.

There is no need to linger on the conjectural aspect of precisely *why* pre-fourth-century legislative documentation is not to be found. More to the point, while no one seriously disputes that (at least in the West) continence after ordination eventually became a standard requirement for all men (married or not) admitted to the diaconate, presbyterate, or episcopate, the *fact* of the absence of such documentation prior to the fourth century constitutes the first major difficulty with Cochini's premise.[14] This absence does not perturb him, for he bases his methodological strategy on what he terms "explaining the obscure by the clear" documentation he purports to have found, beginning in the 380s; it affirms that an apostolic practice and ordinance could have travelled through time as an oral tradition before becoming embodied in legislation. A doctrine or discipline in question has its beginnings in the time of the apostles (78). This is what Cochini means by his "principle of spatio-temporal universality" (85), to which we will return.

A second serious objection to Cochini's position is that legislation regarding the *clergy* exists from well before the late fourth century, as in the *Apostolic Tradition* (c. 217) and the *Didascalia* (c. 250), but without reference to the marital status of clerics, let alone their conjugal activities. Indeed, the great majority of the 210 cases of married clerics that Cochini has inventoried do not mention their ceasing conjugal relations, which opens the possibility that such instances of cessation are mentioned because of the exceptional nature of the event.[15]

As to late-fourth-century bishops and presbyters known to have renounced conjugal intercourse after ordination or never to have married at all, it is important to remember that communities chose their own ministers and that (at least by this time) they had begun to seek candidates whose lives differed from those of average community members. These candidates, once chosen, often staunchly defended virginity and/or continence;[16] but that is not to say that the individuals in question would have sought to impose such an obligation on all the ordained. In any event, individual pronouncements would prove neither a rule nor an apostolic tradition.

Cochini goes to some length to advance the view that the apostles themselves observed continence from the day Jesus called them. To do this he relies (as for most other points) on the "consensus" he perceives in early patristic writings (89–108). In direct contradiction of the claims of Gryson and others, he asserts that it was not the later influence of Hellenistic philosophies and the mystery religions, but rather the Jewish Christian community, that promoted a recapitulation within Christianity of the language and, to some extent, the self-understanding of the Old Testament priesthood (467–468). If the practice of continence appears to be unlegislated before the fourth century, this can be, he says, only because the practice was generally accepted, as illustrated by the same fourth-century legislation—the sort found in the canons of Carthage of 390 and decretals ascribed to Siricius, bishop of Rome.

ii. *Cochini's Deployment of Texts*

To enumerate and examine every text that Cochini cites in defense of his thesis would be tedious and counter-productive. A lengthy study could be made of the way Cochini reworks standard translations of patristic passages or presupposes particular contextual hypotheses in order to read ambiguous texts in the most favorable light possible. Such a study is in this event unnecessary since Cochini is consistent throughout in the way he approaches his texts. Suffice it to focus on his treatment of some key passages as being typical of the way he deploys texts in general. Consider the following examples:

(a) Council of Carthage (390), Canon 2

We begin with the first major piece of ecclesiastical legislation on the subject of clerical continence as highlighted by Cochini, on which he sets great store. The following translation of the second canon of a council held in Roman Africa on 6 June 390 is based on Cochini's French rendition, since it is Cochini's line of argument that is under scrutiny here. The first part of the canon reads, according to him (25): "Bishop Epigonius of Bulla Regius said: In a previous council the rule of continence and chastity was discussed. The three ranks which by virtue of their consecration are bound by the same obligation to chastity, should [now] be instructed more forcefully: I mean the bishop, the priest and the deacon. And they should be taught to preserve purity."[17]

As Cochini interprets this, Epigonius is asserting that a previous (but unidentified) council discussed the rule of continence and chastity (Cochini, 25). But Epigonius is not referring to any rule; he only says that the question has been broached or dealt with (*tractaretur*).[18] Nor does he necessarily mean by *tractatu pleniori* that the same assertion (as one made at a previous council) should now be taught "avec plus de force" (25). What Epigonius rather seems to have meant is "in a more complete fashion," by setting out exactly what is expected of major clerics with regard to chastity, which seems to have been hitherto a rather vague requirement: *constriction quadam castitatis*—a phrase that does not lend itself to Cochini's rendition, "par la même obligation de chasteté."[19] Nor does the Latin text support the claim that the obligation of chastity had been taken on because the members of all three ranks were, by their consecration, "introduits dans un ordre de réalités différent de celui où se déroulait jusqu'alors leur existence" (Cochini, 26). Neither Epigonius nor the joint statement at the canon's conclusion draws a connection between a *constrictio castitatis* and those *qul altario inseruiunt*.[20]

The text of the second episcopal intervention in Carthage's second canon states, in Cochini's reading (25–26): "Bishop Geneclius said: As was said previously, it is fitting that the holy bishops and priests of God, as well as the levites, meaning those who are in the service of the divine mysteries, observe perfect continence so as to be able to obtain in all simplicity what they ask of the Lord: what the apostles taught and antiquity itself has observed, let us also do our part in keeping."[21]

Cochini is fond of repeating the assertion of Geneclius, presider of the council, that the rule of perpetual continence for major clerics is "that which the apostles taught and antiquity itself has observed." He sees in this rule no innovation but rather a custom faithfully adhered to since Christianity's earliest days (28). But he takes liberties with the impact of

Geneclius's intervention, which he himself translates as an advisory (*decet* = "il convient"). He does the same with the final, collective statement of the canon, which he renders (26) as "Unanimously, the bishops declared: we all agree that the bishop, priest, and deacon, [as] guardians of purity, ought to abstain [from conjugal intercourse] with their spouse so that those in the service of the altar may keep perfect chastity."[22]

One supposes, of course, that texts from episcopal gatherings such as this were preserved for a particular reason with even individual interventions seen to express what the gathering (or at least the compiler) wanted said. But what entitles Cochini to give the pronouncements of two individual bishops the same weight as a declaration of the whole synod and to draw from this proof of an apostolic tradition practiced always and everywhere?[23] The synodal statement per se comprises only the final lines of the canon, and its tone is much more circumspect than those of the preceding individual interventions: Members of the ranks in question are "guardians of modesty" (*pudicitiae custodes*) and are "advised" to abstain from conjugal relations (*placet ut . . . se abstineant*) without any precision as to the occasion or the duration of abstention or as to apostolic origins. This latter notion is, "au contraire, une opinion purement privée d'un évêque [Geneclius], que les Pères de Carthage, qui n'etaient pas totalement dépourvus de sens historique, évitent soigneusement de reprendre à leur compte."[24]

Cochini (24) makes much of the fact that Carthage's Canon 2 reappears in the *Codex canonum ecclesiae Africanae* of 419. But there the joint declaration "ab uniuersis episcopis" is limited to Carthage's closing words: "Placet ut in omnibus et ab omnibus pudicitia custodiatur qui altariis (altario) inseruiunt."[25] Yet even were we to accept the entire wording of Carthage's Canon 2 in its strictest possible sense, and to ignore any distinction between joint declarations and individual observations, we would still be left with no more than proof of a perception among a rather small gathering at the end of the fourth century in Proconsular Africa that continence and chastity have apostolic origins. We do not yet have proof that such origins are really the case.

(b) "Siricius"

Cochini's manipulation of history has not been taken seriously by most of his critics and will not delay us longer here. Far more interesting in terms of the continuing debate is his posture in regard to *tradition*;

indeed, his work reveals more about this posture than it does about the objects he treats. This is demonstrable in the way he uses biblical texts and in his presentation of the decretals ascribed to Siricius, bishop of Rome from 384 to 399.

(c) *Epistula 1 ad Himerium* (= *Directa*)

Of the three early Roman decretals invoked by Cochini, the earliest (according to Gryson) dates from 10 February 385. *Directa* purports to be the response of a synod of bishops convened at Rome by Siricius to answer queries sent by Himerius, bishop of Tarragona, to Siricius's predecessor, Damasus (†11 December 384). *Directa* deals with various matters, all of them disciplinary: admission of Arians and apostates to the Catholic communion (chaps. 1 and 3); administration of marriage, baptism, and penance (chaps. 2, 4, and 5); and questions of monastic and clerical discipline (chaps. 6–15). The decretal is among the earliest surviving testimonies to the idea of the apostolic origins of the continence rule for major clerics. Cochini (if it needs repeating) deduces from it a proof of those origins.[26] He focuses on the decretal's seventh chapter, which opens a section on clerical matters (Cochini, 28–30). The pertinent passage reads:[27]

> Why then were the priests [of the Old Testament] commanded to dwell in the Temple, away from their homes, during their year-long tour of duty? Obviously so as not to have carnal intercourse with their wives in order that, resplendent with an unsullied conscience, they might offer a gift acceptable to God (see 1 Pet. 2:5). Once the period of their service had been completed, they could make use of conjugal relations, but only to assure the succession, for no one could be admitted to the ministry of God except from the tribe of Levi (see Lev. 15:16–17; 1 Sam. 21:5–7).
>
> That is why the Lord Jesus, after enlightening us by his coming, affirms in the gospel that he has come not to abolish the Law but to fulfill it (see Matt. 5:17); and why he wishes the beauty of the Church, whose bridegroom he is, to shine again with chastity's splendor so that, when he comes again on the Day of Judgment, he might find her without stain or wrinkle, as was taught through his apostle (see Eph. 5:27). All of us, priests and Levites, are bound by the unbreakable law of these ordinances, that from the day of our ordination we may deliver our hearts and bodies over to sobriety and chastity so as

to be pleasing in all things to our God in those sacrifices we offer day after day.[28]

This first decretal, which also appears to be the least synodal in tone—that is, it sounds more as if written by an individual author and less as if it is a joint statement than the others—is also the most stringent ("insolubili lege constringimur") and the most insistent on the model of the Old Testament priesthood as a justification for Christian clerical practices. There is, then, no doubt where the author stands personally on the issue, and in that sense Cochini understands him correctly.

But the writer of the decretal lacks inner logic in that the second paragraph cited does not follow from the first.[29] Moreover, he fails to describe the precise link between the Old and New Testament views of priesthood. He does not, for instance, choose the obvious path of extending his conclusions to say that "priests" of the New Testament would be free to observe absolute continence since Christian priesthood is no longer "restricted to a tribe or family. Nor does he seem aware of the possibility that the OT could have prescribed that Levites have families before being allowed to officiate at the Temple worship just as minor clerics could before the reception of major orders."[30] The focus on the levitical example is primarily due, it seems, to the necessity of countering the argument that clerics could enter into and use marriage because of Old Testament priestly practices.[31]

Furthermore, the closing reference to "daily" sacrifice is obscure, since a daily celebration of the Eucharist at Rome in this period is far from certain.[32] It is therefore questionable whether the phrase *in his, quae quotidie offerimus* deserves the interpretation "devant offrir quotidiennement le sacrifice" (Cochini, 23), even though the necessity of continence for "daily worship" would not necessarily mean that the eucharistic liturgy was celebrated literally every day (*pace* Dassmann);[33] "the pollution" caused by sex (referred to in the second decretal) need be seen not in formally ritual terms, valid for a precise period of time, such as twenty-four hours, but in more generalized moral terms; and certainly the notion of "being always prepared" is a factor here, as the other decretals show.[34]

On the other hand, if an uninterrupted tradition of continence were provable—or at least generally acknowledged—the author of the first decretal would only have had to remind Himerius of it. He did not; what occurs instead is that, in the other two decretals we will examine, the ritual purity argument gains in intensity, indicating that, though in *Directa* it is not crucial to the defense of absolute continence for major clerics, it becomes more so once it is perceived at Rome that the argument of an unbroken tradition is not having the desired effect on the clergy, at least in Italy.[35]

(d) *Epistula 10 ad Gallos episcopos* (*Dominus inter*)

Though Cochini considers it (34) to belong to the time of Pope Innocent I (†417), the decretal *Dominus inter* was probably written earlier than *Epist. 5*—therefore, sometime in 385,[36] and is a synodal response to queries from bishops in Gaul regarding a variety of pastoral difficulties. The language of this second decretal makes it clear that the synodal decision is encapsulated in the statement that opens the passage (Cochini, 35): "In the first place it was decided, with regard to bishops, presbyters and deacons: that those involved in the divine sacrifices and through whose hands the grace of baptism is conferred and the body of Christ made present (*conficitur*), not we alone but the divine scriptures as well oblige to be most chaste; and the fathers too have commanded that bodily continence be observed."[37]

The justification for this stance then follows (Cochini, 35–36):

> For this reason let us not pass over [this point], but let us pronounce the reason. For with what effrontery would a bishop or presbyter dare to preach integrity or continence to a widow or virgin, or to urge the preservation of a chaste marriage bed, if he himself has been more occupied with offspring for the world than with children for God? . . . Therefore, with regard to these three ranks, of which we read in the scriptures, the precept of purity is to be observed by the ministers of God, and this requirement is always in force; for baptism will always need to be conferred or sacrifices to be offered.[38]

As it stands, this declaration is vague, for it leaves unclear what being "most chaste" and "observing bodily continence" entail. Though some concrete consequences of noncompliance are spelled out, they are clouded by the following section's palpable switch from the plural to the singular, suggesting that an individual has interjected a personal commentary, which begins perhaps with the passage just cited.[39] At any rate, it continues to advance the example of the Old Testament priesthood with, once more, the deduction that priests of the New Covenant must therefore *permanently* abstain from conjugal relations (Cochini, 36):

> Would an unclean person dare contaminate what is holy, when what is holy is such for holy persons? Thus those who offered sacrifices in the Temple, in order to be pure, quite properly remained in the Temple during the entire year of their service, having nothing to do with their own households. Even idolaters, in order to carry out their impious acts and offer sacrifice to demons, impose on themselves abstinence from women and keep themselves untainted by certain foods; and you ask me whether a priest of the true God, who is to offer up spiritual sacrifices (see 1 Pet. 2:5) should be perpetually untainted, whether he should be concerned about the flesh [like someone] totally in the flesh? If intercourse is a pollution, then the priest must stand ready for heavenly duties, as one who is to intercede for the sins of others; otherwise he might himself be found unworthy. For if it is said [even] to laypersons, "Abstain for a time, that you may leave time for prayer" (1 Cor. 7:5), those who apply themselves to the generation of creatures may well carry the name of "priests" but they cannot carry it with honor.[40]

The alleged temporary abstinence from conjugal relations required of levitical priests during their tours of duty in the Temple, and of the Jewish people generally on certain occasions, Cochini (466) believes to be the sole surviving remnant within Christianity of the purity codes of ancient Israel. The exceptional survival of this practice (confirmed, in Cochini's view, by Paul in 1 Cor. 7:5) shows the importance with which it was regarded in the apostolic era (Cochini, 471–472), and the strengthening of this rule to absolute continence for the clergy is characteristic, he says, of "the priesthood of Christ [which] brought the Old Testament to perfection" (Cochini, 31; see also 466 and 468).

In the first (synodal) part of the citation from the second decretal, the rule of continence supposedly demanded of Old Testament priests is applied to those of the New Testament; but here it is also said that the Old Law is perfected and completed by the New. One must then ask what the criteria are according to which one regulation of the Old Law is known to have been abolished and another to have been subsumed into the new dispensation, or, in this instance, "How could Christians again allow the force of ancient laws of purity when Jesus and the New Testament writers revoked the ritual precepts of the Old Testament and declared them void?"[41] According to the author of *Dominus inter*, "The answer must lie in the practice of the Church. When the customs of the Church are parallel to those of the OT, they are to be understood as the final development of earlier usages. Where there is no correspondence, the OT has given way to the NT. Hence the laws in these decretals are not deductions from the OT (or the NT). Rather, it is confidently expected and believed that what the Church is doing will have been prepared for by the OT and described in the NT."[42]

The second (and less clearly synodal) part of the citation contains a statement that is unequivocally ritual.[43] As used here, it makes a weak argument. There is nothing about a daily Eucharist that would have rendered an argument based on cultic abstinence compelling. The mention of both baptism and the Eucharist suggests that neither one was frequent enough or sufficient by itself to ensure absolute continence, even granting that only a cleric ritually pure was allowed to officiate. The use of baptism is particularly unconvincing for an argument based primarily on ritual purity.

Still, here the ritual argument, while not yet paramount, has gained momentum since the first decretal.[44] And, as intimated earlier, there is an assumption here that sex necessarily defiles the body's holiness (*si commixtio pollutio est*); hence it should be voluntarily abandoned by all seeking perfection but must be abandoned by those involved regularly and by ordination in the celebration of the sacred mysteries. We will return to a consideration of ritual purity in the conclusion to this section.

(e) *Epistula 5 ad episcopos Africae* (= *Cum in unum*)

Its title notwithstanding, the third decretal, *Cum in unum*, concerns the Church in Italy, having originally addressed Italian bishops unable to attend a synod held at Rome in January of 386.[45] Cochini (33) terms this decretal "an essential link whereby the bishops of the Roman synod of 386 and Pope Siricius situate themselves in continuity with the apostolic age." But the link appears to be more tenuous than Cochini suggests.

The document first presents eight disciplinary canons (none of them on continence, although one canon forbids a cleric to marry a widow and another bars any aspirant to the clergy who has married a widow). The canons are followed by a brief exhortation on continence, which includes the text on which Cochini focuses (32):

> Besides, as is worthy, chaste and honest, we advise that priests and levites not have intercourse with their wives, because they are preoccupied by the daily demands of their ministry. For Paul writes to the Corinthians, "Abstain, that you may leave time for prayer" (1 Cor. 7:5). If, therefore, abstinence is demanded of laypersons, so that they may be heard when they pray, how much more should the priest, fortified by a spotless purity, be ready at every moment, in case he is called upon to offer sacrifice or to baptize? If he were contaminated by carnal concupiscence, what would he do? Excuse himself? With what shame, in what state of mind would he assume [these functions]? By what act of conscience, by what right would he believe himself heard, when it is said, "All things are clean to the clean, but for those who are tainted and unbelieving nothing is clean" (Tit. 1:15)? That is why I exhort, I admonish, I request that this opprobrium, which even the pagans would be right to charge against [us], be lifted away. Perhaps someone believes it [is permitted] because it is written, "The husband of one wife" (1 Tim. 3:2, 12; Tit. 1:6). But [the text] was not speaking of someone who persists in the desire to procreate, but rather of the continence to be observed from then on.[46]

Again, this passage does not seem to entirely originate from a synod per se, for once more an abrupt shift occurs from the first person plural to the singular, indicating that an individual's views have been interjected. If that is indeed the case, the situation is similar to those related to the preceding decretal and to Carthage, where the compiler took no great care to distinguish between synodal and individual views. Yet in each case the synodal statement is more restrained in its tone and interpretation of scripture than is the individual. In the quotation's opening lines, the same note of *counsel* ("suademus") is employed as in the earlier collective statements, with the same lack of precision as to the duration and circumstance of the practice of continence.

The Old Testament model of the first decretal, while preserved in the second, has been displaced in the third. The precision of absolute continence, emanating from the individual portion of the decretal, is derived from the observance of cultic abstinence, justified not from temple priesthood, but from Paul's enjoinder to laypersons in 1 Corinthians 7:5. The decretal argues that those who offer sacrifice or baptize are much more strictly bound to continence than are the married laypersons whom Paul advised to abstain so that they might devote themselves to prayer. Thus the Pauline counsel is extended to absolute continence.[47]

Even with the disappearance of the Old Testament model, the ritual purity argument is here at its strongest among the decretals—practically the only argument now offered.[48] "The argument by which major clerics are exhorted to perpetual abstinence from their wives is exclusively ritual. Continence is necessary for worship to be acceptable to God, and the daily ministry of major clerics, either baptism or the Eucharist, obliges them to observe perfect continence."[49]

Exegetes today would argue that the recognition in 1 Corinthians 7:5 that spouses may by agreement abstain in order to devote themselves to prayer is more likely a concession than an obligation. The concession probably stems from the view that nothing should distract from the prayers' intensity; at any rate, there is no reference to a ritual motivation.[50] We might also note that the counsel to spouses not to refuse themselves to each other is addressed to all married couples in the community; no exception is made for specially designated ministers.[51] In fact, the Pauline text appears to diametrically oppose Cochini's thesis, for the idea of a basic Christian choice, *either* a life of prayer *or* a sexual life in marriage, is distinctly unpauline.

The same decretal interprets the stipulation of 1 Timothy 3:2, 12 (or Titus 1:6) that the *episkopos* be "the husband of one wife" as a requirement intended to ensure the choice of men whose previous sexual morality was irreproachable and who could therefore be trusted to keep the continence which would be required of them once they assumed office. Cochini admits that this requirement clearly envisioned a married clergy; but he also believes that it excluded those who, by the standards of the time, had rendered themselves suspect with regard to continence by having remarried after the death of the first spouse (Cochini, 31).[52] He approves of the decretal's interpretation of the phrase in the Pastoral Letters; but while this could be the meaning, the text gives no suggestion that it is.[53] And while Siricius may be correct in understanding "the husband of one wife" of 1 Timothy 3:2, 12 (Tit. 1:6) to exclude the possibility of successive marriages, the assertion that this moral requirement is meant to guarantee future continence is questionable.[54] It is therefore far from certain that the final words of the third decretal passage (*propter continentiam futuram*) must be understood in the sense of "en vue de la continence qu'il lui faudrait pratiquer" (Cochini, 32), still less that the same interpretation was intended by the author of 1 Timothy (Titus) or, for that matter, of 1 Corinthians.

Yet the decretal's interpretation of "the husband of one wife" stipulation is crucial to Cochini's argument—particularly in light of the numerous examples of married clerics from the first seven centuries that fill his fifth chapter (Cochini, 112–158). In the case of the more than twenty texts cited that pre-date Ambrosiaster (ca. 385), he consistently reverses standard translations or hypothesizes the contexts of the texts in order to yield readings favorable to his thesis. In short, it is clear that Cochini is determined to harmonize the biblical texts either with the claims of the authorities wherein he found these texts employed or with the claim recorded at the Council of Carthage that the rule of continence was "taught by the apostles." In either case, he shows far more deference to such claims than he does to the meaning of the texts, whether that meaning has been gleaned from the texts themselves or is ascribed to them by modern exegetes.

(f) Elvira, Canon 33, and Arles, Canon 6

Since Cochini sets great store by it (183–186), we pause briefly at the thirty-third of the canons ascribed to the regional Council of Elvira (held at the beginning of the fourth century).[55] The Latin text of the canon in question reads: "Placuit in totum prohibere episcopis, presbyteris et diaconibus uel omnibus clericis positis in ministerio abstinere se a coniugibus suis et non generare filios. Quicumque uero feceret, ab honore clericatus exterminetur."[56]

The text presents an immediate problem with its double negation (*prohibere . . . abstinere se . . . et non generare*). This is possibly meant to reinforce the ideas stated, but it could be taken to mean that clergy are not to be absolutely forbidden to have conjugal relations and to procreate. We will not discuss the precise reasons for the grammatical construction here. Whatever this text's meaning, Gryson has shown that the canon belongs to the end of the fourth century, since only the first twenty-one canons ascribed to the Council of Elvira were actually enacted there.[57]

The thirty-third canon would, then, belong to the same time frame as the four documents already discussed and need delay us no further here.

Nor, for similar reasons, is it necessary to dwell on the sixth canon, ascribed to the Council of Arles (314), another passage highlighted by Cochini (186–194). This canon, too, represents a case of erroneous attribution, a fact Cochini has chosen to ignore.[58]

(g) Augustine, *De baptismo* IV, 24:31

The methodology Cochini considers appropriate to his demonstration he finds primarily (75–87) in hermeneutical criteria furnished through Augustine's *De baptismo* (written ca. 400): "That which is kept by the whole Church and has always been maintained, without having been established by councils, is rightfully believed to have been transmitted only by virtue of apostolic authority."[59]

Cochini argues (76–83) that a point of doctrine may be deemed to have been "kept by the whole Church" if it has been kept by (1) a majority of those exercising the greatest moral and intellectual authority in the Church; (2) individual churches that were founded by the apostles personally or have maintained a "consanguinity of doctrine" with such churches; or (3) the aggregate of bishops (successors of the apostles), most particularly in their synodal and conciliar declarations.

Augustine's second criterion—that a teaching has "always been maintained"—can be considered to have been fulfilled, Cochini says (83–85), if (a) retrojecting from the moment when we can verify that a teaching is being "kept by the whole Church" (in the sense just defined), there is found no decision made by an ecumenical council or by the incumbent of the Apostolic See in Rome to prove the existence of a contrary belief or practice manifest in the whole Church; (b) the teaching in question has never been the subject of a prior contestation in the name of a parallel tradition among the apostolically founded churches; and (c) the teaching is not in formal contradiction with a text of scripture. Cochini (85) terms this expansion of Augustine's formula the "principle of spatio-temporal universality." He then adds two further methodological safeguards: a "principle of progressive explanation," requiring that the earliest text extant in support of a teaching not be identified with the origin of that teaching unless there is positive evidence in favor of the identification, and a "principle of comprehensive interpretation," requiring that obscure historical phenomena, texts, or aspects thereof be interpreted in the light of phenomena, texts, or aspects thereof that are clear.

Eager to expand the import of Augustine's criteria beyond the limits of what they actually comprehend, Cochini fails to address at the outset a crucial element: that the passage in question refers, not to a point of discipline, but to one of liturgy and doctrine.[60] While Augustine's text admittedly deals with the problem of unwritten traditions, the passage belongs to a very particular context—a controversy with the Donatists over who might receive baptism, with the aim of clarifying the Church's understanding of the relationship between the Church's holiness and its ability to mediate God's grace. It is important that in the above citation from *De baptismo* Cochini omits the words that explicitly refer to this context: "tamen ueraciter conicere possumus, quid ualeat in paruulis baptismi sacramentum."[61] He thereby deletes any direct reference to Augustine's immediate concern, the efficacy of baptism in someone (an infant) whose faith consciousness is deemed to be unavoidably but unquestionably absent.[62] Cochini's application of Augustine's text therefore seems particularly inappropriate, especially as the question of infant baptism in early Christianity remains unsettled among scholars.[63]

Cochini anticipates this objection by arguing that, though "the domain of non-written traditions consists before all else of the truths of faith," the elaborations of theological reflection, especially of the major councils over the centuries, have nuanced the distinction so as to make it clear that the place of disciplinary and liturgical customs in this "apostolic deposit transmitted by the living voice" of tradition is also significant (Cochini, 74). In other words, Augustine's application is at least "quasi-disciplinary" (ibid.). A more likely reason is that he finds Augustine to be a more orthodox—and certainly weightier—source of such a principle than Tertullian or Vincent of Lerins, both of whom enunciated similar notions, would have been (see Cochini, 76 n. 19). Still, it remains a mystery how Cochini was inspired to employ the Augustine text in the context of celibacy.[64]

Cochini's "methodological principle"—termed by Balducelli "a hybrid theological-historical methodology"[65]—is also susceptible to the following criticisms: (1) Is it certain that what has been preserved by the whole Church and has always been maintained is derived from apostolic authority? (2) To maintain such a principle, is it sufficient to refer to a number of patristic witnesses (however numerous), in this case to establish that the discipline of clerical continence goes back to a positive will of the apostles? (3) The principle that supposes some sort of apostolic but unwritten legislation is impossible to demonstrate, especially if we give to the biblical expression "husband of one wife" (1 Tim. 3:2, 12; Tit. 1:6) the sense usually given it by exegetes and if we take into account the existence of many unquestionably married "clerics" in the first centuries.[66]

c. Concluding Observations

1. *"Tradition"*

Cochini's approach evinces an understanding of tradition that may be defined, in Jaroslav Pelikan's words, as "submission to the authority of tradition [as though] truth would not dare to appear outside it."[67] Or, to formulate it negatively, it betokens the view that no error—particularly no error involving an interpretation of the tradition itself—could ever have been received by that tradition. His understanding of tradition is also implicit in Cochini's failure (or refusal) to acknowledge the contextual factor (mentioned earlier) pertaining to the text from Augustine's *De baptismo* that functions as the centerpiece of his methodology.

Perhaps the greatest drawback to Cochini's approach is that he reads into the texts of the Christian past his firm conviction that the apostles themselves observed continence from the day of their calling by Jesus. Such a conviction is based on the thesis that the observance of continence that began to be legislated in the West from 385 on was in keeping with a practice derived from the origins of the Church, from the teaching of the apostles, and from ancient custom (Cochini, 89–108). If the Church was silent on this tradition prior to the fourth century, he argues, it is because the practice was generally accepted. This, however, seems highly unlikely in the earliest period, particularly in light of the New Testament insistence that the Temple, its priesthood, and its cult had all been relegated to the past.

Though Cochini cites numerous patristic and conciliar texts from the second, third, and (especially) fourth centuries in support of his position, he has left himself protected in that most are distinctly ambiguous. One may grant that many of the texts he draws on from the period between the Council of Carthage in 390 and that of Trullo (Quinisext) in 691/2 do favor the position that churches in both East and West maintained an absolute rule of continence for major clerics. Yet the earliest texts that unequivocally support the thesis are from Ambrosiaster (c. 385), Ambrose (d. 397), and Jerome (d. 420) (Cochini, 249–253, 261–266, and 324–331), that is, from the period in which most commentators concede that a rule of continence for such clerics began—or at least became widespread.[68]

What happened in the fourth century, then, is not the issue. What *is* at stake is Cochini's claim that Carthage and the decretals were simply articulating a universally acknowledged law, one viewed as unquestionably reaching back to the apostles. It seems far more likely that the decretals were sharing the assumption of a widely held and long-standing tradition, but the assumption does not prove that such a tradition was really the case. "C'est un des points de vue théologiquement les plus faibles de cet ouvrage, par ailleurs documenté. Qui veut trop prouver risqué de ne rien prouver du tout."[69]

Cochini, therefore, has no right to claim that "on ne trouve dans l'histoire des premiers siècles aucune idée d'évolution, selon lequelle la discipline de la continence des clercs ne serait peu à peu impose aux esprits sous la pression des courants favorable à la virginité" (Cochini, 277). This lack of evolutionary awareness is, in fact, as Crouzel remarks (295–296), one of the more troubling aspects of Cochini's book:

> Il est inconcevable que si l'obligation au célibat-continence avait été ressentie comme une loi obligeant strictement tous les clercs, il n'en soit resté de trace plus nette, alors que la "loi de monogamie" venant de *"unius uxoris virum"* paulinien est signalée en tant que loi par Tertullien, Hippolyte, et Origène (Cochini, 460, n. 3) sans aucune trace de l'interprétation qu'on en donnera plus tard. Is est pareillement inconcevable qu'Origène, si sévère, et fréquemment, pour les vices du clergé à son époque, n'ait jamais stigmatisé des situations contraires à l'obligation de la continence, alors que les auteurs ecclésiastiques des siècles suivants et les conciles le feront constamment.[70]

Any text is shaped in its expression by cultural references and historical circumstances. In the case of the first decretal, for instance, the context of Himerius's query was probably the Priscillianist movement then threatening Spain with its promotion of an extreme asceticism.[71] In the case of all three decretals, it is necessary to note the religious climate in Rome at the time of Siricius's response, affected as it was by the interrogations of Helvidius (in 383) against the validity of asserting the superiority of continence to marriage and the necessity of responding to these decretals without sounding like the Manichees, also active in Rome during the 380s.[72]

Moreover, the Roman decretals were reflecting a (by then) general insistence in the church at Rome on absolute continence for major clerics after ordination (Callam, "Clerical Continence in the Fourth Century," 33–34), premised on widespread attitudes in antiquity that all sexual intercourse rendered one somehow less than human.[73] Helvidius is also probably a reflection of a contemporary presumption that clerical continence had apostolic roots, but there is insufficient proof here and elsewhere that such roots actually existed.[74]

Far from having resolved the question concerning traditional claims for clerical continence (if not celibacy), Cochini's main contribution has been simply to introduce a new level of complexity. No specific connection has been shown to exist between ministry and celibacy (or even continence) in early Christianity. The most probable explanation for the fourth-century emphasis on continence is not, as Cochini pretends, that it is due to "an unwritten tradition of apostolic origin which ... first found canonical expression in the fourth century," but that it reflects values which had gradually arisen and were now finding greater scope for expression, including the clergy/laity distinction, the deep suspicion of all sexual acts, the exaltation of virginity,[75] the choice by some individuals of permanent celibacy or continence as an individual initiative,[76] and the growing influence of asceticism on all aspects of church life, including notions of sanctity.[77]

Such notions of asceticism in this period would have had two results: ascetics would have been more and more considered likely candidates for the episcopate,[78] or, at the very least, it would have been claimed that virginity, being superior to marriage, ought to bind clergy to the former.[79] Such was precisely the argument of the second and third decretals.

All of this Cochini ignores, approaching all his texts uncritically. He ignores modern exegesis showing that none of Siricius's scriptural interpretations could pass muster. There is nothing in Eph. 5:27 that permits one to link it to chastity. There is no biblical (or mishnaic) basis for the idea of a year-long temple duty served in continence by Old Testament priests.[80] There is no hint anywhere of protracted continence being required for those in a priesthood which was, after all, hereditary.

ii. *Ritual Purity*
Conscious, perhaps, that the orientation of the three decretals moves steadily toward a justification of continence pinpointed on the argument of cultic purity, Cochini suggests that it is time to do away with the cultic purity argument for maintaining clerical continence. Such a justification,

he says, is "chargée de résonances païennes ou philosophiques (notamment stoïciennes) qui ne sont pas toujours homogènes à l'esprit du christianisme" (280, n. 41). In its place one ought to speak of "service de l'autel" and of "ministère sacerdotal." But the motivation he suggests is still cultic: It is connected with the liturgical function of the priest as eucharistic celebrant in a liturgy "where Christ himself comes to presence and associates his ministers to his own person and sacrifice." These catechetical commonplaces are to rescue clerical continence from obscurity and usher in legitimation to sustain the validity of continence now and into the future.

iii. *Summary*

Many doubt that Cochini's work has proved anything new; still, while some critics have declared his method inadequate, none have branded him as naïve in regard to history, and with good reason. For the work has undoubted value as a reference tool framed by gathering texts that deal with continence. On the other hand, Cochini uses his method in an attempt to contextualize the texts in a way that more often obscures matters than reveals them clearly. And his tendency to draw conclusions from silences in the documentary record do not hold up under scrutiny.

At the end of the book Cochini alleges that, with the exception of churches that followed schismatic movements, extant texts of the second to seventh centuries indicate that there was remarkable unity throughout the oriental and occidental churches in their acceptance of absolute continence after ordination for bishops, presbyters, and deacons (Cochini, 312–318). Even the Council in Trullo, which established *periodic* continence for presbyters and deacons in the East, was in harmony with the spirit of the apostolic rule. Cochini believes Trullo's rule was a misinterpretation of the *Apostolic Canons*, which are today generally regarded not as conciliar but as apocryphal. This brings us to the writings of Roman Cholij.

II. Roman Cholij

a. His Method

Writing as a canon lawyer, Cholij produced a series of articles, culminating in a book, to counter the thesis that "in the Eastern Church (apart from special cases) there exists no law of celibacy, and that this state of affairs has existed since apostolic times" (Cholij, *AHC* 1987, 71, and *CCEW* 1989, 1). In other words, Western Catholic tradition has alone preserved clerical continence as a primitive tradition. The implications of this are far-reaching, suggesting that celibacy cannot be dismissed as merely disciplinary.

Where Cochini's *terminus ad quem* is the seventh century, Cholij deals primarily with Trullo and its aftermath as far as Gratian (twelfth century). In this period he admits that (*AHC* 1987, 136, and *CCEW* 1989, 67) "the discipline of continence was regarded generally as not being of apostolic origin, nor attached in any strictly necessary way to the exercise of orders." Hence, "If the canonists and theologians of the 12th and 13th centuries had not been presented with the difficulty of Greek discipline legitimized above all by Gratian, it is quite conceivable that they would have had little hesitation in attributing the law of continence to the apostles."

The basis of Cholij's argument is that "the various aspects of the legislation regulating clerical marriages form . . . one whole congruous complex" and that after considering the parts of that complex one is certain to conclude in favor of the "early universal discipline of celibacy" (Cholij, *AHC* 1987, 109, 277, and 282, and *CCEW* 1989, 40, 197, and 202).[81] Such arguments would not apply earlier than Trullo, Cochini's *terminus ad quem*. Consequently what has been said about Cochini's thesis and method applies as well to Cholij and requires no repeating here. What I will address is his interpretative practice.

Cholij admits that his method is not strictly historical but rather "critic-interpretative" (*AHC* 1987, 73, and *CCEW* 1989, 3), meaning that he seeks to focus on the origins of the continence rule not in its chronological establishment but in its anthropological import. Legislation reconstructed on the basis of the earliest extant data not only called for deposing clerics who contracted marriage after ordination but also forbade the wife of a cleric to remarry after her husband's death.[82] The only reasonable explanation for a rule of continence binding a clerical widow consists in presuming that she consented to permanent continence on her husband's ordination. Needless to say, her continence had nothing to do with personal service at the altar. Therefore, says Cholij, contrary to the view of many nineteenth- and twentieth-century historians, the rule of clerical continence is not to be ascribed to an "outdated and mistaken anthropology which demanded 'ritual purity' through sexual abstinence for the daily ministry of priests," but rather to a theology of consecration according to which clerical candidates as well as their wives were deemed, upon ordination, to have dedicated their whole selves "for the exclusive use or possession of God" (Cholij, *AHC* 1987, 98, and *CCEW* 1989, 27).

Cholij's work is difficult to assess independently because of its ambiguous though real relation to the work of Cochini. The former is prone to cite the methodological positions of the latter in support of his own positions (e.g., *ACH* 1987, 244–247, and *CCEW* 1989, 164–67) despite the fact that his own argument does not always appear compatible with its author's major positions. He maintains, for example, that the Western rule of continence was not a bulwark of "ritual purity." Yet he glides over those texts (such as the decretals and Gratian) that affirm that this was the motivation. A clear example of such incompatibility is the claim just mentioned: that Christian priesthood is based on a different principle than ritual purity. Admittedly, Cholij has adopted a methodology that, on the surface, much resembles Cochini's. In theory it rests on "the argument of 'cumulative probability'" (*AHC* 1987, 138, and *CCEW* 1989, 199–200), which Cholij ascribes to Cardinal Newman. But "although Cholij invokes Newman's theory of development ... his own view of Christianity is essentially static: What is must always have been" (Callam, review of Cholij, 727). In practice it interprets the obscure by the clear, but this frequently means interpreting a given text in the light of a "praxis" made apparent by contemporary attestations, deductive reasoning, or other evidence (e.g., *AHC* 1987, 90–91 and 173, and *CCEW* 1989, 20 and 100).

At this point Callam rightly argues that "the indignation that Cholij expresses against the bishops of Trullo seems exaggerated.... The bishops chose to follow a tradition—for what is a tradition if not a long-continued practice?—which allowed priests and deacons, but not bishops, a limited use of marriage. Furthermore, the Catholic Church itself has de facto honoured this tradition and the canons of Trullo for its uniate members, a point which causes Cholij considerable embarrassment."[83] As a result of this embarrassment, Cholij not only resorts to calling Roman tolerance of married clergy "indulgent" (*AHC* 1987, 266, and *CCEW* 1989, 186), but even accuses Pope Paul VI's acceptance of them in *Sacerdotalis Caelibatus* (1967) as based on a "material error" (*AHC* 1987, 271, and *CCEW* 1989, 191), by which he means "the insufficiently critical views of the historians of celibacy rather than the positive doctrine of the ordinary magisterium." The irony is that Cholij bases his judgment on an uncritical acceptance of the assertions of Cochini regarding the centuries preceding Trullo. The critique leveled earlier at Cochini's use of documents applies here to Cholij.

Cochini argues that allowing priests and deacons to marry must have been an innovation based on a decline in discipline, prior to which the East was as committed as the West to upholding clerical continence. Yet there is no positive evidence for this whatsoever. The only reasonable reading of the evidence is that the Trullan synod was merely asserting Oriental tradition in explicit terms in reaction to Western pressure to fall in line with papal legislation.

Nevertheless, whenever he is dealing with his own material and not borrowings from, Cholij demonstrates far more respect for the text than does Cochini. His attitude toward tradition is nuanced, reflecting in part his standing[84] as a Ukrainian Catholic questioning the practice of married priesthood within his own church, which has long claimed apostolic authority for it. But more than Cochini, Cholij regards apostolic precepts as evoking assent on the basis of what is humanly possible and reasonable rather than a rule requiring submission to some authority or apparently irreformable discipline.

b. Cholij's Deployment of Trullan Canons

For Cholij clerical continence is closely related to priesthood even in the East. This is exemplified by the fact that in the East, since Justinian at least, celibacy has been compulsory for bishops.[85] Trullo's Canon 3 specifies that one who has been married twice after baptism, or had a concubine, is barred from entering any rank of the clergy. In addition, the council explicitly repeats certain injunctions of Canons 17 and 18 of the *Apostolic Canons*[86] to the effect that one who has espoused a widow, a woman dismissed by her husband or a harlot, servant, or actress may not enter any clerical rank. Canon 6 forbids subdeacons, deacons, and presbyters to marry after ordination. Cholij proposes that, on the basis of logic alone, this law can have no other motive than absolute continence. If this is not the law's basis, it is inexplicable that from the time of its earliest known enactments at synods in Ancyra (314) and Neocaesarea (314–325), no distinction is made to indicate that those who have remained virginal up to ordination are for that reason free to contract marriage (Cochini, 194–203). The only tenable explanation of why the impediment should have applied to them is that they, like men married prior to ordination, would have had to live in perfect continence with their partner. In the case of those already ordained, however, contracting marriage would imply consummating it, thus breaking, even if only once, the continence already enjoined upon them (Cholij, ACH 1987, 106, and *CCEW* 1989, 40).

In reviewing objections to this thesis, Cholij mentions the story of Paphnutius's intervention at the Council of Nicaea in 325 against mandatory continence for clergy,[87] an account he dismisses as inauthentic: thus he argues that, at least from a Roman Catholic standpoint, "the Eastern discipline today can thus at most be considered to have no more force than that of particular law" (*AHC* 1987, 272, and *CCEW* 1989, 192). From this he concludes that "there is obviously no doubt at all that celibacy in its strict sense (of being unmarried) is not demanded by the priesthood itself: apostolic tradition and the witness of the first millennium [*sic*] in the Latin Church are clear proof of this. Nonetheless there would appear to be a more intimate link between celibacy in its wider sense of continence and the priesthood" (*AHC* 1987, 278, and *CCEW* 1989, 198). Thus Canon 13 of Trullo, affirming that total continence is not obligatory for presbyters and deacons, constitutes a rupture with the sense of pre-Trullan marriage laws for clerics: "The law of prohibition of marriage can only be regarded as a vestigial positive discipline expressing that simpler ancient discipline which harmonized the natural relation which exists between the priesthood and celibacy" (Cholij, *AHC* 1987, 137, and *CCEW* 1989, 68). As he concludes, "celibacy, therefore, would seem to be the natural state for the priest, for only then could he be truly considered a minister totally given to his vocation or 'consecrated' to God for the service of the Church. It would seem that in the early Church, since apostolic times, this was how the priesthood was understood in relation to celibacy" (*AHC* 1987, 282, and *CCEW* 1989, 202).

Hastings, however, takes exactly the opposite view of Trullo's implications: "The only reasonable reading of the evidence is that the Trullan synod was merely asserting Oriental tradition in explicit terms in reaction to Western pressure to fall in line with papal legislation" (174). Hence, far from preserving the most pristine tradition in this matter, it is the West that must be judged the innovator.

III. Three Other Authors

a. Roger Gryson

Roger Gryson, whom Cochini portrays as supporting a nineteenth-century thesis that the celibacy law is a perversion of New Testament teaching, makes it clear in his overview that he does not consider historical continuity between the gospel and the traditional continence rule to be the only kind of continuity whereon the rule might validly rest.[88]

b. Daniel Callam

A year before the appearance of Cochini's book, Daniel Callam published an article dealing in part with the Roman decretals,[89] but in a much more careful fashion than Cochini did. Callam's writings dealing with the origin and evolution of the continence rule reflect his rigor in dissipating misconceptions and half-truths when it comes to the relation between clerical continence and ritual purity. As Callam says about this relation:

> It is well known that the early Church ordained married men but did not allow an unmarried man or a widower to marry after ordination. As a result, the first step toward the law of clerical celibacy in the Latin Church was to require married clerics in major orders to refrain completely from conjugal intercourse. The earliest instance known is Canon 33 of the Council of Elvira (ca. 306). About eighty years later the first papal decretals enforcing continence on major clerics were issued, during the episcopate of Pope Siricius (384–399). General observance of ritual purity and evidence that Mass began to be celebrated daily at that time have suggested that Siricius' legislation was simply a logical deduction from these two facts: by the principle of ritual purity intercourse was forbidden the day before a religious rite and, since Mass was said every day, married clerics would obviously, almost automatically, have been bound to total continence.

Callam then interrogates each of these assumptions. He finds that daily eucharistic celebration was not the usual practice in fourth-century Italy and that the Elvira canons represent a collection of canons rather than the statements of a single council, while Canon 33 originally intended a meaning almost directly contrary to the one that has traditionally been assigned to it. He raises the question of what ritual purity meant and what form its observance would have taken in the fourth century. He points out that the polemics of both Ambrose and Jerome against Jovinian are, predictably, concerned with virginity as an expression of what they perceive to be under attack: asceticism. Jerome's *Aduersus Iouinianum* makes it "clear that ritual continence was to be observed both by the laity and clerics before the Eucharist"; even here, however, where (if nowhere else) one would expect to find a basis for the notion of ritual purity, we find instead that the main reason for this temporary continence "is simply to imitate the higher state of virginity" (16). Jerome does not trace even the absolute continence of major clerics "to the demands of cult except in the most general terms"; rather, "his main concern is to show that virginity is practiced, or at least desired, by all serious Christians, ordained or not" (ibid).

In his close reading of the three decretals ascribed to Siricius, Callam finds that their real issue "is better identified as ascetical rather than ritual" (1980: 48). Moreover, he argues that the decretals' treatment of the continence of Old Testament priests is anachronistic since it views absolute continence as an ascetic ideal, which is impracticable in the case of a hereditary priesthood. After placing the decretal *Directa* in its Priscillianist context, Callam notes that *Directa* is free with the language of ritual holiness, seemingly applying the model of the Old Testament priesthood to the contemporary situation, but Callam says it actually moves in the opposite direction. It first invents a biblical description of temple priesthood as involving a year's sexual abstinence at a time before going on to impose upon the Old Testament priests a decidedly anachronistic conception of dedicated continence (27).

Callam admits that the careful construction of *Directa*'s eighth section reveals that the author knew what he was doing. His respect for the subtle obscurities introduced into every text by the particular conditions of its composition is complemented by his reluctance to perceive linear or causal development of practices and their motivations where parallel development is also a feasible explanation. As a result, Callam remains skeptical about abstracting an overall policy on clerical continence from one or even several such texts under consideration.

Nevertheless, Callam moves quickly from the discovery of anachronisms in the Roman decretals to the conclusion that their notions of ritual purity are little more than ideas about consecration in disguise. Callam ends his 1980 article with an observation on the broader context of the Judaic understanding of ritual purity: "the notion that sacred things themselves pollute is . . . an important aspect of the question" (50). The gap between conceiving of this pollution in terms of holiness and conceiving of it as impurity is obviously prodigious, and the extent to which antimaterialistic perceptions of sexuality have brought about misconstruals will have a profound bearing on our understanding of what the absolute continence of clerics in the early Church could have implied.

As to Cholij, Callam says he failed to justify projecting fourth-century (or later) developments onto "the early Church." Cholij permits himself the use of later texts to verify earlier reality. In doing so, Callam charges, Cholij has betrayed his vocation as an Eastern Catholic to bridge misunderstandings between East and West, instead demonstrating that "the voice of uniate Christianity has acquired a strong Roman accent" (Callam, 728).

c. Peter Brown

A book chapter by Peter Brown titled "Late Antiquity" and his full-length study of sexual renunciation have contributed to the understanding of celibacy in general and clerical continence in particular,[90] with a sensitivity to the way social and cultural codes mediate symbolic meanings. Brown acknowledges that continence among clergy became associated with altar service in the West in the early fourth century and became entrenched later in the same century. But Brown's recognition of this development has little to do with the dynamic he considers to have promoted the emergence of a continent church leadership.

Brown insists on "the importance of sexual renunciation as a means to singleness of heart in the radical Judaism from which Christianity emerged" (1987, 266). Since Christians lacked the clear ritual boundaries provided by Jewish dietary laws and circumcision, they instead highlighted "their exceptional sexual discipline" as "expressing the difference between themselves and the pagan world" (1987, 263). Thus "sexuality became a highly charged symbolic marker precisely because its disappearance in the committed individual . . . was thought to register, more significantly than any other human transformation, the qualities necessary for leadership in the Christian community" (1987, 267). Such developments were often eschatologically motivated, with Christians seeing continence as a way of highlighting "the fragility of a seemingly changeless order" (1988, 64).

In addition, continence was sought by Christian leaders as a means of demonstrating that the Church was "ruled and represented in public by celibate males, over against the society of the world, in which double-hearted pride, ambition, and the stubborn solidarities of family and kin group raged unchecked" (1987, 269). This was especially true in more remote, "more insecure and warlike provinces of the Western Empire" where clerics who converted from a life of wielding power and violence could prove their newfound trustworthiness by agreeing "to abandon sex" (1988, 359). In sum, Brown suggests that "nothing . . . is more striking to an observer of the Christian churches of the second century than is the variety of meanings that had already come to cluster around the mute fact of sexual renunciation" (1988, 64).

IV. Final Remarks

It should be apparent by now that the celibacy debate is part of a series of larger questions: for example, how written revelation relates to tradition and how that tradition is formed, reformed by circumstances, and understood at any given moment. The writers whose works have been reviewed here understand developments of the continence rule differently. Cochini understands it in terms of mediatory intercession, distinguishing it sharply from an esteem for consecrated virginity (which he concedes evolved gradually). Cholij, on the contrary, favors consecration as the rule's first principle, while Callam clearly believes the decretals' promulgation of the rule to have had consecratory rather than ritual motives. In a sense, the only difference between views such as Callam's or Brown's and those of Cochini and Cholij is that neither of the former displays any expectation of finding a simple truth unadorned by the mediations of formulation or praxis. Instead their interpretive approaches imply that we cannot assess the meaning of celibacy, or any other traditional practice, by abstracting it from what Angela Tilby has called the "whole system of living and believing" within which the tradition first made sense.[91]

In passing I may briefly note that some papal documents from 1978 to 1992 have tended to refer to celibacy from the standpoint of Cholij and Cochini.[92] However, the biblical reference (Matt. 19:12) has been virtually abandoned by authors, even those defending celibacy. Cochini, for instance, readily concedes that the verse (which has no synoptic parallel) has nothing to do with celibacy as an *intrinsic* requirement of Christian priesthood. During the October 1990 synod held in Rome, a series of proposals released included support for reaffirming celibacy. But it was also revealed during the synod that the pope had approved the ordination of two married men in Brazil under certain conditions, including that of "total separation from the wife in the matter of cohabitation."[93] This would appear to be firmly in line with the view that perpetual continence was required of all candidates for major orders, but the textual evidence of this is affirmed only for the West, and then only beginning in the late fourth century. The case for an earlier history of the requirement has yet to be made.

Indeed, based on the existing evidence, the case for the apostolic origins of a *married* Christian ministry appears to be at least as plausible as the case for continence/celibacy. In the end, neither Cochini nor anyone else has satisfactorily demonstrated a connection between ministry and celibacy in early Christianity. The apostolic origins of clerical continence/celibacy are therefore far from proven. Indeed, in their attempts to so prove, Cochini and his supporters may have achieved the opposite objective, showing that a *historical* demonstration of celibacy's validity is a fruitless quest.[94] The arguments for maintaining mandatory clerical celibacy will, then, have to be sought elsewhere than in an "apostolic tradition."

Notes

Editor's note: As I mentioned in the introduction, this is a slightly abbreviated version of a long article that was published in 1993 in a journal that had limited circulation and has long been out of print but deserves another reading and further consideration. I have cleaned up a number of typographical errors, eliminated a very few and very short passages no longer relevant, and added a few notes to clarify historically obscure or recondite references and revised others for clarity.

1. See R. Hotz, "Soll jeder Priester Mönch sein? Zur ostkirchlichen Tradition des verheierateten Priesters und des Zölibats," *Diakonia* 16 (1985): 404–411. Even some bishops have proposed that married *viri probati* be considered for presbyteral ordination, arguing that the right of God's people to regular eucharistic celebrations outweighs the need for a celibate clergy. See the pastoral letter "Facing the Future with Hope" of Archbishop Rembert Weakland of Milwaukee of 1 November 1991 (draft version in *Origins* 20 [24 January 1991]: 535–540, par. 8–10). See also episcopal interventions at the international synod in Rome in October 1990 (e.g., *Origins* 20 [1 November 1990]: 338–339), and later: *The Tablet* (16 November 1991): 1420–1421. The revised *Code of Canon Law* of 1983 (Canons 1031, art. 2, and 1042, art. 1) already permits the ordination of married "proven men" to the diaconate. See R. Puza, "Viri uxorati—viri probati. Kanonistisch-historische Überlegungen," *Theologische Quartalschrift* 172 (1992): 16–23.

2. See, e.g., *The Report of the Archdiocesan Commission of Enquiry into the Sexual Abuse of Children by Members of the Clergy*, 3 vols. (St. John's, NF), 1990.

3. E.g., A.W.R. Sipe, *A Secret World: Sexuality and the Search for Celibacy* (New York, 1990).

4. Besides Hotz in n. 1 above, see S. H. Pfüer, "Der Zölibat—Ein Instrument 'heiliger Herrschaft'?" *Diakonia* 20 (1989): 89–100. See also the series of articles in *The Tablet* for 12, 19, and 26 August 1989 by (respectively) A. Tilby, R. Foxcroft, and A. Greeley.

5. R. Gryson, "Dix ans de recherches sur les origins du celibate ecclésiastique: Réflexion sur les publications des années 1970–79," *Revue théologique de Louvain* 11 (1980): 157–185.

6. R. Gryson, *Les origins du celibate ecclésiasique du premier au septième siècle* (Gembloux, Belgium, 1970).

7. See, e.g., Aidan Nichols, *Holy Order: Apostolic Priesthood from the New Testament to the Second Vatican Council* (Dublin, 1990), 155–165.

8. For this reason, since each is a reprint of a work that first appeared in the 1970s, I exclude H. Crouzel's *Mariage et divorce, celibate et caractère sacerdotaux dans l'Eglise ancienne: Etudes diverses* (Turin, 1982), and Charles A. Frazee, "The Origins of Clerical Celibacy in the Western Church," *Church History* 57, supplement (1988): 108–116. Two unpublished licentiate theses in canon law defended at the Catholic University of America (Washington, DC) offer only a summary treatment of the historical data: L. T. Persico, "The Law of Celibacy for the Ukrainian and Ruthenian Churches in the United States: A Historical Development" (1982) and P. Weinhoff, "The Celibacy of Deacons" (1983), 3–25.

9. Christian Cochini, *Origines apostoliques du celibate sacerdotal* (Paris: Lethellieux/Namur: Culture et Vérité, 1981). English translation by Nelly Marans: *Apostolic Origins of Priestly Celibacy* (San Francisco, CA: Ignatius Press, 1990), 71. Roman Cholij, "Clerical Celibacy in the Western Church: Some Clarifications," *Priest and People* 3 (1989): 310–312; citation at 301–303.

10. On this expression, see L. Hödl, "Die 'lex continentiae': Eine problemgeschichtliche Studie über den Zölibat," *Zeitschrift für katholische Theologie* 83 (1961): 325–244. Hödl, however, takes an uncritical approach to early Christian sources; see 332–335.

11. Cochini was reacting to two works in particular, both published in Paris in 1967: J.-P. Audet, *Mariage et celibate dans le service de l'Eglise: Histoire et orientation;* and E. Schillebeeckx, *Autour du celibate du prêtre: Etude critique,* a translation of *Het ambtscelibaat in de branding* (Bilthoven, Netherlands, 1966). English translation by C.A.L. Jarrott: *Celibacy* (New York, 1968).

12. This is not new in itself, having been frequently uttered since at least the latter part of the past century (Cochini, *Origines apostoliques*, pp. 54–56 and 72; Cholij, "Married Clergy and Ecclesiastical Continence in Light of the Council

in Trullo [691]," *Annuarium Historiae conciliorum* 19 (1987) (*AHC* 1987): 71–230, 241–296, citation at 139. See also Cholij, *Clerical Celibacy in East and West* (Leominster/Herefordshire: Fowler Wright Books, 1989) (reprint of *AHC* 1987) (*CCEW* 1989), 70–71.

13. Cochini, *Origines apostoliques*, 475, his emphasis; see also 277.

14. Anne Llewellyn Barstow, *Married Priests and the Reforming Papacy: The Eleventh-Century Debates* (Lewiston, NY: Edwin Mellen Press, 1982), 21 and 28. Her focus is on the medieval canonical prohibition of marriage for clerics rather than on the concern of earlier centuries with clerical continence. This leads her to some misleading statements, such as the following: "Not until after 250 did numbers of clergy begin to live out the ideals of singleness and virginity" (20). Barstow sees (on 22 and 30) the fourth-century legislation as a manifestation of the influence of asceticism as well as of another influence—"a need for the liturgy to provide the basis for great imperial celebrations. The priesthood presiding over these mysteries gradually became a spiritual elite whose role was defined in strongly sacral terms" (30–31).

15. It is worth mentioning in this respect that celibacy was subject to financial and social penalties until Constantine's repeal of the Augustan marriage laws in 320. See Max Kaser, *Roman and Private Law* (Durban, South Africa: Butterworths, 1968), a translation of a German original published in 1959. Even if it is assumed for the sake of argument that clerical continence was an important issue to Christians of the first three centuries, the discretion enjoined by these laws on the subject seriously complicates Cochini's scenario and should give even more pause than usual in the deployment of an *argumentum e silentio*.

16. Ambrose, for instance, in *De officiis* I, 50 (J. P. Migne, ed., *Patrologia Latina* [Paris, 1841–1855] [*PL*] 16, cols. 97–98). Decretals ascribed to Siricius, bishop of Rome.

17. Conc. Carthaginense, Can. 2 (Corpus Christianorum, Series Latina [Turnhout, 1953–] [*CCL*], 149, p. 13.26–30): "Epigonius episcopus Bullensium regionum dixit: Cum praeterito concilio de contientia et castitate tractaretur, gradus isti tres qui constriction quadam castitatis per consecrationem adnexi sunt, episcopus inquam, presbyter et diaconus, tractatu pleniori, ut pudicitiam custodian, doceantur."

18. See Roger Gryson's review of Cochini in *Revue d'Histoire ecclésiastique* 78 (1983): 90–93.

19. Ibid., 91.

20. Ibid.

21. Can. 2 (*CCL* 149, p. 13.31–36): "Geneclius episcopus dixit: Vt superius dictum est, decet sacros antistites ac dei sacerdotes necnon et leuitas uel qui sacramentis diuinis inseruiunt, continents esse in omnibus, quo possint simpliciter quod a domino postulant impetrare, ut quod apostolic docuerunt et ipsa seruauit antiquitas nos quoque custodiamus."

22. Can. 2 (*CCL* 149, p. 13.37–40): "Ab uniuersis episcopis dictum est: Omnibus place tut episcopus, presbyter et diaconus, pudicitiae custodies, etiam ab uxoribus se abstineant ut in omnibus et ab omnibus pudicitia custodiatur qui altario inseruiunt."

23. See Gryson's review, *Revue d'Histoire ecclésiastique*, 91.

24. Ibid., 91. In his commentary, Cochini (*Origines apostoliques*, 27) interjects an expression, "*qui sacramenta contrectant*," one indeed more precise than the others, but one that does not appear in all manuscript versions of the synodal declaration (as Gryson's review, p. 91, argues) and has not been included in the critical text as established by the "Corpus Christianorum" edition, the edition Cochini uses (p. 25, n. 9).

25. *CCL* 149, pp. 102.30–31 and 118.34–35.

26. Cochini, 31. "La décrétale *Directa* ne fait pas explicitement reference à une tradition apostolique, mais c'est néanmoins avec les origins de l'Eglise qu'elle fait coïncider les origins de la loi de continence exigée des prêtres de Jésus-Christ."

27. For this and the remaining patristic citations I follow my own translation. Note that a critical edition of these early decretals has yet to be made.

28. *Epist. 1 ad Himerium* 7:9–10 (*PL* 13, cols. 1138–1139): "Cur etiam procul a suis domnibus, anno uicis suae, in templo habitare iussi sunt sacerdotes? Hac uidelicet ratione, ne uel cum uxoribus possent carnale exercere commercium, ut conscientiae integritate fulgentes, acceptabile Deo munus offerent (cf. I. Pet. 2:5). Quibus expleto deseruitionis suae tempore, uxorious usus soliussuccessionis causa fuerat relaxatus, quia non ex alia, nisi ex tribu Leui, quisquam ad dei ministerium fuerat praeceptus admitti (cf. Lev. 15:16–17; I Sam. 21:5–7). Vnde et dominus Ieusus cum nos suo inlustrasset aduentu, in euangelio protestatur, quia legem uenerit implore, non soluere (cf. Matt. 5:17). Et ideo ecclesiae, cuius sponsus est, formam castitatis uoluit splendore radiare, ut in die iudicci, cum rursus aduenerit, sine macula et ruga eam possit, sicut perapostolum suum instituit, reperire (cf. Eph. 5:27). Quarum sanctionum omnes sacerdotes atque leuitae insolubili lege constringimur, ut a die ordinationis nostrae, sobrietati ac pudicitiae et corda nostra mancipemus et corpora dummodo per Omnia deo nostro in his, quae quotidie offerimus, sacrificiis placeamus."

29. Daniel Callam, "Clerical Continence in the Fourth Century," *Theological Studies* 41 (1980): 3–50, here at 28.

30. Ibid., 28. Further, see *Epist.* I 9:13 (*PL* 13, col. 1142).

31. See *Epist.* I 7:8 and 11:15 (*PL* 13, cols. 1138 and 1143–1144). In fact, it is more accurate to say that the decretal is even more interested in opposing clerical marriage than it is in defending ritual abstinence: "To Siricius, ordination implies a mind and body totally and exclusively subjected to what God wants of his clergy" (Callam, "Clerical Continence," 28–29). The author does not bother to inquire why God did not find some other way—as in the New

Testament priesthood—to ensure succession so that celibacy could be practiced totally among Old Testament priests.

32. Callam, "Clerical Continence," 31–32.

33. Ernst Dassmann, "Diakonat und Zölibat," in Josef G. Plöger and Hermann J. Weber, eds., *Der Diakon: Wiederentdeckung und Erneuerung seines Dienstes* (Freiburg im Breisgau: Herder, 1980), 57–67, here at 63–64.

34. Adrian Hastings, "The Origins of Priestly Celibacy," *Heythrop Journal* 24 (1983): 171–177 (review of Cochini), here 173, and Joseph A. Komonchak, "Celibacy and Tradition," *Chicago Studies* 20 (1981): 5–17, esp. 6–9.

35. See Callam ("Clerical Continence," 47–48), who adds that Siricius's main concern throughout "was with other motives for absolute continence."

36. Ibid., 36. Komonchak (n. 34 above) makes this the earliest of the decretals, while Dassmann (p. 63) ascribes it to Damasus, as does E.-Ch. Babut, *La plus ancienne décrétale* (Paris, 1904), 32. The latter also perceives (74) the strong influence of Jerome on the passage.

37. Epist. 10 ad Gallos episcopos 2:5 (col. 1184): "Primo in loco statutum est de episcopis, presbyteris, et diaconibus, quos sacrificiis diuinis necesse est interesse, per quorum manus et gratia baptismatis traditur, et corpus Christi conficitur; quos non solum nos, sed et scriptura diuina compellit esse castissimos, et patres quoque iusserunt continentiam corporalem seruare debere."

38. Epist. 10 2:5–6 (cols. 1184–1185): "Qua de re non praetereamus, sed dicamus et causam. Quo enim pudore uiduae aut uirgini ausus est episcopus uel presbyter integritatem uel continentiam praedicare, uel suadere castum cubile seruare, si ipse saeculo magis institit filios generare quam deo? ... De his itaque tribus gradibus, quos legimus in scripturis, a ministris dei munditia praecepta est obseruari, quibus necessitas semper in promptu est. Aut enim baptisma tradendum est, aut offerenda sunt sacrificial."

39. Callam, "Clerical Continence," 37: "Although the title mentions a synod, Siricius seems to have replied on his own."

40. Epist. 10 2:6 (cols. 1185–1186): "Numquid immundus ausus erit contaminare quod sanctum est, quando quae sancta sunt, sanctis sancta sunt? Denique illi, qui in templo sacrificia offerebant, ut mundi essent, toto anno in templo, solo obseruationis merito, permanebant, domus suas penitus nescientes. Certe idolatrae, ut impietates exerceant, et daemonibus immolent, imperant sibi continentiam muliebrem, et ab escis quoque se purgari uolunt: et me interrogas, si sacerdos dei ueri, spiritalia oblaturus sacrificia (cf. 1 Pet. 2:5), purgatus perpetuo debeat esse, an totus in carne carnis curam debeat facere? Si commixtio pollutio est, utique sacerdos stare debet ad officium coeleste praeparatus, qui pro alienis peccatis est postulaturus: ne ipse inueniatur indignus. Nam si ad laicos dicitur, 'Abstinete uos ad tempus, ut uacetis orationi' (1 Cor. 7:5), et illi creaturae utique generatione deseruiunt; sacerdotes tale possunt habere nomen, meritum habere non possunt."

41. Edward Schillebeeckx, *The Church with a Human Face: A New and Expanded Ministry of Theology* (New York: Crossroad, 1985), 242.
42. Callam, "Clerical Continence," 38.
43. Ibid., 40.
44. Ibid., 42–43.
45. Ibid., 44.
46. Epist. 5 ad episcopos Africae 3 (cols. 1160–1161): "Praeterea quod dignum et pudicum et honestum est suademus, ut sacerdotes et leuitae cum uxoribus suis non coeant; quia in ministerio, ministerii quotidianis necessitatibus occupantur. Ad Corinthios namque sic Paulus scribit, dicens, 'Abstinete uos, ut uacetis orationi' (1 Cor. 7:5). Si ergo laicis abstinentia imperatur, ut possint deprecantes audiri: quanto magis sacerdos utique omni momento paratus esse debet, munditiae puritate securus, ne aut sacrificium offerat, aut baptizare cogatur? Qui si contaminatus fuerit carnali concupiscentia, quid faciat? Excusabit? Quo pudore, qua mente usurpabit? Qua conscientia, quo merito hic exaudiri se credit, cum dictum sit, 'Omnia munda mundis, coinquinatis autem et infidelibus nihil mundum' (Tit. 1:15)? Qua de re hortor, moneo, rogo, tollatur hoc opprobrium, quod potest iure etiam gentilitas adcusare. Forte hoc creditur, quia scriptum est, 'Vnius uxoris uirum' (1 Tim. 3:2, 12; Tit. 1:6). Non permanentem in concupiscentia generandi dixit, sed propter continentiam futuram."
47. Callam, "Clerical Continence," 46.
48. But the argument remains weak, in the view of Callam in ibid., 46–48.
49. Ibid., 45.
50. See H. Conzelmann, *1 Corinthians: A Commentary on the First Epistle to the Corinthians* (Philadelphia, 1975), 117 (trans. of *Der erste Brief an die Korinther*, Göttingen, 1969).
51. Hastings, "The Origins of Priestly Celibacy," 175.
52. See Hans-Jurgen Vogels, "The Community's Right to a Priest in Collision with Compulsory Celibacy," *Concilium* 133 (1980): 88. Even Jean Galot (*Theology of the Priesthood* [San Francisco: Ignatius, 1985], 153), who is generally favorable to Cochini's thesis, takes exception to this interpretation.
53. Hastings, "The Origins of Priestly Celibacy," 175.
54. See, for example, Richard Kugelman, "The First Letter to the Corinthians," in J. A. Fitzmyer and R. E. Brown, eds., *The Jerome Biblical Commentary*, vol. 2 (Englewood Cliffs, NJ, 1968), 263.
55. Several authors, including Cochini, date it to "ca. 305."
56. In the edition by José Vives, *Concilios visigo'ticos y hispano-romanos* (Barcelona and Madrid, 1963), 7.
57. Komonchak, "Celibacy and Tradition," 5, seems unaware of this. See Gryson, "Dix ans," 161 and 164, following M. Meigne, "Concile ou Collection d'Elivre?," *Revue d'Histoire ecclésiastique* 70 (1975): 48; Callam, "Clerical Continence," 3 n. 2; Schillebeeckx, *Celibacy*, 241; and Jesus Superbiola Martinez, *Nuevos*

concilios hispano-romanos de los siglos III y IV. La colección de Elvira (Malaga, 1987), 14 and 85–104. For all these authors, Canon 33 is an anachronism.

58. See *CCL* 148, p. 25 (Can. 29), to which Cochini alludes without comment.

59. Aug., *De baptismo* IV, 24:31 (*Corpus Scriptorum Ecclesiasticorum Latinorum* [Vineea, 1866–] [*CSEL*] 51, p. 259.1–4): "Quod uniuersa tenet ecclesia nec conciliis institutum, sed semper retentum est, non nisi auctoritate apostolica traditum rectissime creditor."

60. See Y. Congar, *La Tradition et les traditions*, vol. I (Paris, 1960), 67.

61. Aug., *De baptismo* IV, 24:31 (*CSEL* 51, p. 259.4–5).

62. The same application to liturgico-doctrinal issues is made in II, 7:12; IV, 6:9; and V, 23:31.

63. See A. Benoit, "Le problème du pédobaptême," *Revue d'Histoire et de Philosophie religieuses* 28 (1948): 132–141; J. Jeremias, *Infant Baptism in the First Four Centuries* (London, 1960); J.B.C. Didier, ed., *Le baptême des enfants dans la tradition de l'Eglise* (Paris, 1959) and *Faut-il baptiser les enfants? La réponse de la tradition* (Paris, 1967); K. Aland, *Did the Early Church Baptize Infants?* (London, 1963); J. Jeremias, *The Origins of Infant Baptism: A Further Study in Reply to Kurt Aland* (London, 1963); P. A. Gramaglia, *Il battesimo dei bambini nei primo quattro secoli* (Brescia, 1973); R. de Latte, "Saint Augustin et le baptême: Etude liturgico-historique du rituel baptismal des enfants chez saint Augustin," *Questions liturgiques* 56 (1975): 177–223, and 57 (1976): 41–55; V. Grossi, "Battesimo dei bambini e peccato originale: La problematica storica e teologica nei Padri," *Vita monastic* 34 (1980): 10–24; D. F. Wright, "The Origins of Infant Baptism–Child Believers' Baptism," *Scottish Journal of Theology* 40 (1987): 1–23; and P. Riché, "Faut-il baptiser les enfants?," in P. de Clerck and E. Palozzo, eds., *Rituels: Mélanges offerts au Père Guy* (Paris, 1990), 447–453.

64. Possibly the answer lies in the third chapter of J. H. Newman's *An Essay on the Development of Christian Doctrine* (1844), whose methodological principles Cochini accepts (85–87), even if no explicit reference is made to Newman's work. R. Cholij, *AHC* 1987, 71–230 and 241–296, here at 138–184, and in *Clerical Celibacy in East and West*, 69–105, is explicit in connecting Newman's work to the methodological principle of cumulative responsibility argued by Cochini.

65. Roger Balducelli, "*The Apostolic Origins of Clerical Continence:* A Critical Appraisal of a New Book," *Theological Studies* 43 (1982): 693–705 (a review of Cochini), here at 695–698 and 704–705.

66. For similar criticisms of Cochini's methodology, see the review of Cochini by Alexandre Faivre in *Revue d'Histoire et de philosophie religieuses* 63 (1983): 471–472, and Hastings, "The Origins," 173–174.

67. J. Pelikan, *The Vindication of Tradition* (New Haven, CT, 1984), 55.

68. Edward Schillebeeckx, *The Church with a Human Face: A New and Expanded Ministry of Theology* (New York: Crossroad, 1985), 241; see Cholij, *AHC* 1987, 72, and *CCEW* 1989, 2.

69. Gustave Martelet, *Deux mille ans de l'Eglise en question*, vol. II (Des martyrs à l'Inquisition) (Paris: Ed. du Cerf, 1990), 374–377, here 376, n. 54.

70. Henri Crouzel, "Une nouvelle étude sur les origines du célibat sacerdotal," review of Cochini, *Bulletin de Littérature ecclésiastique* 83 (1982): 293–297.

71. David G. Hunter, "Resistance to the Virginal Ideal in Late Fourth-Century Rome: The Case of Jovinian," *Theological Studies* 48 (1987): 45–64 and 57–58, and Callam, "Clerical Continence," 16–25 and 32.

72. Hunter, "Resistance to the Virginal Ideal," 49–62. Similarly, hostility to Bonosus (c. 390) and Jovinian (c. 391) must in part account for certain Roman decretals, beginning with Siricius's *Epist. 7 ad diuersos episcopos* (*PL* 13, cols. 1121–1123): See Callam, "Clerical Continence," 6–16. In the matter of Jovinian, see Hunter, "Resistance to the Virginal Ideal," 45–64, and A. J. Budzin, "Jovinian's Four Theses on the Christian Life: An Alternative Patristic Spirituality," *Toronto Journal of Theology* 4 (1988): 44–49. Cochini seems premature in his conclusion that the decretals addressed to Spain and Gaul were in part a reaction to "le raz-de-marée jovinianiste" (277).

73. Peter Brown, *The Body and Society: Men, Women, and Sexual Renunciation in Early Christianity* (New York: Columbia University Press, 1988), 18–23 et passim.

74. Hastings, "The Origins," 173–174: "The trouble is that while there may be no patristic evidence absolutely incompatible with such a thesis, there is very little either clearly in favour of it. Time and again Cochini simply interprets unsure evidence in the light of the fourth-century Western consensus, claiming that this is in principle the right thing to do: ecclesiastical history should be presumed to be consistent. It is a large presumption. It can well be admitted that many married priests and bishops may have practiced total continence from ordination long before the fourth century; in most cases it is impossible to prove it and still less to prove any sort of law."

75. Joseph Komonchak, "Celibacy and Tradition," *Chicago Studies* 20 (1981): 5–17.

76. Brown, *The Body and Society*, 33–64.

77. See A. Rousselle, *On Desire and the Body in Antiquity* (Oxford, 1988); P. Brown, *The Making of Late Antiquity* (Cambridge, MA, 1978); R. Rader, *Breaking Boundaries: Male/Female Friendship in Early Christian Communities* (New York, 1983); and W. J. Sheils, ed., *Monks, Hermits, and the Ascetic Tradition* (Oxford, 1985). On resistance to these developments, David G. Hunter, in *"On the Sin of Adam and Eve*: A Little-Known Defense of Marriage and Childbearing by Ambrosiaster," *Harvard Theological Review* 82 (1989): 283–299, here 298, remarks: "Ambrosiaster's relatively untroubled attitude towards human sexual relations was probably typical of that held by most of the Roman clergy."

78. Adrian Hastings, "The Origins of Priestly Celibacy," review of Cochini, *Heythrop Journal* 24 (1983): 171–177, here 175, and Peter L'Huillier, "Episcopal

Celibacy in the Orthodox Tradition," *St. Vladimir's Theological Quarterly* 35 (1991): 271–300, here 286–287.

79. Hastings, "The Origins of Priestly Celibacy," 176, and L'Huillier, "Episcopal Celibacy," 295.

80. Callam, "Clerical Continence," 27. The only rabbinic directive here is that the high priest was to be separated from his spouse during the week before Yom Kippur (*M. Yoma* 1:1). See Raymund Kottje, "Das Aufkommen der täglichen Eucharistiefeier in der Westkirche und die Zölibatsforderung," in *Zeitschrift für Kirchengeschichte* 82 (1971): 225 n.

81. Daniel Callam, review of Cholij, *CCEW* 1989, *Journal of Theological Studies* n.s. 41 (1990): 725–729, here 726: "This bold statement is the single thread on which his thesis dangles; cut the threat and the argument comes crashing down."

82. Cholij, *AHC* 1987, 91. In "Clerical Celibacy in the Western Church" he wrote: "There is one reason to suppose that the legislation prohibiting re-marriage to a cleric's widow was not an expression of earlier praxis." Cited in support of this is Elvira's Canon 33, which Cholij calls "the first known legislation on celibacy" (Cholij, "Clerical Celibacy in the Western Church: Some Clarifications," *Priests and People* 3 [1989]: 301–312, here 208, and "The 'Lex continentiae' and the Impediment of Orders," *Studia Canonica* 21 (1987): 391–418, here 393, which he dates "c. 305" (see also *AHC* 1987, 106, and *CCEW* 1989, 37). But the precise dating is not the issue here; the issue is the authenticity of these canons.

83. Callam, review of Cholij, *CCEW* 1989, 727.

84. *Editor's note*: Cholij's standing at the time of this writing, that is. He has since been widely reported as having married and renounced both his book on celibacy and his own celibate priesthood. He is working in the legal field now.

85. It is interesting that Cholij's position—that Trullo chap. 12 (which forbids already married bishops to cohabit with their wives after their ordination) is at variance with earlier, even apostolic, practice—should reflect the same concern as that of some Orthodox, but with the opposite objective of removing the celibacy requirement for episcopal ordinations. See Peter L'Huillier, "Episcopal Celibacy in the Orthodox Tradition," *St. Vladimir's Theological Quarterly* 35 (1991): 271–300, here 297, for a sample of this debate; see also P. I. Boumes, "Married Bishops," *Greek Orthodox Theological Review* 29 (1984): 81–93.

86. These canons form part of the eighth book of the *Apostolic Constitutions* (ca. 380), which were repudiated as a whole as not apostolic and not orthodox. But their inclusion in Trullan legislation increased their respectability.

87. Socrates, *Historia ecclesiastica* I, II (J. P. Migne, ed., *Patrologia Graeca* [PG] [Paris, 1867–1866], 67, cols. 161–163); Sozomen, *Hist. eccl.* I, 23 (*GCS* 50, pp. 44.10–45.3).

88. Gryson, "Dix ans," 195.

89. Daniel Callam, "Clerical Continence in the Fourth Century," *Theological Studies* 41 (1980): 3–50.

90. Peter Brown, "Late Antiquity," chap. 2 in P. Veyne, ed., *History of Private Life*, vol. 1 (Cambridge, MA: Harvard University Press, 1987), 237–311, and *The Body and Society: Men, Women, and Sexual Renunciation in Early Christianity* (New York: Columbia University Press, 1988).

91. Tilby, "The Pastor's Wife," *The Tablet*, 12 August 1989, 916.

92. Given Cochini's claim (in *Origines apostoliques*, 91) that Cardinal Daniélou encouraged him to expand and publish his doctoral work (on which claim see the severe remarks of Kannengiesser, 621, endorsed by Gryson in his review of Cochini, 92–93) and introductory remarks in the books of both Cochini and Cholij by Alfons Stickler, sometime prefect of the Vatican Library and later cardinal, the whole enterprise "may be seen as a major scholarly expression of the present Roman campaign to vindicate the existing discipline" (Hastings, "The Origins," 171; see also 175). Indeed, Stickler has called the books of Cochini and Cholij "the two definitive studies of celibacy of the clergy in the Christian Church" (in Cholij, *CCEW* 1989, vii).

93. See *Origins* 20 (1 November 1990), no. 21, p. 334 and also *La documentation catholique* 2017 (9 December 1990): 1061.

94. See Hastings, "The Origins," 171: "One must indeed be grateful to the author for so sustained, erudite and charitable a work. If the thesis here presented is unconvincing, then, one might reasonably conclude, no further approach on these lines is ever likely to satisfy."

Bibliography

Balducelli, Roger. "*The Apostolic Origins of Clerical Continence*: A Critical Appraisal of a New Book." *Theological Studies* 43 (1982): 693–705 (a review of Cochini).

Barstow, Anne Llewellyn. *Married Priests and the Reforming Papacy: The Eleventh-Century Debates*. Lewiston, NY: Edwin Mellen Press, 1982.

Brown, Peter. "Late Antiquity." Chap. 2 in P. Veyne, ed., *History of Private Life*, vol. 1 (Cambridge, MA: Harvard University Press, 1987), 237–311.

———. *The Body and Society: Men, Women, and Sexual Renunciation in Early Christianity*. New York: Columbia University Press, 1988.

Callam, Daniel. "Clerical Continence in the Fourth Century." *Theological Studies* 41 (1980): 3–50. Unless otherwise specified, all citations of Callam in this appendix refer to this article.

———. Review of Cholij, *Clerical Celibacy in East and West*. *Journal of Theological Studies*, n.s. 41 (1990): 725–729.

Cholij, Roman M. T. "The 'Lex continentiae' and the Impediment of Orders." *Studia Canonica* 21 (1987): 391–418.

———. "Married Clergy and Ecclesiastical Continence in Light of the Council in Trullo (691)." *Annuarium Historiae Conciliorum (AHC)* 19 (1987): 71–230, 241–296.

———. "De caelibatu sacerdotali in Ecclesia Orientali nova historica investigatio." *Periodica de re morali canonica liturgica* 77 (1988): 3–31.

———. "Celibacy: A Tradition of the Eastern Churches." *Priests and People* 2 (1988): 208–222.

———. "Celibacy in the Eastern Church: The Historical Evidence." *Canadian Catholic Review* 7 (1989): 17–26. Abridged version of the preceding.

———. *Clerical Celibacy in East and West.* Leominster/Herefordshire: Fowler Wright Books, 1989. Reprint of *AHC* 1987 = *CCEW* 1989.

———. "Clerical Celibacy in the Western Church: Some Clarifications." *Priests and People* 3 (1989): 301–312.

Cochini, Christian, *Origines apostoliques du célibat sacerdotal.* Paris: Lethellieux/Namur: Culture et Vérité, 1981. Trans. by Nelly Marans: *Apostolic Origins of Priestly Celibacy.* San Francisco: Ignatius Press, 1990.

Crouzel, Henri. "Une nouvelle étude sur les origines du célibat sacerdotal." *Bulletin de Littérature ecclésiastique* 83 (1982): 293–297. Review of Cochini.

Dassmann, Ernst. "Diakonat und Zölibat." In Josef G. Plöger and Hermann J. Weber, eds., *Der Diakon: Wiederentdeckung und Erneuerung seines Dienstes.* Freiburg im Breisgau: Herder, 1980, 57–67.

Favre, Alexandre. Review of Cochini. *Revue d'Histoire et de philosophie religieuses* 63 (1983): 471–473.

Galot, Jean. *Theology of the Priesthood.* San Francisco: Ignatius Press, 1985. Trans. of *Teologia del sacerdozio.* Florence: Libreria Editrice Fiorentina, 1981.

———. Review of Cochini. *Gregorianum* 64 (1983): 152–153.

Gryson, Roger. Review of Cochini. *Revue d'histoire ecclésiastique* 78 (1983): 90–93.

Hastings, Adrian. "The Origins of Priestly Celibacy" (review of Cochini). *Heythrop Journal* 24 (1983): 171–177.

Hunter, D. G., "*On the Sin of Adam and Eve*: A Little-Known Defense of Marriage and Childbearing by Ambrosiaster." *Harvard Theological Review* 82 (1989): 283–299.

Hunter, David G. "Resistance to the Virginal Ideal in Late Fourth-Century Rome: The Case of Jovinian." *Theological Studies* 48 (1987): 45–64.

Kannengiesser, Charles. Review of Cochini. *Recherches de science religieuse* 70 (1982): 620–621.

Komonchak, Joseph A. "Celibacy and Tradition." *Chicago Studies* 20 (1981): 5–17.

Lawrence, C. H. "Unconvincing Arguments against a Married Priesthood." Review of Cholij, *CCEW* 1989. *The Tablet* 244 (6 January 1990): 14.

L'Huillier, Peter. Review of Cholij, *CCEW* 1989. *Sobornost* n.s. 12 (1990): 180–182.

———. "Episcopal Celibacy in the Orthodox Tradition." *St. Vladimir's Theological Quarterly* 35 (1991): 271–300.

Marchetto, Agostino. Review of Cochini. *Rivista di Storia della Chieasa in Italia* 37 (1983): 186–190.

Margerie, Bertrand de. Review of Cochini. *Science et Esprit* 35 (1983): 260–261.

Martelet, Gustave. *Deux mille ans de l'Eglise en question*, vol. II (Des martyrs à l'Inquisition). Paris: Ed. du Cerf, 1990, 374–377.

Martin, Charles. Review of Cochini. *Nouvelle Revue Théologique* 105 (1983): 437–438.

Marzotto, Damiano. "Il celibate nel Nuovo Testamento." *La Scuola Cattolica* 110 (1982): 333–370.

Schillebeeckx, Edward. *The Church with a Human Face: A New and Expanded Ministry of Theology*. New York: Crossroad, 1985.

Trémeau, Marc. Review of Cochini. *Esprit et Vie* 92 (1982): 106–109.

Vogels, H. J. "The Community's Right to a Priest in Collision with Compulsory Celibacy." *Concilium* 133 (1980): 84–92.

CONTRIBUTORS

EDWIN BARNES was the Anglican bishop of Richborough in the Church of England from 1995 to 2001, when he retired. In January 2011 he and his wife, Jane, were received into the Catholic Church, and he was ordained deacon and then priest later that year in and for the Personal Ordinariate of Our Lady of Walsingham. In 2012 he was made a monsignor and papal chaplain. He died in February 2019.

J. KEVIN COYLE was a sometime priest, scholar of Augustine and antique North African Christianity, and longtime professor in the faculty of theology at Saint Paul University, Ottawa, before his sudden death in 2010.

LAWRENCE CROSS, a widower with children, is an archpriest in the Russian Byzantine Catholic Church serving pastorally in Melbourne, Australia.

NICHOLAS DENYSENKO, a deacon in the Orthodox Church of America, is Emil and Elfrieda Jochum University Professor and Chair at Valparaiso University in Valparaiso, Indiana.

ADAM A. J. DEVILLE is associate professor of theology and director of humanities at the University of Saint Francis in Ft. Wayne, Indiana. He is editor-in-chief of *Logos: A Journal of Eastern Christian Studies* and author and editor of numerous other works including, most recently, *Everything Hidden Shall Be Revealed: Ridding the Church of Abuses of Sex and Power* (Brooklyn, NY: Angelico Press, 2019).

JAMES S. DUTKO is a married protopresbyter of the American Carpatho-Russian Orthodox Diocese of the USA.

IRENE GALADZA is a retired Catholic schoolteacher in Brampton, Ontario, where she and her husband, the mitered archpriest Roman Galadza, founded St. Elias Ukrainian Greco-Catholic Church in 1976. They raised six children together and now have a number of grandchildren.

PETER GALADZA recently retired as professor and director of the Metropolitan Andrey Sheptytsky Institute of Eastern Christian Studies at St. Michael's College in the University of Toronto. A priest of the Ukrainian Greco-Catholic Church, he and his wife, Olenka, have three grown children.

JULIAN HAYDA comes from a large Ukrainian Greco-Catholic family going back to the time of the Union of Brest. He is finishing his master's degree in International Studies at DePaul University, where he researches religious identities in the post-Soviet space. He is currently a radio producer for Worldview, the daily global-issues talk show on WBEZ, Chicago's NPR station.

DELLAS OLIVER HERBEL earned a PhD in historical theology from St. Louis University and currently serves as a full-time chaplain in the North Dakota Air National Guard. He is a priest in the Orthodox Church of America and the author of *Sarapion of Thmuis: Against the Manicheans and Pastoral Letters* (2011) and *Turning to Tradition: The Making of an American Orthodox Church* (2013). He and his wife, Lorie, have three children.

DAVID G. HUNTER is the first occupant of the Cottrill-Rolfes Chair of Catholic Studies at the University of Kentucky. His academic interests lie in the early history of Christianity and the history of Christian thought. He has published several books and numerous articles on Greek and Latin writers of the early Church. Other publications include *Marriage, Celibacy, and Heresy in Ancient Christianity: The Jovinianist Controversy* (Oxford: Oxford University Press, 2007), and *Marriage and Sexuality in Early Christianity*, a part of the series *Ad Fontes: Early Christian Sources* (Minneapolis: Fortress Press, 2018).

JOHN HUNWICKE, after seven years at Oxford reading Greek and Latin language and literature, history, philosophy, and theology, was ordained in the Church of England in 1968 and served two parishes before moving to Lancing College in West Sussex, UK, as head of theology. Upon retirement, he served part-time in two parishes and was senior research fellow at Pusey House. He entered the Catholic Church via the Ordinariate and was ordained a Catholic priest in 2012. He and his wife, Pamela, have five children and five grandchildren.

ANDREW JARMUS, originally from Canada, is the son of a priest in the Ukrainian Orthodox Church and is himself a priest in the Orthodox Church of America, serving as pastor of St. Nicholas Church in Fort Wayne, Indiana.

ALEXANDER M. LASCHUK is a married Ukrainian Greco-Catholic priest and canon lawyer working in the tribunal of the Archdiocese of Toronto.

THOMAS J. LOYA is currently the pastor of Annunciation of the Mother of God Byzantine Catholic Parish in Homer Glen, Illinois. He is also the host of *Light of the East Radio*, heard on EWTN Radio and other networks. He is a member of the Tabor Life Institute (www.taborlife.org) and one of the founders of www.easternchristianmedia.com and www.oltv.tv. He was ordained to the priesthood in 1982.

DAVID MEINZEN was ordained a priest in the Orthodox Church of America before becoming a priest in the Ukrainian Greco-Catholic Church. He is the full-time bi-ritual chaplain at VA Hospital in Fort Wayne, Indiana. He and his wife, Elizabeth, have three daughters.

WILLIAM C. MILLS is a priest in the Orthodox Church of America. Married, with two daughters, he is a prolific author. His most recent book was *Losing My Religion: A Memoir of Faith and Finding*.

BASILIO PETRÀ is a Roman Catholic priest of the Diocese of Prato, Italy. He received a doctorate in moral theology from the Alfonsiana in Rome. He also studied at Greek Orthodox schools in the United States and Greece, including a semester under the theology faculty at the University of Thessaloniki. He has taught Orthodox theology at the Pontifical Oriental Institute and served as a consultor for the Congregation of Oriental Churches. His numerous publications on married priests have been published in several languages.

VICTOR POSPISHIL was an archimandrite in the Ukrainian Greco-Catholic Church. Born in Vienna in 1915 he received his theological training in Croatia and then Rome, where he earned a doctorate at the Gregorian University. Author of many studies in several languages, he was made a monsignor by Pope John XXIII and later made an archimandrite by Patriarch Josyf Cardinal Slipyj. Pospishil died in New Jersey in 2006.

PATRICK VISCUSO is a professor of canon law at the Antiochian House of Studies and a priest of the Greek Orthodox Archdiocese of America. His doctorate from the Catholic University of America concentrated on Byzantine and Eastern canon law and history. He is the author of numerous scholarly articles and five books: *A Quest for Reform of the Orthodox Church* (2006), *Orthodox Canon Law: A Casebook for Study* (2007), *Sexuality, Marriage, and Celibacy in Byzantine Law: The Alphabetical Collection of Matthew Blastares* (2008), *Guide for a Church under Islam, The Sixty-Six Canonical Questions Attributed to Theodoros Balsamon* (2014), and *The True Significance of Sacred Tradition and Its Great Worth, by St. Raphael Hawaweeny* previously unpublished (2017).

INDEX

abstinence. *See* clerical continence
Ad Gallos episcopos, 20n.32, 308, 332n.37
Ambrose of Milan, 4, 11, 20n.31, 316, 324, 330n.16
Ambrosiaster, 313, 316, 335n.77
Anglican ordinariates, xii, xvii, 91, 97–98
   Anglicanorum coetibus, 81–84, 87n.42, 91, 100
   canonical status of, 97–100
   financial costs of married priests in, 98–99, 104, 106
anthropology, theological, 201–2, 320
asceticism, 69n.14, 94, 209n.3, 252, 317–18, 324, 330n.14
Athenagoras, Patriarch, 32–33, 36, 46, 49
Audet, Jean-Paul, 13, 16n.5, 20n.39, 329n.11
Augustine of Hippo, 314–16

Balsamōn, Theodōros, 54–62, 68n.4, 69n.17, 70n.20, 70n.27, 71nn.36–37
Balthasar, Hans Urs von, 117–19
Barron, Robert, xii
Basilian Order, 273–74
Bea, Augustine, 127–28

Benedict XVI (pope). *See* Ratzinger, Joseph
Bickell, Gustav, 4–5, 15n.3
Borecky, Isidore, 77, 258, 293n.1
Brent, Allen, 26, 31n.21
Brown, Peter, 326–27
Budka, Nicetas, 262, 292, 295n.15
Byzantine Catholics/Catholic Church, xvi, 30n.5, 34–38, 40, 46–47, 75–80, 83, 204, 258, 260–62, 267–72

Callam, Daniel, 131n.10, 318, 321, 324–27, 331n.29, 332n.32, 336n.81, 337n.89
canon law
   Byzantine canon law, 53–55, 60, 67, 69n.14, 70n.19
   Code of Canons of the Eastern Churches (1990), 77, 82, 86n.15, 86n.17, 87n.33, 120, 121, 129n.2, 149, 217, 234
   Code of Canon Law (1983), 227n.16, 328n.1
   decretals, 129n.7, 303, 306–12, 317–18, 324–27, 335n.72
   faculties, 75, 87n.36, 98, 261
   role of *oikonomia* in, 67, 72n.43, 146–57

Cholij, Roman, 53–55, 60, 63, 110, 129n.7, 134n.55, 300, 319–23, 327, 336n.84, 338
Chornock, Orestes, 36–37, 44, 45, 292
Church of England, 93
  parish culture, 95–96
  wives of clergy in, 102–3
Clement of Alexandria, 10, 19n.26
clerical continence, 3–7, 9–12, 14, 16n.5, 17n.6, 19n.25, 19n.29, 20n.33, 53–54, 62–63, 109–11, 122, 130n.9, 139, 210, 300–328
Cochini, Christian, 9–11, 14, 16n.6, 19n.25, 67n.1, 109–10, 128, 130n.9, 300–18, 320, 321–27
Collins, Raymond, 6–7, 17n.10, 18n.14, 18n.21
Coptic Catholic Church, 41, 113
Council of Arles, 314
Council of Carthage, 19n.24, 265, 303–5, 310, 313, 316–17
Council of Elvira, 15n.2, 68n.3, 313–14, 324, 336n.82
Council of Nicaea, 213, 323
Cum Data Fuerit, 35–37, 42, 44, 76–77, 80, 83, 119, 203, 261, 292

Damasus, and Siricius of Rome, 11, 20n.32, 306
Denzler, Georg, 4, 13, 14, 16n.5, 20n.41
Didascalia, 9, 302

Ea Semper, 34, 261
ecclesiology, 25–29, 138, 202, 247, 294n.18
ecumenical dialogue
  enforced celibacy as stumbling block to, 109, 111, 128
  North American Orthodox-Catholic dialogue, 33, 74
Ecumenical Patriarchate of Constantinople, 32, 34, 36, 64, 213, 276, 279

Epigonius, 304, 330n.17
ethnicity, xvii, 30n.9, 148, 267, 273–74, 292
Evdokimov, Paul, xxii, 158, 162, 165, 207, 251–54

Francis (pope), 74, 78–85, 141, 202
  Amoris Laetitia, 247, 250–51
  views on celibacy as Cardinal Bergoglio, 108, 121–24, 129n.3
Funk, Franz Xaver, 4, 15n.3

Galicia, 23, 128, 264, 273–74, 292, 295n.20
Greek Orthodox Archdiocese of America, 36
  requirements for ordination in, 63–67
Gregory VII (pope) (Hildebrand), 94–95
Gryson, Roger, 16n.5, 20n.39, 130n.9, 299–300, 301–3, 306, 313, 323–24, 329nn.5–6, 330n.18, 331n.23, 333n.57, 336n.88, 337n.92, 338

Heid, Stefan, 5, 7–8, 11, 14, 17n.6, 18n.21, 111, 129n.6, 132n.18
Hermaniuk, Maxim, 260, 294n.11
Hermas
  The Shepherd, 8
historiography
  of celibacy, 3–20, 299–309
  of ecumenical relations, 32–52
Hoyos, Darío Castrillón, 212, 230

Ignatius of Antioch, 22, 26, 29, 32n.21
immigration
  from Austro-Hungarian Empire, 34, 266
  to Canada, 75, 76–77
  to the United States, 22, 26, 30n.11, 37, 75, 267

Ireland, John, xviii, 21–24, 35, 37, 75, 267–68

Jadot, Jean, 289–90, 298n.41
Jerome, 4, 316, 324–25
John Paul II (pope), 82, 98, 201, 212, 215, 232, 242
   Familiaris Consortio, 218, 220–21, 247–51
   Orientale Lumen, 207
   Pastores dabo vobis, 111–13, 211, 216, 225, 226n.4, 244n.2
Johnson, Luke Timothy, 7

Krindatch, Alexei, 26

L'Huillier, Peter, 116, 131n.10, 335n.78, 336n.85
Lutheran Church (Missouri Synod), xix, 140–41

Mariology, 155–58, 165–66
Maronite Church, 86n.25, 270, 271, 274, 280
marriage
   liturgies of, 156, 182–83, 208, 252, 257n.23
   theology of, 70n.25, 113, 123, 219, 239, 246–55
Melkites, 40, 50n.13, 78, 86n.24, 263, 270, 274, 280, 282, 288
   Patriarch Maximos V, 288–89
mental health of clergy/clergy families, 149, 161–64, 187–89
Merton, Thomas, 48–49

Nazianzus, Stephanos Charalambidis of, 217, 235
Nedungatt, George, 86n.17, 110–11, 120, 123, 129n.2, 131n.10, 132n.41, 133n.50
Newman, John Henry, 91–93

North African Christianity, 304, 305, 310

ontology, xxii, 115, 214, 247, 253
Origen of Alexandria, 9–10, 18n.19, 19n.28, 19n.30, 317
Orthodox Church of America, 76, 268
Ortynsky, Soter Stephen, 261, 262, 292

Palmas, Angelo, 260, 293n.4, 293n.9
Parish, Helen, 94, 101n.3
pastoral epistles, 6–8, 17nn.12–13
Paul VI (pope), 12, 13, 39, 248, 264
   interference in Canadian ordinations, 260, 275
   relations with the Orthodox, 32, 46, 276–77, 288
   Sacerdotalis caelibatus, 125, 128, 134n.57, 154
Pharos, Philotheos, 217, 226n.10, 235, 244n.4
Phillips, Adam, xv
Piacenza, Mauro, 109
Polycarp of Smyrna, 26, 27, 29
Priscillianist movement, 317, 325

Ratzinger, Joseph, xiv, 44, 78, 83, 84, 125, 255n.4
Redemptorists, 258, 272–74
Roman Curia, 117, 127, 266–68, 275, 277–78, 281, 287, 291
Rusnak, Michael, 77, 258–59
Russian Orthodox Church, 21, 35, 266, 268, 294n.18, 296n.29
Ruthenian Church. *See* Byzantine Catholics/Catholic Church

Sarah, Robert, xiii, 53, 68n.3
Schillebeeckx, Edward, 13, 16n.5, 20n.39, 329n.11, 333n.41, 334n.68, 339

Second Vatican Council
  Presbyterorum ordinis, xiv, 3–4, 12, 15n.1, 121–23, 127, 215, 224, 226, 231
  Optatam Totius, 125–26
  Orientalium Ecclesiarium, 39, 87n.37, 255n.5, 276, 280
seminaries, 83, 140–41, 187, 208, 260, 282–85
Sepe, Crescenzio, xxiv, 115–16
Sheptytsky, Andrey, 264
Siricius, 4, 11, 19n.24, 20n.33, 303–6, 310–12, 317–18, 324–25, 330n.16, 331n.31, 335n.72
Slipyj, Josyf, 77, 154n.1, 263, 294n.10, 294n.18, 296n.29
Stickler, Alfons Maria, 5–6, 9, 11, 14, 17n.6, 19nn.23–24, 67n.1, 237, 337n.92
Syro-Malabar Church, 78
Syro-Malankar Church, 78

Taft, Robert, xii, xvii, 295n.21
Takach, Basil, 35–37, 261, 277
Tertullian, 9–10, 18n.19, 19n.27, 315

Theodore of Mopsuestia, 7, 18n.15
Theodoret of Cyrrhus, 7–8, 18n.16
Toth, Alexis, 21–23, 29n.1, 30n..7,8, 35–37, 44, 75, 268
transference/countertransference dynamics, 189–90
Trullo, Council/Synod of, 53–55, 60, 110, 126, 131n.10, 131n.15, 210, 265–66, 280, 316, 319–23

Ukrainian Greco-Catholic Church, xii, 75, 295n.21
Ukrainian Orthodox churches, 76, 154n.1, 167, 169, 172, 269
Union of Brest, 37, 75, 85n.1, 277, 296n.32
Union of Uzhorod, 34–37, 40, 44, 45, 47

Verkamp, Bernard, 13
Vigneron, Allen, 116–17, 125, 131n.13, 132n.29
Volianskyi (Volans'kyĭ), Ivan, 23, 75

www.ingramcontent.com/pod-product-compliance
Lightning Source LLC
Chambersburg PA
CBHW050429240426
43661CB00055B/2315